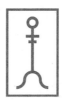

WILDERNESS
A TO Z

AN ESSENTIAL GUIDE TO THE GREAT OUTDOORS

"I went to the woods because I wished to live deliberately,
to front only the essential facts of life. . . ."

Henry David Thoreau, *Walden* (1854)

RACHEL CARLEY

A FIRESIDE BOOK

PUBLISHED BY SIMON & SCHUSTER

NEW YORK • LONDON • TORONTO • SYDNEY • SINGAPORE

FIRESIDE
Rockefeller Center
1230 Avenue of the Americas
New York, NY 10020

Library of Congress Cataloging-in-Publication Data

Carley, Rachel.
   Wilderness A to Z: an essential guide to the
great outdoors / Rachel Carley.
      p.   cm.
   Includes bibliographical references
   1. Outdoor recreation—Handbooks, manuals,
etc. 2. Outdoor life—Handbooks, manuals, etc.
I. Title.
GV191.6.C37 2001
796.5—dc21   2001034409

ISBN 0-7432-0057-8 (alk. paper)

Manufactured in the United States of America

10   9   8   7   6   5   4   3   2   1

Produced by Archetype Press, Inc.,
Washington, D.C.

Diane Maddex, Project Director
Gretchen Smith Mui, Editor
Robert L. Wiser, Designer
Carol Peters, Editorial Assistant

My thanks go to Dee Shapiro and Shirin Zade
for their help and good cheer in researching this
book; to Jeanne Van Etten for her illustrations;
to Neeti Madan; and to Diane Maddex and the
staff of Archetype Press.—*Rachel Carley*

Cover: Color block print *Winter Looks Down
on Spring*, by Frances H. Gearhart (1869–1958).
Courtesy JMW Gallery, Boston

Back cover: Postcard of a private camp in the
Adirondacks (ca. 1900). Hugh C. Leighton Company

Passages from *The Everglades: River of Grass*
(fiftieth anniversary edition, 1977), by Marjory
Stoneman Douglas, are used by permission of
Pineapple Press, Inc. Passages from *The Journey
Home: Some Words in Defense of the American
West*, by Edward Abbey (E. P. Dutton, 1977),
appear courtesy of Penguin Putnam, Inc.

Words highlighted within text entries refer to
separate entries in the book.

For information regarding special discounts for
bulk purchases, please contact Simon & Schuster
Special Sales at 1-800-456-6798 or business@
simonandschuster.com

FOR MY PARENTS

"IN WILDNESS IS THE PRESERVATION OF THE WORLD."

Henry David Thoreau (1851)

Introduction

The idea for a compendium of essays and related resource information touching on the diverse range of topics and personalities found in *Wilderness A to Z* grew out of an appreciation for how the American wilderness has been a defining theme for so many aspects of enterprise, achievement, and debate throughout the country's history. No single volume can definitively cover such a rich and complex subject, and organizing it into alphabetical entries has both advantages and limitations. For one thing, there is always the risk of leaving something out, not to mention the challenge of compartmentalizing topics that do not necessarily fall willingly into categories. Such a format is nonetheless an intriguing means of highlighting the web of relationships that emerge when one examines any whole in terms of its individual parts. Because this book is designed to serve a multitude of interests and uses, the result of that endeavor is itself hard to categorize: part reference book, part practical manual for responsible wilderness recreation, *Wilderness A to Z* is also presented as a joyful gazetteer of history, geography, and facts both usual and unusual. That readers may encounter something as different as an analysis of the 1906 Antiquities Act, a guide to viewing glaciers, and a short discourse on the first treatise on angling (written in the 1400s by an English nun) is precisely the point.

Why wilderness? In his famous "frontier thesis" of 1893, the historian Frederick Jackson Turner (1861–1932) credited the unique pioneering course westward across the American wilderness as the single defining experience to shape our democratic institutions. The debate is ongoing, but the Turner thesis is rarely dismissed out of hand. It would certainly be difficult to argue that America's wildlands are not a significant part of both our national and our popular culture if the vast body of literature, art, photography, scientific research, religious and philosophical discourse, and legislation relating to the value and preservation of the wilderness is any measure of its influence. More than a century after the 1890 U.S. Census declared the frontier extinct, the West remains America's particular embodiment of swagger and independence. Daniel Boone (1734–1820) and Buffalo Bill Cody (1846–1917) are still instantly recognizable folk heroes—and anyone who has not read Owen Wister's 1902 potboiler, *The Virginian* ("When you call me that, *Smile*") has probably seen the television show. Indeed, with its impossibly grand landscape and heritage of frontier lore, the potency of the West as mental and physical safety valve has never really diminished.

But the truth is that all of America's wilderness regions, from the Adirondacks to Alaska, represent an increasingly important refuge and retreat. The next question might be how best to undertake the stewardship of that refuge. One recurring theme in the work of nineteenth-century artists and thinkers as diverse in their expression as Henry David Thoreau (1817–62), Frederic Remington (1861–1909), and the painter and ethnographer George Catlin (1796–1872)—father of the national park concept—is the idea of loss. Or more precisely, the enormity of the loss were Americans to squander what might be considered this country's greatest gift.

That concept resurfaces continually today as the basis of discussion of virtually any wilderness preservation effort. It is notable that the Wilderness Act (1964), the only federal statute to define wilderness, does so as an area "where the earth and its community of life are untrammeled by man" and "where man himself is a visitor who does not remain." The mere existence of wild country raises the question of what the human impact on that wilderness is and should be and whether human life is dependent on the existence of wild areas even if the reverse is not true.

This specific issue may not be a fundamental component of our cultural heritage, but the process and character of the debate are. That is because the debate, itself encouraged by the essentially American institution of national advocacy, underscores many of the oft-conflicting ideals inherent in the

American way. The two men who did most to forge the foundation of the current U.S. policy of natural resource management, Theodore Roosevelt (1858–1919) and his chief forester, Gifford Pinchot (1865–1946), for example, adhered to a precept of use and benefit that is basic to a democratic society: management and exploitation for the greatest good of the greatest number of people. Although Roosevelt was instrumental in declaring numerous national monuments and forest preserves, the notion of preserving nature, or wilderness, for its own sake did not enter into the equation. "Forest protection is not an end in itself," declared Roosevelt. "It is a means to increase and sustain the resources of our country and the industries which depend on them."

The larger question, of course, is what defines the "greatest good." Thoreau, himself an early advocate of woodland preserves, saw setting aside such tracts as essential to the preservation of society. The implicit transcendentalist credo— that nature does in fact have "its own sake"—had profound implications. The beauty and morality inherent in the natural world were not only evidence of God; each individual's direct connection with nature also put him or her closer to God. In that kind of intellectual context it was possible for such eloquent literary naturalists as John Muir (1838–1914), John Burroughs (1837–1921), Aldo Leopold (1887–1948), and Rachel Carson (1907–64), all critical voices in the first national environmental reform movement, to present an ethical argument for the care and protection of wilderness (or nature in one of its purest forms). The standpoint that humans do not exist apart from nature means that our existence depends on preserving the balance and complexities of the greater community of life, as well as that the responsibility for that preservation falls specifically on us. In this sense, caring for the environment is putting the needs of civilization first.

But what happens when that philosophy is balanced against the American dream of material progress? When progress is measured in terms of cost and benefit, the justification for wilderness protection in America is always equated with use. This is partly because it is so difficult to assess such benefits as beauty, ecological harmony, and mental sustenance, none of which can be quantified in numbers of visitors or dollars. Many people do not realize that America's first national park, Yellowstone (1872), was set aside not to protect an unsullied tract of wilderness but rather as a public "pleasuring ground" and potential location for hostelries, concessions, and other tourist attractions. Indeed, the designation came only after Congress had been assured that the high altitude

Wilderness as Idea

and bizarre geology of the Yellowstone Valley precluded farming or settlement; creating a park would thus do "no harm to the material interests of the people."

Nearly a century passed after the creation of Yellowstone National Park before the value of preserving wilderness as wilderness was recognized broadly in a federal statute. In 1964 the Wilderness Act created the National Wilderness Preservation System, which aims to protect large tracts of public domain from road building, mining, logging, and other types of development. Nevertheless, detractors of the U.S. Forest Service, the primary agency responsible for administering national wilderness areas, point out that these tracts are nearly always the "leftovers" of the public domain—land already relatively useless in terms of resource development—so that what is left to preserve and protect for posterity and recreation is wilderness that no one else wants anyway.

And when "use" does not mean extracting resources for the benefit of the populace whose taxes support the management of the public domain, it almost always means use for recreation. Few federal reserves in the United States do not invite or accommodate leisure activity. Be it hiking, canoeing, hunting, fishing, birding, or all-terrain vehicle use, public "play" is usually a reason, if not the primary reason, for reserving federal lands from development. It is not easy to argue that the public should not have access to public lands. But recreation itself is an increasing threat to American wilderness areas worn down and out by the estimated 13 million hikers who annually set out for backcountry trails.

But as Wallace Stegner (1909–93) wrote, we would be wise to acknowledge that there are other reasons for protecting wildlands. One is the reassurance that wilderness "is good for our spiritual health even if we never once in ten years set foot in it." It is good "for use when we are young," said Stegner, "because of the incomparable sanity it can bring briefly, as vacation and rest, into our insane lives. It is important to us when we are old simply because it is there—important, that is, simply as an idea."

A rguably the most familiar of the twentieth-century photographers who explored the western landscape, Ansel Adams (1902–84) celebrated nature in both its monumentality and its minute detail. His viewpoint—as artist, photographer, teacher, musician, activist, and individual—paralleled the transcendentalist philosophy of the nineteenth-century literary figures RALPH WALDO EMERSON and HENRY DAVID THOREAU: the presence of God is immanent in the harmony of nature (☞ WRITERS (NINETEENTH CENTURY)). Associations with the great modern photographers Paul Strand (1890–1976) and Alfred Stieglitz (1864–1946) encouraged Adams to explore photography subjectively, as an interpretive art form, rather than as a means of cold documentation. The abstract images that resulted from his nature studies—a sunlit cloud formation or a snow-crusted mountain peak—were often devoid of human scale. "*What* and *who*," he once explained, "make small difference in the presence of the eternal world."

Adams's views of nature were drawn from the lush vistas of YOSEMITE VALLEY, the Big Sur coast, and the SIERRA NEVADA RANGE in California; from the snow fields of ALASKA; and from the more barren and mysterious desert landscape of the Southwest (☞ DESERTS). He was born in San Francisco and maintained a close relationship with the Sierra Club (☞ ADVOCATES) throughout his life, serving as a director from 1934 to 1971. Sierra Club outings often incorporated readings, lectures, and

Ansel Adams

Through images like this 1942 view of Montana's Lake McDonald, Ansel Adams hoped to inspire viewers to seek the "inexhaustible sources of beauty" in nature.

related activities involving such writers and environmental leaders as JOHN MUIR. The photographer also held regular summer workshops in Yosemite Valley from 1955 to 1981. As an alternative to cheap postcards, he offered high-quality 8-by-10-inch "special edition" prints of his photographs at his Yosemite studio. Thousands were sold, making thousands of people familiar with Adams's work. ☞ *also* PHOTOGRAPHERS

Adirondack Mountains

"New York has her wilderness within her own borders."

Henry David Thoreau, "Ktaadn" (1848)

Often referred to as the country's first wilderness, the Adirondacks are as much a state of mind as they are a place. These are the wildest wilds of the eastern United States—a rugged landscape of mountain, lake, and sky fanning northwest from Albany, New York, toward the Canadian border that takes its name from the Adirondack Mountains (when people say "Adirondacks" they mean the whole region). The writer Bill McKibben has said that to experience the Adirondack backcountry is to "see what the world must have looked like." The strangely parallel sense of remoteness and revelation embodied by the ancient mountains, which began to rise about 15 million years ago, has drawn explorers—of geography, intellectual frontiers, and life's outdoor pleasures—to the region since the Frenchman Samuel de Champlain (1567–1635) sailed up the St. Lawrence and Richelieu Rivers and became the first European to set foot on Adirondack soil near present-day Ticonderoga,

New York, in 1609. Jesuit missionaries encountered Iroquois warriors, RALPH WALDO EMERSON and Winslow Homer (1836–1910) found their muses—and it was in this region that Americans of all ranks first discovered the potential of the wilderness as refuge.

A southern appendage of Canada's Laurentian Highlands, the Adirondacks are the only peaks in the eastern United States that are not part of the APPALACHIAN MOUNTAINS. The range is bounded on the east by Lakes George and Champlain and sweeps from the foothills near the St. Lawrence River in the north down to the Mohawk River valley in the south. The highest peak is Mount Marcy, at 5,344 feet the tallest in the state. Before 1838 the mountains were known as the Black or Peru Mountains, and the larger Adirondack region was referred to as the Great Northern Wilderness. Indians had another name for their winter hunting ground: Couchsarge, or Dismal Wilderness.

Wilderness it was. Although the wilds begin only about 200 miles north of New York City, forays into the Adirondacks were fairly sporadic into the 1830s. Even the source of the Nile was discovered before that of the Hudson River, which originates at Lake Tear of the Clouds near Mount Marcy. Beginning in the early 1800s, however, word of vast resources such as timber and ore—virgin white pine grew 6 feet in circumference—lured business entrepreneurs. By midcentury the Adirondacks had made New York the leading lumber state in the country. The glory days of the Gilded Age rustic pleasure palaces, later known as GREAT CAMPS, followed on the heels of post–Civil War railroad development.

By the early 1900s the region lost some of its allure as sizable areas were reduced to stumpage by large-scale mining and logging: some 3.5 million trees were felled on private tracts by

An 1861 camp scene— *Hunters Shanty. In the Adirondacks*—was one of several lithographs published by Currier and Ives in response to growing interest in this wilderness region.

the turn of the century. Most of the existing forest is second or later growth, although pockets of virgin forest are found scattered throughout the 6.1-million-acre ADIRONDACK PARK, subject to some of the most restrictive forest protection regulations in the country. These include the "forever wild" designation protecting the 2.7 million noncontiguous acres in the Adirondack Forest Preserve (☞ NEW YORK STATE FOREST PRESERVE).

Contacts

Adirondack Architectural History ✉ Box 159, Raquette Lake, NY 13436. ☎ 315-354-5832
■ Devoted to enhancing appreciation of the architectural heritage of the Adirondack region, this nonprofit membership group sponsors historic preservation efforts, tours, and educational and cultural programs.

Adirondack Mountain Club ✉ 814 Goggins Road, Lake George, NY 12845. ☎ 800-395-8080. 🖥 www.adk.org
■ This membership group created in 1922 and known as ADK is committed to the protection and responsible recreational use of the New York State Forest Preserve, parks, and other wildlands and waters in the Adirondacks. The ADK guide to the Adirondack High Peaks region was published in 1934; ever since, the club's trail guides and detailed topographic maps have set the standard and constitute some of the best trail references in the country.

Adirondack Museum ✉ P.O. Box 99, Blue Mountain Lake, NY 12812-0099. ☎ 518-352-7311. 🖥 www.adkmuseum.org
■ Set on 32 acres overlooking Blue Mountain Lake, the museum features indoor and outdoor exhibits on logging, boating, hunting, and camp life in the Adirondacks. It has an exceptional collection of freshwater boats. Representative wilderness artwork and more than 66,000 historic photographs document regional culture.

An Adirondack icon, the three-sided lean-to was typically built as a makeshift shelter for parties of hunters and fishermen—and ladies. Adapted elsewhere in the country, it became a standard overnight accommodation for adventurers in the woods.

Association for the Protection of the Adirondacks ✉ 30 Roland Place, Schenectady, NY 12304. ☎ 518-377-1452. 🖥 www.global2000.net/protectadks/organiz.html

■ This nonprofit citizens organization works for the protection of the New York State Forest Preserve, Adirondack Park, and Catskill Park; maintains the Adirondack and Catskill Research Library; sponsors programs; and works on legislative issues.

📖 Alfred L. Donaldson, *A History of the Adirondacks* (1921, 1992). 📖 Nathan Farb, *The Adirondacks* (1985). 📖 Barbara McMartin, *The Great Forest of the Adirondacks* (1994). 📖 Paul Schneider, *The Adirondacks: A History of America's First Wilderness* (1997). 📖 Philip Terrie, *Contested Borders: A New History of Nature and People in the Adirondacks* (1997). 📖 Carl E. Heilman and Bill McKibben, *Adirondacks: Views of an American Wilderness* (1999).

Reading

Adirondack Art

If the American landscape school of painting was the ideal expression of nature as the antidote to civilizing forces, then the majestic wilderness vistas of the Adirondacks were the ideal inspiration. As early as the 1830s, Thomas Cole (1801–48), the leading light of the HUDSON RIVER SCHOOL ARTISTS, was making forays into the region "in search of the picturesque." Until the 1860s Cole and fellow landscape painters, including Asher B. Durand (1796–1886) and John Kensett (1816–72), visited Keene Flats (now Keene Valley) on their summer tours of the American wilds, helping establish the High Peaks region as a summer artists colony. After the Civil War it began to draw a coterie of painters and illustrators who set up permanent studios there. Frederic Remington (1861–1909) (☞ WESTERN ILLUSTRATORS) stayed in Cranberry Lake. Winslow Homer visited the Adirondacks in the 1870s as an illustrator for *Harper's Weekly*. Beginning in the mid-1800s, paintings by Arthur Fitzwilliam Tait were reproduced as lithographs by Currier and Ives, and wood engravings based on images by Henry Fenn appeared in Bryant's *Picturesque America* (1872).

Photography also brought the scenic wonders of the area to national attention in the post–Civil War era. Edward Bierstadt, the brother of the Hudson River School artist Albert Bierstadt (1830–1902) (☞ ROCKY MOUNTAIN SCHOOL ARTISTS), worked extensively in the Adirondacks during the 1870s and 1880s, when he was hired by the real estate developer William West Durant (1850–1934), builder of the first GREAT CAMPS. Bierstadt made a business of producing brochures, artotype sets, and albums of Adirondack views, which were sold at local hotels and in his own New York City studio. WILLIAM HENRY JACKSON, an Adirondack native, made several return tours to New York State to shoot resorts for his own publishing company and for the D&H Railway. One of the most prolific early landscape photographers in America, Seneca Ray Stoddard

Henry Fenn's painting of Ausable Chasm illustrated William Cullen Bryant's *Picturesque America* (1872).

(1843–1917) concentrated his career in the Adirondacks, where in 1873 he began publishing a long series of illustrated maps, almanacs, and guidebooks. An outspoken supporter of protection for the region, he addressed the state assembly in 1892 in favor of the creation of the ADIRONDACK PARK and subsequently toured New York with his pro-conservation lecture illustrated by handtinted lantern slides. ☞ *also* PHOTOGRAPHERS

Adirondack Literature

By the late nineteenth century the Adirondacks had inspired more published works than any other wilderness area in the United States, maintaining a hold on the public's imagination even as frontier expansion was creating a distinctive genre of adventure writing in the West (☞ WESTERN FICTION). An unbroken Adirondack literary tradition began with the novels of JAMES FENIMORE COOPER, historical accounts by Ethan Allen (1738–89) and Francis Parkman (1823–93), and the poems of RALPH WALDO EMERSON. Cooper may have been the first eastern writer to use New York's wild backcountry as the backdrop for a work of fiction: *The Last of the Mohicans* (1826) is set in the Lake George area south of the present ADIRONDACK PARK. Much of the credit for the widespread press coverage that drew a procession of nineteenth-century intelligentsia to the Adirondacks goes to Charles Fenno Hoffman (1806–84). A poet, novelist, and gentleman journalist, the one-legged Hoffman was editor of the *American Monthly Magazine* and the *New York Mirror*, in which he published a serialized account of a spiritually regenerating 1837 excursion to the Adirondacks; this was reissued in Hoffman's two-volume *Wild Scenes in the Forest and Prairie* (1839 and 1843).

Dozens of writers followed suit with essays and poems in magazines and journals such as *Atlantic Monthly*, *Scribner's Monthly*, *Saturday Evening Post*, and *Forest and Stream*. Engravings of scenes by Winslow Homer and Samuel Colman often accompanied the articles, which frequently appeared under romantic "Indian" pen names such as Nessmuk and Wachusett. A succession of guidebooks also tantalized the imagination of armchair travelers. Most notable was the hugely successful *Adventures in the Wilderness: or Camp-Life in the Adirondacks* (1869) by William H. H. Murray (1840–1904). "Adirondack Murray" was a Congregationalist minister from Boston who preached the spiritual and physical benefits of outdoor life from the pulpit. ("The wilderness provides that perfect relaxation which all jaded minds require.") Written after a camping trip on Racquette Lake, his *Adventures*, a complete guide to clothing, hotels, trails, and the like, quickly went through eleven printings and precipitated a surge in Adirondack tourism, dubbed "Murray's Rush."

By contrast, the Hartford, Connecticut, writer and news-paperman Charles Dudley Warner (1829–1900), of Mark Twain's Nook Farm circle, poked gentle fun at the area's idiosyncrasies. One object of Warner's musings was the legendary guide "Old Mountain" Phelps, a grizzled character whose clothes, penned Warner, "seemed to have been put on him once for all, like the bark of a tree." ☞ *also* WRITERS (NINETEENTH CENTURY)

Blueline ⊠ 125 Morey Hall, Department of English and Communication, SUNY   *Contact*
Potsdam, Potsdam, NY 13676. 🖳 www.potsdam.edu/ENGL/blueline/default.
html#History
■ This literary journal publishes poems, stories, and essays relating to the
Adirondacks and regions similar in geography and spirit, as well as literary pieces
concerned with the shaping influence of nature.

The Adirondack Review. Poetry and short stories by writers from the Adiron-   *Web Site*
dack Mountains and other North Woods regions are included in this online literary journal. 🖳 www.suite101.com/myhome.cfm/adkrev

📕 William H. H. Murray, *Adventures in the Wilderness* (1869). 📕 Charles Dudley   *Reading*
Warner, *In the Wilderness* (1878). 📕 Anne LaBastille, *Woodswoman* (1976). 📕 E. L.
Doctorow, *Loon Lake* (1980). 📕 Joyce Carol Oates, *Bellefleur* (1980). 📕 Russell
Banks, *Affliction* (1989). 📕 Paul Jamieson, ed., *The Adirondack Reader* (1998).

Adirondack Park

With its 6.1 million acres, the state-owned Adirondack Park in New York is the largest park of any kind outside ALASKA—encompassing more land than Grand Canyon, Yellowstone, and Yosemite National Parks put together (☞ GRAND CANYON, YELLOWSTONE NATIONAL PARK, YOSEMITE VALLEY). This vast state park was created by the state assembly in 1892, when it became clear that widely dispersed parcels within the Adirondack Forest Preserve (☞ ADIRONDACK MOUNTAINS, NEW YORK STATE FOREST PRESERVE) did not constitute sufficient land to protect the forest and watersheds. The boundaries were originally defined by the so-called blue-line border, drawn with a blue pencil on a map of New York. The area included the existing forest preserve as well as land that the state planned to acquire. At the time, four-fifths of the total 2.8 million acres was privately owned, meaning that the park was essentially a park on paper only.

Since it was established, the Adirondack Park has expanded threefold in size through state and private purchases to become a complex jigsaw puzzle of public and private lands. Roughly the size of Vermont, it contains more than 2,800 lakes and ponds, the headwaters of the Hudson River, more

Adirondack Park tourists in the early 1900s could enjoy the sights from the relative comfort of an open-air bus.

In an engraving from William Cullen Bryant's *Picturesque America* (1872), Henry Fenn depicted hikers at the park's Indian Pass.

than 30,000 miles of brooks and rivers, some 2,500 Adirondack Mountain peaks, and about 90 percent of all animal species in the Northeast. The state-owned land, including the forest preserve, accounts for about 39 percent. More than one-half of the park land (about 3.5 million acres), however, is still privately owned. Despite the mixed ownership, 80 percent of the park remains open space. Many of the large private tracts belong to major timber corporations and are logged for profit: the International Paper Corporation is the largest landowner within the park after the state. Other tracts are preserved as open recreational space by private clubs and individual home-owners. Hiking trails are maintained by both the state and private groups. State-purchased recreational easements permit hiking, camping, canoeing, and other outdoor activities on thousands of acres of private land.

In addition to its enormous size, the Adirondack Park is exceptional in that it encompasses such a complex mix of residential, recreational, and commercial uses while supporting a permanent population of 130,000 residents plus about 110,000 seasonal visitors. Numerous towns and villages are located within the expanded blue-line boundaries. Because of the park's immensity, stringent preservation regulations, and a long history of economic disparity between the local and seasonal populations, it has been a template—and a battle-ground—for national environmental issues.

Outside the forest preserve, most of the park land was not subject to preservation regulation until a 1973 use and development plan drafted by the Adirondack Park Agency, an independent, bipartisan state forum responsible for developing long-range policy. The most ambitious effort ever to

An Adirondack guide-boat portage (carry) between two lakes was recorded around 1902 by the famous landscape photographer William Henry Jackson, a native of the woodsy region.

address such a large multiuse region, this state plan set up a classification system that dictates land use and development activities on the public land and the 3.5 million acres of private land within the park. Most of this has been classified for protection as open space.

New York State Adirondack Park Agency ⊠ P.O. Box 99, Ray Brook, NY 12977. 𝄢 518-891-4050. 🖳 www.northnet.org/adirondackparkagency ■ This independent, bipartisan state agency develops long-range park policy. The 1971 state law creating it authorized it to regulate development on private and public lands.

Contact

Advocates

Environmental advocacy groups in America operate within the private and public sectors on local, state, and national levels. Efforts concentrating on wilderness and wildlife preservation, responsible scientific research, policy development, and information dissemination tend to be undertaken within the private sector by special-interest groups acting as a grassroots movement. Many of the hundreds of private nonprofit societies and independent clubs devoted to canoeing (☞ CANOES), HIKING, MOUNTAINEERING, trail building, and other outdoor activities serve as watchdogs, often banding together to create a louder voice on Capitol Hill. State environmental lobbies consist of local and regional groups as well as individual members.

Anyone interested in lobbying individually can reach the office of any member of Congress in Washington, D.C., by calling the Capitol switchboard (𝄢 202-224-3121) and asking for a U.S. representative by name. If you are not sure which congressional or legislative district you are in or who your representative is, call your county clerk's office. The ENVIRON-MENTAL PROTECTION AGENCY is the primary advocacy group responsible for the environment at the federal level.

The nation's leading private national wildlife and wilderness advocacy groups are listed below. Several can be counted among the oldest conservation groups in America and have been instrumental in shaping the environmental movement over the last century by campaigning for the creation of national parks and monuments, supporting environmental legislation, and litigating against threats and violations. All foster national activist networks and maintain comprehensive Web sites that post news alerts and fact sheets.

Contacts

American Geological Institute ⊠ 4220 King Street, Alexandria, VA 22302-1502. (703-379-2480. ▯ www.agiweb.org

■ A federation of professional earth science organizations, the institute promotes a united voice for the geoscience community, advocating responsible resource management and the appropriate use of science in public policy. It also maintains the U.S. National Geoscience Data Repository and the GeoRef database of published information. Publications include *Spotlight* and *GeoSpectrum* and the Environmental Awareness book series.

American Trails ⊠ P.O. Box 11046, Prescott, AZ 86304-1046. (520-632-1140. ▯ www.outdoorlink.com/amtrails

■ This national organization works on behalf of all trail interests, including hiking, bicycling, mountain biking, horseback riding, water trails, cross-country skiing, snowshoeing, trail motorcycling, ATV use, and snowmobiling. It also trains advocates, lobbies on behalf of trail issues, implements the Universal Trail Access Information System, and sponsors the National Trails Symposium. Publications include *Trail Tracks*. The Web site provides state-by-state links to trail information.

Center for Environmental Citizenship ⊠ 1611 Connecticut Avenue, NW, Suite 3B, Washington, DC 20009. (202-547-8435. ▯ www.envirocitizen.org

■ Founded by young activists in 1992, this nonprofit educates and trains a national network of young leaders in environmental protection. Programs include Campus Green Vote, EarthNet, and NEWS.

Earth Island Institute ⊠ 300 Broadway, Suite 28, San Francisco, CA 94133. (415-788-3666. ▯ www.earthisland.org ▯ www.earthinfo.org

■ A global activist group supporting environmental conservation and restoration, the institute was founded in 1982 by the environmentalist David Brower and now aids about thirty grassroots projects worldwide. U.S. efforts include the Bay Area (California) Wilderness Training Program, Campaign to Safeguard America's Waters (Alaska), and Estuary Action Challenge, designed to inspire children. The Web sites post conservation alerts and encourage environmental activism.

Environmental Defense ✉ 257 Park Avenue South, New York, NY 10010. ☏ 212-505-2100. ⌨ www.edf.org

■ Staffed by scientists, economists, and attorneys, the former Environmental Defense Fund promotes economic incentives for environmentally sound packaging and the reduction of all types of pollution. Action Network is an online clearinghouse for information on public policy issues. Other projects include the Pollution Prevention Alliance, targeted at the Great Lakes region. It also advocates habitat restoration and was an important influence on the return of gray wolves in the mid-1990s to their historic range in Wyoming and Idaho. Online publications include *E* and *Green Living*.

Friends of the Earth ✉ 1025 Vermont Avenue, NW, Washington, DC 20005. ☏ 202-783-7400. ⌨ www.foe.org

■ The mission of this coalition-building group—the largest international environmental network in the world—is to empower citizens to have a voice in decisions affecting their environment. The group fights toxic dumping and works for enforcement of environmental laws. Litigation successes include suits compelling the EPA to set pollution standards for Washington, D.C., waterways and to protect Mississippi River coastal areas from floating casinos. Publications include *Atmosphere*.

Greenpeace USA ✉ 702 H Street, NW, Suite 300, Washington, DC 20001. ☏ 202-462-1177. ⌨ www.greenpeace.org

■ This independent activist organization uses nonviolent confrontation to expose global environmental problems. Its mission is to force solutions that are essential to a green and peaceful future.

League of Conservation Voters ✉ 1920 L Street, NW, Suite 800, Washington, DC 20036. ☏ 202-785-8683. ⌨ www.lcv.org

■ This bipartisan watchdog group aims to hold Congress accountable on issues concerning environmental, wildlife, natural resource protection, and public land management. It is the only national environmental group dedicated to informing the public about congressional voting records on these matters.

National Parks Conservation Association ✉ 1300 Nineteenth Street, NW, Suite 300, Washington, DC 20036. ☏ 800-NAT-PARKS; 202-223-6722. ⌨ www.npca@npca.org

■ Established as the National Parks Association in 1919 "to defend the National Parks and Monuments fearlessly against the assaults of private interests and aggressive commercialism," its founders included Stephen T. Mather, the first National Park Service director. It is now the only private nonprofit group concerned solely with protecting the National Park System from dam building, mining, logging, and other threats, serving as both a watchdog for existing parks and a promoter of new ones. Publications include *National Parks* and an online press room.

National Wilderness Institute ✉ P.O. Box 25766, Washington, DC 20007. ☏ 703-836-7404. ⌨ www.nwi.org

■ This environmental think tank founded in 1989 leads a nonadversarial education campaign based on reliable scientific data, maintaining that a healthy environment cannot exist without a healthy economic base. The group advocates wise resource protection, the preservation of private property rights, and the reduction of government regulations. Publications include *Fresh Tracks* and the *NWI Resource* magazine.

Natural Resources Defense Council ✉ 40 West Twentieth Street, New York, NY 10011. ☎ 212-727-2700. ⌨ www.nrdc.org

■ A defender of endangered plant and animal systems, the council is committed to giving the public a voice in decisions that affect the natural environment. Programs target clean air and water quality, pesticides, energy efficiency, habitat preservation, improved management of national parks and public and private forests, and protection of waterways and ocean life. Initiatives are under way in the Everglades, San Francisco Bay, and San Joaquin River. Publications include *The Amicus Journal.*

In 1972 Environmental Action used Mother Earth as a familial metaphor for a dramatic Earth Day poster.

Preservation Action ✉ 1350 Connecticut Avenue, NW, Suite 401, Washington, DC 20036. ☎ 202-659-0915. ⌨ www.preservationaction.org

■ This full-time national citizens' lobby for historic preservation causes maintains a list of state lobbying coordinators. Its Web site posts updates on current bills and issues and offers lobbying tips.

Scenic America ✉ 801 Pennsylvania Avenue, SE, Suite 300, Washington, DC 20003. ☎ 202-543-6200. ⌨ www.scenic.org

■ Scenic America is committed to preserving the American countryside and works at the federal level and with state affiliates in California, Florida, Kentucky, Michigan, Missouri, North Carolina, and Texas to advocate legislation that empowers communities to preserve and enhance their distinctive scenic character. Initiatives include the fight to reduce billboard blight in America and to keep highways scenic.

The Sierra Club ✉ 85 Second Street, Second Floor, San Francisco, CA, 94105-3441. ☎ 415-977-5500. ⌨ www.sierraclub.org

■ The club's mission is to "explore, enjoy and protect the wild places of the earth," a credo shared by the conservationist John Muir and other founders of this society created in 1892 in part to explore and map the Sierras. Club hikes, climbing expeditions, and ski trips "to hear the trees speak for themselves" were also an early feature of the club, which still offers outings. It has also been a leader in the campaign for all major U.S. legislation affecting the environment, federal protection of wildlands, and the creation of numerous wilderness areas, national parks, national preserves, and national monuments. Current priorities also include the issues of urban sprawl, global warming, pollution, commercial logging, and responsible trade.

The Wilderness Society ✉ 1615 M Street, NW, Washington, DC 20036.
☎ 800-THE-WILD (843-9453). 🖥 www.wilderness.org
■ The society was founded in 1935 by some of the nation's leading environmental advocates, including the Alaskan explorer Robert Marshall, wildlife ecologist Aldo Leopold, and Benton MacKaye, creator of the Appalachian Trail. The society has been instrumental in major wilderness legislation; advocacy efforts have added 104 million acres to the National Wilderness Preservation System and created national monuments, one of the society's major causes. An online newsroom and fact sheets and the *Wild Alerts* newsletter provide updated information on current wilderness issues.

Worldwatch Institute ✉ 1776 Massachusetts Avenue, NW, Washington, DC 20036. ☎ 202-452-1999. 🖥 www.worldwatch.org
■ The institute fosters the evolution of an environmentally sustainable society in which human needs are met in ways that do not threaten the natural environment's health. It conducts interdisciplinary nonpartisan research on emerging global environmental issues, disseminating the results worldwide.

📕 Bruce C. Wolpe et al., *Lobbying Congress: How the System Works* (1996). *Reading*
📕 Paul Hermson, ed., *The Interest Group Connection: Electioneering, Lobbying and Policymaking in Washington* (1997). 📕 Donald E. Dekieffer, *The Citizen's Guide to Lobbying Congress* (1997). 📕 Ken Kollman, *Outside Lobbying: Public Opinion and Interest Group Strategies* (1998). 📕 Jeffrey M. Berry, *New Liberalism: The Rising Power of Citizen Groups* (1999). 📕 Robert L. Guyer, *Guide to State Legislative Lobbying* (1999).

Alaska

It is said that wilderness is a state of mind, but in Alaska it is also hard reality. America's northern frontier is set apart both physically and psychologically by its formidable but often inhospitable beauty, its climate (among the coldest on earth), and its sheer vastness. Covering some 586,000 square miles, this single state occupies an area more than twice the size of Texas. Half of it is treeless, 90 percent of it is roadless, and 85 percent is covered with permafrost, which can reach depths of 1,000 feet or more. So distant and apparently impenetrable, Alaska was largely unexplored for many years after the territory became a U.S. possession in 1906. That this was a land every bit as unimaginable, and seemingly imaginary, to most Americans as was the trans-Mississippi West before the Lewis and Clark expedition of 1804–6 (☞ CORPS OF DISCOVERY) has contributed to the unshakable impression that Alaska is the country's last frontier. That—and the fact that its climate and geography make Alaska so much less accessible to human control and development than almost any other part of America—turns it into a frontier by default, perhaps, but a frontier nevertheless.

**The Last
Conservation
Frontier**

When Alaska became a state in 1959, almost 99 percent of its land was already federally owned. Two-thirds of Alaska's 372 million acres are now under federal management, an extraordinary amount by any measure. Most of the remaining land is owned by state corporations (90 million acres) or by native groups (37 million acres), with only 1.3 percent in private hands. One-third of Alaska's total land mass (and one-half the public lands) consists of some form of conservation system unit, largely because of designations made under the Alaska National Interest Lands Conservation Act (1980). Eighty-six percent (about 76.8 million acres) of the country's entire NATIONAL WILDLIFE REFUGE SYSTEM and 60 percent (about 52.7 acres) of the entire NATIONAL PARK SYSTEM is located in Alaska, which contains fifteen national parks or preserves and four NATIONAL MONUMENTS. Within these units and the Tongass National Forest, about 56.2 million acres are designated wilderness, making up 54 percent of the NATIONAL WILDERNESS PRESERVATION SYSTEM. The Tongass (earmarked mainly for timber production) in the southeast and the Chugach National Forest in south-central Alaska are the two largest in the nation (☞ NATIONAL FOREST SYSTEM), while the Yukon Delta National Wildlife Refuge (20 million acres) is the largest wildlife refuge. Contained within all these are complete Arctic ecosystems, tundra and boreal forests, sedimentary rocks deposited some 1.6 billion years ago, active glaciers and volcanoes, and the archaeological remains of nomadic hunters' camps dating back at least 9,000 years. The Alaskan mountain ranges are still unexplored for vast stretches.

**The "Last
Chance to Do
Things Right"**

The Alaska National Interest Lands Conservation Act is the most broad-reaching piece of wilderness preservation legislation in the world. Signed into law in 1980 by President Jimmy Carter, the act created more than 100 million acres of new national parks, wildlife refuges, forests, monuments, wild and scenic rivers (☞ NATIONAL WILD AND SCENIC RIVERS SYSTEM), and NATIONAL RECREATION AREAS, as well as national conservation areas. The law has its roots in the Alaska Native Claims Settlement Act (1971), which required the withdrawal from the public domain of "national interest" lands earmarked for future preservation and called for $1 billion and a 44-million-acre allotment to Alaska natives to settle aboriginal land claims.

The provisions of this monumental and controversial piece of legislation underscore the uneasy relationship among hunters and sports enthusiasts, foresters and miners, private and public landowners, and natives and outsiders, who all regard the state as theirs. Some tracts of Arctic tundra, boreal forest, and coastal rain-forest ecosystems were set aside to

The first major scientific expedition to Alaska was led by Edward Henry Harriman in 1899. Images of the icy wilderness, like this one of Glacier Bay, riveted the American public.

preserve them unaltered, but the law provides for the use of snowmobiles, complex rifles, and motorboats on protected lands as well. The act also allows Alaska natives to use federal reserve lands for hunting, fishing, and other traditional subsistence activities.

A strong opposing argument to federal control, as the wilderness historian Roderick Nash points out in *Wilderness and the American Mind* (3rd ed., 1982), would have it that there is more wilderness in Alaska than can ever be ruined by tourism or eaten up by resource development; under this theory—a sort of Darwinian code of wilderness survival of the fittest—the state will take care of itself. (Or as one state politician put it: "Anybody who says the ecology is fragile is an ignoramus or a goddamned liar.") But the act affirmed that Alaska is bigger than the sum of its individual interests. Preserving it, says Nash, was "the nation's last chance to do things right for the first time." ☞ *also* ALASKA RANGE, ALEUTIAN RANGE, BROOKS RANGE, GLACIERS, IDITAROD

Alaska Department of Natural Resources ✉ 550 West Seventh Avenue, Suite 1260, Anchorage, AK 99501-3557. ☏ 907-269-8400. ▣ www.dnr.state.ak.us ■ The department manages all state land (much of it used for mineral and oil development) and water resources (except fish and game), is responsible for 34,000 miles of coast, and owns freshwater resources that constitute about 40 percent of the nation's fresh water. It also houses the office of the state pipeline coordinator, part of the joint state-federal program to oversee the 800-mile Trans-Alaska Pipeline.

Alaska Public Lands Information Centers ✉ 605 West Fourth Avenue, Suite 105, Anchorage, AK 99501. ☏ 907-271-2737. ✉ 250 Cushman Street, Suite 1A, Fairbanks, AK 99701. ☏ 907-456-0527. ✉ P.O. Box 359, Tok, AK 99780.

Contacts

(907-883-5667. ⊠ 50 Main Street, Ketchikan, AK 99901. (907-228-6220.
⌨ www.nps.gov/aplic
■ These four centers serve the public on behalf of the Bureau of Land Management. They offer information on history, conservation legislation, travel, and recreation, as well as special events, including geological walks and "Celebrating Wildflowers" month. The main Web site provides detailed information on bear-watching sites.

Alaska Wildlife Alliance ⊠ P.O. Box 202022, Anchorage, AK 99520.
⌨ www.akwildlife.org
■ This nonprofit organization is devoted to protecting wildlife and habitats.

Web Site

AlaskaGuidebook.com. This site is an excellent source of information on backpacking, bicycling, dog mushing, fishing, "flightseeing," mountaineering, snow sports, and sea kayaking. ⌨ www.alaskaguidebook.com

Reading

📕 George Bird Grinnell, *Alaska 1899: Essays from the Harriman Expedition* (1899, 1995). 📕 Jack London, *The Call of the Wild* (1903). 📕 Sally Carrighar, *Icebound Summer* (1951). 📕 Roderick Nash, *Wilderness and the American Mind* (1967, 1973, 1982). 📕 John McPhee, *Coming into the Country* (1985). 📕 Nancy Lord, *Green Alaska: Dreams from the Far Coast* (1999). 📕 Lois Chrisler, *Captive Wild* (2000).

Mount McKinley in the Yukon region of Alaska is the tallest peak in North America. Known locally as Denali, it is the centerpiece of Denali National Park and Preserve. The mountain was first summited successfully in 1913.

Alaska Range

An extension of the Pacific Coastal Range, the south-central Alaska Range traces a 600-mile arc from the Alaska Peninsula on its southwestern end to the Wrangell Mountains and the Yukon border at the southeastern limit. The crest of these extremely rugged, glaciated mountains averages about 8,000 feet, creating the major barrier to the Alaskan interior's great plateau and the drainage divide for the state's northward-flowing rivers (into the Yukon system) and those flowing south (into the Gulf of Alaska). The range rises to the summit of Mount McKinley, which, at

20,320 feet, is the highest point in North America and the focal point of Denali National Park and Preserve. Lake Clark National Park is also located in the Alaska Range, where spectacular valley GLACIERS dominate the dramatic tundra landscape; permanent ice caps crown the highest peaks. The Alaska Range Overlook on Yukon Drive in Fairbanks offers a view of the entire north side of the range. ☞ *also* ALASKA, ALEUTIAN RANGE, BROOKS RANGE

Aleutian Range

This Alaskan mountain range, an extension of the Coast Mountains, is a chain of about eighty semiactive volcanoes, part of a larger submarine volcanic system separating the Pacific Ocean from the Bering Sea. Merging with the Alaska Range to the northeast, the Aleutians trace a route from the west end of the Alaska Range along the entire Alaska Peninsula from Mount Spurr west of Anchorage and continue west partially submerged as the Aleutian Islands as far as Attu Island. About half of the volcanoes are active, including Mount Spurr, Mount Redoubt (the tallest Aleutian peak at 10,200 feet), and Mount Augustine, which last erupted in 1976. The Katmai National Park and Preserve contains the Valley of Ten Thousand Smokes, the remnant of a tremendous 1912 Aleutian eruption. The Becharof National Wildlife Refuge, Aniakchak National Monument and Preserve, and Alaska Peninsula Wildlife Refuge are also found in this range. ☞ *also* ALASKA, ALASKA RANGE, BROOKS RANGE

Angling

It is remarkable, to say the least, that the first known discourse on angling—the sport of fishing with rod, line, and hook—was written by a fifteenth-century English nun. Attributed to Dame Juliana Berners, *The Treatise of Fishing with an Angle* was introduced to readers in the second *Book of St. Albans* in 1496 and remained the primary word on sport fishing in England for the next 150 years. Berners's pensive primer on the deportment and technique of sport fishing not only ranked angling as a sport for the first time, but it also went so far as to present it as the superior of all hunting sports. Moreover, while the sister sports of hunting, hawking, and fowling were limited to the noble classes, the *Treatise* presented angling as a gentle leisure pursuit open to any country resident who could learn how to tie a fly by hand, thus making it a classless pastime.

Berners's book is believed to be the model for its much better known successor, *The Compleat Angler* (1653). This famous discourse on "the contemplative man's recreation" by

About 1875 the noted landscape painter Thomas Moran tried his hand at angling from a geological formation known as the Fish Pot, located in the hot springs of Montana's Yellowstone Lake. His effort was captured by the photographer William Henry Jackson.

the English biographer Isaak Walton (1593–1683) is still in print 350 years after the first edition appeared—outnumbered in copies, some say, only by the Bible and Shakespeare's plays. Written during a violent period of civil war, Walton's book was offered as both a fishing guide and a commentary on the tumultuous Restoration era. In arguing for the peaceful pursuit of fishing as physical and moral sustenance, Walton draws on the wisdom of Pliny, Aristotle, and Plutarch; quotes the shepherd king David ("they that occupy themselves in deep waters see the wonderful works of God"); and makes a point of noting that four of the twelve apostles were fishermen. Included are observations on catching salmon, trout, grayling, bream, pike, perch, eel, and carp; practical lessons on tying flies and casting techniques; and an analysis of every possible kind of worm living in English soil. The two main characters in this gentle morality play are the fisherman (Piscator), whom the author casts as master to the hunter (Venator). Initially a skeptical pupil, the hunter is soon won over to the virtues of the play's real protagonist: the fine art of angling itself. Above all, Walton makes clear that the patience, hope, and observation demanded by angling are all-consuming, and his underlying sermon was that a certain value can be found in giving oneself up to something so completely.

Angling was a gentleman's pursuit in America as early as 1732, when the Schuylkill Fishing Company of Schuylkill, Pennsylvania, became the country's first private hunting and fishing club. It was not until the 1800s, however, that sport fishing gained widespread popularity in this country, partly as a respite from the urbanization of the Industrial Revolution. In part, the fad for fishing coincided with the romantic-era enthusiasm for any outdoor pursuit that would lead one on an adventure in the wilderness. By the mid- to late nineteenth century, the fashion for angling had become a gentle rural pastime against the gritty backdrop of industrialization. The writer WASHINGTON IRVING was an early convert, devoting a chapter to the angler in his *Sketch-Book of Geoffrey Crayon, Gent.* (1819–20). Irving relates how, after studying the seductive pages of Walton's *Compleat Angler,* he set forth to a mountain brook in the Hudson River highlands to try his hand at the sport, "as stark mad as was ever Don Quixote from reading books of chivalry." Enthusiasm was not a good teacher: Irving hooked himself, tailed his line in a branch, splintered his rod, and finally gave up fishing to read "old Izaak" under a tree.

Contact

American Museum of Fly Fishing ⊠ 3657 Main Street, Manchester, VT 05254. (802-362-3300. ▱ amff.com
■ Exhibitions and extensive collections of angling-related materials, including flies, rods, manuscripts, and photographs, document the history of fly fishing. Publications include *The American Fly Fisher.*

Reading

▱ Izaak Walton, *The Compleat Angler: Or the Contemplative Man's Recreation* (1653, 1998). ▱ Mary Orvis Marbury, *Favorite Flies and Their Histories: With Many Replies from Practical Anglers to Inquiries Concerning How, When, and Where to Use Them* (1892, 1988). ▱ Norman Maclean, *A River Runs Through It* (1976). ▱ Paul Schullery, *American Fly Fishing: A History* (1987). ▱ James Prosek, *The Complete Angler: A Connecticut Yankee Follows in the Footsteps of Walton* (1999).

Appalachian Mountains

It may take a geographer's understanding of heaving tectonic plates, glacial slides, and crustal folds dating to the Paleozoic era to recognize that whether you are climbing a peak in New England's WHITE or GREEN MOUNTAINS, hiking the CATSKILL MOUNTAINS or the Alleghenies, driving the BLUE RIDGE, or exploring spurs "back of beyond" in the GREAT SMOKY MOUNTAINS or the Cumberland Plateau, you will find yourself in the single chain of geological land known as the Appalachians. In 1728, when William Byrd (1674–1744) surveyed the border of North Carolina and Virginia, he described these mountains as "Ranges of Blue Clouds rising one above the other." The prodigious parade of worn, forested peaks traces a line along the half-billion-year-old Appalachian plateau extending from the Gaspé Peninsula southwest as far as the Gulf Coast plain in Alabama. The range supports one of the globe's greatest and most diverse hardwood FORESTS—filled with oak, ash, chikapin, Fraser fir and pine, giant tulip magnolias, hawthorn, blackberry, and phosphorescent jack-o-lantern mushrooms (forty rare types of wildflower inhabit the southern Appalachians alone).

Hernando De Soto (1496?–1542) was likely the first European to enter the southern portion of the Applachian range, on a 1539–40 Spanish expedition north from what is now Georgia, crossing into the Tennessee River valley near Chattanooga. In the north Samuel de Champlain (1567–1635) recorded a sighting of the Green Mountains in Vermont. To limit Indian contact, consolidate fur trade, and maintain control over an orderly line of English plantations on the eastern seaboard, the British Crown declared the Appalachian range the official western boundary of the thirteen colonies, beyond which it was illegal to settle. This and the few transverse passes made the Appalachians a physical and a psychological obstacle to the western wilderness and frontier expansion. The first English expedition across the Blue Ridge, led by Governor Alexander Spotswood (1676–1740) of Virginia, was not organized until 1716.

The best known of the early explorers of the southern mountains was DANIEL BOONE, who led his first hunting trip to the Cumberland Mountains of the Kentucky Territory in 1769, and in 1773 he began forays to colonize Kentucky in a direct challenge to the British proclamation. George Washington (1732–99) was the great explorer of the central Appalachians. A skilled surveyor and capable mountaineer, he piloted several surveys across the Alleghenies, a western ridge extending from Pennsylvania southwest to Virginia, and scouting expeditions. These included a 1,000-mile wilderness journey across Pennsylvania to the French outpost at Venango (present-day Franklin) and back through the Blue Ridge to Williamsburg, Virginia, in 1754. The pioneering botanist William Bartram (1739–1823) (☞ NATURALISTS) explored the southern Appalachians in the 1770s, remarking on the primeval wilderness he found.

Following the Swiss and German palatinate settlers west, it was primarily the tough, independent-minded Scots-Irish, or Ulstermen, who piled up along both sides of the mountain border in south and central Appalachia, which saw a million settlers by 1830. The stubborn separateness of the Southern Highlanders was perpetuated by an unforgiving wilderness of sloughs, creeks, and boulders that exacted a particular brand of self-reliance and kept the Appalachian mountaineers isolated. Or unforgiving at least as far as any farmer was concerned. (As the saying goes: "Goin' up, you might nigh stand up straight and bite the ground: goin' down, a man wants hobnails in the seat of his pants.") Some claimed that an Appalachian farmer could break his neck falling out of his own cornfield. ☞ also APPALACHIAN NATIONAL SCENIC TRAIL

Appalachian Mountain Club ✉ 5 Joy Street, Boston, MA 02108. ☎ 617-523-0636. ▢ www.outdoors.org

Contacts

■ Founded in 1876, the club is the oldest recreational organization in America as well as the oldest conservation group. Its mission is to promote responsible recreational use of the mountains, rivers, and trails in the American Northeast. Twelve local chapters sponsor guided hikes, canoe outings, outdoor skills training, and social events and are responsible for maintaining 1,400 miles of trails through a massive volunteer effort. The club publishes several respected hiking and camping guides, along with the magazine *AMC Outdoors*, chapter newsletters, and *Appalachia Journal*, a compendium (issued continuously since 1876) of outdoor writing, trip and gear reports, and conservation news.

Appalachian Trail Conference ✉ P.O. Box 807, Harpers Ferry, WV 25425-0807. ☎ 304-535-6331. ▢ www.atconf.org

■ This volunteer-based nonprofit coalition of private citizens and public agency leaders was founded in 1925 to oversee the connection of new and existing trails to form what would later become the Appalachian National Scenic Trail. That accomplished, its main purpose now is the ongoing purchase of additional corridor land and pursuit of permanent protection for the trail in tandem with the Trust for Appalachian Lands and stewardship of the trail itself. In 1984 the National Park Service turned over to the conference management of the lands it acquires for the trail corridor. The organization and its member clubs publish detailed topographical maps, eleven guides to the trail by section (also available on CD-ROM), and the *AT Data Book*, an information guide to all aspects of hiking the trail. Regional offices and affiliated clubs offer legal advice and fund-raising help.

The Appalachian Trail's northernmost section extends into Maine, where this view in Baxter State Park reveals a more austere landscape than that of the Great Smokies at the southern end of the route.

Appalachian National Scenic Trail

"Wilderness is two things—fact and feeling. It is a fund of knowledge and a spring of influence. It is the ultimate source of health."

Benton MacKaye, founder
Appalachian National Scenic Trail

Give or take a few miles, this 2,160-mile-long public hiking trail follows the crest of the Appalachian chain from Mount Katahdin in Maine to Springer Mountain in Georgia. Under the National Trails System Act (1968) (☞ NATIONAL TRAILS SYSTEM), the route was established as the country's first national scenic trail. About 96 percent falls under state and federal ownership and runs through fourteen states, eight national forests, Great Smoky Mountains and Shenandoah National Parks, and sixty state parks, forests, and game lands.

Although this unique linear recreation area is technically a unit of the NATIONAL PARK SYSTEM, it is managed primarily by club volunteers, a legacy of the original Appalachian Trail, created by Benton MacKaye (1879–1975). It was the goal of MacKaye, a research forester for the U.S. FOREST SERVICE and a planner for the Tennessee Valley Authority, to unite a disparate group of hiking clubs as the Appalachian Trail Conference. Through their volunteer efforts, the first part of the trail was built and marked during the 1920s and 1930s. The U.S. Forest Service, NATIONAL PARK SERVICE, CIVILIAN CONSERVATION CORPS, and state and local organizations were active partners. A continuous trail was opened in 1937; after a series of interruptions it was reopened and completed in 1951.

The legislation creating national scenic trails also authorized about $170 million to purchase private lands to create a buffer zone against incompatible uses. As a result the trail passes almost entirely through protected public lands and encompasses some of the most valued natural and scenic resources in the East. More than 4 million day hikers use it each year. Through-hiking was never advocated by MacKaye, and except in the northernmost hundred miles, it is easy to enjoy a day hike on a short section because roads cross or provide access via side trails to the main route. Nevertheless, the trail has a peculiar hold on hikers' imaginations and has fostered a strong brotherhood of kindred spirits who make it their mission to walk the entire path in a single year. Only about one-fifth of the 1,500 persons who attempt it annually succeed.

Developed in the 1930s, the Appalachian Trail grew from its envisioned length of about 1,200 miles to more than 2,000 miles, stretching from Georgia to Maine. Study centers planned for the route were never built.

Reading

📖 David Emblidge, ed., *The Appalachian Trail Reader* (1996). 📖 Bill Bryson, *A Walk in the Woods: Rediscovering America on the Appalachian Trail* (1998). 📖 Noah Adams, *Far Appalachia* (2001). 📖 Scott Weidensaul, *Mountains of the Heart: A Natural History of the Appalachians* (2001).

Inspired by the discovery of burial mounds and earthworks, the first systematic archaeological investigation in America began shortly after the Revolution, when THOMAS JEFFERSON directed a controlled excavation of an ancient Indian mound in Virginia in 1784. Over the next century the American Antiquarian Society, American Philosophical Society (☞ LEARNED SOCIETIES), Smithsonian Institution, and Archeological Institute of America promoted the first serious archaeological investigations and published accounts. Adolph Bandelier's alarming reports of vandalism at the highly valued Pecos site in New Mexico spurred the first congressional debate over the preservation of archaeological sites in the early 1880s. In 1889 the federal government appropriated $2,000 to conserve the Casa Grande ruins near Florence, Arizona.

Today archaeological parks featuring above-ground artifacts, ruins, and cultural remains are maintained by state and federal park systems, historical societies, museums, and universities. Many focus on America's paleo-Indian history, including the pueblos of the Southwest and the ancient mound complexes of the Southeast and Midwest. Digging and collecting materials including arrowheads, fossils, and rocks is typically prohibited. ☞ also NATIONAL PARK SYSTEM, NATIVE AMERICANS

Archaeological Parks

Colorado's Mesa Verde National Park, created in 1906, was the first national park established to preserve the works of humans. It encompasses thousands of ancient Indian archaeological sites, including cliff dwellings and mesa-top villages built between A.D. 450 and 1300, when the area was abandoned.

Society for American Archaeology ✉ 900 Second Street, NE, Suite 12, Washington, DC 20002. ☎ 202-789-8200. 🖥 www.saa.org
■ Founded in 1934, this international society is devoted to the research, interpretation, and protection of the archaeological heritage of North, South, and Central America. Advocacy efforts focus on site conservation and the opposition to the sale of looted artifacts. A government affairs network is involved in federal legislative and regulatory issues. Publications include the journal *Antiquity*.

Society for Historical Archaeology ✉ P.O. Box 30446,Tucson, AZ 85751. ☎ 520-886-8006. 🖥 www.sha.org
■ Founded in 1967, this is the largest scholarly society devoted to archaeological research in the modern world. The group supports the preservation and research of archaeological sites underground and under water.

Web Sites

Archaeological Parks in the U.S. Maintained by the Arkansas Archaeological Survey to provide links to state and federally managed archaeological sites by state and region. 🖥 www.uark.edu/misc/aras

National Archeological Database. A vast computerized communications network administered by the National Park Service for the archaeological and historic preservation community. 🖥 www.cr.nps.gov/aad/nadb.htm

John James Audubon

Born in Haiti and educated in France, John James Audubon (1785?–1851) traveled extensively in the American West, Florida, and Labrador from 1818 to the 1840s. His exhaustive journals from those frontier expeditions provided the substance for *The Birds of America*, brought out in elephant folio in London between 1827 and 1838. The accompanying text was entitled *Ornithological Biography* (1831–39) and was edited by William MacGillivray, who is credited with providing the technical details.

HENRY DAVID THOREAU commented that he "read in Audubon with a thrill of delight." Audubon's informal essays were remarkable in that they made his science so accessible. His watercolors were equally extraordinary in their record of American wildlife in a natural habitat complete with flowers, grasses, and all the minutest details of the locale. Like many of his contemporaries who traveled to the frontier, Audubon was ambivalent about the inexorable impact of the march west. "Whether these changes are for the better or worse," he wrote,"I shall not pretend to say."
☞ *also* BIRDS, NATURALISTS

Selected Works

📕 *The Birds of America* (1840–44). 📕 *The Viviparous Quadrupeds of North America*, with John Bachman (1845–46).

"About ten o'clock, as we stood around our campfire, we were startled by a brief but striking display of the aurora borealis. My imagination had already been excited by talk of legends and of weird shapes and appearances, and when, on looking up toward the sky, I saw those pale phantasmal waves of light chasing each other across the little opening above our heads, and at first sight seeming barely to clear the treetops, I was as vividly impressed as if I had caught a glimpse of a veritable spirit of the Neversink. The sky shook and trembled like a great white curtain."   John Burroughs (1837–1921)

Aurora Borealis

Occurring during the equinoxes, the aurora borealis is best seen in the United States near the Canadian border and in Alaska. These natural light shows explode. in shades of blue, green, yellow, and violet.

Occurring in oval bands moving around the northern geomagnetic pole, the aurora borealis (Latin for "northern dawn") is a series of luminous patterns created when subatomic particles showered from sunspots and solar flares rain down into the upper atmosphere. As they strike a particular type of atom or molecule, the particles briefly lose some of their electrons, creating glowing atmospheric gases when they absorb and lose energy. The fantastic results are the striated arcs, ripples, streamers, and hanging curtains of color known as the northern lights. (The aurora australis in the Southern Hemisphere is known as the southern lights.)

The oval path of the northern aurora passes most often through northern Norway, across Hudson Bay, through Point Barrow in Alaska, and through northern Siberia. Farther away from the average oval, the geomagnetic disturbances are more unpredictable. Closer to it, one has a better chance of seeing the aurora. The northern lights may be visible several times a year in New England, for example, but only a few times a century in the Southeast. The best location in the United States to view this polar phenomenon is the north coast of Alaska, where the northern lights are visible 300 nights of the year—barring pollution and the interference of artificial lights, that is. In this northern region, the optimum

Opposite: John James Audubon's illustration of an adult female golden eagle (*Falco crysaetos*) shows the bird with her prey. An engraving of the image, which displays the artist's characteristic attention to detail, appeared in Audubon's 1833 *Birds of America*.

viewing time is at midnight around the spring and fall equinoxes. Summer night skies are not usually dark enough for background contrast, and winter viewing is just plain cold. Summer skies also reveal the aurora borealis across the northern United States, but seeing them is often a matter of luck.

Web Site   **Geophysical Institute, University of Alaska, Fairbanks.** Forecasts of auroral activity are posted here. 🖳 www.pfrr.alaska.edu/ ~ pfrr/AURORA

Avalanches

The most dangerous type of avalanche occurs when a plate of snow breaks off and slides as a cohesive slab down the surface of a weaker snow mass. These "dry slab" avalanches travel about 70 to 80 miles an hour and are far more hazardous than slower-moving wet avalanches, caused by rapidly warming temperatures, or loose-snow "sluff" avalanches. Slab avalanches can occur naturally when wind or a new snowfall deposits a fresh layer of snow on a weaker layer that eventually gives way under the weight. The majority of fatal slab avalanches, however, are the result of human activity—by hikers, mountaineers, snowboarders, skiers, or snowmobilers (the leading cause of fatal avalanches)—and almost always occur in the backcountry. Fatal avalanches within official ski-area boundaries are rare because such areas practice vigilant control measures, such as setting off potentially dangerous slides with explosives. ☞ *also* GLACIERS, ICE SAFETY, MOUNTAINEERING, SNOW CAMPING, SURVIVAL STRATEGIES

The glacial environment of North Cascades National Park in Washington creates the right conditions for snow avalanches. In the Picket Range an avalanche flows out from the base of the cliffs (right center).

Made in a multitude of designs, backpacks are available as smaller daypacks and larger packs designed for trips of several days. Many camping stores rent the larger packs, which is a good way to test one before committing to a purchase that might make you miserable. Look for the lightest weight in the desired size. Check for tight stitching and reinforcing bar tacks at stress points, and avoid puckers, which will chafe. Beware of too many straps, pockets, and extras.

A daypack should have these basic features: adjustable padded shoulder straps, a foam-padded back or a built-in plastic back-support panel and a padded waist-hip belt, and a zipper pocket for stowing small items. Better models have adjustable compression straps used to snug up the load; these are handy for lashing on a lightweight camera tripod or a collapsible fly rod.

The greater challenge is choosing a large pack, because the designs offer so many variations in pocket size and location, storm flaps, closure type, and the like. Look for a full-size pack that comes with a range of interchangeable belts and harnesses so you can fit it with those in the right size for your body. The critical element is the frame, which is designed to distribute weight down to a padded hip belt, shifting the burden away from the neck, shoulders, and back to the hips, buttocks, and thighs. General-purpose internal-frame packs are built around flexible integral stays (aluminum, graphite, or polycarbonate)

Backpacks

that typically meet at the small of the back and may be supplemented by a polyethylene panel. These packs are usually made of urethane-coated nylon duck, Cordura® nylon, or ballistics nylon. Good for moderate loads and off-trail rambling, they are relatively narrow and fit snugly to the back. Internal-frame packs are recommended for activities such as skiing and snowshoeing (☞ SNOWSHOES) because they are stable yet adapt to your own movement; however, they can be uncomfortably hot in hot weather.

Backpacks are now made for canine hikers as well as for their masters. Adjustable dog packs are designed not to interfere with the animal's stride.

Typically less expensive, external-frame packs are better for heavy loads and long distances. The rigid cross-bar frame (usually aluminum or plastic) is designed as a separate component and holds the pack away from the body to allow air circulation. A wider, flatter pack and more elevated center of gravity permit a more upright body posture than an internal-frame pack (in which the weight rides a bit lower), but the rigid frame means that the pack has a tendency to sway. Stabilizer straps at the bottom corners can be tightened to help. You can check the strength of the frame by setting one lower corner of the pack on the floor, and then pressing down diagonally from the other corner. If it gives, it is not well made.

Both internal- and external-frame packs come in a variety of sizes. Short trips (two or three days) will require a 3,000- to 3,500-cubic-inch pack; 4,500 to 6,000 cubic inches hold enough gear for about a week; 5,000 cubic inches is a good middle ground. Avoid packs with a hybrid internal-external frame and one-size-fits-nobody models.

Fitting a Pack

■ Many of the better backpacks come in specific sizes. The key to the fit is not in your height but in the length of your torso.

■ Have someone measure the distance from the bony protrusion at the base of the neck (the seventh vertebra) to the point in the small of the back that is level with your hip bones. If this measurement is less than 18 inches, you want a small pack; 18 to 20 inches indicates medium; and a longer torso calls for large.

■ One key adjustment is that all-important torso length: the objective is the right relationship between the shoulder-strap position and the hip-belt placement. A high-riding hip belt indicates that the torso is too short, a low-riding belt the reverse. Depending on the pack style, torso length may be adjusted by moving the attachment points of the shoulder straps or hip belts. Sometimes simply switching to a different-size frame is called for.

■ Check to see that the lumbar pad fits firmly slightly below the small of the back.

■ Check that the hip belt is stiff but not so stiff that it chafes. A good hip belt is made with several layers of foam in different grades for fine-tuned compression. The belt should tuck over the hip bones to maximize weight-bearing capacity. Snugging it up should make the pack rise slightly on your back; otherwise the pack itself is probably too short. In this case, adjust the torso length so the belt cradles your hip bones and the pack weight rides primarily on your hips. On an internal-frame pack, you can do this by changing the height of the shoulder yoke.

■ Next, check the shoulder-strap fit. Extra-soft straps may feel good in the store, but they will probably give too much on the trail. On an external-frame pack, adjust the lift straps and check to see that the shoulder-strap padding extends about 2 inches below the armpit. The top of the shoulder straps should meet the frame at the exact level of your shoulder tops. The sternum strap, which connects the shoulder straps, should ride below the collar bone. When you tilt your head back, it should not hit the frame or the bag. You should also be able to move freely without feeling off balance or noticing any irritating hot spots.

■ Never make a final purchase without loading the pack and walking around the store. Climb stairs and sit down with it on.

■ Once you get home, the pack may need a week or two of tinkering to get the fit just right. Whatever else, don't fail to take it on a test run.

Barkcraft

In Indian lore the thunderbird is the mythical bird believed to bring on thunder and lighting. Legend has it that one day when Nanabojou, the great North Woods sorcerer, was fleeing the thunderbird's rage, he took refuge in the hollow trunk of a fallen birch tree. Because the birch is believed to be the offspring of the thunderbird, harming Nanabojou would have meant hurting the child first, and the infuriated bird was forced to retreat. Saved, Nanabojou vowed, "As long as the world stands, this tree shall be a protection and a benefit to man." For Indians, the sorcerer's declaration was proof of why lightning never strikes a birch tree.

The Iroquois and Algonquian Indians, including the Chippewas, who inhabited the dense transitional FORESTS that once spread unbroken from the North Woods to New England, prized the paper birch (*Betula papyrifera*) indigenous to this region for its strength and imperviousness to water. This natural parchment's pliability also made it an essential element of the barkcraft that was so fundamental to the forest-based Indian cultures. The natives used the bark for their superbly engineered CANOES and toboggans, as well as for utensils, baskets, waterproof vessels, fishing creels, haversacks, quivers, torches, and many other articles essential to warfare, hunting, and domestic life.

Indians are said to have believed that the lenticels (slits) distinguishing the bark of the paper birch were the strikes made by Nanabojou to identify the tree for their use and that the bark's "winged" dark spots were the image of the thunderbird itself. The romantic associations are a primary reason why the art of barkcraft has outlived the native cultures themselves. From the 1800s onward, woodland guidebooks often

The white birch, valued by Native Americans for its pliable bark, was also an elegant subject for William J. Linton's engraving *White Birches of the Saranac* (1873), based on by a drawing by John Augustus Hows.

featured birch-bark projects, and few children have ever finished a stay at scout or summer camp without a home-made bark napkin ring or wallet to show for it.

Gathering the Birch

■ The best bark for barkcraft is paper birch, which is white on the outside and tan on the underside.

■ Gathering bark requires particular care. There is no justification for stripping it from a live tree, which can damage or kill it. Fallen logs and dead standing trees are the proper source for bark, which is so resistant to insects and decay that it stays intact long after the tree itself has died and rotted to dust.

■ The bark of a dead tree can be harvested by cutting a lengthwise slit down the trunk and carefully snapping away the bark in a sheet with a penknife or fingers. (Take only what you need, because dead trees serve as habitats for insects.)

■ To avoid creating tears at knots or at the "thunderbird" black spots where bark tends to stick, gently pound them to loosen the bark.

■ Roll the sheets white side in, against the natural curve of the bark, to prevent a permanent curl from setting in.

■ If you need to store the bark for any length of time, unroll the sheets, pile them inner side down on the ground, and weight them to flatten.

One of many popular handbooks on woodland activities published before World War II, Bernard S. Mason's *Woodcraft* (1939) featured directions for this birch-bark bowl.

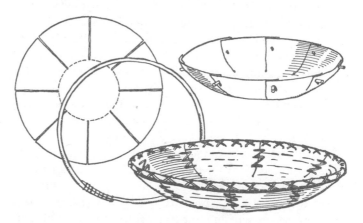

Making a Birch-Bark Bowl or Basket

Chippewa baskets, called *makuks*, were traditionally made from a single piece of birch bark that was folded into the desired form and often lashed with sweet grass or basswood bark lacing. The shallow circular design described here was a standard type of food bowl. In basketmaking the bark should always be used white (outer) side in.

■ When you are ready to use a piece of bark, soak it first in hot water and clean it with soap to remove the powdery resin if you are planning to decorate the surface with paint or ink.

■ Using heavy shears, cut a circle of bark 18 inches in diameter.

■ With the white side up, lightly pencil a circle measuring about 9 inches in diameter in the center of the circle. (Draw a smaller circle for a deeper bowl or a larger circle for a more shallow bowl.)

- At even intervals cut eight slits from the outer edge to the pencil line.
- Gently bend each of the resulting sections upward (brown side out), overlapping at the top edges by one inch. At the corner of each overlap, use an ice pick to make a hole by holding the bark against a flat surface and carefully twisting the point through both layers. Secure the layers by inserting toothpicks into the holes.
- Make a hoop by cutting a long pencil-thick switch of maple or ash. After soaking the switch in water until it is flexible, cut it to a length measuring four inches longer than the circumference of the basket top. Bend the switch into a circle, overlapping the ends by two inches, and lace together the ends with raffia or yarn.
- Slip the hoop over the basket top and lash it to the bark with raffia or yarn using a darning needle, neatly tying off the ends.
- In the same manner, lace each overlap, removing the toothpicks as you work.

Bears

Two species of the *Ursidae* family inhabit North America below the Arctic Circle: the black bear (*Ursus americanus*) and the grizzly, or brown, bear (*Ursus arctos*). The average adult male black bear weighs 200 pounds and measures about 5 feet from nose to tail. The grizzly rears up to 8 or 9 feet tall and weighs in at an average of 500 to 800 pounds. The Alaskan brown bear, or Kodiak bear, a northwestern coastal strain of grizzly bear, is the largest species of land carnivore, sometimes weighing in excess of 1,500 pounds. Both *Ursus americanus* and *Ursus arctos* are good waders, fishers, and swimmers. They walk with a clumsy, lumbering gait (the grizzly swings its head), but they can also move with bursts of surprising speed—up to as much as 30 miles per hour.

Both bear types are omnivores and have an excellent sense of smell, good hearing, and awesome power: a single blow of a grizzly's 30-pound paw is enough to kill a moose, and the bears have been known to use their claws like crampons to scale a vertical 30-foot cliff to get at a carcass. The fur of both bear species can range in color from blond to brown to black (black bear fur even occurs in white and blue-gray), so color is not necessarily a surefire identifying feature—although if you get close enough to a brown bear (not a good idea), you will see that white fur tips are what make it look grizzled. The two species are better distinguished by physical attributes: the grizzly differs from the black bear primarily in its muscular shoulder hump, dished-in face, and longer, straighter foreclaws, which are designed for digging for roots and burrowing animals.

Usually found in forested areas, the far-ranging black bear has been recorded in all states except Hawaii, whereas grizzlies are limited primarily to Alaska and parts of Montana,

Longer, crampon-like claws distinguish the grizzly (above) from the less ferociously manicured black bear—not that you should ever be close enough to tell the difference.

Range

Wyoming, Washington, and Idaho. ALASKA claims more than 98 percent of the U.S. brown bear population, including the Kodiak. Katmai National Park and Preserve contains about 2,000 Alaskan brown bears, which is the world's largest protected population. It is estimated that there are now only about 1,000 grizzlies in the lower forty-eight states, and the population—reduced over the last two centuries by disease, poaching, intermittent breeding, and starvation—occupies only about one percent of its original range.

Black bears tend to prefer mountain forests. Grizzlies favor forests as well as more open country in coastal areas and river valleys. After holing up for a period of winter dormancy, the bears emerge in spring when food is again available and are most likely seen through early to mid-summer. Feeding sites include logs and stumps turned over or clawed apart for insects and grubs, clawed and chewed tree trunks, torn-up berry patches, and gaping pits where grizzlies have dug for rodents. Both bear types are primarily nocturnal.

Endangered Bears

In 1975 the grizzly bear was listed as threatened under the Endangered Species Act (1973) (☞ ENDANGERED SPECIES). An Interagency Grizzly Bear Committee comprising representatives from the NATIONAL PARK SERVICE, U.S. FISH AND WILDLIFE SERVICE, U.S. FOREST SERVICE, BUREAU OF LAND MANAGEMENT, and several state game and fish departments was created in 1983 to oversee a recovery effort. The goal is to restore truly wild, self-sustaining grizzly populations in six ecosystems in the contiguous forty-eight states.

A clear threat to bears is the trade in bear viscera. Bear bile and gall bladders, used in traditional Asian medicines and in some luxury cosmetics, bring extremely high prices in some international markets, despite the fact that a synthetic version is available. Overhunting in Asia has led to an increase in poaching in America. States such as Idaho permit the sale of bear galls, and unless caught in the act of poaching, merchants can claim the viscera originated in a state that allows their sale.

Bear Safety

In most cases bears are not usually aggressive unless they are hurt or defending their cubs or a kill. But there really is no sure way to predict bear behavior: both species have been known to attack unprovoked. All bears should thus be considered potentially dangerous and accorded due respect. It is not unusual to encounter black bears near garbage dumps and fish-drying racks; there are yearly reports of their wandering into downtown Juneau, Fairbanks, and Anchorage, Alaska. Grizzlies are usually shy and difficult to spot but can certainly be tenacious when it comes to satisfying their appetites. If you plan to do any backcountry hiking or animal watching in grizzly territory, get information from park or wildlife authorities in advance and carefully follow instructions.

Black bears and grizzlies can be safely observed only from a minimum distance of 100 yards. Above all, you want to avoid a surprise meeting. Most bear encounters happen off the well-trod trails and rarely involve groups of more than two people. To announce their presence, hikers should talk loudly, sing, ring a bell, or rattle a can full of stones. If you do have a close encounter, the bear will likely retreat first.

Confronting a Bear

- Stop whatever you are doing. Do not run or move abruptly. If you are fishing and have a fish on a line, quietly cut it loose.
- Talk to your companions in low, quiet tones.
- Toss something like a water bottle to one side of the bear to distract it, but hold on to your backpack.
- In an attack situation, capsicum-based bear pepper spray is a good deterrent. If possible, spray a cloud between yourself and the bear when the bear is 50 feet away. In dire straits, spray it in the bear's face.

If It's a Black Bear . . .

- If a black bear charges, it probably smells food but can be scared away by yelling.
- The general wisdom is to chase a black bear, loudly banging pots or otherwise making noise—but do not corner it.
- If the bear is wily enough to get your food, leave it alone until it is done dining.

A cardinal rule in bear country is never get between a mother and her cubs. Young brown bears like these two are nimble and quick, but after their first year they lose their ability to climb—and cannot follow human intruders up trees.

■ Because they have bad eyesight, grizzly bears typically stand upright and squint to focus on a sound or a smell. This posture is often mistaken for the first move in an attack. In fact, grizzlies readying to charge do not rear but instead drop to all fours, cock their ears with head low, and gnash their formidable teeth.

■ Avoid making noise. Walk slowly over to a tall tree and climb it. (Grizzlies over a year old generally do not climb.)

■ Never turn and run.

■ If a grizzly appears to be attacking, fall to the ground face down with your legs slightly spread and your arms folded over your head and the back of your neck. Even if the bear comes at you, keep your face down and resist the urge to yell.

■ Remain still and hold the position for at least 20 minutes after the bear retreats.

Storage and Bear Bagging

One of the chief ways to keep bears away is proper food and garbage storage, which is required by federal law in national parks. (Visitors to the Brooks Camp in Katmai National Park, Alaska, are required to attend the Brooks Camp School of Bear Etiquette.) Depending on the rules, mandated storage might be in the trunk of a vehicle or in air-tight bearproof containers and dumpsters provided in the parks. Bearproof canisters made of sturdy plastic can also be rented at many locations. Avoid packing in aromatic foods such as cheese, bacon, and fish. Camp away from natural watering

Strict procedures for food and garbage storage are mandated in national parks. Waterproof camping packs are now available for safely storing food in a method called bear bagging.

holes, prepare meals in a separate area located downwind from tents, and keep bearproof containers at least 100 yards away from the sleeping area. Use them for food, garbage, and all cosmetics, including toothpaste and sunscreen. In grizzly hot spots it is also necessary to seal up your stove, utensils, water containers, and even the clothes you have worn while cooking because they will be permeated with food odors. Seal food supplies as you cook and use them; do not wait until the end of the meal. Never bring food or water into a tent. Shake out backpacks and hang them outside. Keep a can of capsicum-based bear pepper spray in your tent and in the cooking area. Clean all traces of food from grills and tabletops so that bears will not become habituated to food smells at the camp site. Such acclimation makes them lose their natural fear of humans and become aggressive problem bears.

In the absence of containers, suspending air-tight bags out of bear reach is the preferred means of storing food and belongings. This method, known as bear bagging, involves rigging two equally weighted bags of provisions from a tree branch to deter climbing bears. (Grizzlies lose the ability to climb after a year, but black bears, especially the nimble cubs, are good climbers.)

■ Find a slender tree branch at least 12 feet off the ground and well away from the tree trunk.

■ Using a piece of cord about 40 feet long, weight one end with a hammer or another tool and toss that end over the branch.

■ Untie the weight and tie a bag to one free end of the cord, hauling it up to hang about a foot below the branch.

■ Tie the second bag as far up the cord as possible, then tuck the tail into the bag, leaving a loop sticking out.

■ Use a long stick to work the bags to even height.

■ To retrieve the bags, snag the loop with the stick, pull down the cord, and then keep pulling gently, catching the bags as they fall.

Setting Up Bear Bags

Great Bear Foundation ✉ P.O. Box 9383, Missoula, MT 59807. ☎ 406-829-9378. ▯ www.greatbear.org

■ The Great Bear Foundation was established in 1982 to promote conservation of wild bears and their habitat around the world. Its efforts include scientific research, education, monitoring government agencies responsible for land management decisions affecting bear survival, and litigation in defense of bears and bear habitat.

Contact

▤ Charles Dudley Warner, "How I Killed a Bear," *In the Wilderness* (1878). ▤ Andy Russell, *Grizzly Country* (1967). ▤ John McPhee, "A Textbook Place for Bears," *Table of Contents* (1980).

Reading

Birds

Birdwatching as a popular outdoor pursuit developed alongside the American bird conservation movement, which coalesced in 1886 when some 38,000 persons responded to a call by George Bird Grinnell (1849–1938), editor of *Forest and Stream*, to help form the first Audubon society (☞ JOHN JAMES AUDUBON). That instant enthusiasm reflected the growing dismay over the widespread loss of bird populations to sport hunting and commercial harvesting in the absence of federal game laws and bag limits. Among the worst threats was the market for colorful plumage and stuffed birds used to decorate hats.

Although reportedly half as many songbirds can be found in the country today as in 1948, only four of about 160 bird species known to have nested in eastern forests are extinct: the Carolina parakeet, ivory-billed woodpecker, Bachman's warbler, and passenger pigeon (☞ ENDANGERED SPECIES). These species fell prey primarily to professional market hunters and habitat destruction. The most stunning statistic involves the eradication of the passenger pigeon, whose flocks in the hundreds of thousands once literally darkened the sky. At the height of migration there were an estimated 9 billion passenger pigeons in America—about double the number of all land birds today. By 1914 the population had been reduced to a single bird, named Martha, which died that year in an Ohio zoo. Every last one of the others had been shot, netted, clubbed, or starved into extinction.

By the late 1800s ornithologists had essentially finished the task of identifying and recording America's birds. The first sighting of Worthen's sparrow in New Mexico in 1884 was among the last discoveries until the 1973 identification of the Hawaiian po'ouli, a previously unknown species and genus of honeycreeper. The American Ornithologists' Union was formed in 1883, followed in 1896 by the Massachusetts Audubon Society, whose vociferous women members began lobbying politicians for a boycott of feather-decorated ladies' wear. New York State's Audubon Plumage Law (1910) was the first in a series of state laws that shut down the plumage market by 1913. The federal Migratory Bird Treaty Act (1918) mandated bag limits and hunting seasons for migratory species.

Birding

Sixteen states had formed Audubon chapters by 1899. The main forum for discussion was the magazine *Bird Lore,* whose founder, Frank Chapman, instituted the first national Christmas Bird Count in 1900. According to the National Audubon Society, Chapman's idea was that "it was better to count birds than shoot them." The survey put hundreds of birders into the woods, and more than 42,000 participate in the annual

The overhunted passenger pigeon, depicted by John James Audubon in his 1827–30 *Birds of America*, was dealt a death blow when a vast area of its Great Lakes habitat was harvested to provide timber for rebuilding Chicago after the 1871 fire. The bird was extinct by 1914.

count today. That effort spawned local birding clubs and the 1910 Junior Audubon Club, responsible for educating more than four million children about bird conservation over the next twenty-five years. Roger Tory Peterson (1908–96), considered the father of modern birdwatching, published the first contemporary field guide, to birds of the eastern United States, in 1934. His system of identification incorporated black-and-white illustrations and descriptive text that focused on a characteristic "field mark" for each bird.

Contacts

American Bird Conservancy ✉ P.O. Box 249, The Plains, VA 20198. ✆ 888-Bird-Mag. 🖥 www.abcbirds.org
■ This national nonprofit organization dedicated to bird and habitat conservation builds coalitions of conservation groups, scientists, and members of the public through its policy council and Partners in Flight program. Publications include *Bird Calls* and *Bird Conservation*.

American Birding Association ✉ P.O. Box 6599, Colorado Springs, CO 80934. ✆ 719-578-9703 🖥 www.americanbirding.org
■ The association promotes the environmental values of birdwatching and encourages conservation of birds and habitat. Publications include *Birding* and *Winging It*.

American Ornithologists' Union ✉ c/o National Museum of Natural History, Division of Birds, MRC 116, Washington, DC 20560. ⌨ www.pica.wru.umt. edu/AOU/AOU.html

■ The oldest organization (1883) in North America devoted to the scientific study of birds, the American Ornithologists' Union is primarily a professional society, but the membership of about 4,000 includes many amateurs dedicated to the advancement of ornithological science. An online checklist of birds gives scientific and English names, taxonomic status, and ranges of all known bird species in North America.

Ducks Unlimited ✉ One Waterfowl Way, Memphis, TN 38120. ☎ 800-45DUCKS. ⌨ www.ducks.org

■ This groups works to protect and restore waterfowl habitat in America and promotes public education about waterfowl and wetland management.

National Audubon Society ✉ 700 Broadway, New York, NY 10003. ☎ 212-979-3000. ⌨ audubon.org/nas

■ This leading national advocacy group has local affiliates devoted to the conservation of birds and other wildlife. Publications include *Audubon*.

Roger Tory Peterson Institute ✉ 311 Curtis Street, Jamestown, NY 14701. ☎ 800-758-6841. ⌨ rtpi.org

■ A national nonprofit educational organization focusing on educating children about birds and the natural world, the institute offers programs and exhibits and houses the library of the naturalist Roger Tory Peterson.

Web Sites

BIRDNET. This online service of the Ornithological Council provides comprehensive information about ornithology and birding, a state-by-state listing of bird observatories, and links to ten North American professional ornithological societies. ⌨ www.nmnh.si.edu/BIRDNET

Birdwatching.com. Birdwatching tips can be found here, along with links to online bird-listing databases. ⌨ www.birdwatching.com

Reading

📖 John Farrand, *How to Identify Birds: An Audubon Handbook* (1988). 📖 Roger Tory Peterson, *A Field Guide to the Birds* (1988). 📖 John Bull et al., *National Audubon Society Field Guide to North American Birds* (1994). 📖 Donald Stokes, *Stokes Field Guide to Birds* (1997). 📖 John Dunn, *National Geographic Field Guide to the Birds of North America* (1999). 📖 David Allen Sibley, *The Sibley Guide to Birds* (2000).

Bison

One of the most shocking statistics of frontier history is surely the near extinction of the American bison. Before European settlement, great herds of American bison, commonly known as buffalo, roamed the western plains in numbers estimated at 60 to 70 million. The first reports of the large herds came from the Lewis and Clark expedition (☞ CORPS OF DISCOVERY) in 1804. A century later the count was down to 500—this, the largest mammal in North America and an animal that had been evolving with the plains since the last Ice Age. Although NATIVE AMERICANS had long hunted bison without lasting impact, the animals do not fear humans and were no match for hunters and guns that moved west with the line of the frontier. The bison was sought for its hide, tongue (considered a delicacy), bones (used for making bone china), and its meat, which was used to feed thousands of railroad workers and soldiers. In the mid-1800s roughly two million buffalo were systematically slaughtered each year.

The English botanist Mark Catesby made this painting of the American bison during a frontier expedition about 1722, when millions still roamed the plains. A century later, although buffalo once occupied most of the continent, there were none east of the Mississippi River.

The first federal legislation to protect the buffalo was enacted in 1894, just three years before the last of the wild plains bison (two bulls, a cow, and her calf) were shot in Colorado and put on display at the Denver Museum of Natural History. A lost herd of wood bison, however, was discovered in northern Alberta, Canada, in 1893. Around 1910 a group of alarmed conservationists including THEODORE ROOSEVELT founded the American Bison Society and began efforts to regenerate herds by transferring animals to new locations. The current population of wild bison in ALASKA is descended from twenty animals released there near Delta Junction in 1928. Protected in game preserves, bison were initially bred and ranched like cattle to increase numbers, but by the 1960s revived herds were being allowed to grow, decrease, and migrate naturally and are thus considered truly wild. An estimated 125,000 wild bison now roam the country. ☞ *also* ENDANGERED SPECIES, YELLOWSTONE NATIONAL PARK

The central section of Skyline Drive, from Thornton Gap to Swift Run Gap in Virginia, drew a parade of Blue Ridge sightseers when it opened in 1934.

Blue Ridge Mountains

Blue Ridge is the perfectly eponymous name for the velvet blue skyline created by this eastern rampart of the APPALACHIAN MOUNTAINS, which runs from northwestern Maryland to northern Georgia. The ridge is noted for two scenic drives built as part of the CIVILIAN CONSERVATION CORPS program in the 1930s. Skyline Drive runs the length of Shenandoah National Park in Virginia from Front Royal to Rockfish Gap, near Waynesborough. The Blue Ridge Parkway picks up its own route at Rockfish Gap and covers 469 miles, passing through the Black Mountains, Craggies, Pisgahs, and Balsams to the GREAT SMOKY MOUNTAINS. Designated viewing spots are recommended for the autumn hawk and monarch butterfly migrations that distinguish this region. No commercial traffic is permitted.

Contact

Shenandoah National Park ⊠ 3655 U.S. Highway 211 East, Luray, VA 22835. ☎ 540-999-3500. ⌨ www.nps.gov.shen
■ The park contains 101 miles of the Appalachian National Scenic Trail.

Daniel Boone

Hunter, marksman, legislator, scout, and trail guide, Daniel Boone (1734–1820) was one of the country's most celebrated nineteenth-century frontiersmen: a master of the wilderness ennobled by deed in his own time and a folk hero so completely recast by future generations that the legend has long outweighed the man.

Around 1761 Boone began guiding hunting parties into the Watagua Valley of what is now eastern Tennessee, heretofore explored only sporadically by British and French Indian traders. In 1775, after earlier colonizing attempts were repelled by Indians, Boone entered Kentucky—then Cherokee country by royal treaty—as an advance agent for the Transylvania Company, blazing the Wilderness Road through the Cumberland Gap into the Great Grant of Kentucky, and founded Boonesboro on the Kentucky River.

Boone first gained notoriety in print in the 1784 biographical account *The Discovery, Settlement and Present State of Kentucke*, by John Filson, a Kentucky speculator. Filson's widely read volume, reprinted many times through the 1850s, was actually a thinly veiled piece of propaganda intended to generate land sales in the Kentucky Territory. The author offered Boone as the heaven-sent hero figure. On one level his story helped convey some of the real peril frontier settlement entailed. On another he symbolized the unimpeachable messenger of Divine Providence, "sent to answer the important designs of heaven," that legitimized the pursuit of the new western empire—and with it the seizure of territory and conquest of "savages" for the greater good of the more civilized settlers who were advancing ever westward.

Boone's image makers nurtured a legend that surpassed the man. In his *Leatherstocking Tales*, JAMES FENIMORE COOPER modeled the famous backwoodsman character Natty Bumppo on the frontiersman, portraying him as a reluctant conqueror of a wilderness in which he could see an inherent aesthetic value that might best not be conquered. In *Don Juan* (1818), the British

Daniel Boone was a logical subject for a genre artist like George Caleb Bingham, a frontier native and ardent adherent of the democratic process. Bingham's painting *Daniel Boone Escorting Settlers through the Cumberland Gap* (1851–52) remains the most famous of all images of the hero.

poet Lord Byron (1788–1824) went further, casting Boone as a romantic hero rather than a conquering pioneer. Until the Civil War, Boone was also portrayed as a folk symbol by numerous artists, including JOHN JAMES AUDUBON, Thomas Cole (1801–48) (☞ HUDSON RIVER SCHOOL ARTISTS), and George Caleb Bingham (1811–79) (☞ FRONTIER GENRE PAINTERS). After Andrew Jackson's election as president in 1828, the market for "Boonealia" traveled west of the Mississippi with the pioneer movement.

Brooks Range

As far as anyone knows, the first non-native to explore central ALASKA's Brooks Range was Robert Marshall, who first ventured into the north fork drainage of the Koyukuk River in 1929. It was a place, declared the environmentalist, "two hundred miles beyond the edge of the Twentieth Century." As the major northern Alaskan mountain system, the Brooks Range comprises a number of smaller ranges, including the DeLong, Baird, Schwatka, Endicott, Philip Smith, Romanzof, Shublik, and Davidson Mountains. All reach across the full width of Alaska above the Arctic Circle to form the great barrier between the Arctic plain and the rest of the state to the south. From the base of the Brooks Range, the Northern Slope unfolds to the Arctic Ocean and the Beaufort Sea. The sun never rises in winter or sets in summer on this vast sweep of frozen tundra, the spring feeding ground for hundreds of thousands of migrating caribou and a critical habitat for wolves, grizzlies, musk oxen, polar bears, and other Alaskan wildlife. Large portions of the Brooks Range are located in the Cape Krusentern National Monument, Noatak National Preserve, Kabuk Valley National Park, Gates of the Arctic National Park and Preserve, and Arctic National Wildlife Refuge (☞ NATIONAL WILDLIFE REFUGE SYSTEM).

William Cullen Bryant

"The groves were God's first temples."

William Cullen Bryant, "A Forest Hymn" (1860)

William Cullen Bryant (1794–1878), a poet, literary critic, and journalist, practiced law in Massachusetts before moving to New York in 1825. He joined the *New York Evening Post* the following year, and during his half century at the newspaper's helm, he exercised a cultivated voice as advocate for a cultural tradition separate and distinct from that of Europe. Of Mayflower stock, Bryant advocated the extension of U.S. laws into the new territories to protect against European encroachment; he also supported forest protection and the creation of national parks.

As one of the country's first men of letters to find inspiration in the American wilderness, Bryant published several of his best-known poems—"Thanatopsis," "A Forest Hymn," "To

The panoramic Catskill landscape, familiar to William Cullen Bryant and friends such as the Hudson River painter Thomas Cole, was captured in this engraving by S. V. Hunter. It was based on Henry Fenn's painting *Sunrise from South Mountain*, published in Bryant's *Picturesque America* (1872).

a Waterfowl," "The Yellow Violet"—before he was twenty-one. Profoundly influenced by the work of the English poet William Wordsworth (1770–1850), his romantic odes to nature celebrated as art the same elements of nature that inspired Thomas Cole (1801–48) and the other HUDSON RIVER SCHOOL ARTISTS, with whom Bryant was so closely associated.

Bryant saw nature as proof of God, but for him God remained a divine being, separate from the nature he created. Among his muses were forests, stars, summer winds, and the new moon. One poem celebrates the mosquito ("Fair insect!"); several find inspiration in the sorrows of weeping Indian maidens. His articles and editorials in the *Evening Post* also opened a literary window on the many expeditions he made into the CATSKILL, ADIRONDACK, and WHITE MOUNTAINS. After an 1846 steamer trip to the remote outposts of Sault Ste. Marie and Mackinac Island, Michigan, Bryant lamented the proliferation of summer colonies and tourist resorts that would supplant the "wild and lonely woods" of the GREAT LAKES wilderness. He declared the nation's natural wonders to be "wilder and more beautiful than any in the world" and found meaning in the essential tension that these assets presented in the face of progress, which he viewed as part of Americans' historical destiny. ☞ *also* WRITERS (NINETEENTH CENTURY)

Selected Works

📖 *Poems* (1832). *Tales of Glauber-Spa* (1832). *The Fountain* (1842). *The White-Footed Deer* (1844). *A Funeral Oration, Occasioned by the Death of Thomas Cole* (1848). *Memorial of James Fenimore Cooper* (1852). *A Forest Hymn* (1860). *Thirty Poems* (1864). *Picturesque America* (1872). *The Story of the Fountain* (1872). *The Little People of the Snow* (1873). *Among the Trees* (1874). *A Popular History of the United States* (1876–81).

Contact

William Cullen Bryant Homestead ✉ Bryant Road, Cummington, MA 01026 ☎ 413-634-2244. 🖥 www.berkshireweb.com/trustees/bryant

Buffalo Bill

"Young, sturdy, a remarkable specimen of manly beauty, with the brain to conceive and the nerve to execute, Buffalo Bill par excellence is the exemplar of the strong and unique traits that characterize the true American frontiersman."

Playbill, Buffalo Bill's Wild West Show (1893)

There is no question that William Frederick Cody (1846–1917) possessed brains and nerve, but his real genius was that of any consummate showman: the ability to blur the distinction between fiction and history so that the performance itself becomes the reality. That, of course, is the essence of the frontier legend, and Buffalo Bill was arguably the greatest legend-maker of his time. Born in Iowa and raised in Kansas, this "remarkable specimen of manly beauty" worked variously as railroad man, Pony Express rider, army scout, and buffalo hunter before the adventurer and pulp-fiction writer Ned Buntline (☞ DIME NOVELS) persuaded him to act in his play, *The Scouts of the Plains*, in 1872. Once on stage, the flamboyant Cody never looked much beyond the footlights again, except to serve as scout for the Fifth Cavalry. In 1883 he established Buffalo Bill's Wild West Show. This toured widely in America and abroad, featuring an assortment of "rough riders" (a name co-opted by THEODORE ROOSEVELT) and starring the sharpshooter Annie Oakley from 1885 to 1902.

The Wild West Shows invariably reversed history to present the Indian as territorial aggressor and the army and frontier settler (always the victim) as the vanquishing heroes. Cody's performances were a reversal of their own sort, shamelessly crossing the frontier between reality and fiction in both directions. During Custer's doomed confrontation with Sitting Bull at Little Big Horn in 1876, Buffalo Bill left the stage for the field actually dressed in one of his stage costumes (a Mexican *vaquero* suit in black velvet). After killing a Cheyenne warrior known as Yellow Hand in a skirmish, the showman put the Indian's scalp to use on stage in *Life on the Border*. In 1893 Buffalo Bill was a guest performer at the World's Columbian Exposition in Chicago, where he performed his Wild West Show to a grandstand audience of 18,000 twice a day. Appearing at the same exposition was FREDERICK JACKSON TURNER, who delivered there his famous lecture on the passing of a frontier that Cody also believed had vanished.

Buffalo Bill Museum, Buffalo Bill Historical Center ✉ 720 Sheridan Avenue, Cody, WY 82414. ☎ 307-587-4771. ⌨ www.bbhc.org
■ The museum interprets the legend of Buffalo Bill in the context of the history of the West. Collections also cover the history of dude ranching, western conservation, and frontier entrepreneurship.

Contact

Buffalo Bill's Wild West Show at the 1893 World's Columbian Exposition in Chicago, as a program cover indicates, captured the action-packed excitement of frontier life. Who could possibly resist? Some eighteen thousand ticket holders filled the grandstand to see him twice daily.

Bureau of Indian Affairs

Although it acts as a trustee of federal Indian assets, this bureau of the U.S. DEPARTMENT OF THE INTERIOR has long been plagued by an embarrassing history of broken treaties and fallout from the forced relocation program it ran when it was part of the War Department in the early 1800s. Now staffed mostly by NATIVE AMERICANS, the bureau is set up to mobilize public and private aid for the advancement of Indians and Alaska natives and to promote self-determination by encouraging tribal involvement. Programs include education, social services, law enforcement, agriculture and range management, and resource protection. The bureau publishes a list of federally recognized Indian tribes in the Federal Register.

Contact **Bureau of Indian Affairs** ⊠ U.S. Department of the Interior, 1849 C Street, NW, Washington, DC 20240. ☎ 202-208-3710. ▯ www.doi.gov/bureau-indian-affairs.html

Bureau of Land Management

Created in 1946 when President Harry Truman merged the General Land Office and the U.S. Grazing Service, the BLM, under the auspices of the U.S. DEPARTMENT OF THE INTERIOR, is the steward of about 264 million acres of the nation's PUBLIC LANDS (located primarily in the West and ALASKA) and another 300 million acres of subsurface mineral estate. As the government's largest landowner, the BLM manages 20 percent of the NATIONAL WILD AND SCENIC RIVERS SYSTEM (2,038 miles) and 85 percent of the NATIONAL TRAILS SYSTEM (more than 4,000 miles), as well as about 5.24 million acres in the NATIONAL WILDERNESS PRESERVATION SYSTEM. Sites of rare or fragile natural, historical, cultural, or scenic value are designated by the BLM as Areas of Critical Environmental Concern and receive special management. Designation does not necessarily prevent recreation within the area. Tent Rocks in Peralta Canyon, New Mexico, for example, is still a popular spot for hikers and sightseers.

The agency is responsible for surveying all federal land boundaries; administering mineral, energy, and grazing leases; and overseeing numerous wildlife habitats, watersheds, and riparian-wetland areas. It also manages a wild horse adoption program (☞ WILD HORSES AND BURROS). At the National Interagency Fire Center in Boise, Idaho, the BLM additionally oversees a wildland fires research program and coordinates the dispatch of firefighters, equipment, and supplies in response to natural disasters.

Opposite: Established as part of the War Department in 1824, the Bureau of Indian Affairs was transferred to the Interior Department in 1849. For a department mural, Ansel Adams photographed the Hopi pueblo Walpi atop a mesa near Flagstaff, Arizona, in 1941, but World War II prevented its completion.

Bureau of Land Management ⊠ U.S. Department of the Interior, 1849 C Street, NW, Room LS-406, Washington, DC 20240. ℂ 202-452-5125. ▤ www.blm.gov

National Information Resources Management Center ⊠ P.O. Box 25047, Denver, CO 80225-0047. ℂ 303-236-6965

National Interagency Fire Center ⊠ 3833 South Development Avenue, Boise, ID 83705-5354. ℂ 208-387-5447

National Science and Technology Center ⊠ P.O. Box 25047, Denver, CO 80225-0047. ℂ 303-236-6454 ▤ www.blm.gov/nstc

National Training Center ⊠ 9828 North Thirty-first Avenue, Phoenix, AZ 85051-2517. ℂ 602-906-5500

Contacts

Providing irrigation for the seventeen contiguous western states, this arm of the U.S. DEPARTMENT OF THE INTERIOR was created under President THEODORE ROOSEVELT in 1902 to aid homesteaders by harnessing water supplies in the nation's arid regions. A major hand in settling the West, it has built more than six hundred federally funded reservoirs and dams, including the Hoover and Grand Coulee, and is one of the country's major producers of hydroelectric power. In recent years, policy emphasis has shifted from dam building to water recycling. Most of the pilot programs are currently in

Bureau of Reclamation

California to ease the demand of growing urban areas on watersheds such as the Mono Lake Basin, a spectacular scenic area that supplies water to Los Angeles. The bureau also works on wetland restoration projects and with the National Fish and Wildlife Foundation (☞ U.S. FISH AND WILDLIFE SERVICE) to restore native fish species (☞ ENDANGERED SPECIES).

Contact **Bureau of Reclamation** ✉ U.S. Department of the Interior, 1849 C Street, NW, Washington, DC 20240. ✆ 202-513-0575. ▯ www.usbr.gov

John Burroughs

"Each of you has the whole wealth of the universe at your very door."

John Burroughs

Regarded as the father of the nature essay, John Burroughs (1837–1921) earned his place in the evolution of conservation ethics as one of the most widely read authors of his day: his life's work accounts for 1.5 million copies in print. Some two dozen volumes established the nature essay as a literary genre and had such a huge popular following that many of his books remained a staple of the American public school curriculum well into the 1920s.

Something of a cult figure, Burroughs attracted a steady stream of admirers to Slabsides, his bark-covered cabin in the CATSKILL MOUNTAINS, with visitors ranging from fawning Vassar girls to his friends WALT WHITMAN and THEODORE ROOSEVELT. Burroughs, who shared Roosevelt's passion for birdwatching, was in turn a frequent visitor to the White House and Pine Knot, the president's Virginia retreat; the two also camped together in the Yellowstone River valley (☞ YELLOWSTONE NATIONAL PARK). Burroughs referred to the country around Slabsides as "Whitman land" and took on his poet friend as the subject of his first book. He particularly connected with Whitman's approach to nature as spiritual influence rather than divine entity. Whitman in turn used Burroughs's description of a hermit thrush in an 1865 essay, "In the Hemlocks," as inspiration for the thrush in "When Lilacs Last in the Dooryard Bloom'd" (1865).

Burroughs made his living by turns as a journalist, treasury clerk, bank examiner, and fruit farmer in his native Catskills. He garnered an early following through his writing for periodicals such as the transcendentalist review, *The Dial,* and *Atlantic Monthly.* "From the Back Country," the first of many nature essays for the *New York Leader,* appeared in 1861. His popular *Field and Study* (1919) mourned man's hand in the extinction of the passenger pigeon (☞ BIRDS). *Accepting the Universe* (1920) quietly extolled the spiritual solace to be experienced in nature. The self-taught naturalist's great gift was for observation, and his simple, genuine prose inspired a love of natural history in a generation of readers who were encouraged to experience the outdoors for themselves.

📖 *Notes on Walt Whitman as Poet and Person* (1867). *Wake-Robin* (1871). *Birds and Poets* (1877). *Locusts and Wild Honey* (1879). *Fresh Fields* (1884). *Signs and Seasons* (1886). *Life of Audubon* (1902). *Ways of Nature* (1905). *Leaf and Tendril* (1908). *Gospel of Nature* (1912). *Under the Apple Trees* (1916). *Field and Study* (1919). *Accepting the Universe* (1920). *Under the Maples* (1921). *My Boyhood* (1922). *The Art of Seeing Things: Essays by John Burroughs*, ed. by Charlotte Zöe Walker (2001).

American Museum of Natural History ✉ 175–208 Central Park West (at West Seventy-ninth Street), New York, NY 10024-5192. ℂ 212-769-5100. 🖳 nimidi.amnh.org/burroughs/burroughs
■ The museum houses a permanent exhibit on the life and work of John Burroughs and maintains the Burroughs Pages, an online resource for students and scholars.

John Burroughs Association ✉ West Park, NY 12493. 🖳 www.johnburroughs.org
■ The association maintains Slabsides, Burroughs's rustic 1895 Hudson Valley cabin (open to visitors twice a year), and the adjoining John Burroughs Preserve. It also sponsors an annual award for a distinguished book in natural history.

The naturalist and author John Burroughs spent many a reflective moment at the rustic retreat in the Hudson River valley he called Slabsides. Among his guests were Walt Whitman and Theodore Roosevelt.

Campfires

"Within the circle of its light, camaraderie melts to friendship—close, sincere, fraught with deeper meaning than elsewhere in all the world. There is truth in the friendship symbol.

"In its dancing flame, its glowing and fading embers, there are pictures—the food of imagination, the wine of creativity. Tonic for artist, poet, composer, inventor—for you and me—it is the charm of fertile fancy.

"Alone beside the sacred fire, then it is that we hear the Voices, and the secret message of the Great One comes to us. So it was with the vigil Indian in yesteryears, so with the most practical in an external world today. In potent symbol fire transcends the mundane world."

Bernard S. Mason, Woodcraft (1939)

Campfires may indeed call up Indian spirits and bond friendships, but much has changed since Bernard S. Mason waxed poetic in his guide to wilderness woodcraft in 1939 (the Dark Ages by contemporary CAMPING standards). Current wilderness wisdom holds that of all camping practices, lighting fires has the most detrimental environmental impact. Fires are prohibited or restricted in many camping areas. Scavenging for fuel wears out the terrain, and harvesting the wrong wood can be unhealthy for the ecosystems at hand, particularly in a treeline area, where fuel supplies are limited and slow to regenerate. Other problems are the sterilized soil and general trampling that tend to occur around a campfire site. And no hiker enjoys encountering a dirty fire ring piled with ashes and the charred remnants of a meal.

There are essentially two types of campfire—COOKING fires and those lit for the pure cheer and sociability of it—and no agreement on whether either is appropriate. Several organizations, including the National Outdoor Leadership School (☞ HIKING), now take an official position against campfires and advocate using a portable stove (☞ COOKING) instead. Some would argue that the cooking fire, by definition, is the lesser of two evils, but it has also been said that an occasional pleasure fire (again, in the proper site and circumstances) is in keeping with the romantic spirit of camping and has less adverse impact than a multitude of cooking fires that put constant wear and tear on camping sites.

All of that said, campfires are considered acceptable by some authorities if the following guidelines are followed:

Siting a Campfire

■ Use an existing ring. Rarely will a circumstance warrant building a new fire ring, and creating one will only attract other new rings. Look for a small (hat-sized) ring on bare ground away from camping equipment, logs, dry leaves, other plant material, and overhanging tree limbs.

■ An emergency may require a new fire ring. If so, make it on a sandy or gravely spot where it will be easy to erase the traces. Do not make a fire ring with stones or dig a hole.

■ Always check the seasonal restrictions and be aware of the potential hazard of forest fires, particularly in the summer and dry autumn months. Determine the prevailing breeze and make sure that the fire will not blow sparks in the direction of anything flammable. Never light a fire in windy conditions.

■ Build the fire on dry ground, never on humus or evergreens. Be sure that there are no tree branches hanging lower than 20 feet from the ground.

■ Keep a can of water and a trowel close at hand, and never leave a fire or smoldering embers unattended.

■ Make sure that the fire is absolutely cold before leaving camp. Douse it thoroughly with water, dig up the ashes with a stick, and then douse again. Dispose of the ashes by scattering them in small batches in several locations well away from the campsite. Do not smother the fire with earth, because it can smolder underground for hours or even days.

Fuel for the Fire

■ Pick up only dry windfall and deadwood. Do your foraging in small amounts in scattered areas well beyond the picked-over areas that are likely to be found nearest a campsite. Pieces should be small enough to break with your hands and to burn completely to ash; never cut firewood with an ax or a saw. If it must be cut to be gathered, it should not be gathered at all.

■ Avoid green or punky wood and leave larger logs and rooted pieces for the birds and animals that are likely using them as hunting or nesting ground.

■ Look for hardwoods, which burn slowly and evenly and produce glowing

Sharing a fire was a sign of Native American hospitality at the time Alfred Jacob Miller made an expedition to the Rocky Mountains in 1837 and sketched scenes like his *Campfire—by Moonlight*.

embers that last after the flame is gone. If you can find and identify them, hunt for black and yellow birch; they ignite quickly and burn evenly and long. White ash, another slow burner, is also a good choice given that it splits easily. Other recommended woods are hickories, white oak, sugar maple, beech, and white birch.

■ Avoid softwoods such as balsam, spruce, and white or pitch pine, because they burn fast and furiously. They also go out just as fast, and there is always the dispiriting possibility that you might set your hair on fire in the fast flames.

Natural Tinders

A fuzz stick—tinder deeply shaved but with shavings still attached—allows air to circulate well under a fire.

■ **Bark and cones.** The "torch of the Indian," birch bark is one of the best natural tinders to be found in the woods and even ignites when wet. One of the beauties of this resinous bark is that only a small slip of it is needed to start a fire, so it is never necessary to strip the bark off a tree. Loose coils can be picked up from the ground or peeled off deadfall. Other hardwood barks, such as hemlock, are suitable because they produce coals, which are good for cooking. Dry evergreen cones are also good for tinder and for making a slow-burning fire burn hotter for cooking.

■ **Fat pine.** Harder to come by than birch bark, this pitch-soaked wood also makes excellent tinder. Fat pine is typically found in aging tree stumps where the pitch has settled and hardened. The brittle pine breaks easily, and one chip will start a fire.

■ **Fuzz sticks.** These are the traditionalist's firestarters for wet weather. A fuzz stick is made by using a knife to shave a dry stick so that the shavings are still attached; a stick cut in this manner will burn more easily than a round stick. Start with a piece of softwood about a foot long. Whittle one end to a point, and then, while bracing the other end against a log or tree, work down the shaft with the knife, cutting in deeply at the base of each cut so that the shaving does not detach. Stuck into the ground tripod fashion, three fuzz sticks make good supports for kindling.

■ **Twigs.** To be sure that they are dry, snap twigs off deadwood branches rather than picking them up directly from the ground. Limit foraging to twigs no larger than pencil size. For tinder this small, the type of wood does not matter.

■ **Starting the fire.** A fire burns best when it has something to climb up. It should be laid so that it is compact but packed loosely enough for air to circulate. In wet weather, it may be necessary to use a piece of candle, a cork, a small log of wax-drenched newspaper, a bit of porous wood soaked in white gas, or the reliable (but heavy) magnesium block firestarter that can be found at camping-supply stores.

■ **Size.** Keep the fire small: you do not need a bonfire to fry a few pieces of bacon or boil a pot of coffee.

■ **Tipi shape.** This tall slender construction is good for light but less effective for cooking because the coal area is too small. Stack the kindling vertically in a cone shape, starting with three evenly spaced pieces, and then fill in around a small amount of tinder in the center of the fire ring; leave a small opening to light the tinder. Next add a layer of firewood pieces in the same manner. Keep the tipi small, no larger than a foot high and a foot in diameter at the base.

■ **Log cabin shape.** This construction of wood courses stacked in alternating directions capitalizes on air circulation and creates an even bed of wood. Start with a 6-inch tipi construction. Around this, place four pieces of wood about 2 inches thick, log cabin style, to create a one-foot square, and then stack in alternating courses.

Camping

amping guides published just two or three decades ago invariably celebrate the romance of the crackling campfire or of bushwhacking off the beaten path to find a secluded site to enjoy a starlit sky in complete privacy. Yet as the dramatic increase in backcountry recreation has begun to affect both the health of the environment and the quality of the experience, a strong code of ethics has emerged for environmentally responsible hiking and camping. In a way, things have gotten more complicated. CAMPFIRES are now an issue of contention, and the authorities overseeing parks and FORESTS usually designate minimum camping distances (100 to 300 feet) from private property, shorelines, water sources, and trails to help prevent pollution, habitat disturbance, and wearing of the ground (anything that wears down a site, such as keeping hiking boots on in camp, is frowned on).

The fact is, hikers face a fundamental conflict every time they camp in the backcountry, because it is nearly impossible to experience the wilderness they wish to enjoy and preserve without having an impact on it at the same time. Every aspect of making, using, and breaking a low-impact camp thus requires compromise. ☞ *also* CAMPFIRES, COOKING, HIKING, SLEEPING BAGS, SNOW CAMPING, TENTS

■ Leave enough time to find a site and set up camp while there is still plenty of daylight.

■ Follow the rules and use common sense. If camping-only areas are designated, use them. If they are not, don't camp in an untouched area unless you are

absolutely sure that you are able to leave no trace of your presence. It is better to choose an established campsite over one that has never been used. By the same token, however, avoid a site where erosion, picked-over firewood, exposed roots, and trammeled ground clearly indicate overuse.

■ Find the right campsite for your needs rather than altering one to suit them by building new fire rings or hauling around logs or stones or sawing branches to create windbreaks and "furniture."

■ Take into account a site's natural advantages, disadvantages, and potential dangers. Because warm air rises, for example, an elevated site can be 10 degrees warmer than one located in a basin (good in cold weather but maybe not so great in midsummer). Look for a site providing a natural windbreak against the prevailing breeze. Avoid swales and gullies because runoff from a heavy rainstorm can fill them surprisingly quickly. Dry riverbeds are also dangerous—during rainstorms they can become deadly washes in a matter of minutes. Avoid abandoned cabins and shelters, which tend to be infested with rodents and insects.

■ No matter how appealing it looks, don't camp on a site carpeted with live, leafy plants or disturb the sensitive alpine plants above the treeline that are slow to regenerate. The best flooring for a tent is forest duff, which offers a natural cushion of dried pine needles, leaves, and twigs. The next choice is bare ground or sand (or, depending on location or season, deep snow). Meadows are also off limits, although some parks permit camping on dry mountain meadow grass that wears down slowly.

■ Respect the local animal population. Avoid any area where crushed plants or scat indicate that bears and other animals are nearby. In a bear hot zone, the site must include a suitable tree for bear bagging if bear-proof containers are not available (☞ BEARS).

From their campsite in Colorado's White River National Forest, members of the Maroon Snowmass Trail Riders club take in a view of Snowmass Mountain and Snowmass Lake about 1950.

Reading

📖 Karen Berger, *Hiking and Backpacking: A Complete Guide* (1995). 📖 John Hart, *Walking Softly in the Wilderness: The Sierra Club Guide to Backpacking* (1998). 📖 Mark W. T. Harvey, *National Outdoor Leadership School Wilderness Guide: The Classic Handbook* (1999). 📖 Cliff Jacobson, *Basic Essentials: Camping* (1999). 📖 Glenn Randall, *The Outward Bound Backpacker's Handbook* (2000).

Canoes

The oldest continually used type of watercraft in North America, the canoe is the gift of the Iroquois- and Algonquian-speaking tribes of the Northeast, eastern sub-Arctic, and GREAT LAKES. The term *canoes*, which technically defines both canoes and KAYAKS, derives from *canoa*, the word first recorded by Christopher Columbus (1451–1506) as being used by the West Indians he encountered in Hispaniola for their dugoutlike boats. The dugout, a primitive form in which the boat is carved or chipped out of a single log, is a canoe form best suited for large bodies of water; it was used by native peoples, usually coastal tribes, in North America as well. The seagoing dugouts of the Clatsops and Chinooks along the Pacific Coast measured 50 feet long and made a vivid impression on Lewis and Clark (☞ CORPS OF DISCOVERY) during their western expedition in 1804–6. "I have seen the natives near the riding waves in these canoes with safety and apparently without concern," reported Meriwether Lewis (1774–1809) in his journal, "where I should have thought it impossible for any vessel of the same size to live a minute."

The king of all native North American canoe types was the birch-bark canoe, which was perfected by the Algonquians for use on interior rivers and lake systems. It is is believed to have evolved from the heavier dugout form but was specifically adapted as a lighter canoe supremely suited to rivers, streams, lakes, and the many portages in between. The journals of European explorers record admiration for the highly developed bark canoes, which were made by folding huge sheets of birch bark over a ribbed frame (usually pine) to create a boat light enough to be carried but sturdy enough to support extraordinary loads. The Algonquian canoes encountered by Samuel de Champlain (1567–1635) when he explored the St. Lawrence River in 1609

Birch-Bark Canoes

A Seminole Indian family paddles a dugout canoe in Florida's Everglades about 1910. This canoe type was also used by natives of the West Indies.

measured as much as 20 feet long and 50 inches across the beam and could carry half a ton of cargo. Considered a great spoil of war by other native tribes that did not have access to birch, the streamlined design was adopted by the seventeenth-century French Canadian *voyageurs*. The French introduced canvas to the Great Lakes region and devised sailing canoes to navigate the fur trade corridors through the lakes. The Montreal *canot du maître* measured 40 feet long, supported a crew of fourteen, and was perfectly capable of carrying several tons of furs.

Pleasure Craft

The sturdy dugout canoe (below, top), made from a hollowed log, was used by many Native American tribes but only for deep-water travel in northern regions, where the lighter birch-bark canoe was ideal for carrying during overland portages (below, bottom). Canoe-inspired commercial designs in the 1950s included the ribbed double-end rowboat and the sleek "war canoe" (opposite, top and bottom).

Directions on how to make bark canoes began appearing in trappers' guides around the time of the Civil War. Not long after, the demand for pleasure craft was met with great success by one of the first and most famous canoe manufacturers, John Henry Rushton of the backcountry ADIRONDACKS. Rushton issued his first catalogue in 1877, inspiring immediate competition as handsome canoe catalogues became a new genre of boating literature.

Canoe clubs took off at about the same time. In 1880 Nathaniel Holmes Bishop of Lake George, New York, called a "Canoe Congress" of paddlers at his Adirondack resort to form the first national canoeing club. The congress was the genesis of the American Canoe Association, founded in 1880, whose first official organ was *Forest and Stream* magazine. Although canoeing was more affordable than other types of yachting, most of the early aficionados were "sporting men" of a certain social class who could afford the rather steep $125 price tag of Rushton's model cruising canoe. Women who attended canoe meets were relegated to separate "squaw camps" and excluded from ACA membership until the 1940s.

☞ *also* NATIONAL WILD AND SCENIC RIVERS SYSTEM, WATER TRAILS

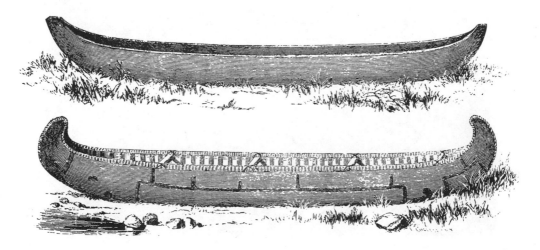

American Canoe Association ✉ 7432 Alban Station Boulevard, Suite B-232, *Contacts*
Springfield, VA 22150. ✆ 703-451-0141. 🖳 www.aca-paddler.org
■ America's largest nonprofit paddle-sports association (more than 35,000 members) promotes recreational canoeing, rafting, and kayaking; sponsors races; and serves as a federal and state conservation advocate on issues from water use to jet-ski threats. Its Web site lists affiliated ACA clubs by state. Publications include *Paddler* magazine.

American Whitewater Association ✉ 1430 Fenwick Lane, Silver Spring, MD
20910. ✆ 301-589-9453. 🖳 www.awa.org
■ Membership in this national nonprofit includes more than 160 paddling clubs. It maintains a state-by-state inventory of whitewater rivers (the River Pages Project), monitors conservation threats, organizes events, and promotes education and boating safety. Publications include *American Whitewater*.

Wooden Canoe Heritage Association ✉ P.O. Box 226, Blue Mountain Lake,
NY 12812. 🖳 www.whca.org
■ This nonprofit membership organization is devoted to the study, use, and preservation of wood, wood-canvas, and birch-bark canoes.

United States Canoe Association. The association fosters paddling as a rec- *Web Site*
ognized competitive sport, hosts national marathon championships, offers canoe instructor certification courses, and holds online auctions. Its mission is to promote competition, cruising, conservation, camping, and camaraderie.
🖳 www.uscanoe.org

📕 William Picard Stephens, *Canoe and Small Boat Building: A Complete Manual for* *Reading*
Amateurs (1883). 📕 Calvin Rutstrum, *North American Canoe Country: The Classic Guide to Canoe Technique* (1964, 1992). 📕 Dave Harrison, *Canoeing: The Complete Guide to Equipment and Technique* (1988). 📕 John McPhee, *The Survival of the Bark Canoe* (1989). 📕 Herbert Gordon, *The Complete Book of Canoeing* (1992, 1997).
📕 Laurie Gullion, *Ragged Mountain Press Woman's Guide to Canoeing* (1999).

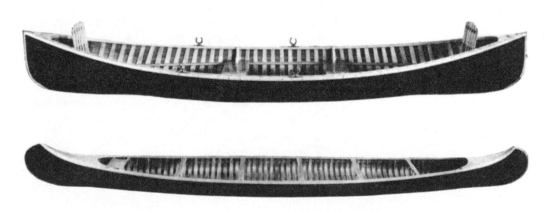

Rachel Carson

The illustration on the title page of Rachel Carson's *Silent Spring* (1962) alluded to the DDT threat to songbirds.

Silent
Spring

by Rachel Carson
Drawings by Lois and Louis Darling

HOUGHTON MIFFLIN COMPANY BOSTON
The Riverside Press Cambridge
1962

Rachel Carson (1907–64) was trained in the natural sciences and earned a master's degree in marine biology from Johns Hopkins University, pursuing a career teaching zoology at the University of Maryland and working for the U.S. FISH AND WILDLIFE SERVICE. Three books on sea life preceded her most provocative study, *Silent Spring* (1962).

First published in serial form in *The New Yorker* magazine, this last book, which popularized the term *ecosystem,* issued a public alert to the dangers of commercial pesticides and underscored the new threats of a post–World War II technology: DDT and other toxic chemicals, nuclear emissions, and acid rain. The title referred to the result of the imminent extermination of BIRDS through pesticide use. *Silent Spring* was an extraordinary event in that it not only stirred up unprecedented public outcry over ecological abuses but also did so with a scientifically based argument. Carson's message was especially shocking because it alerted a public relatively unattuned to the idea that scientific progress might not always be a good thing. The book was slammed by the chemical industry, which tried to persuade Carson's publisher, Houghton Mifflin, to abandon publication and branded the author a crazed zealot. *Silent Spring* was nevertheless an instant best-seller.

Selected Works

📖 *Under the Sea Wind* (1941). *The Sea Around Us* (1951). *The Edge of the Sea* (1954). *Silent Spring* (1962).

Cascade Mountains

A 700-mile-long segment of the Pacific mountain system, the Cascades stretch from Lassen Peak in northern California through Oregon and Washington to the Fraser River in British Columbia. The north-south string of peaks—many higher than 10,000 feet—is a headstream region for the Willamette River and runs about 100 to 150 miles inland from the Pacific Ocean to create a barrier between two distinctive climatic zones: the arid desert region of the interior (☞ DESERTS) and the moist forested regions to the West (☞ FORESTS), where the annual rainfall averages 100 inches. Lewis and Clark (☞ CORPS OF DISCOVERY) passed through the Oregon Cascades by way of the Columbia Gorge (now America's only national scenic area) on their approach to the Pacific in 1805. The mountains were not named, however, until late 1841, when the range was surveyed by the expedition led by Charles Wilkes (1798–1877), which played a critical role in settling the Oregon border and determining the 49th parallel as the country's northwestern boundary.

The Pacific side of the Cascades nurtures some of the tallest and most diverse evergreen forests on the globe—with a mix of hemlocks, cedar, spruces, and firs. These account for the last primeval forests in America and are thus the battle-ground for many current environmental wars. The great aristocrat of the Cascade forests is the Douglas fir (*P. menziesii*). The state tree of Oregon, this fir was named for David Douglas, the Scottish botanical collector for the Royal Horticultural Society who catalogued much of the Northwest's flora for the first time in the 1820s. The Douglas fir, which can exceed 300 feet in height and live for more than 1,000 years, is considered one of the best timber trees in the country.

The mountains themselves technically make up two overlapping volcanic ranges. The older western Cascades (now known as the foothills) erupted into a jagged string of peaks about 45 million years ago, while the younger (by about 20 million years) High Cascades, which dominate the range's eastern ridge, account for most of the tallest summits, including Mount Hood (11,235 feet) in Oregon and Mount Rainier (14,410 feet) in Washington. Among the recently active volcanoes are Mount Baker and Mount St. Helens; Mount Hood last erupted in 1790.

At 14,410 feet, Mount Rainier (seen from the west) is the tallest peak in Washington's Cascades and the centerpiece of the eponymous national park. The volcanic peak, which contains numerous glaciers, was discovered and named by Captain George Vancouver in 1792.

Much of the range, including the majority of the Oregon Cascades, are federally owned PUBLIC LANDS, including North Cascades, Crater Lake, and Mount Rainier National Parks (☞ NATIONAL PARK SYSTEM) and Lassen Volcanic National Monument. The U.S. FOREST SERVICE manages 15.5 million acres in Oregon alone, including six contiguous national forests (☞ NATIONAL FOREST SYSTEM), thirty-five national wilderness areas, and the Columbia Gorge National Scenic Area. According to the Wilderness Society, about 90 percent of the ancient forests west of the Cascades in Washington and Oregon have been logged. The remaining 10 percent of old-growth stands are contained almost exclusively in the region's national forests.

Catskill Mountains

Offering an unparalleled view of Hudson Valley scenery, the Mountain House, drawn by W. H. Bartlett, was the fashionable Catskills retreat.

"Whoever has made a voyage up the Hudson must remember the Kaatskill mountains. They are a dismembered branch of the great Appalachian family, and are seen away to the west of the river, swelling up to a noble height, lording it over the surrounding country. Every change of season, every change of weather, indeed, every hour of the day, produces some change in the magical hues and shapes of these mountains, and they are regarded by all the good wives, far and near, as perfect barometers. When the weather is fair and settled, they are clothed in blue and purple, and print their bold outlines on the clear evening sky; but sometimes, when the rest of the landscape is cloudless, they will gather a hood of gray vapors about their summits, which in the last rays of setting sun, will glow and light up like a crown of glory."

Washington Irving, "Rip Van Winkle"
The Sketch-Book of Geoffrey Crayon, Gent. (1819–20)

"There is no summer resort more conveniently situated, and at the same time more pleasant and agreeable, than the neighborhood of the Catskills. The trip up the Hudson, towards this beautiful region, is most exquisite. The river is celebrated for its extreme beauty, and the voyage up is one of the most enjoyable features of our trip to the Catskills."

T. Nelson and Sons, *Our Summer Retreats:*
Katskill Mountains–Saratoga–Trenton–Caldwell, &c.&c. (1859)

With the ADIRONDACK MOUNTAINS, the Catskills are often called America's first wilderness. This "dismembered branch" of the APPALACHIAN MOUNTAINS, bounded north and east by the Mohawk and Hudson River valleys in southeastern New York, takes its name from "Kaaterskill" (Wildcat Creek), which is what Dutch settlers called one of the many streams that drain the Catskill range. The dark ruggedness and grand panoramic views inspired many of the leading lights of the romantic movement. Birthplace of the HUDSON RIVER SCHOOL ARTISTS, the region attracted tourists to its wilderness resorts as early as the 1820s. The precipitous cliff 2,000 feet above the Hudson River that was the setting for the Mountain House Hotel in Pine Orchard moved JAMES FENIMORE COOPER'S Natty Bumppo (Hawkeye in *The Pioneers*, 1823) to describe it as a place where "creation" might be seen at a single glance. Nearby was the spot overlooking the "fairy mountains" that WASHINGTON IRVING used as the setting for Rip Van Winkle's lengthy nap.

The Catskills contain thirty-five peaks higher than 3,500 feet and rise to their highest elevation at Slide Mountain (4,204 feet). Because they were so inaccessible, several of the old-growth Catskill forests escaped the effects of the late-nineteenth-century logging (☞ CLEAR-CUTTING), tan-barking, and charcoal industries that so scarred the Adirondacks to the north. In 1885 the 34,000-acre Catskill Forest Preserve was established as part of the NEW YORK STATE FOREST PRESERVE under the same "forever wild" provision applying to the Adirondack Forest Preserve. Expanded to almost 300,000 acres, the preserve constitutes about 40 percent of the larger Catskill Park, designated by the state in 1904 and now embracing about 700,000 acres. ☞ *also* FORESTS

Civilian Conservation Corps

In 1933 an army of unemployed young men fanned out to take jobs in forestry, erosion prevention, flood control, grazing, emergency relief, and other similar projects to benefit the country without competing with the open job market. The Civilian Conservation Corps was established during the Great Depression by Congress to promote President Franklin D. Roosevelt's New Deal. The men, who earned

A poster designed as part of the Federal Art Project touted the benefits of the Civilian Conservation Corps. It was issued in 1941, near the end of the program.

$30 a month plus room, board, and clothing, had to be between eighteen and twenty-five years of age and unemployed. Only three months after the president proposed the corps, more than 300,000 enrollees were established in 15,000 forest camps of about 2,000 men each. They were at work building fire towers and dams and planting trees in forests, state and national parks, and rangelands under the supervision of the U.S. DEPARTMENT OF THE INTERIOR and U.S. DEPARTMENT OF AGRICULTURE. CCC camps were located in every state, as well as Alaska, Hawaii, Puerto Rico, and the Virgin Islands.

The corps cleared 5,000 miles of truck roads and built 2,500 miles of road, 5,000 miles of foot and horse trails, thousands of check dams, about 1,000 cabins, almost 14,000 shelters, and 16,000 acres of picnic grounds, as well as parking areas, overlooks, bridges, fire towers, camp grounds, lodges, and administrative buildings. Some viewed this enormous public works program as a substantial threat to America's wild areas, despite the fact that "Uncle Sam's forest army" also transplanted half a billion seedlings in 10,000 acres of new forest. The CCC was abolished in 1942, and many of its recreational facilities began to deteriorate. By 1956 the problem was so bad that the NATIONAL PARK SERVICE established the Mission '66 program to develop new facilities during the next decade. The U.S. FOREST SERVICE followed with a five-year program, Operation Outdoors.

Clear-Cutting

A controversial system of silviculture, clear-cutting of FORESTS prescribes a one-cut sweep of all trees in a given area, followed by regeneration (artificially or naturally) with an even-aged timber stand. Along with seed-tree, shelterwood, and selection harvesting, it is one of four primary types of timber harvest and regeneration in the United States. In seed-tree management, selected seed trees are left in the clear cut; in the shelterwood system, the timber is cut in phases; and in selection harvesting, trees are carefully cut singly and in small clusters over time. All but this last method are even-aged production systems in which the new growth is essentially the same age and size.

As the fastest and least expensive method, clear-cutting is defended by the wood-products industry as healthy and efficient if managed properly. It was the principal means of timber harvesting in the NATIONAL FOREST SYSTEM from the 1960s to the 1990s; before then, the selection method dominated. Proponents argue that clear-cutting is an effective tool for disease and quality control and advantageous for certain shade-intolerant species—the Douglas fir and Sitka spruce, for example—because new seedlings benefit from full exposure to sunlight. Clear-cutting also provides the U.S. FOREST SERVICE with enormous flexibility in its management of the national forests and in interpreting the Multiple Use Sustained Yield Act (1960).

Opposition to the practice, however, is almost universal among environmental groups, many of which advocate a complete ban in favor of selective harvesting. Although all of the silviculture methods are invasive and affect a forest system's wildlife habitats and overall ecological balance, critics cite clear-cutting as especially abusive: the associated road building, skidding, and stacking are major causes of soil erosion and water degradation; the sweeping cuts leave ugly gashes and destroy animal habitats; and the even-growth regeneration replaces hardy and diverse forests with inferior monocrops. Regeneration significantly transforms a forest by shifting the dominance in a short period from old-growth to young trees, while putting at risk of extinction the flora and fauna that depend on old-growth habitats for survival.

Loggers in northern Michigan float harvested timber to mills about 1900, when the state led the nation in lumber production. So many trees were cut down that the Michigan lumber industry was all but over by 1910.

Between 1984 and 1991 clear-cutting accounted for more than 60 percent of tree harvesting in the national forest system. From the 1960s to the early 1990s, thousands of square miles of old-growth forests were harvested by this means in the Pacific Northwest. In the early 1990s several hundred acres of old-growth stands in Oregon's Umpqua National Forest, including a grove of trees almost 1,000 years old, were slated for clear-cutting. The controversy in this period over protecting old-growth forests as habitat for northern spotted owls was a catalyst for intensified debate. Several bills banning clear-cutting and other even-age silviculture systems have since been introduced in Congress.

Clothing

What to wear?—that nagging fashion question—has never had more significance than in the great outdoors. The right clothing from head to foot not only makes the difference between misery and a rewarding wilderness experience; it can also save your life. The first basic rule in dressing for the wilds is to hope for the best and expect the worst. The second rule is to think before you buy and use your common sense. Simple, well-made clothing is generally a wiser investment than shiny new gear with all the bells and whistles. Look for tuck-away hoods, loose-fitting sleeves, and details such as armpit or "gill" zippers (angled from chest to lower back), zipper baffles, and mesh-backed pocket zippers that let you easily fine-tune ventilation. Zippers should have pull-tabs so you can pull them with gloves on.

Despite the overwhelming selection of modern hiking gear now available, deciding on any single item often means compromise: the heavier the boot, the more protection but the less flexibility; the more waterproof a garment, the less it will breathe. Here are several rules of thumb:

■ Shop at a reputable retailer that specializes in outdoor gear rather than at a department store or large chain outlet. Salespeople in wilderness specialty shops are usually experienced outdoorspeople themselves and can offer invaluable advice.
■ Ask for advice, and be forthright about your level of experience (ego has doomed more than a few hikers to sore backs and feet).
■ Discuss the kind of activities you are planning, expected conditions, and trail type. If salespeople aren't willing to talk, you are in the wrong store.
■ Buy the best quality your budget allows and take plenty of time to make decisions.

Layering Body Wear

The principle of layering clothes made of comfortable, lightweight fabrics is based on the relationship of heat and moisture on your skin. That balance is constantly changing, even as a hiker passes from sun to shade or from flat to incline. The idea is to trap the warm air created by body heat while encouraging perspiration to escape before it cools down and creates a chill as activity decreases.

The ideal layering system offers ventilation, wicking, rapid drying, insulation, wind and water resistance, and freedom of movement. Wearing thinner, lighter layers anticipates a variety of conditions and helps control body temperature far more efficiently than taking off or putting on one heavy garment. Both wool and polyester have the great advantage of acting as insulators when wet. The combination obviously varies depending on the person, the activity, the location, and the time of year.

This is the "wicking layer," the inside line of defense designed to deflect moisture away from skin. The best fabrics for underwear and socks are silk or synthetic fibers such as nylon or a polyester-wool blend, rather than cotton or wool, because they conduct moisture and also feel good to the touch. Cotton is fine—until it gets wet, so it is really a good choice only for a hot, dry desert climate, where an evaporative cooling mechanism is desirable (☞ DESERT HIKING). **Layer One**

Long underwear comes in three weights: lightweight for active wear in cool temperatures; medium weight to provide extra warmth and wicking in cold weather; and expedition weight for extremes. Cotton retains moisture; silk wicks it away. Polypropylene does not wick away moisture, so polypropylene longjohns work only if worn with a layer of wool or fleece immediately on top. Polyester does not wick either. Polyester-wool blends and polypropylene-wool blends are better, but the wool increases drying time. An alternative is treated polyester, such as Capeline,® blended with Lycra® and nylon.

Too much or too little sock can affect boot support and cause irritating friction. For moderate terrain, one medium-heavy sock in wool, a wool-synthetic blend, or waterproof-breathable Gore-Tex® should be fine. Layer it over a light wicking sock to help prevent blisters. Avoid cotton. Remove your boots and socks and air your feet whenever you take a hiking break.

For cold weather, light wool or polyester glove liners can be worn inside a mitten and water-repellent mitten shells.

The next one or two layers should trap warmth when you need it by creating dead air space but also vent when the body starts to warm up. Depending on the weather, this might mean wearing a wool shirt or sweater, a lightweight **Layers Two and Three** polyester fleece jacket, or an insulated vest and socks made of polypropylene or polyester or of a wool-polyester blend, worn over lighter wicking liners.

Nylon or polypropylene-cotton hiking shorts are great for warm weather, but a hiker should pack a pair of lightweight long pants as well—for sun and insect protection and temperature changes. You should also have two shirts on hand: one short-sleeved and one long-sleeved in lightweight wool. Nylon leg gaiters, which fit over the shins and boot uppers, keep out snow, mud, and gravel and protect legs from thorny plants and underbrush.

Layers Four and Five

A pullover anorak with a zippered neck for easy ventilation is a good choice for an outer layer. Lightly quilted shoulders add padding for backpack straps.

All outerwear should be loose enough to comfortably accommodate the underlayers of clothing and allow air to circulate. An all-in-one jacket will not provide as much flexibility as a light shell worn over several single-purpose garments. The wide range of performance materials used in making outerwear is designed to provide water protection while ventilating. *Microfiber* usually refers to a fabric made with a polyester microfilament that is woven very tightly to deflect wind and rain. Microfiber garments are lightweight and good for aerobic activity but will not keep you warm under extreme conditions. Activent® and Pneumatic® are two frequently encountered trademark names for special synthetics designed to emphasize breathability while providing a good level of water resistance. Gore-Tex® is the best-known laminate (membrane) used to treat a fabric to make it waterproof without compromising its breathing power. The code *WB Coated* means Waterproof and Breathable; the code *DWR* means Durable Water Repellent, an applied finish that causes water to bead up on an outer shell. In two-layer construction, a synthetic outer shell and an inner layer of laminate sandwich a loose layer of lightweight wicking fabric. In three-layer construction the shell, laminate, and wicking layers are meshed together—lighter but stiffer than two layers.

In moderate weather the last layer should be a thin protective shell. In a brief rainstorm, a urethane-coated nylon poncho or jacket and rain pants are fine, but they do not offer enough ventilation for extended use. In a downpour, you will actually get wetter wearing a completely waterproof jacket that makes you perspire than you would wearing a good water-repellent garment that may get you damp but also breathes. The usual choice is a loosely fitting jacket (anorak, wind shell, or parka) and rain pants made of a quick-drying microporous "performance" fabric such as Gore-Tex® or Kilmate® that is designed to protect from wind and wet but also allows moisture to escape. For winter hiking, heavy-duty microporous parkas are designed to ventilate moisture. Down is one choice for cold, dry weather, but it can be risky because wet feathers lose their warming capacity.

Footwear

Good footwear is essential to a good HIKING experience. It is actually possible to walk on rough terrain in any comfortable rubber-soled shoe, including sneakers and even high-tech sandals. Specialized MOUNTAINEERING footwear, however, is designed for support, durability, stability, traction, and warmth.

There are dozens of reputable brands but only two really important criteria for choosing hiking boots: comfort and protection. The more protection a boot offers the heavier it is, so the goal is to find a pair that is suited to the desired type of hiking but weighs no more than is absolutely necessary. Why? Because hiking one level mile means picking up and putting down your boots 2,500 times. An extra pound on your feet may feel like 5 more pounds on your back.

As with other types of outdoor footwear, there is no such thing as a true all-purpose boot that is ideal for every condition, so stay away from anything that claims to be. Buy the best you can afford. Cheap boots tend to have poor linings—usually a slow-drying cushiony foam that soaks up blister-causing moisture instead of wicking it off—and will not give your feet enough support to keep your toes from sliding forward.

Good Hiking Boots

■ **Lightweight trail boots.** Good for relatively easy hiking and most backpacking in moderate weather, these are fairly light and flexible on the foot. The uppers are made of leather, nylon packcloth, a textured nylon called Cordura® canvas, or a combination of the above. Lightweight boots weigh from 2 to 3 ½ pounds per pair. They are comfortable, cool, and moderately priced, but they are also only moderately durable and tend to wear out in a single season. They come in walking-shoe styles and ankle-height boot style; the latter is recommended if you are carrying any kind of load.

■ **All-terrain boots.** Heavier and stiffer, these midweight boots are designed for more rugged trails, moderate-to-heavy backpacking, and freezing temperatures. They are usually all leather, weigh about 2 ¾ to 4 pounds a pair, and are generally more expensive but will last several seasons. The boot should feel stiffer than a lightweight model and more resistant to thumb pressure, particularly at the heel.

■ **Trekking boots.** Designed for heavy backpacking and off-trail hiking, trekking boots are extremely stout and supportive; completely waterproof, they are made of sturdy leather or tough plastic and are grooved to fit crampons. These mountaineering boots offer great protection, but weight averages 5 pounds a pair. They are also harder on the trail and take miles to break in.

Choosing Boots

For anything other than the occasional day hike on a well-groomed trail, leather boots are recommended. Leather uppers may be full grain (the full thickness of the hide—the stiffest, most durable, and most expensive type of leather), used smooth or rough side out; top grain (the outer, naturally oiled surface of the tanned cowhide); or split grain (the bottommost, least durable, and least expensive layer of a hide that has actually been split). The fewer the seams the better.

A good heel cup is also important. Test by twisting the boot on its long axis; it should resist. The heel and toe should be rigid and the neck opening soft on the ankle but sturdy enough to give good support. In a lighter boot, the insole should be soft and flexible; for heavier duty it can have a shank support. The sole should be made of stiff rubber with lugs for traction. Light lugs are fine for light terrain, while deep lugs are designed for rough hiking but are also stiffer to walk on and cut up the trail. Look for a heel with a real step up from the instep for good gripping power and close lug placement at the toe and heel.

For rugged climbs, heavy boots with deep lugs and ankle reinforcing provide traction and support. On lighter hikes, heavy boots wear out both hiker and trail.

The boots should have moisture-wicking, breathable linings, such as Gore-Tex,® Cambrelle,® or Sympatex.®

Check for a sturdy gusset of flexible leather, sewn to both the tongue and the upper to keep out sand, water, and stones. A "bellows" tongue and wide gussets will make the boot easier to get into. Metal- or plastic-coated metal (but not all-plastic) lacing hardware is recommended; the fasteners may be grommeted eyelets, D-rings, hooks, or a combination. Eyelets are less likely to break but can be harder to lace.

Fitting Boots

For best results, try on boots late in the day with toenails trimmed and your regular hiking socks on. When deciding between two pairs, try one of each at the same time; one will soon feel better than the other.

The ideal measure is about ½ inch longer than the stockinged foot. To test, push your foot forward into the toe before lacing. It should be possible to fit an index finger between your heel and the boot back. (You can also check this by taking the liner out and putting your foot on it.) Reposition your foot to the boot center, and be sure you can wriggle your toes.

A too-snug boot will restrict circulation, which can cause cold feet and even frostbite.

Next, lace the boots, pulling the laces firmly outward on each side until the slack is gone; if the closure pulls together at the neck, the fit is too loose. With the boot tied, have the salesperson hold your foot down to the floor; you should not be able to lift your heel more than 1/4 inch or rotate the ball of the foot sideways. Kick forward and down; if your toe hits the tip, the boot is too short. Finally, with the boots laced and tied, walk around the store for at least 10 minutes to test comfort and flexibility. Walk up and down stairs and stand on a sharp edge to test arch support. Roll your ankles to the side to test ankle support. If you are planning to hike with a heavy load, try on a loaded pack.

Breaking In Boots

While boots with fabric uppers are usually readily flexible, all-leather boots need breaking in. The process also breaks down the resins in new leather, making it easier for waterproofing sealants to soak in and work. Start with short walks and expect a few blisters. If you blister easily, try leaving the topmost hooks or eyelets unlaced for the first few miles. Be sure the tongue lies straight under the laces; otherwise it can settle in permanently at the wrong angle. Stout boots may need between 10 and 50 miles of walking to mold to the foot. Some experts recommend a breaking-in period of 50 miles on any new boots, in short trips, before attempting a serious hike. This will help prevent blisters and identify fit problems.

Sealing and Caring for Boots

After breaking in leather boots, it is a good idea to seal the seams with a urethane sealant, which is available at sporting goods stores. (Lightweight combination-fabric boots can be treated with a spray-on silicone-based water repellent.) Scrub the seams until clean with water and a toothbrush, let dry thoroughly, and then reclean with rubbing alcohol. When the alcohol has evaporated, apply a narrow bead of the sealant and let it dry overnight. Finally, treat the entire upper. If you don't, the leather will tend to sponge up moisture in wet conditions and crack in dry ones. Brush the leather uppers with a stiff brush, and then apply an oil- or beeswax-based conditioner, rubbing it on with your fingers. Apply two thin coatings of the wax, wiping off the excess with a clean cloth. Each time leather boots are used they should be cleaned with saddle soap and treated with conditioner. For best results, gently warm the boots a good distance from the heat source. Overheating will crack leather, ruin the sealant, and shorten the life of the boot. Stuff the boots loosely with crumpled newspaper and store them in a cool dry spot.

Eyewear

Sunglasses are a personal choice. There is a theory that dark lenses can actually cause eye strain by tricking the eyes into staying open wider than they should. A suggested alternative is to acclimate eyes naturally by wearing a brimmed hat. This may mean squinting for a day or two, but your eyes will soon adjust on their own to sun conditions and will not be dependent on dark lenses. Extreme conditions, however, are another matter. The higher the altitude, the more intense the sun's ultraviolet rays, which can damage the retina. Reflection off snow intensifies the effect.

Both sunglasses and goggles should prevent 100 percent of UV rays from reaching the eye. Some manufacturers also offer infrared radiation protection, although there is no definitive proof that this is necessary. Goggles, designed to fit snugly on the face (over eyeglasses, if necessary), protect eyes from direct and indirect radiation, as well as from ice, flying snow, and wind. Better models have double, thermal-barrier lenses to reduce fogging. Vents and antifogging lens treatments are designed to do the same. The more air space (i.e., the larger the lenses) the less prone goggles are to fogging.

Headwear

A brimmed hat protects from glare, keeps in warmth on cold days, and deflects sun in the heat. A good winter hat is a wool stocking cap, while a good summer hat is a havelock, with a long front visor and a neck protector in the back.

Online and Mail-Order Purchases

Buying online or by catalogue has two obvious disadvantages: you can't touch the product, and you can't try it on. Yet there are good reasons for logging on to an online shopping guide. In an instant you can see the full range of products, read about construction and materials, familiarize yourself with the lingo, and get a sense of prices. Many people prefer to go online or browse through catalogues before shopping in a store. If there is a flexible return policy, ordering by catalogue or Web does let you try gear without any time pressure. Many online suppliers also have retail stores. ☞ *also* CAMPING, DESERT HIKING, HIKING, MOUNTAINEERING, SNOW CAMPING

Continental Divide

Sometimes called the Great Divide, the Continental Divide forms America's backbone. A ridge of peaks in the ROCKY MOUNTAINS, it serves as the boundary line between the continental watersheds, separating westward- and eastward-flowing rivers. Several national parks—Glacier, Rocky Mountain, and YELLOWSTONE NATIONAL PARK—fall on the divide. The Continental Divide National Scenic Trail

(☞ NATIONAL TRAILS SYSTEM) was designated by Congress in 1978 to provide a continous route from Mexico to Canada, passing through Montana, Idaho, Wyoming, Colorado, and New Mexico. About 70 percent is complete.

A view of Glacier National Park in Montana shows the Rockies just west of the Continental Divide.

"Smile not, kind lady reader, at the depth of ignorance that the following notes presume on the part of the reader. You are perhaps not aware that the male ignoramus will be surprised if his directions are so incomplete as not to contain an injunction against allowing the water to burn. How much of each article of diet must the camp take? The following statement will assist; it shows the amount of various articles consumed by six men in two weeks: 20 lbs. bacon, 2 lbs. ham; 1 lb. spiced beef, 4 lbs. bologna, 70 lbs. bread, 6 lbs. beans, 6 lbs. rice, 24 lbs. sugar, 20 tins of condensed milk, 6 lbs. flour, 6 lbs. raisins, 6 lbs. rolled oats, 3 lbs. cornmeal, 2 lbs. weatlets, 7 lbs. prunes and apricots, 6 candles, 6 tins salmon, 2 tins sardines, 1 package cornstarch."

James Edmund Jones, *Camping and Canoeing: What to Take, How to Travel, How to Cook, Where to Go* (1903)

Cooking

Responsible camp cooking is a matter of balancing the desire for pleasant meals with an effort to minimize refuse, animal-attracting odors, and soap pollutants. Cook only the food you need for any given meal to reduce the garbage that must be packed out and to eliminate the need for bear proofing leftovers (☞ BEARS). The rule of thumb is about 2 pounds of food per day per person. Don't wipe your hands on your clothes; use a dishcloth that can be washed or bear bagged, and reserve an apron or a set of clothes for cooking to minimize the number of garments that soak up odors. ☞ *also* CAMPFIRES, CAMPING

Camp Stoves

Opting for a lightweight portable stove instead of building a fire is not only environmentally sound practice; it is safer and more practical. Rain and wind can make it impossible for all but the most experienced camper to light a fire. A stove precludes the problem altogether—at least if it is a stove with a push-button igniting mechanism. Camp stoves have a reputation for being finicky, but such amenities as self-cleaning jets, adjustable heat levels, and built-in sparkers have significantly improved designs.

There are two basic types: liquid fuel and cartridge. A limited choice of solid-fuel stoves, which burn Sterno® or fuel pellets, are also available, but these do not burn hot enough for any real cooking. (One alternative is a specialty model that burns pine cones and other tinder using a battery-operated fan.) Make sure that the stove has an adjustable flame and check the burn (fuel-depletion) time. Be aware that the weight noted on the hang tag almost never accounts for the fuel tank or cartridge (each of which weighs about 10 ounces). Most models will burn two to four hours on one fuel supply; a liquid-fuel stove with a built-in tank may go only an hour,

Cooking over the open fire, as depicted in this nineteenth-century drawing by Felix Octavius Farr Darley, was both the custom and a necessity in frontier days. Current trail wisdom, however, favors camp stoves.

which is true also of small-canister stoves. Because it is illegal to carry cartridge or tank fuel on an airplane, fuel must be bought at your hiking destination. Keep in mind that fuel prices are generally higher at campgrounds and specialty camping stores than they are at large discount department stores. Kerosene stoves and many white-gas stoves require priming with a separate fuel such as solid fuel or denatured alcohol, which should be packed as well.

Once you have chosen a stove type, there is one primary rule to follow and a few others:

- Practice, practice, practice.
- Carefully read the directions and run through the lighting routine several times before you even think of taking any stove out on the trail.
- Burn a tank or a cartridge of fuel so you understand how hot it burns and how long the fuel lasts between feedings.

Liquid-Fuel Stoves

The basic components of a liquid-fuel stove are a refillable fuel tank (either built-in or removable), a vaporizing tube, a pump, and burner(s) or a burner plate, which come in a variety of configurations. Most of these stoves use a refined, clean-burning fuel known as white gas, which is commonly called Coleman® fuel. Some multifuel models take a variety of fuels, such as kerosene, methyl alcohol, and even automobile gas, but they may require changing a tube or a jet to adapt to the fuel change. Some liquid-fuel stoves burn only kerosene or only alcohol (nonvolatile but less efficient). However, in the United States and Canada white gas—plentiful and inexpensive—is the standard fuel of choice.

Liquid-fuel stoves burn more efficiently (and at lower outdoor temperatures) than cartridge stoves. They also burn hotter and faster. The down side is that liquid-fuel stoves are heavier and more cumbersome and often more expensive to buy, although your fuel expense will be lower in the long run. They are also typically trickier to operate, usually requiring assembly, pumping, and priming, which can be incredibly annoying. Moreover, you cannot relight a liquid-fuel stove while it is hot, which can be equally annoying if you run out of fuel in the middle of cooking.

Some liquid-fuel stoves come with a built-in needle for cleaning; otherwise you can run a thin wire through the burner orifice. It is also necessary to periodically remove and soak the jet in white gas to clean it and to check both the tube and the jet for blockages. To prevent pressure leaks, the rubber pump seal must be checked to make sure that it has not dried out and cracked (a dab of oil can help).

Liquid-fuel stoves come with a refillable tank. They run on refined liquid gas, typically white; Coleman is the most common brand.

Cartridge (Bottled-Gas) Stoves

Detachable cartridges of pressurized blended fuel (usually a mix of propane and butane) make these simple, clean-burning stoves easy to use. Cartridge stoves vary in size and configuration, but they are generally a compact valve-and-burner arrangement weighing less than a pound without the fuel tank. Choose a simple model and consider one with a self-cleaning flow-jet to avoid annoying cleaning jobs. In a cartridge stove, the compressed liquid fuel is released as a burnable vapor. The silent flame can be adjusted, and in most weather, except windy conditions, the stove is easy to light with a match or a lighter; no priming is necessary.

Most American manufacturers make the cartridges with reusable seals so that a partially used cartridge can be carried in a backpack with no fear of leaking. The cartridges of some European-made stoves, however, are designed to stay installed until the fuel is used up. Some fuels will not vaporize in freezing temperatures; straight butane, for example, refuses to turn to gas under 30 degrees Fahrenheit. For cold-weather camping, opt for a butane-propane mix, which will light at 20 degrees, or isobutane, which lights at 12 degrees.

Cartridge stoves use prefilled, disposable fuel cans. They run on propane, butane, or a mix of the two.

When using a cartridge stove in extreme temperatures, make sure that it is equipped with a heat exchanger. Otherwise the cartridge may have to be warmed by holding it against your body, putting it in a sleeping bag, or setting it in the sun. The emptier the cartridge the colder the tank, the weaker the flame, and the slower the stove. Regardless of the freezing point, cartridge stoves lose their dependability much earlier than the designated cutoff temperature indicates, because the chilled gas expands much less vigorously. That problem is compounded by the fact that the cartridge itself gets cold as it loses fuel. This, however, is not such an issue in high altitudes, because the lower air pressure lets gas expand faster. A butane stove will still work in below-freezing temperatures at 10,000 feet.

Stove Safety

■ Never use a camp stove inside a tent or in an unventilated area; all fuels produce carbon monoxide and consume oxygen when they burn.

■ Set up the stove in a level, protected spot that is out of the way of everyone in your camping party. Also keep it away from any dry vegetation and camping gear.

■ Shelter the stove from the wind, or it will not work right.

■ Check for stability.

■ In snow, you must keep the stove warm, while preventing it from melting itself into a hole. Set it on an insulated pad or a piece of wood.

■ Never refill a tank or change a cartridge near a source of heat or sparks. In refilling a liquid-gas stove, use a funnel to avoid spills that could accidentally ignite later.

■ Never refuel a liquid-fuel stove when it is hot.

■ Use the minimum amount of priming fuel to avoid overpriming, which can cause overheating and flareups.

■ Alcohol is a less volatile fuel than butane and white gas and a good choice if small children are on hand; it does not burn as efficiently as white gas, however.

■ Do not store a white-gas tank without emptying it and letting it dry thoroughly. (Funnel the gas into the gas tank of your car.)

■ Do not use a camp stove as a space heater, and never leave it unattended.

Cookware

Choosing cookware for camping is a matter of common sense, depending on menu preferences, trip length, and the size of the camping party. A single pot, for example, can do fine for a pair of hikers; if you bring more pots and pans, be sure they nest. Full camping cooksets usually include two pots (one small, one bigger), a couple of lids that can double as frying pans, and a gripper handle, altogether weighing less than 2 pounds. Other useful kitchen gear includes mess kits, plastic containers, and a collapsible water carrier. Cord and sturdy sacks or containers for bear bagging are also necessary (☞ BEARS).

Materials

■ **Bi-metal.** Pros: The black aluminum coating promotes fast heat absorption, and the stainless steel lining adds durability. Con: Can be expensive.

■ **Enamel.** Pros: The enamel-coated steel is easy to clean. Cons: The enamel can chip, and the steel will rust.

■ **Stainless steel.** Pros: Durable and cleans easily. Cons: Stainless steel is heavy and is not an even heat conductor, so food can cook unevenly and scorch.

■ **Titanium.** Pros: Light and strong, this is the king of cookware materials. Con: expensive.

■ **Uncoated aluminum.** Pros: Light, cheap, and a rapid heat conductor. Cons: Dents easily; burned food sticks and is hard to clean; may react to acidic foods.

Washing Up

The use of soap to clean cookware is an issue of contention. The strictest opinion holds that for a truly green campsite, no soap should be used—ever. Soap is hard to rinse away completely, and even biodegradable soap can pollute. The safest method is to clean pots and dishes with water and a soapless scouring pad; sand, pine cones, and snow are the recommended natural alternatives.

That said, biodegradable, phosphate-free, nondetergent liquid soaps are made for camping. Boiling soapy water in the cookware will kill bacteria. Never wash dishes, with or without soap, directly in a stream or in any other body of water. Strain the dirty wash water, and put the solids in a garbage bag. Scatter the wash and rinse water widely among brush or stones at least 100 feet away from ponds, streams, and lakes. In a grizzly bear area, it is safer to drain dishwater into a small hole and cover with soil or put it into the current of a sizable stream.

Reading

📖 Dorcas S. Miller, *Good Food for Camp and Trail: All-Natural Recipes for Delicious Meals Outdoors* (1993). 📖 Dale Burk, *Camp Cookbook* (1994). 📖 Claudia Pearson, ed., *National Outdoor Leadership School Cookery* (1997). 📖 Teresa Marrone, *The Back-Country Kitchen: Camp Cooking for Canoeists, Hikers and Anglers* (1998).

James Fenimore Cooper

"Extremes of habits, manners, time and space
Brought close together, here stood face to face
And gave at once a contrast to the view
That other lands and ages never knew."

James Fenimore Cooper,
Epigraph, *The Pioneers* (1823)

The Last of the Mohicans, illustrated by E. Boyd Smith in 1910, portrayed the frontier scout as an American hero.

James Fenimore Cooper (1789–1851) was the first popular American novelist to take exception to the Puritan concept of wilderness as the scourge of the New World. His early literary success was established with the best-selling *The Spy* (1821) and confirmed with the epic series of affectionate backwoods adventure novels known as the Leatherstocking Tales, which were initiated with *The Pioneers* (in print continuously since 1823) and completed intermittently with *The Last of the Mohicans* (1826), *The Prairie* (1827), *The Pathfinder* (1840), and *The Deerslayer* (1841). The series, whose extravagant and formulaic plots centered on pioneer heroics, features the famous backwoods protagonist known variously as Hawkeye and Natty Bumppo. A fictional incarnation of DANIEL BOONE, Bumppo is cast as a self-sufficient scout and pathfinder who is raised from childhood in the forest by Indians and finds sustenance in his fierce resentment of would-be civilizers. As hunter, moralist, and lonely wanderer, he personifies the courage and simple virtue now threatened by progress, and his adventures underscore the inevitable clash between civilization and the wilds.

Cooper himself deplored the loss of the frontier, but he ultimately saw the advance

of civilization as the greater of two goods. He did not foresee the coexistence of Indians and whites, but he did support a proposed plan to establish a formal Indian territory west of the Mississippi and its provision for sending delegates to Congress. In this way the decimation of a noble culture would be checked and the Indians offered the opportunity "to continue to advance in civilization. . . ." ☞ also WRITERS (NINETEENTH CENTURY)

📄 *Precaution* (1820). *The Spy* (1821). *The Pioneers* (1823). *The Pilot* (1823).   *Selected Works*
Lionel Lincoln (1825). *The Last of the Mohicans* (1826). *The Red Rover* (1827). *The Prairie* (1827). *Homeward Bound* (1838). *The American Democrat* (1838). *Home as Found* (1838). *The Pathfinder* (1840). *The Deerslayer* (1841). *The Redskins* (1846). *Oak Openings* (1848). *The Sea Lions* (1849). *The Ways of the Hour* (1850).

James Fenimore Cooper Society ✉ 8 Lake Street, Cooperstown, NY 13326.   *Contact*
🖥 www.oneonta.edu/ ~ cooper
■ An organization of students, scholars, and readers devoted to the lives and work of James Fenimore Cooper and his daughter Susan Fenimore Cooper, the society publishes a newsletter and papers and hosts a weeklong Cooper conference every two years.

Corps of Discovery

No greater story of American wilderness adventure probably surpasses that of the Lewis and Clark expedition of 1804–6. This three-year odyssey from the Mississippi River valley to the Pacific Ocean covered a monumental distance in both miles and knowledge gained. At a time when two-thirds of the non-native population lived within 50 miles of the Atlantic Ocean, so little was known of the trans-Mississippi West that it was believed that the APPALACHIAN MOUN-TAINS were the tallest peaks in the country and that the Mandans were a tribe of misplaced Welshmen.

"Ocian in View! O! The joy."

Lieutenant William Clark (November 6, 1805)

The independent infantry company co-commanded by Captain Meriwether Lewis and Lieutenant William Clark—known as the Corps of Volunteers for North West Discovery—were the first Americans other than indigenous peoples to lay eyes on a coyote (Clark called it a "Prairie Wolf"); the first to describe a Rocky Mountain Indian nation (the Shoshones); the first to slay a grizzly bear (with considerable difficulty); and the first to see and chart the Yellowstone River (☞ YELLOWSTONE NATIONAL PARK) and the Missouri Great Falls. Covering some 10,000 miles round trip, their extraordinary route of exploration took them up the upper Missouri River, across the ROCKY MOUNTAINS by Indian pass, and down the Clearwater, Snake, and Columbia Rivers to the Pacific. In 1806 the group traveled in separate parties via alternate routes

(north to the Missouri's Great Falls and south along the Yellowstone River), reconnoitering at the confluence of the Missouri and Yellowstone before returning by water to St. Louis.

Although the corps encountered bitter winters, near starvation, and some fifty unfamiliar Indian tribes, every member of the permanent party of thirty-three survived. By all accounts the expedition owed its success to the complementary skills of its two leaders. William Clark (1770–1838), an expert marksman and resourceful negotiator, was the chief surveyor and cartographer. His maps of the Missouri and the route to and from Fort Clatsop constitute the first codified picture of the trans-Appalachian West. Meriwether Lewis (1774–1809) was an informed ethnographer and first-rate naturalist, illustrator, and celestial navigator of equal accomplishment. During the winter bivouac (1805–6) in Fort Clatsop on the Pacific Coast, Lewis classified at least ten previously unknown plant species, including the Sitka spruce. His ethnographic accounts of little-known Indian tribes, including the Shoshones, Mandans, Clatsops, and Chinooks, provided a significant resource of information on nations that would be eradicated by disease only a few decades later.

A primary motive of the Lewis and Clark expedition, which was sponsored by Congress and the American Philosophical Society (☞ LEARNED SOCIETIES) under pressure from THOMAS JEFFERSON, was to explore the northern boundaries of the Louisiana Purchase (1803) and secure a direct trade route from the East to the Pacific and ultimately to Canton. The discovery that such a northwest passage required a 340-mile overland interval conclusively proved that the hoped-for

cute apex, which is mostly but not entirely
with a smale subrelate thorn. they are jointed a
pointed consisting of 6 par and terminating in
[this form.]
like   sessile
                                                                        the teeth
saw, each   point term.
~ a smale subulate spine, being from 25 to 27 in numb
oth, plane and of a deep green, their points
obliquely towards the extremity of the rib or

water corridor between the Mississippi River valley and the
Pacific did not in fact exist. The spoils of the expedition,
however—in the form of seeds, soil samples, minerals, animal
skins, and skeletons, as well as detailed information on the
geography, climate, ethnography, and natural history of the
previously unexplored West—were of inestimable value. The
expedition also helped establish the upper Missouri River as
an important transportation artery to the Northwest and set
into motion a successful bid for Oregon. Equally important,
the reports furnished by corps members provided the public
with a vivid image of the western wilderness that still has a
hold on the American consciousness.

Upon his return to St. Louis, William Clark was appointed superintendent of Indian Affairs in 1807 and served
as governor of the Missouri Territory from 1813 to 1821.
Meriwether Lewis, who had served as Jefferson's private secretary just before the expedition, was appointed governor
of the Louisiana Territory. On his way to Washington in
1809, he died under mysterious circumstances at an inn on
the Natchez Trace, possibly a suicide. Lewis's journals were
edited posthumously, and the first official account appeared
as *The History of the Expedition under the Command of Captains
Lewis and Clark, 1804–5–6*, edited by Nicholas Biddle and Paul
Allen in 1814. The Sierra Club (☞ ADVOCATES) is marking the
bicentennial of the Corps of Discovery expedition with the
Wild America Campaign for permanent protection of
thirty-four undesignated areas of wild territory along the
explorers' route.

Among the great
bounties of the Lewis
and Clark expedition
were botanical speci-
mens. William Clark's
records depict a sample
of Oregon grape leaf
collected on the Pacific
Coast, measured almost
perfectly to actual size.

Selected Supplies Used on the Lewis and Clark Expedition, 1804–6

■ Beads (33 pounds) ■ Brass kettles (8) ■ Chisels ■ Chronometer ■ Cloth (150 yards, to be oiled and made into tents) ■ Dr. Rushes Patented Pills (50 dozen) ■ Face paint (vermilion) ■ Fishing hooks and lines (10½ pounds) ■ Flannel shirts (45) ■ Gunpowder (176 pounds) ■ Hand compass ■ Hand saws ■ Hatchets ■ Knives (288) ■ Mosquito curtains ■ Muzzle loaders (15) ■ Pliers ■ Plotting instruments (one set) ■ Pocket mirrors (12 dozen) ■ Portable soup (193 pounds) ■ Rifles (.54 caliber) ■ Salt (3 bushels) ■ Sewing needles (4,600) ■ Sextants (2) ■ Surveyor's compass ■ Telescope ■ Thermometers ■ Tobacco (130 rolls)

Contact

Lewis and Clark Trail Heritage Foundation ✉ P.O. Box 3434, Great Falls, MT 59403. 🖳 www.lewisandclark.org
■ The foundation supports education and research about the Lewis and Clark expedition, promotes awareness and appreciation of native tribes, and assists with interpretation of the historic and natural resources of the Lewis and Clark National Historic Trail. Publications include the quarterly journal *We Proceeded On*.

Reading

📕 Bernard DeVoto, ed., *Journals of Lewis and Clark* (1953). 📕 Gary Moulton, ed., *The Journals of the Lewis and Clark Expedition* (1988). 📕 Stephen E. Ambrose, *Undaunted Courage: Meriwether Lewis, Thomas Jefferson, and the Opening of the American West* (1997). 📕 Dayton Duncan and Ken Burns, *Lewis and Clark: The Journey of the Corps of Discovery* (1999).

Council on Environmental Quality

Requiring public involvement on land management plans and issues, the National Environmental Policy Act (1969) established the Council on Environmental Quality within the president's office and called on the federal government to cooperate with state and local governments and private groups in declaring "a national policy which will encourage productive and enjoyable harmony between man and his environment." The act further directed all federal agencies to prepare environmental impact statements, which are reviewed by the council, pending development on PUBLIC LANDS. The council also advises the president on environmental policy matters, prepares an annual environmental quality report to Congress, and includes the Office of Environmental Quality.

Contact

Council on Environmental Quality ✉ Old Executive Office Building, Room 360, Washington, DC 20501. ☎ 202-456-6224. 🖳 www.whitehouse.gov/ceq

Edward S. Curtis

Edward Sheriff Curtis (1868–1952) spent more than thirty years photographing Indians in distant parts of the United States and Canada in an attempt to visit all the North American tribes and document their vanishing cultures. His North American Indian Project fell short of that goal, but beginning in the 1890s the photographer did encounter at least eighty major tribes, commencing with the Apache, Navajo, and Jicarilla and ending with native peoples in the ALASKA territory. In the process he covered more than 40,000 miles and produced a similar number of negatives, working primarily in a massive 14-by-17-inch format.

In 1899 Curtis joined the Harriman expedition to Alaska. This journey alone yielded 5,000 negatives and produced a significant body of photographs of GLACIERS as well as images of Inuits. With the help of the financier J. P. Morgan (1837–1913), Curtis's life's work was published as the twenty-volume series *The North American Indian* (1907–30), which included detailed text on art, culture, and custom. In the course of this massive endeavor Curtis gained THEODORE ROOSEVELT as a supporter, and in 1906 the president asked him to photograph Geronimo and five other chiefs on the White House lawn. The following year the first volume of the series—part photographic essay, part ethnographic survey—was issued with a foreword by Roosevelt. ☞ *also* NATIVE AMERICANS, PHOTOGRAPHERS

The Eagle Catcher, a photograph taken by Edward S. Curtis around 1908 and first published in his multivolume work *The North American Indian* (1907–30), conveys the proud bearing of a Hidatsa Indian with an eagle he has caught.

Desert Hiking

By practical definition *desert hiking* and *desert camping* refer to any wilderness experience in a hot, arid location that does not offer a ready supply of water. The extreme conditions are one good reason why desert hikers often use a vehicle (well stocked with drinking water, food, and dry clothes) as a base for short forays into the wilds. Consult a detailed map before you depart, and inform someone of your route and date of return.

The desert may look inhospitable and tough, but the ecosystems are fragile (☞ DESERTS). In particular, the desert floor's blackish cryptobiotic crust (made up partly of algae and tiny plants), which helps prevent erosion and promotes taller plant growth, is vulnerable to fracture underfoot. This crust is slow to regenerate, so hikers should avoid walking on it; the cactus that you knock over with a boot has likely taken two decades to grow. ☞ *also* ARCHAEOLOGICAL PARKS, CAMPING, CLOTHING, DESERTS, HEALTH AND FIRST AID, HIKING, NATIVE AMERICANS, SLEEPING BAGS, TENTS

Weather

■ Check the weather forecast and familiarize yourself with the general conditions of any desert region, and don't forget to take altitude into consideration.

■ Because of the extreme heat, hiking in the Chihuahuan and Sonoran desert lowlands (usually 3,000 feet or less), for example, is practicable only in winter. However, in the higher altitudes (3,500 to 5,000 feet), freezing temperatures can occur at night in the coldest months.

■ Hiking in air temperatures that exceed your body temperature is akin to walking through a giant convection oven. Hike the desert when the sun is low, in the early morning or late afternoon, and look for cooler air temperatures near water or in sheltered areas like caves. Rest in shade for 10 minutes every hour. Reapply sunscreen often.

■ Keep a close eye on the sky for thunderheads; if there is the least threat of a downpour, stay away from canyons, washes, and gullies, where July and August thunderstorms often cause flash flooding.

■ Common wisdom holds that breezes cool you down by aiding sweat evaporation; in scorching temperatures, however, a strong, steady wind can create blast-furnace conditions that result in too much moisture loss.

■ Consider the time of year. The annual rainfall in the Mojave Desert, for example, is less than 5 inches and occurs in the winter, producing a blast of blossoms in early spring. Both climate and colors make these two seasons the best for hiking there. Summer is brutally hot, dry, and windy; temperatures in Death Valley go above 120 degrees Fahrenheit in the shade.

Water

■ Hiking in arid regions means bringing in all water. Research shows that a healthy person can expect to live five to seven days without water in temperatures around 90 degrees Fahrenheit. A hiker who starts out hydrated should be able to cover 7 to 10 miles in desert conditions without water.

■ Because of the threat of dehydration, you will need huge water supplies: the conservative rule of thumb is a 1.5-gallon base requirement and an additional quart for every 5 miles covered—more for intense temperatures.

■ In spite of what a map might indicate, never depend on a local water source; there is a good chance that it has dried up since the last field check.

■ Although water intake can come in part from eating fruit and other moist foods, you will need more than you can reasonably carry. One tactic is to cache a supply of water bottles at intervals along the route by tucking them in a shallow hole or under a small pile of stones; map each cache adequately with compass bearings. Because a hiker's life depends on finding these caches on the return, the convention is to document them with Polaroid pictures or careful notes.

■ In a water emergency, head back to your starting point at a slow, even pace; if you must go farther than 10 miles, wait until dark. Limit your food intake to a few carbohydrates, and avoid cigarettes, alcohol, and coffee. Keep a lookout for birds or converging animal tracks, which may indicate a natural water source.

Clothing and Gear

■ Deserts present one of the rare hiking situations in which all-cotton garments—loose and comfortable—are preferred. Wear a light-colored, long-sleeve shirt and long pants to protect against insects, wind, sun, and painful encounters with stinging shrubs and cactus needles.

■ Don't forget sunglasses and a hat with a visor and a neck-shielding havelock.

■ Bring a flashlight to see nocturnal desert life; a black light will pick out scorpions and other desert critters.

■ Desert campers often prefer sleeping under the stars. Otherwise limit yourself to a lightweight tent, or a tarp, which can be quickly pitched to provide shade during a midday rest stop as well; a basic three-season sleeping bag should suffice.

■ Because of the possibility of flash floods, never pitch camp in a dry river or stream bed or gully. Do not try to cross a flooding area by foot or car.

Deserts

"In my case, it was love at first sight. This desert, all deserts, any desert."

Edward Abbey, "The Great American Desert," *The Journey Home* (1977)

"The Great American Desert is an awful place. People get hurt, get sick, get lost out there. Even if you survive, which is not certain, you will have a miserable time. The desert is for movies and God-intoxicated mystics, not for family recreation."

Edward Abbey, "The Great American Desert," *The Journey Home* (1977)

Desert conditions exist across most of Utah, including this region south of the High Uintas (visible in the distance), recorded by the WPA photographer John Vachon in 1942.

Deserts, as Edward Abbey (1927–89) testifies, are an essay in ambiguity. Their complex geological makeup, disparate climatic conditions, and delicate balance of plant, animal, and insect life mean that these arid wildernesses do not fall neatly into categories, despite certain qualifying characteristics, such as the rate of evaporation versus rainfall and the amount of moisture the soil conveys to vegetation. Scientists disagree over precisely which plant and animal life

define a desert. Moreover, boundaries of a specific desert are likely to shrink and spread with cycles of rain and drought. Simply put, what one expert calls a desert another may not.

That said, the prevailing geological classification accounts for four major American deserts defined roughly by type and location: Great Basin, Mojave, Sonoran, and Chihuahuan. All but the Chihuahuan fall mostly in what is known as the Basin and Range province, a western region of parallel mountain ridges and intervening valleys with no coastal outlet lying between the Pacific Coast ranges and the ROCKY MOUNTAINS. The region covers about 200,000 square miles in California, Idaho, Nevada, Oregon, Utah, and Wyoming.

Great Basin Desert

The northernmost desert is the eponymous Great Basin Desert, which spreads over southeastern Oregon, the southern third of Idaho, most of Nevada, western and southern Utah, and a northeastern bit of Arizona. It is considered a "cold desert" in that elevations up to 6,500 feet produce low annual temperatures and more than half of the precipitation is snow. Juniper and piñon trees grow in the higher elevations. Shrubs—sagebrush, saltbush, blackbrush, shadscale, Mormon tea, and greasewood—are plentiful, while the cacti, agaves, and yuccas of the southern deserts are rare to nonexistent. The southeastern section of the Great Basin Desert dips into the highlands of the Colorado plateau, where the dry climate has exposed mineral-laden sedimentary rocks from 50 to 500 million years old. This semiarid "canyon country" of southwestern Colorado, northeastern Arizona, southeastern Utah, and northwestern New Mexico is defined by dramatic mesas and gorges (the GRAND CANYON being the largest) and is often, but not always, referred to as the Painted Desert.

Mojave Desert

The Mojave, Sonoran, and Chihuahuan Deserts are characterized by more extreme heat and aridity than the Great Basin Desert. This is the result of cool Pacific currents and high atmospheric pressure, which limit rainfall to less than 10 inches a year. Once an inland sea, the Mojave covers southern Nevada, part of southern California, and northwestern Arizona. Cactus is found in the low-lying *bajadas;* yucca, desert Spanish bayonet, creosote bush, shadscale, big sagebrush, bladder-sage, bursages, and blackbrush are the common shrubs. Unique to the Mojave is the Joshua tree (*Yucca brevifolia*), a treelike type of yucca—protected in the Joshua Tree National Park—said to have been named by Mormons who thought that the outspread branches resembled the wide-spread arms of Joshua, leading them out of the wilderness of the California desert. The lowest point in the country (282 feet below sea level) occurs in the Mojave Desert, in the Death Valley National Monument (California). The Mojave National Preserve at the intersection of the Sonoran, Mojave, and Great Basin Deserts contains prehistoric petroglyphs and dinosaur tracks.

Sonoran Desert

To the south of the Mojave, the Sonoran Desert (106,000 square miles) extends over southern Arizona, the tip of California, and part of northwestern Mexico, as well as most of the Baja Peninsula. Cacti (notably the saguaro) are the defining feature of this, the hottest and driest of the North American deserts, characterized by low-slung mountain ranges. Expanses of true desolation are particularly evident in the Organ Pipe Cactus National Monument and the Cabeza Prieta National Wildlife Refuge near the Mexican border. By contrast, in the western Sonoran, sometimes called the Colorado Desert, moisture from Pacific storms can produce a spectacular show of flowers in the spring. The Sonoran habitat also supports chollas and ocotillo, desert saltbush in the lowlands, and dense growths of honey mesquite and cottonwoods.

Chihuahuan Desert

The easternmost desert is the Chihuahuan Desert (175,000 square miles), which spreads over extreme West Texas and the Rio Grande valley, extending north into New Mexico and south into Mexico. The wildest section of the Chihuahuan is found in Big Bend National Park. Most of this desert lies at elevations between 3,500 and 5,000 feet. Most precipitation (about 10 inches a year) is in the summer growing season of this shrub desert, which produces a rich range of plant life, including yuccas and agaves, grasses and creosote bushes, prickly pears and chollas, Mormon tea, tarbush, white-thorn acacia, Allthorn, and ocotillo. Honey mesquite thrives in the washes and playas.

Desert Preservation

One of the largest pieces of wilderness legislation ever passed in America is the California Desert Protection Act (1994), which was the culmination of a long battle to protect California's deserts from excessive off-road vehicle use, open-pit mining, and grazing and to rescue bighorn sheep and golden eagles threatened by compromised habitats. The law created nine BUREAU OF LAND MANAGEMENT areas totaling 3.6 million acres; established the 1.6-million-acre Mojave National Preserve, including 695,000 acres of national wilderness area; expanded the Death Valley and Joshua Tree National Monuments into national parks; reserved 326,000 acres as wilderness study areas; set aside as wilderness some 95,000 acres OF U.S. FOREST

SERVICE land and 9,000 acres on the Havasu and Imperial National Wildlife Refuges; transferred 20,500 acres of BLM land to Red Rock Canyon State Park; and created the 2,000-acre Desert Lily Sanctuary. ☞ *also* DESERT HIKING, NATIONAL MONUMENTS, NATIONAL PARK SYSTEM, NATIONAL PRESERVES, NATIONAL WILDERNESS PRESERVATION SYSTEM, NATIONAL WILDLIFE REFUGE SYSTEM

Selected Deserts

Although agreement may be lacking over what defines a desert, these names are commonly used to designate certain desert areas within the four larger deserts:

- **Arizona Upland Desert.** A plateau of the Sonoran Desert in southern Arizona where saguaro cactus predominates.
- **Black Rock Desert.** A subdesert of the Great Basin Desert in northwestern Nevada, northeast of Pyramid Lake, notable for its *playas*.
- **Borrego Desert.** A western portion of the Sonoran Desert area in southeastern California.
- **Colorado Desert.** The California section of the Sonoran Desert, west of the Colorado River.
- **Escalante Desert.** A subdivision of the Great Basin Desert located just west of Cedar Breaks in southwestern Utah.
- **Great Sandy Desert.** The part of the Great Basin Desert that is located in southeastern Oregon.
- **Painted Desert.** The badlands on the northeastern bank of the Little Colorado River in northern Arizona, unfolding south from the Grand Canyon to include the Petrified Forest National Park.
- **Red Desert.** The semiarid region of southwestern Wyoming.
- **Sevier Desert.** A subdivision of the Great Basin Desert in south-central Utah.
- **Smoke Creek Desert.** A section of the Great Basin Desert in northwestern Nevada that borders the north end of Pyramid Lake.
- **Trans-Pecos Desert.** The Chihuahuan Desert west of the Pecos River in Texas.
- **Yuha Desert.** The portion of the Sonoran Desert extending between Ocotillo and El Centro, California, south into Mexico.
- **Yuma Desert.** The Sonoran Desert east of the Colorado River near Yuma, Arizona.

The hallmark desert plant of Arizona's Saguaro National Park is its namesake succulent. Ansel Adams's photograph helped make the saguaro the most recognizable cactus in the world.

Arizona-Sonora Desert Museum ✉ 2021 North Kinney Road, Tucson, AZ 85743. ☎ 520-883-1380. 🖳 www.desertmuseum.org

Contacts

- This natural history museum has ongoing research projects about desert habitats and plant and animal life, including a number of endangered species, and runs a tortoise adoption program.

Desert Fishes Council ✉ P.O. Box 337, Bishop, CA 93515. ☎ 760-872-8751. 🖳 www.desertfishes.org
- The council's mission is to preserve the biological integrity of aquatic ecosystems in the desert Southwest. The group holds symposia to report on related research and management endeavors.

Desert Tortoise Council ⊠ P.O. Box 3141, Wrightwood, CA 92397. (909-884-9700. 🖳 www.deserttortoise.org

■ The private, nonprofit council encourages conservation of the wild desert tortoise (a threatened species) in the deserts of the Southwest and Mexico. The group advises fish and wildlife agencies, holds workshops, and initiates recovery actions.

Dime Novels

Cheaply printed, formulaic adventure stories were a spectacularly successful genre that flourished in America during the Civil War era—the brainchild of brothers Erastus and Irwin Beadle, who issued the first dime novel in 1860. Within months, *Malaeska*, the tragic tale of a star-struck Indian girl wed to a white settler, sold more than 65,000 copes. The Beadles' next venture, *Seth Jones; or, the Captives of the Frontier* (said to be a favorite of Abraham Lincoln), sold 600,000 copies and was translated into several languages. A rapid succession of novel-length pamphlets followed, turned out as often as once every two weeks by Irwin P. Beadle and Company (later renamed Beadle and Adams) and many other publishers, including Frank Tousey and Street and Smith.

Capitalizing on the success of dime novel westerns, Erastus Beadle's weekly pulp magazine *Half Dime Library* featured stories by Prentiss Ingraham.

Sold for a dime at newsstands and dry goods stores, the books featured tales of tomahawk-wielding savages, innocent maidens in distress, and virile backwoodsmen and frontier scouts who came to the rescue. Although other sagas were popular, the favorites were westerns, which typically followed a hackneyed plot in which some moral dilemma was resolved—often as industry and capitalism triumphed over frontier backwardness.

The writing was generally second-rate, and the use of frequently changing pen names helped camouflage the embarrassing speed with which the books were churned out. Among the most prolific dime novel authors was one Colonel Prentiss Ingraham, who spun wild tales about BUFFALO BILL. Ingraham wrote a story per week of about 60,000 words, usually raking in $250 for each tale. ☞ *also* WESTERN FICTION

Disturbed Lands

Public land agencies including the NATIONAL PARK SERVICE have begun trying to restore so-called disturbed lands—lands that have been used and abandoned or scarred by interventions such as roads, excavations, reservoirs, dams, diversion channels, oil fields, railway grades, and irrigation ditches associated with mining, mineral development, water reclamation, and logging. Such disturbances often cause erosion, attract dumping, and alter wildlife habitats.

Restoration is a complex concept, in part because of disagreement over whether the goal is a return to the natural system that preceded the disturbance or one that "belongs" to the region but did not previously exist there. And some advocates contend that whatever was used to disturb the area originally—pick and shovel or heavy machinery—be used to restore it, which itself may be inappropriate or infeasible.

A ccepting paying guests at a working ranch is a uniquely American enterprise. Some trace the seeds of the idea to Bill Sublette, a famous mountain man who in 1844 agreed to take a group of easterners to Brown's Hole in Montana for the summer for a genuine taste of the western wilderness. The first ranch to take in paying guests is believed to be the Custer Trail Ranch near Medora, North Dakota. Located on land where General George Armstrong Custer camped just before his last stand at Little Big Horn in 1876, this 7,000-acre spread was owned by Alden, Willis, and Howard Eaton, former meat suppliers for Northern Pacific Railway construction crews. Claiming their land with squatter's rights, these three brothers from Pittsburgh established

Dude Ranches

Image is everything: a group of dudines at the Valley Ranch in Wyoming pose about 1935 for a photograph decked out in chaps and other western garb for a cattle roundup.

a successful cattle and horse ranch and lured visitors from back East with reports of excellent buffalo hunting (☞ BISON). The term *dude*, which in the West refers to a city slicker—specifically an easterner—was formally coined in YELLOWSTONE NATIONAL PARK in 1886; female dudes were properly known as *dudines* and children as *dudettes*.

The enormous popularity of DIME NOVEL westerns and BUFFALO BILL's Wild West Show in the late 1800s only embellished the romantic lure of the West. In this early era "duding" was a privilege limited to those who could spare the expense and time required to travel; the Valley Ranch in Wyoming maintained its own Pullman and dining cars in trains running from New York to Cody, and the owner greeted arriving greenhorns dressed in full cowboy regalia. When World War I precluded the traditional grand tour of Europe, the dude ranch became a fashionable alternative. While enjoying the wide-open western landscape of mountain and sky, guests pitched in to help with cattle roundups and horse branding. Pack trips, barbecues, square dances, and hayrides rounded out the roster of cowboy activities.

The real heyday for the dude ranch came in the 1920s, as the advent of automobile tourism brought thousands of visitors west just at a time when many working ranches began converting to "duding" to make ends meet. In the 1920s and 1930s, ranches reduced cattle stock to accommodate more guests. That trend reversed during World War II, when the war effort required increased beef and crop production. As visitation fell off, some ranches closed, while others tried special promotions. The Valley Ranch advertised "victory vacations," in which youngsters were offered six- to eight-week stays at reduced cost in exchange for joining the ranch's own effort "to increase war productions" by working in the hay fields and vegetable gardens and doing their own housekeeping. In the postwar years colorful brochures and the wide publication of promotional photographs in national magazines regenerated a business that has thrived ever since.

Contact   **The Dude Ranchers' Association** ⊠ P.O. Box F-471, LaPorte, CO 80535. ℂ 970-223-8440. ▯ www.duderanch.org

■ This organization, founded in 1926, maintains a directory of 100-plus dude ranches in twelve western states, offers travel services, and supplies information on internships and seasonal employment for wranglers, cooks, and other ranch workers.

One of the best descriptions of Ralph Waldo Emerson (1803–82) in the wilds comes from the writer and artist William James Stillman (1828–1901). In his essay "The Philosophers' Camp," in which Stillman recalled a now-famous 1858 Adirondacks (☞ ADIRONDACK MOUNTAINS) camping trip taken by a group of Cambridge philosophers and literati, he marveled at his friend's kinship with the forest in what was the Concord author's first visit to real "Wilderness" (Stillman's capitalization). "He seemed to be a living question, perpetually interrogating his impressions of all there was to be seen," wrote Stillman. "The rest of us were always at the surface of things—even the naturalists were only engaged with their anatomy; but Emerson in the forest or looking at the sunset from the lake seemed to be looking through the phenomena, studying them by their reflections on an inner speculum." Emerson himself commemorated the camping trip in a poem entitled "The Adirondacs," which was published to great success in 1860.

A quarter of a century earlier, the poet and essayist had outlined the main tenets of transcendentalism in his anonymous essay "Nature" (1836). In it he repudiated materialism and called for spiritual renewal through an individual experience of nature—uncompromised by history and tradition—which he presented as the temporal proof of a higher spiritual being. That man, God, and nature do exist in spiritual harmony was

Ralph Waldo Emerson

"And theft from satellites and rings
And broken stars I drew,
And out of spent and aged things
I formed the world anew."

Ralph Waldo Emerson, "Song of Nature" (1867)

an idea that Emerson revisited in numerous works, including "The American Scholar" (1837), "The Method of Nature" (1841), and "The Young American" (1844). ☞ *also* WRITERS (NINETEENTH CENTURY)

Endangered Species

As defined by the Endangered Species Act (1973), an endangered species is one that is in danger of extinction throughout all or a significant part of its ranges; a threatened species is likely to become vulnerable in the foreseeable future. One can only guess at the total number of native species that actually exists in America, but to date more than 100,000 (land and freshwater) have been identified. The federal Endangered Species List currently designates some 632 endangered species and 190 threatened species, but it is widely acknowledged that the full number at risk is greater. The Nature Conservancy estimates that about one-third of America's wild flora and fauna is "of conservation concern." According to a 1990 Conservancy study, the most threatened fauna populations are fish, with a full 40 percent of fish species in grave danger of immediate or foreseeable extinction. Fish are followed in order of danger by reptiles (18 percent are threatened), mammals (17 percent), and birds (15 percent). Hawaii has the world's largest proportion of extinct or endangered species, and the state is believed to have lost half of its birds and dozens of plant and invertebrate species. Among other problem regions are Arizona and the southern regions of Florida (☞ EVERGLADES), California, Texas, and the APPALACHIAN MOUNTAINS.

By the time the Spanish conquistadors began exploring the country in the 1540s, many North American species—including camels, horses, mammoths, mastodons, saber-toothed cats, and giant ground sloths—had already been extinct for about 7,500 years, possibly the victims of climate change and overhunting by paleo-Indians at the close of the last Ice Age. The Wilderness Society (☞ ADVOCATES) estimates that five hundred-plus native plant and animal species have vanished in America since the time of European settlement.

One early threat was the impression that there was an endless source of plenitude. Who could conceive of anything running out in a land where more tree types grew in a single mountain range (☞ GREAT SMOKY MOUNTAINS) than in all of Europe and where lobsters, found beached in heaps 2 feet high, were so numerous they were regarded as a trash food? Hunting—for such market commodities as furs, bird feathers and eggs (☞ BIRDS), and buffalo tongue (☞ BISON)—had a significant impact on animal species as early as the 1700s. Some, like the Labrador duck, vanished completely. Others were driven so far out of their natural ranges that it is now difficult to imagine that caribou once roamed in Maine and the northern GREAT LAKES, that elk was a Virginia native, and that woods bison, gray wolves, and mountain lions thrived in the forests of the Mid-Atlantic seaboard.

The worst period for species destruction came in the late 1800s and early 1900s. Jaguars and timber wolves were targeted primarily because of fear and superstition and because they preyed on crops and livestock. Eastern mountain lions, hawks, owls, BEARS (New Hampshire's black bear population was reduced to an astounding fifty in 1900), and bald eagles were all victims of state-sponsored "varmint" campaigns. As late as the 1940s, West Virginia offered an annual college scholarship to the young man who bagged the highest number of animals deemed to be farm pests. Government-sponsored campaigns helped achieve the near extermination of wolves, bison, grizzly bears, and prairie dogs.

The primary threat to animal and plant species in America now is habitat destruction, compounded by fire suppression, POLLUTION, and competition from exotic (alien) species (a major concern in Hawaii). One problem is policy: wildlife protection

Opposite: In 1858 *Frank Leslie's New Family Magazine* invited readers into the Philosophers' Camp in the Adirondacks, showing how Ralph Waldo Emerson, Louis Agassiz, and James Russell Lowell "amuse themselves in the summer."

Lost Habitats

has been traditionally considered secondary to recreation and development interests in the United States, particularly in the NATIONAL FOREST SYSTEM, where logging, mining, camping, and other activities must compete under the prevailing mixed-use management policy.

The loss of habitat is another factor. According to the ecologist David S. Wilcove in *The Condor's Shadow* (2000), more than 85 percent of the country's virgin FORESTS (☞ CLEAR-CUTTING) has been harvested, 90 percent of the tallgrass prairies plowed or paved, and 98 percent of the rivers and streams dammed or diverted since the seventeenth century. Particularly deadly to birds, woodland destruction is the major cause of the near-extinction of whooping cranes and the total eradication of the Carolina parakeet and the passenger pigeon (☞ BIRDS).

Beach development is a more recent threat to coastal habitats, endangering the leatherback turtle, western snowy plover, and California least tern. Arguably the most famous victim of water pollution, reclamation projects, and commercial fishing is the Pacific salmon—vanished from about 40 percent of its former breeding grounds in California, Washington, Oregon, and Idaho. In 1990 not a single sockeye salmon got all the way past the eight hydropower dams blocking the Columbia and Snake Rivers to reach its Idaho spawning grounds; the sockeye was added to the Endangered Species List in 1991.

Endangered Species List

The list was created under the broad-reaching Endangered Species Act (1973), the grandchild of the first Endangered Species Act (1966). Whereas the first offered protection only on a discretionary basis, the 1973 law provides for the protection, restoration, and propagation of endangered and threatened plants, fish, and other wildlife, their habitats, and the ecosystems on which they depend. Protection extends to federal, state, and private lands, including federal purchase of land for species protection; most states also have their own lists.

A species is officially designated as endangered or threatened through listing on the Endangered Species List, maintained by the U.S. FISH AND WILDLIFE SERVICE. Both the secretary of the interior and the secretary of commerce (in charge of the National Marine Fisheries Service) may list species and change designations. All federal agencies are responsible for carrying out the act's huge mandate. Federally listed species, for example, are found in 120 units of the NATIONAL PARK SYSTEM. The Fish and Wildlife Service expected in one recent year to be involved in more than 550 habitat conservation plans covering more than 20 million acres and two hundred species. These plans are increasingly demanded by landowners, state

and local governments, and developers. Any member of the public may petition the Fish and Wildlife Service to include a species on the list or to prevent some activity, such as logging, mining, or dam building, in a habitat area. Federal listing can be, and has been, suspended: in 1995 Congress imposed a one-year moratorium, reportedly because there were not enough votes to actually kill the act, which has many industry detractors.

Getting on the Endangered Species List, of course, does not guarantee survival. The Fish and Wildlife Service has reported that, in part because of budget restraints, no more than 10 percent of the listed flora and fauna has a safe future. Recently, however, replenished forests, particularly in the Northeast, and reintroduction programs have resulted in the increase of white-tail deer, black bears, beavers, buffalo, and wild turkeys. Among the recovered species removed from the list in the last twenty years are the American alligator (1987), American peregrine falcon (1999), Arctic peregrine falcon (1994), brown pelican (1985), and gray whale (1994). ☞ *also* ADVOCATES, NATIONAL WILDLIFE REFUGE SYSTEM

Defenders of Wildlife ⊠ 1101 Fourteenth Street, NW, Suite 1400, Washington, DC 20005. (202-682-9400. ▯ www.defenders.org
■ This organization is dedicated to protecting all native wild flora and fauna in their natural habitats, particularly predators such as grizzly bears and wolves. It advocates preventive approaches designed to keep species from becoming endangered.

Fund for Animals ⊠ 200 West Fifty-seventh Street, New York, NY 10019. (212-246-2096. ▯ www.fund.org
■ The author Cleaveland Amory founded this advocacy organization in 1967 to fight cruelty to wild and domestic animals. Efforts center on education, legislation, litigation, and hands-on care, with facilities including a wildlife rehabilitation center in California for such native species as bobcats, coyotes, and raptors.

Contacts

National Wildlife Federation ✉ 11100 Wildlife Center Drive, Reston, VA 20190. ☎ 703-438-6000. 🖥 www.nwf.org
■ This member-supported conservation group increases public awareness about issues concerning wildlife and natural resource conservation through education initiatives, with a focus on school programs.

Native Habitats ✉ 17287 Skyline Boulevard, Suite 102, Woodside, CA 94062. ☎ 650-941-1068. 🖥 www.nativehabitats.org
■ Native Habitats supports efforts to restore and preserve native ecosystems through information dissemination and support networks.

The Nature Conservancy ✉ 4245 North Fairfax Drive, Suite 100, Arlington, VA 22203-1606. ☎ 800-628-6860. 🖥 www.tnc.org
■ Founded in 1951, the Nature Conservancy is the world's largest private international conservation group. It takes a nonconfrontational approach to creating partnerships of landowners, businesses, and government agencies. Its network of some 1,300 preserves is the largest private nature sanctuary system. Excursions are offered through regional and state offices.

Wildlife Advocacy Project ✉ 1601 Connecticut Avenue, NW, Suite 700, Washington, DC 20009. ☎ 202-518-3700. 🖥 www.WildlifeAdvocacy.org
■ This nonprofit group aids grassroots activists in achieving long-term protection of wildlife and the environment, as well as in preventing abuse and exploitation of animals held in captivity. The project advocates the "recognition and respect for the innate wild nature of all animals."

Web Sites
The Invasive Species Home Page. Describes the threat of exotic (alien) species. 🖥 invasives.fws.gov

U.S. Endangered Species Home Page. Offers extensive information on endangered species. 🖥 endangered.fws.gov

U.S. Fish and Wildlife Service. Posts fact sheets on endangered and invasive species. 🖥 species.fws.gov

Reading
📕 Peter Matthiessen, *Wildlife in America* (1995). 📕 David S. Wilcove, *The Condor's Shadow: The Loss and Recovery of Wildlife in America* (2000).

Environmental Funds

Funds earmarked for environmental protection exist in both the private and the public sector. Private environmental funds consist of monies raised for advocacy (☞ ADVOCATES), habitat preservation, and wilderness protection and are usually supported by individuals and corporate donors who wish to advance the particular mission of the group administering the fund. Federal funds include government funds that have been set up by specific government offices and councils as well as appropriations from federal spending bills directed toward departmental programming for PUBLIC LANDS.

Most private funds operate by raising money and then distributing it. This money often takes the form of grants, usually to community and local organizations rather than individuals. Many private funds work as revolving funds with a purchasing arm that allows them to acquire wildlands for the specific purpose of preventing development there.

Private Funds

Access Fund ✉ P.O. Box 17010, Boulder, CO 80308. ☎ 303-545-6772. 🖥 www.outdoorlink.com/accessfund
■ This fund, also an environmental policy advocate, promotes sound climbing practices on private and public lands, purchases threatened property, and provides grants for building trails, environmental restoration, and climber education.

America the Beautiful Fund ✉ 1730 K Street, NW, Suite 1002, Washington, DC 20006. ☎ 202-638-1649. 🖥 www.america-the-beautiful.org
■ Started in 1965, this clearinghouse aids community projects to save natural and historic areas and operates as a catalyst for new projects. Programs include Operation Green Plant, Rediscover America, and American Landscapes.

The Columbia River flows 1,210 miles to the Pacific. Because only forty-two free-flowing river segments longer than 125 miles still exist outside Alaska, raising funds to protect such unspoiled stretches of riverways has become an increasing priority.

The Conservation Fund ⊠ 1800 North Kent Street, Suite 1120, Arlington, VA 22209-2156. ☏ 703-525-6300. ▯ www.conservationfund.org
▪ This fund raises money to purchase ecologically significant property under imminent threat. Its goal is to conserve land as open space, mainly by creating parks, wildlife refuges, and greenways in collaboration with public land stewardship agencies, foundations, corporations, and private citizens. Programs include the Conservation Leadership Network and American Greenways Program.

Environmental Support Center ⊠ 4429 Connecticut Avenue, NW, Suite 2, Washington, DC 20008. ☏ 202-966-9834. ▯ www.envsc.org
▪ The center underwrites training, consultants, and fund-raising loans to help local, state, and regional grassroots groups become better managed and equipped.

New England Grassroots Environment Fund ⊠ P.O. Box 1057, Montpelier, VT 05601. ☏ 802-223-4622. ▯ www.grassroots.org
▪ Grants from the fund aid established activist groups working on hometown environmental problems.

Government Funds

Public funds often support administrative costs, but some, like private funds, may also be used to purchase land and support grant giving.

Ongoing Funds

Land and Water Conservation Fund
▪ Based on the idea that money earned by extracting nonrenewable resources should be reinvested in the protection and restoration of those that are renewable, this fund uses revenues from offshore oil and gas leasing (as well as federal motorboat fuel taxes and outdoor recreation user fees) to purchase land and water properties. Its goal is to support the creation of national and community parks, forests, wildlife refuges, and open spaces. Since 1964 some 7 million acres of parkland, water resources, and open spaces have been purchased and more than 37,000 local projects supported with matching grants; the Clinton administration used the fund to acquire more than one hundred natural and historic sites. Although $900 million is earmarked for this fund annually, Congress must appropriate the money before it can be spent. If the appropriations are not made, the revenues can be used elsewhere—and Congress has diverted much of the money for nonconservation purposes, including deficit reduction.

Lands Legacy Initiative
▪ Created in 1999 by the COUNCIL ON ENVIRONMENTAL QUALITY, this initiative was designed to provide money for federal acquisition of privately owned lands to protect them as environmental resources, increasing federal land acquisition funding through the Land and Water Conservation Fund. Matching grants (moribund in the fund in recent years) would go to acquisition of land and easements for urban parks, greenways, recreational areas, wildlife habitats, and coastal wetlands. Separate funds include the Cooperative Endangered

Species Conservation Fund, Forest Legacy Program, and North American Wetlands Conservation Fund; these service components are a major source of the financial assistance that the U.S. FOREST SERVICE and other agencies provide to states and communities.

Central Hazardous Materials Fund

■ This BUREAU OF LAND MANAGEMENT fund finances remedial investigations, feasibility studies, and hazardous-waste cleanup.

Cooperative Endangered Species Conservation Fund

■ Grants to states to conserve threatened and ENDANGERED SPECIES are provided under this U.S. FISH AND WILDLIFE SERVICE program.

Historic Preservation Fund

■ State historic preservation efforts are furthered by this NATIONAL PARK SERVICE–administered fund.

National Wildlife Refuge Fund

■ Payments are provided under the Refuge Revenue Sharing Act (1935) to counties in which national wildlife refuges are reserved from the public domain or purchased and managed by the U.S. FISH AND WILDLIFE SERVICE.

North American Wetlands Conservation Fund

■ Administered by the U.S. FISH AND WILDLIFE SERVICE, this fund protects wetlands ecosystems harboring migratory game and nongame BIRDS.

Wildlife Conservation and Appreciation Fund

■ Supported projects—involving fish and wildlife and their habitats—bring together the U.S. FISH AND WILDLIFE SERVICE, state agencies, and private organizations and individuals through matching grants to states.

Environmental Networks

Environmental networks function primarily as information clearinghouses for activists. Online resources offer news alerts, calendars, and directories. Many post articles, report on protests, and present program proposals covering U.S. and global issues. The following networks are a sample:

ActivistNet ✉ 4505 University Avenue, NE, Suite 537, Seattle, WA 98105. ☎ 206-320-9864. 🖳 www.activistnet.org
■ This comprehensive Internet resources directory posts a network of thousands of Web sites and also includes chat rooms and message boards.

Citizens League for Environmental Action and Recovery ✉ P.O. Box 92, Manville, RI 02838. ☎ 401-769-7085. 🖳 www.ultranet.com/ ~ clear/index.shtm
■ CLEAR is a clearinghouse for the exchange of environmental materials. A video and software library is geared to K–12 students.

Earth Day Network ✉ 91 Marion Street, Seattle, WA 98104. ☎ 206-682-1184. 🖥 www.earthday.net

■ This group coordinates Earth Day events and runs a clean-energy campaign and activist network.

EnviroLink Network ✉ 5805 Forbes Avenue, Second Floor, Pittsburgh, PA 15217. 🖥 www.envirolink.netforchange.com

■ EnviroLink offers the latest news and information about the global environmental movement. It posts breaking news stories, offers links to radio and television shows, and maintains a directory of organizations and a topic-search network.

Environmental Protection Agency

An independent executive branch agency, the EPA was created in 1970 in response to public pressure to reform pesticide pollution spurred by the 1962 publication of RACHEL CARSON's *Silent Spring*. The idea was that the agency would be the leader in environmental protection and would have no obligation to promote commerce or agriculture. Its directive was to treat air pollution, water pollution, and solid wastes (☞ POLLUTION) "as different forms of a single problem." In the last thirty years, the agency has been responsible for banning the use of DDT, limiting the raw sewage discharged into the nation's waterways, setting the first national standards limiting industrial water pollution, initiating the phaseout of PCBs and lead gasoline, establishing auto emission standards, recommending amendments to the Clean Air Acts to preserve clean air in national parks and national wilderness areas, and promoting state and national recycling initiatives.

Contacts

Environmental Protection Agency ✉ 401 M Street, SW, Washington, DC 20460. ☎ 202-260-2090. 🖥 www.epa.gov

National Service Center for Environmental Publications ☎ 800-490-9198, 513-489-8910. 🖥 www.epa.gov/ncepihom

Everglades

"There are no other Everglades in the world. They are, they have always been, one of the unique regions of the earth, remote, never wholly known. Nothing anywhere else is like them: their vast glittering openness, wider than the enormous visible round of the horizon, the racing free saltness and sweetness of their massive winds, under the dazzling blue heights of space. They are unique also in the simplicity, diversity, and the related harmony of the forms of life they enclose."

Marjory Stoneman Douglas, *The Everglades: River of Grass* (1947)

"Our traditional Seminole cultural, religious, and recreational activities, as well as commercial endeavors, are dependent on a healthy south Florida ecosystem.

In fact, the Tribe's identity is so closely linked to the land that Tribal members believe that if the land dies, so will the Tribe."

Congressional testimony by the Seminole Indian tribe, 2000

"The truth is that we're not exactly sure all this stuff will work."

Florida Governor Jeb Bush's Everglades restoration team, 2000

The largest remaining subtropical wilderness in the continental United States, the Everglades comprise a network of lakes and wetlands covering the greater part of south Florida from Lake Okeechobee to the tip of the peninsula at Florida Bay. This series of ecosystems—called Pa-hay-okee ("Grassy Waters") by the ancient Calusa Indians—is dominated by a freshwater river that measures 40 to 60 miles wide, averages just 6 inches deep, and nowhere rises more than a few feet above sea level.

As it washes slowly toward the coast over an almost imperceptible incline of oolitic limestone formed in the last Ice Age, the shallow sheet of water nourishes a diverse group of plant and animal communities, including saw grass (sedge) marshes, cypress and mangrove swamps, wet prairies, coastal lagoons, sloughs (the main avenues of water

The broad, slow-flowing "river of grass" that feeds the Everglades and nourishes its unique ecosystem is only inches deep. Migrating herons and other species make the region a birdwatchers' paradise.

flow), pinelands, wetland tree islands, and small tropical hammocks. The name *Everglades* refers to the vast glades created by the washed-over sedge marshes, which are maintained by a natural fire cycle that keeps hardwoods at bay. Not surprisingly, the diverse ecological communities of this ecosystem—the only one in the world shared by both the crocodile and the alligator—support more than six hundred species of wildlife, including mink and river otter, several rare bird species, the endangered Florida panther, eleven turtle species, and twenty-six snake types.

The southernmost glades are contained in Everglades National Park (1947) (☞ NATIONAL PARK SYSTEM), covering 1.5 million acres at Florida's southwestern tip. At its north end, the park—a WORLD HERITAGE SITE, an INTERNATIONAL BIOSPHERE RESERVE, and a Wetland of International Importance—borders on the Big Cypress National Preserve (☞ NATIONAL PRESERVES), set aside in 1974 (and now expanded to cover 729,000 acres) to thwart a plan to drain and develop the swamp. The preserve contains a portion of the 2,400-square-mile Big Cypress Swamp. The Everglades are also home to Miccosukees and Seminoles on the Big Cypress and Brighton Indian Reservations.

Changing Nature's Course

The freshwater "tidal" basin of the Everglades begins with the flow of the Kissimmee River from the central lake region south into Lake Okeechobee, where the "river of grass" seeps into an expanse of marshland extending to Florida Bay. Before dam building altered the water level, the southern rim of the enormous freshwater lake overflowed each wet season to create a shallow water flow; together this river, the lake, and the overflow itself worked as one integrated watershed unit. Ever since the first state legislature declared the glades "wholly valueless" in the mid-1800s, however, the flood-flow balance has been compromised by a series of drainage and diversion programs that have made the south Florida ecosystem one of the most imperiled wilderness areas in the country. The complex network of locks, pumps, and drains means that the movement of water through the Everglades watershed is now engineered entirely by mechanics rather than by force of nature.

The problems and controversy surrounding these troubled waters have resulted as much from corrective measures as they have from the initial drainage efforts. Drainage of the glades for sugarcane cultivation and other agricultural uses led to massive flooding: some 2,400 people drowned during a 1928 hurricane when Okeechobee overwashed its artificial levee, and two hurricanes in 1947 left 90 percent of south Florida under water. A remedial effort, instituted by the U.S. Army

Corps of Engineers, produced a patchwork of natural and drained areas by creating 1,000 miles of levees and 720 miles of canals and locks over an 18,000-square-mile expanse; a single 100-mile levee in the eastern Everglades completely blocked the river flow.

The benefit has been a $2-billion economy for south Florida by making coastal areas safe for development and permitting the sugar industry to thrive. The cost has been the ecological health of the Everglades. In the fifty years since the flood-control plan was initiated, the population of the region has risen from 500,000 to 6 million. The size of the Everglades, in turn, has been reduced by half. Runoff causes an explosion of non-native species; clean water cannot get to the estuaries and bays that nourish wildlife; an estimated 95 percent of the wading birds have died or disappeared; and hardwoods are disappearing. Off-road vehicles and air boats are other hazards.

The Comprehensive Everglades Restoration Plan, a remedial plan approved by the U.S. Senate, calls for the recapture of the 6.7 billion gallons of water now disgorged daily into the sea, improved water delivery to rivers and bays, and removal of more than 240 miles of levees and canals. The east-west Tamiani Trail (U.S. 41), which currently blocks the Everglades' natural southerly course, would be raised. About 80,000 acres of man-made marshes are intended to capture runover and filter invading fertilizer and pesticide toxins from nearby cities and farmlands. Land acquisitions would include at least 100,000 acres in the Everglades Agricultural Area.

Comprehensive Everglades Restoration Plan

The CERP project is to be managed by the U.S. DEPARTMENT OF THE INTERIOR, the Army Corps of Engineers, and the state at a cost of $7.8 billion over thirty to forty years. The plan's sheer magnitude, which has been called the most complex environmental restoration plan in the world, has raised questions about the wisdom of taking on such a complicated and untested project.

One cornerstone of the restoration plan is the 1999 Multi-species Recovery Plan, devised by the U.S. FISH AND WILDLIFE SERVICE. It proposes to recover sixty-eight threatened and endangered native plants and animals in the Everglades watershed by restoring twenty-three diverse ecological areas over 26,000 square miles in the nineteen southernmost counties. The initial goal is to remove seventeen south Florida species from the Endangered Species List by 2020. The state also maintains the lesser "species of special concern" status, which has been assigned to a number of wading birds, including the little blue and tricolored heron.

Endangered South Florida Species

■ **American Crocodile** (*Crocodylus acutus*). The population of this cousin to the American alligator has been reduced to a few hundred, which live in the brackish saltwater of mangrove inlets at the state's tip. Fewer than twenty females nest each year.

■ **Atlantic Green Turtle** (*Chelonia mydas*). This is the only sea turtle that is primarily a herbivore.

■ **Cape Sable Seaside Sparrow** (*Ammodramus maritimus mirabilis*). A small nonmigratory bird that lives in freshwater or brackish marshes, its population is estimated to have decreased by 95 percent between the mid-1950s and mid-1970s. A dusky seaside sparrow of the Cape Canaveral area was declared extinct in 1991.

■ **Florida Panther** (*Felis concolor coryi*). South Florida is the only remaining eastern habitat of the panther (known as the puma, cougar, or mountain lion in the West), but fewer than forty may survive. None is found in the Everglades National Park, as they have retreated to the Big Cypress Swamp area. Many have been killed by motor traffic, although underpasses on I-95 have been built to ameliorate the problem.

■ **Snail Kite** (*Rostrhamus sociabilis*). This dark hawk formerly known as the Everglades kite feeds on apple snails, whose eggs are being drowned in flood runoff from water-control gates. Probably fewer than 900 remain in Florida.

The endangered Florida panther is no longer found in Everglades National Park. Habitat destruction is the primary threat to the panther, now the target of a recovery plan.

■ **West Indian Manatee** (*Trichechus manatus*). Known also as sea cows, these gentle sea mammals are often maimed or killed by propellers or caught and drowned in the gates of flood-control structures.

■ **Wood Stork** (*Mycteria Americana*). The most endangered wading bird in Florida has been jeopardized by failed nesting seasons because it is highly dependent on a concentrated food source. Drought conditions kill off its staple fish, while artificially high water levels cause the birds to delay nesting.

Everglades National Park ✉ 40001 State Road 9336, Homestead, FL 33034.
☎ 305-242-7700. 🖥 www.nps.gov/ever
■ The park is known for its large winter population of migrating birds.

Everglades Restoration Movement ✉ 2215 NW Thirtieth Place, Pompano Beach, FL 33069. ☎ 954-979-5028. 🖥 www.glades.org
■ Formed in 1990, this nonprofit volunteer organization assists in removing destructive non-native plants from the Everglades.

Florida Panther Society ✉ P.O. Box 1895, White Springs, FL 32096. ☎ 904-397-2945. 🖥 www.atlantic.net/ ~ oldfla/panther/panther/html
■ This membership group is dedicated to the complete recovery and delisting of the Florida panther from the Endangered Species List.

Friends of the Everglades ✉ 7800 Red Road, Suite 215K, Miami, FL 33143. ☎ 305-669-0858. 🖥 www.everglades.org
■ This grassroots volunteer organization was founded in 1969 by the conservationist and author Marjory Stoneman Douglas to protect and restore the greater Kissimmee-Okeechobee-Everglades ecosystem. The group is a watchdog for legislative and development projects that affect the Everglades and is prepared to legally challenge any practice that threatens the survival of the Everglades.

Governor's Commission for the Everglades ✉ 1550 Madruga Avenue, Suite 412, Coral Gables, FL 33146. ☎ 305-669-6973. 🖥 fcn.state.fl.us/everglades
■ This advisory body to the South Florida Ecosystem Restoration Task Force helps evaluate implementation of the restoration plan and serves as a public forum.

South Florida Ecosystem Restoration Task Force ✉ c/o Office of Public Affairs, Florida International University, University Park, OE 148, Miami, FL 33199. ☎ 305-348-1665. 🖥 www.sfrestore.org
■ The task force was founded in 1993 to coordinate the development of consistent policies and plans addressing environmental issues in south Florida. It includes representatives from the Miccosukee and Seminole tribes, governor's office, South Florida Water Management District, and local government.

Comprehensive Everglades Restoration Plan. Posted by the U.S. Army Corps of Engineers. 🖥 www.evergladesplan.org/index

Everglades Information Network. A collaborative digital library led by Florida International University, providing information on research, restoration, and resource management of the Everglades, including scientific and technological reports, natural history writings, maps, and photographs. 🖥 everglades.fiu.edu

📕 Marjory Stoneman Douglas, *The Everglades: River of Grass* (1947).
📕 Steven M. Davis and John C. Ogden, eds., *Everglades: The Ecosystem and Its Restoration* (1994). 📕 Thomas E. Lodge, *The Everglades Handbook: Understanding the Ecosystem* (1994).

Federal Government

All of the federal offices concerned with PUBLIC LANDS and the environment in the United States fall under the executive branch. The four agencies primarily responsible for managing wilderness and natural areas are the NATIONAL PARK SERVICE, U.S. FISH AND WILDLIFE SERVICE, and BUREAU OF LAND MANAGEMENT (all U.S. DEPARTMENT OF THE INTERIOR) and the U.S. FOREST SERVICE (U.S. DEPARTMENT OF AGRICULTURE). In addition to administering the lands under their jurisdiction, these agencies are required by the Endangered Species Act (1983) (☞ ENDANGERED SPECIES) to conserve endangered and threatened species and their critical habitats and to avoid actions that may jeopardize survival of the listed species.

Their activities are overseen by the House and Senate Committees on Interior and Insular Affairs, Senate Committee on Agriculture and Forestry, and House Committee on Agriculture. The Committees on Interior and Insular Affairs are responsible for most legislation affecting forestry and land management. Historically, the majority of members of these committees represent western states, which have the highest proportion of public lands and the most at stake in terms of resource development. Southerners traditionally dominate the two agriculture committees. ☞ *also specific federal agencies, related topics, and entries from* NATIONAL FOREST SYSTEM *to* NATIONAL WILDLIFE REFUGE SYSTEM

Relatively young by geological measure, North American forests are largely the product of a kind of push me–pull you growth phenomenon of the last Ice Age. As the glacial ice sheets began moving down over the continent during the Pleistocene epoch beginning about a million years ago (☞ GLACIERS), plant life was pushed in front of the glacial range downward from the Arctic Sea. This in effect modernized existing forests through a Darwinian survival process that both preserved forms of old species (the sycamore, for example, came through relatively unchanged) and introduced new ones (twenty-six new species of the birch family alone). About 15,000 years ago the polar ice cap covered more than half of the continent, and virtually no forest grew north of the Ohio River. As the ice sheet retreated (at the rate of about 50 miles per century) about 10,000 years ago, new forests were pollinated when seeds were transported back toward the Arctic by wind and wildlife.

At the time of European settlement, forest covered about half of the continent. Trees grew on about 950 million acres in the present-day contiguous forty-eight states, stretching over a virtually unbroken expanse from Florida to Maine and from the Atlantic coast to the Great Plains. The nineteenth-century historian Francis Parkman (1823–93) described the astonishing forest of America as a majestic canopy of trees that "shadowed the fertile soil, covering the land as the grass covers the garden lawn, sweeping over hill and hollow in endless undulation, burying mountains in verdure, and mantling brooks and rivers from the light of day."

The sheer vastness of the forest had a legendary impact on the Puritan consciousness, first as an enemy to be vanquished and eventually as a resource to be exploited. By the end of the 1800s, clearing for farmland (a practice started by NATIVE AMERICANS) and logging had reduced the American woodlands to one-fifth of the original acreage. A major casualty was the great white pine, which was sought for its straight grain and actively harvested from the colonial period onward. The species all but vanished from the North Woods by 1900, although it is now making a slow comeback. One of the last great stands of old-growth forest in America was set aside by President THEODORE ROOSEVELT in 1909 in the Mount Olympus National Monument (Washington) (☞ NATIONAL MONUMENTS). Less than 2 percent of the eastern virgin forest still exists.

Through replanting and natural regeneration, forest (second growth and beyond) now covers about one-third of the total acreage in the contiguous forty-eight states, or some 750 million acres. About 300 million acres of it are in private hands; about 67 million acres are owned by lumber companies; and

Forests

"I like trees because they seem more resigned to the way they have to live than other things do."

Willa Cather,
O Pioneers! (1913)

about 92 million acres are contained in the NATIONAL FOREST SYSTEM. Some 15 million acres are managed by other federal landowners, including the BUREAU OF LAND MANAGEMENT and the U.S. Department of Defense. The remainder is under the aegis of state and local governments.

Softwood Forests

Forests are categorized by type of tree: softwood (evergreen) and hardwood (deciduous). The relics of trees that grew at least as early as the Jurassic era, softwoods constitute the most ancient tree family in America. More than one hundred evergreen species are indigenous; able to thrive in poor, dry soil and rocky heights, they account for about four-fifths of large saw-timber trees. The species found within a given forest vary depending on the limits of tolerance dictated by climate and geography. Ponderosa pine, for example, predominates in the primarily coniferous ROCKY MOUNTAINS forest belt. Another inland forest of softwoods comprising loblolly, longleaf, and shortleaf pines spreads across a sandy soil habitat from Virginia to Texas. The Pacific forest belt—rich in redwoods, sequoias (with trunks up to 35 feet in diameter), Sitka spruce, Pacific yew, western hemlock, western red cedar, and Douglas fir—supports the heaviest stands of conifers in the country, if not in the world.

Oregon's Rogue River National Forest is known for its dense population of conifers, which thrive in the northwestern climate. Its native species include Douglas fir and ponderosa pine.

In the sixteenth century about 74 million acres of southeastern America (from Virginia south to Florida and west to Texas) was under a canopy of longleaf pine. Beginning in the early 1700s, the softwood stands were decimated by logging and the market for resin-based naval stores; longleaf pines today cover only 3 percent of the same region. Heavy logging in the early 1900s also decimated most of the giant cypresses that once proliferated in the Great Cypress Swamp; dwarf cypresses and saw grass prairie predominate today (☞ EVERGLADES). The largest softwood forest in North America is now the northern boreal forest, a dense belt of conifers (primarily spruce and fir) arcing from Newfoundland to ALASKA. Other major softwood forests include the New Jersey pine barrens and the southern pinelands, which extend from the Jersey barrens south to Florida, then west across the Gulf states to the Big Thicket of Texas. These pinelands actually consist of hundreds of smaller groves of various pines, sometimes pure, sometimes mixed with oaks and other hardwoods.

The world's consummate hardwood forest is that of the southern APPALACHIAN MOUNTAINS, extending from the southern BLUE RIDGE MOUNTAINS through the GREAT SMOKY MOUNTAINS and the surrounding uplands. Here the range of environments found from lowlands (yellow poplar, sycamore, black tupelo, black locust, mountain silverbell, sugar maple, yellow birch, magnolia, hickory) to lower slopes (oaks and pines) to peaks (virgin stands of hardwoods and evergreen forests) reproduces nearly every type of habitat found from Georgia to Canada. The southern Appalachian forest claims the greatest number of species concentrated anywhere in North America, including many trees with record proportions, such as the yellow poplar (30 feet in circumference), yellow buckeye (16 feet), and yellow birch (14 feet).

With its more moderate climate, the region between the boreal north and the Deep South sustains what is known as transitional forest. This includes conifers as well as deciduous, broadleaf hardwoods that cannot survive severe cold and need a moister loam than most pines. Mixed deciduous forests sweep down from southern New England through middle Appalachia and west across Ohio and Indiana, into Illinois and the southern GREAT LAKES region, and across West Virginia, Kentucky, and Tennessee to the Mississippi. The western limit is the oak-hickory woodlands of the Boston, Ouachita, and OZARK MOUNTAINS of Missouri, Arkansas, and

Hardwood Forests

Deciduous hardwoods dominate in the middle Appalachian Mountain states, a region noted for its extraordinary variety of trees. The foliage of Blackhorse Gap in Virginia, where the Appalachian Trail crosses the Blue Ridge Parkway, is strikingly colorful in both spring and fall.

Oklahoma. The temperate climate produces a long growing season in the transition forest, creating a patchier canopy than found in the boreal region and thus a more open "roof" that leaks in more sunlight. Transitional forest trees in the Midwest include yellow birch and maple, hemlock, and American basswood. Aspens grow in western lake and bog communities. Eastern hemlock thrives in the north. Red spruce and gray birch are keynote trees of the East, as are the oaks and tulip trees of the Hudson River valley and the sugar maples that produce fall color in New England.

Subtropical and Rain Forests

America's only subtropical forest grows in Florida, where porous soil and a cycle of dry seasons prohibit the type of deciduous growth that would define the region as true tropics. The woodlands of north and central Florida consist of mixed deciduous forest, dominated by pine and oak (with such distinctive species as the flowering dogwood, live oak, sweet gum, and southern magnolia), along with individual forest communities including piney flatwoods (loblolly, longleaf, slash, and pond pines), scrub forest (sand pines predominate), sandhill forest in the central highlands (longleaf pine and oaks), slash pine forest, and the hardwood hammocks (islands of deciduous trees) so characteristic of the EVERGLADES. Olympic National Forest (Washington) and Tongass National Forest (Alaska) are temperate rain forests. ☞ *also* CLEAR-CUTTING, NATIONAL FOREST SYSTEM, TREES, U.S. FOREST SERVICE

Contacts

American Forests ⊠ 910 Seventeenth Street NW, Suite 600, Washington, DC 20006. (202-955-4500. 🖳 www.Americanforests.org
■ Dedicated to establishing "a sustainable future for our nation's forests," the group was founded in Chicago in 1875 as the American Forestry Association—the country's first nonprofit citizens conservation organization. It started one of the first ecotourism programs in America (1933), "Trail Riders of the Wilderness," which led horseback excursions into the Flathead and Lewis and Clark National Forests in Montana. Other initiatives included memorial tree plantings after World War I and the Dixie Crusader forest-fire prevention program (1928–31). The Global Releaf Program is responsible for planting more than 11 million trees.

American Lands Alliance ⊠ 726 Seventh Street, SE, Washington, DC 20003. (202-547-9400. 🖳 www.Americanlands.org
■ The alliance supports grassroots conservation networks and advocacy (the Western Ancient Forest Campaign is a priority) and works to protect and recover native forests, grasslands, and aquatic ecosystems; preservation of biological diversity; watershed restoration, all with "the promotion of environmental justice."

Ancient Forest International ✉ P.O. Box 1850, Redway, CA 95560. ☎ 707-923-3015. 💻 www.ancientforests.org
This group aids philanthropies and communities in acquiring and protecting forest lands, such as California's coniferous forests.

The 500-Year Forest Foundation ✉ 1133 Old Abert Road, Lynchburg, VA 24503. 💻 www.500yearforest.org
■ In return for a commitment to maintain healthy woodlands and share their forests with the public, the foundation provides long-range planning, species inventory, and other services to forest landowners.

Heartwood ✉ P.O. Box 1424, Bloomington, IN 47402. ☎ 812-337-8898. 💻 www.heartwood.org
■ A coalition of groups and businesses concerned with regional forest health, the organization posts action alerts and maintains a news database on national forests.

Heritage Forests Campaign ✉ 1901 Pennsylvania Avenue, NW, Suite 1100, Washington, DC 20006. ☎ 202-861-2242. 💻 www.ourforests.org
■ This alliance of conservationists, scientists, and private citizens has launched a major campaign to preserve the country's unprotected wild forests. The campaign, organized under a grant to the National Audubon Society, posts e-postcards to facilitate communication with lawmakers and welcomes "virtual volunteers" online.

Save America's Forests ✉ 4 Library Court, SE, Washington, DC 20003. ☎ 202-544-9219. 💻 www.saveamericasforests.org
■ The mission of this nonprofit lobbying coalition is to end clear-cutting on federal lands and protect America's wild forests. It was instrumental in moving Congress to hold the first vote on clear-cutting and related road building in national forests.

The Hoh Rain Forest in Washington's Olympic National Park is the most accessible of three rain forests on the Olympic Peninsula. High rainfall levels, fog, and ocean-moderated temperatures produce ideal growing conditions for Sitka spruce.

With its evocative cast of regional characters—the fur trader, the barge captain, the Indian chief, the buckskin-clad pioneer—the American frontier provided an entire generation of artists from the United States and abroad with much of their best subject matter for depicting everyday scenes. The popularity of this genre painting, which began to flourish in the 1820s and 1830s, coincided with the era of western expansion.

Frontier Genre Painters

Artist-Explorers

The Long Island–born William Sidney Mount (1807–68) was the first genre painter to achieve widespread fame with his lively compositions of tavern raffles, horse trading, and cider making. His contemporary George Caleb Bingham (1811–79) is known for scenes of river life. Bingham's most famous work, *Fur Traders Descending the Missouri* (1844), portrays a fur trader and his half-breed son in a dreamlike scene, floating away from the wilds with a bale of furs bound for market—quietly symbolizing the tension between rural frontier life and encroaching civilization.

Working in the field added a fresh immediacy to these artists' work, and many of them became explorers as they traveled the frontier in search of material. Alfred Jacob Miller (1810–74) was the first of the genre artists to journey deep into the ROCKY MOUNTAINS, traveling in 1837 with a contingent of American Fur Company trappers along the future Oregon Trail. The lonely wilds impressed the artist with the sense of being one of the first whites to see the dramatic vistas of the Far West and to record the Indians of the region in their native landscape. The mountains and lakes, he thought, had been waiting for him thousands of years and, wrote Miller, "could afford to wait thousands of years longer, for they are now as fresh and beautiful as if just from the hands of the Creator."

A gifted genre artist, George Caleb Bingham studied in Paris and Düsseldorf between trips to Missouri. *Fur Traders Descending the Missouri* (1844) reflects his ability to capture the indigenous flavor of the frontier with the skill of an academic painter.

As an ethnographer, George Catlin made a serious effort to accurately record native cultures. His oil portrait *Two Apache Warriors and a Woman* (1855/69) carefully depicts details of clothing, jewelry, and hair adornments.

The first pictorial account of Indian life in America dates to as early as the 1500s, when it was customary for European and English colonizing expeditions to include artists in charge of documenting flora, fauna, and the exotic North American savage. Among the best-known of these men is John White, the English artist who accompanied three expeditions to Virginia on behalf of Sir Walter Raleigh between 1577 and 1590. Works from this early era of documentation tend to portray the natives as Europeans in caricature, often set against a backdrop of violent encounters with their would-be conquerors. Yet in their detailed depiction of plants, domestic life, weapons, and clothing, many also reveal an attempt at scientific record making.

The first broad pictorial documentation of Indians by such artists as Seth Eastman (1808–75), Charles Deas (1818–67), Charles Wimar (1824–62), Karl Bodmer (1809–93), and Alfred Jacob Miller (1810–74) occurred in the early nineteenth century in response to the growing realization that failure to make a record would mean that these cultures would be forever lost. Portraits of Indians as noble savages conveyed a sense of mystery and dignity, while battle and hunting scenes incorporated the western landscape in larger perspective and evoked a sense of history in the making. John Mix Stanley (1814–72), the most celebrated artist of the Pacific Railway surveys of the 1850s (☞ SURVEYS), developed a particularly intimate knowledge of western geography and cultures.

Arguably the most infatuated of the genre artists who concentrated on Indian life was George Catlin (1796–1872). In 1832 Catlin joined the first American Fur Company steamboat heading up the Missouri River from St. Louis. The artist spent eight years living among native peoples, traveled widely,

Indian Chroniclers

and eventually gathered information and artifacts from as many as 128 tribes in the Western Hemisphere. Catlin was consumed with the imminent loss of Native American culture, and as early as 1832 he exhorted Congress to create a "nation's park" west of the Mississippi where the vanishing Indian nations might be preserved. The artist eventually took his traveling Indian gallery to London, where he staged a series of popular Wild West shows. Showmanship aside, he was a gifted ethnographer, and his many publications, including *Letters and Notes on the North American Tribes* (1841), complement his paintings to form an important record of wilderness history. ☞ *also* WESTERN ILLUSTRATORS

Contacts

De Young Museum ✉ 75 Tea Garden Drive, Golden Gate Park, San Francisco, CA 94118. ☎ 415-863-3330. 🖥 www.thinker.org/deyoung
■ Among the collection's highlights is George Caleb Bingham's *Boatmen on the Missouri* (1846).

Joslyn Art Museum ✉ 2200 Dodge Street, Omaha, NE 68102. ☎ 402-342-3300. 🖥 www.joslyn.org
■ The collection represents Karl Bodmer and Alfred Jacob Miller, as well as works by George Catlin and Frederic Remington.

Museum of Nebraska Art ✉ 2401 Central Avenue, Kearney, NE 68847. ☎ 308-865-8859. 🖥 monet.unk.edu/mona
■ Many of the great artist-explorers traveled through the Nebraska Territory. This collection covers the exploration period (1819–77), as well as John James Audubon, Albert Bierstadt, Karl Bodmer, George Catlin, and Alfred Jacob Miller.

Furniture

The rustic and western furnishing styles that are closely associated with a wilderness aesthetic in America found their first widespread expression in the nineteenth century. The Victorian appetite for novelty and overt embellishment exemplified the contemporary fashion for eclecticism and put a new emphasis on accessories. The mid-1800s marked the first time in America that a single style did not dominate interior design. Twiggy furniture and western-inspired decorations were just two of many choices now permitted by a newly liberal decorating code that embraced with equal relish historical revivals (from Jacobean to Hepplewhite), the Mission style, and Japanese, Chinese, Byzantine, and Moorish influences.

Deliberately rough-hewn, "wilderness" furnishings actually reflected a sophisticated artfulness in their artifice, and it was only a matter of time before birch bark was fashioned into lampshades and a stuffed moose head replaced the ancestral portrait over the fireplace. Gnarled chairs, antler chandeliers, Navajo blankets, and hunting trophies were usually mixed with other types of pieces, including bamboo, rattan, and wicker, and their use was not necessarily limited to the backwoods. Nevertheless, these trappings of the wilderness had a logical place in ranches, woodland camps, and the cavernous lobbies of the great resort hotels (☞ PARK ARCHITECTURE) because they so perfectly evoked the sense of adventure and fun that inspired such retreats. Exotic accessories like a tomahawk on the mantelpiece or a bear skin on the floor also suggested the ability to go on the big hunt or to explore wild territory inaccessible to the less fortunate. Indeed, if not for the travel and leisure time made possible by an era of Gilded Age affluence, it is doubtful that the wilderness styles would have flourished as they did—or sustained such lasting power.

Lodgepole pine chairs, Indian weavings, and the requisite antlers furnish Pahaska Tepee Lodge, the 1904 hunting lodge of Buffalo Bill Cody, located near the southeast entrance to Yellowstone National Park in Wyoming.

In 1883 the publication *Artistic Houses* intrigued readers with a photograph of a bizarre-looking room filled with buffalo robes, animal trophies, serapes, crude three-legged stools, and a few SNOWSHOES propped consciously in the corner. The surprise was that this unusual interior—deemed "artistic to a high degree"—was located not in the Wild West but in the heart of Philadelphia. It was the sitting room of Frank Furness

Western Furnishings: Cowboy Style

(1839–1912), a society architect motivated by summers spent in the ROCKY MOUNTAINS to recreate the setting of his western idylls on more familiar stomping grounds.

The popularity of the western genre in the Victorian era depended on a public fascination with cowboy life and Indian artifacts, introduced by popular tastemakers and perpetuated by dude ranch decor (☞ DUDE RANCHES). One of the great progenitors was the Fred Harvey Company, concessionaire for the Atchison, Topeka and Santa Fe Railway. By the late 1800s Harvey was actively peddling Indian handicrafts as souvenirs, and in the early 1900s the concessionaire opened a special Indian department to sell artifacts to would-be decorators. The Santa Fe Railway's own Alvarado Hotel in Albuquerque, New Mexico, actually featured an Indian Building, where Navajo weavers and silversmiths performed in a living-history exhibit for rail passengers. Gustav Stickley (1858–1942) was one of the contemporary tastemakers of the day who also promoted Indian accessories. Stickley, for one, advocated Indian rugs ("no form of drapery harmonizes quite so well"), while *The Decorator and Furnisher*, a decorating journal, went so far as to suggest a "wigwam style" room in which the owners, dressed head to toe in buckskin, served as human accessories in the perfectly furnished room. One of the best known of the fashionable socialites to embrace the "Indian" decorating mode was Marjorie Merriweather Post, who furnished her Adirondack camp, Topridge, with Chief Crazy Horse's war bonnet and an assortment of KAYAKS that she hung from the living room ceiling (☞ GREAT CAMPS).

The acknowledged master of "cowboy style" in the American West was the Wyoming designer and furniture maker Thomas Canada Molesworth (1890–1977). Molesworth, whose talents ran from making caskets to coyote-head sconces, cultivated a high-society clientele of eastern "dudes" whom he met through a hunting guide in Cody. From his Shoshone Furniture Company (open 1931–61) in Cody, Molesworth sold hundreds of furnishings designed to evoke the western mystique through rugged materials, western silhouettes, and a color palette inspired by the local landscape. A canny businessman, Molesworth increased his market with displays in the Fifth Avenue show window of Abercrombie and Fitch, the New York adventure outfitter.

In a Molesworth interior the delight was in the conceit: one might find leather walls, horsehide draperies, suede bedcovers, upholstery made of Chimayo weavings, cowboy andirons, and wagon trains silhouetted on parchment lampshades. First-rate craftsmanship and details such as gnarled burls, bullet-shell lamp pulls, and animal-paw drawer knobs were the designer's signature. Molesworth was responsible for furnishing numerous hotels and ranch houses during his lifetime, and his influence remains unsurpassed.

The rustic style emerged in Europe as part of an eighteenth- and nineteenth-century fashion for twiggy garden furnishings and follies. The mode came to America primarily from England, where designs for rustic chinoiserie were published as early as the 1750s and gained momentum during the nineteenth-century picturesque landscape movement in England and the United States. Beginning in the 1830s, rustic designs were pictured in home furnishing guides ranging from Shirley Hibberd's *Rustic Adornments for Homes of Taste* (London, 1856) to William Wicks's *Log Cabins: How to Build and Furnish Them* (New York, 1889). They also appeared in the popular press and such professional journals as *The Horticulturist*, founded in 1846 by the landscape designer Andrew Jackson Downing (1815–52). Widespread public exposure in America to rustic garden ornament, designed to blend naturally with the landscape, began in public parks—most

Rustic Furnishings: The Log Cabin Look

At Camp Cedars in the Adirondacks, a bedroom featured Japanese lanterns, fans, and other accoutrements popularized by an exhibit at the Centennial Exhibition, held in Philadelphia in 1876. Such pieces were freely mixed with other types of furniture.

notably, New York's Central Park (1857), designed by Calvert Vaux (1824–95) and Frederick Law Olmsted (1822–1903).

The rustic furnishings favored for wilderness camps (☞ GREAT CAMPS) directly echoed the garden ornaments, bridges, and pavilions of picturesque showcases such as Central Park in their use of roots, burls, branches, and bark to suggest the form and detail of the piece itself. The most ingenious pieces were often made by local guides and caretakers who were commissioned by an architect or owner to furnish a particular woodland camp. There were no rules, reported one 1860 article in *Moore's Rural New-Yorker* that extolled cheapness as one advantage of rustic work. It was not necessary that "every piece used in its construction should be marked out with rule and square, and fitted together with the utmost nicety; for it is merely a combination of limbs and branches in their natural state, so adjusted as to present a variety of pleasing forms."

At its simplest, wilderness furniture was a model of form and function, as illustrated by the angular Westport "bungalow" lawn and porch chair, an Adirondack classic constructed of sawn boards and introduced around 1900. At its most complex, a rustic piece might sprout tree branches or have an intricate veneer of birch bark or a twig mosaic. By nature the twiggiest pieces did not lend themselves well to mass production, although a few firms, such as the Rustique Work Manufacturing Company of Niagara Falls, New York, did sell rustic cedar furniture and planters. Another manufactured type of woodland furniture that proliferated in camps and hotels was the hickory furniture turned out by such Indiana factories as the Old Hickory Furniture Company (Martinsville) and the Rustic Hickory Furniture Company (La Porte). Sold in department stores and through mail order, pieces were shipped by the boxcar to all corners of the country. ☞ *also* LOG CABINS

Reading   📖 Craig Gilborn, *Adirondack Furniture and the Rustic Tradition* (1987). 📖 Elizabeth Clair Flood, *Cowboy High Style: Thomas Molesworth to the New West* (1992).

Set aside in the Gila National Forest ([☞ NATIONAL FOREST SYS-TEM) by the U.S. FOREST SERVICE in 1924, this site embracing ancient Mogollon cliff dwellings in southwestern New Mexico was the world's first designated wilderness area. Originally a roadless tract of 770,000 acres, today the Gila Wilderness combines two wilderness areas: the Gila Wilderness (557,873 acres) and the Aldo Leopold Wilderness (202,025 acres). It was ALDO LEOPOLD who led the campaign for the Gila's initial "primitive area" designation, which withdrew the area from commercial development and preserved it for wilderness recreation. A combined effort with the Isaak Walton League and the Sierra Club ([☞ ADVOCATES) won the classification as an administrative designation under the regional office of the U.S.

The average adult Gila monster grows to about 23 inches long and weighs 3 pounds. The two primary threats to the population are habitat destruction and pet trade in the reptile, which is associated with mystical powers.

Forest Service, and by 1933 sixty-three of these "primitive areas" were established. The Gila National Wilderness Area, which now has eight hundred trails, was designated in 1964 as part of the new NATIONAL WILDERNESS PRESERVATION SYSTEM.

An extraordinarily rich geological and biological profile defines this former Apache territory, which includes parts of the Sonoran and Chihuahuan Deserts (☞ DESERTS) and is the terminating point for both the ROCKY MOUNTAINS and the Sierra Madre, Mexico's major mountain system. The region preserves Mogollon petroglyphs, traces of Spanish copper mines, and the habitat of the Gila monster, the only poisonous lizard in America.

Glaciers

Creased with crevasses, Muir Glacier in Alaska's Glacier Bay National Park and Preserve measures about 2 miles wide. The naturalist John Muir made his first visit to the fjord now known as Glacier Bay in 1879.

A storehouse for more than 75 percent of the world's fresh water, glaciers are moving ice masses formed in polar regions and high mountains by a natural process in which snow is compacted into granular ice and then set into motion by the increasing pressure of the accumulating mass. A true glacier consists of three layers: snow, a mix of snow and ice known as *névé*, and a relatively flexible base of pure ice that permits the mass to move.

The glacier type known as the alpine, or valley, glacier is formed when more snow falls in the cold months than can melt in the summer; as a result, tongues of moving ice are propelled from mountain snow fields into U-shaped valleys formed by streams. High-altitude piedmont glaciers are created

when valley glaciers converge or spread out at the point of emergence from a valley. Ice-cap glaciers are flatter ice sheets that spread horizontally both on mountains and within valleys. The only two continental glaciers now in existence are the ice sheets covering most of Greenland and Antarctica.

Constantly moving, an active mass of glacier ice scours and erodes the terrain it passes over, all the while picking up rocks and gravel that act as abrasives as the mass moves onward. Glacial ice is thus the great sculptor of the landscape, carving U-shaped troughs, fjords, hanging valleys (created as tributary glaciers work into side canyons), and horns (steep peaks shaped when several glaciers work on different sides of the same mountain); forming moraines (mounds of debris, often covered with forest or meadow), *arêtes* (long narrow walls formed by two opposing glaciers), and *cirques* (bowl-shaped depressions that can form lakes); and flattening valley floors or pushing streams into cascades and waterfalls.

Glacial movement depends on complex relationships among the internal and external temperatures, incline, amount of friction, and amount of water contained in the ice. A glacier can move as slowly as 200 yards in a year or as quickly as 100 miles in a day, often creating lakes that fill and drain as the glacier advances and retreats. Sudden, rapid glacial movement is known as a surge, thought to occur when melted water is trapped under the ice mass and acts as a lubricant. Surges can last from a few months to a few years.

Ice Age weather conditions that shaved off entire mountain ranges, sculpted lakes, and seeded and reshaped the great North American FORESTS are the product of a relatively recent glacial period, or Ice Age, known as the Pleistocene epoch. During the height of the Pleistocene, which began to wind down 15,000 to 20,000 years ago, continental glaciers covered Antarctica, large parts of Europe, North and South America, and smaller portions of Asia—or about 30 percent of the globe. In North America ice sheets up to a mile deep stretched from Canada south to a line running westward from New Jersey through Pennsylvania, along the Ohio and Missouri Rivers to North Dakota, and then on to northern Montana, Idaho, and Washington. The Pleistocene Ice Age ended with the slow, reverse retreat north of the ice sheets (it took about 4,000 years for the ice to move north from present-day Connecticut to Vermont). The last phase, known as the Wisconsin glaciation, began its movement from the present-day Minneapolis area toward the polar region about 7,800 years ago.

The Ice Age

A rock table stands on the back of Muir Glacier in Alaska. John Muir described Alaska as "pure" wilderness.

Hikers cautiously cross a crevasse on a Washington glacier. Hiking over glaciers requires specialized gear, experienced guides, and a high level of outdoor skill.

A Work in Progress

Before it was understood that the Pleistocene was a separate glacial epoch that began about one million years ago, the prevailing theory was that the earth's climate was undergoing a progressive cooling. This was disproved by the discovery that a number of Ice Ages had occurred before the Pleistocene epoch, with intervening warming periods. We are now living in an interglacial period known as the Holocene epoch, which began about 15,000 years ago. What causes the extreme cold that brings on glacial epochs is still not known. Among other things, climatic upheaval has been attributed to boulder-heaving tidal waves, earthquakes, and continental shifts, as well as to global cooling caused by massive clouds of volcanic dust or by a shifting axis that changes the earth's position relative to the sun.

That such cataclysms correlate with Old Testament teaching had an enormous impact on the interpretation of geological history in the nineteenth century. In 1837 the Swiss-born geologist Louis Agassiz (1807–73), "discoverer" of the Pleistocene epoch, first presented to American scientific circles the theory that ice had carved the distinctive features of the northeastern geological landscape. A dominant figure in natural history education, Agassiz substantiated his theory with exacting field studies. Yet as an anti-Darwinian, he was one of many geologists who still believed that the earth's history constituted separate large-scale upheavals in which creation occurred entirely anew during each cataclysm.

Confronted with the geological wonders of the western wilderness, many of the great nineteenth-century surveyors, including Clarence King (1842–1901) in his survey of the 40th parallel (☞ SURVEYS), held to a prominent theory that the land had been shaped by cataclysmic events. Studies by the California naturalist JOHN MUIR of residual glaciers in the YOSEMITE VALLEY led him to theorize that it was inexorable movement, rather than one giant upheaval, that carved out the valley. The current prevailing geological theory is in fact that the earth and its life systems are a continual work in progress, in which the distinct Ice Ages are part of a much larger process of formation, change, and evolution. One reason this concept was hard for the nineteenth-century mind to grasp was that it did not put humans at the center of the temporal universe. Instead, the cold reality is that the earth can and will continue to form and re-form, depending neither on the hand of humans nor on their survival.

Climbing on glacial ice is a specialized MOUNTAINEERING skill requiring specialized equipment and experienced guides. Snow-bridged crevasses are a particular hazard, and no one should attempt glacier travel alone (☞ ICE SAFETY). In many regions, however, hiking trails provide access to glaciers; flyovers are also possible.

Observing Glaciers

Denali National Park and Preserve (Alaska)
■ The country's most substantial glacial complexes are in ALASKA, and some of the largest of these are in this 6-million-acre park, where glacial ice blankets about one million acres. Of the many glacial surges occurring in the last century here in the icy peaks of the ALASKA RANGE, one is currently taking place on the north side of Denali ("The Great One"), also known as Mount McKinley. Glacier pilots fly charter flights out of Talkeetna to the Ruth Glacier and Great Gorge, filled with hanging glaciers.

Gates of the Arctic National Park and Preserve (Alaska)
■ A small number of alpine glaciers flow from the north sides of the higher peaks (about 7,000 feet) in the BROOKS RANGE. The park and preserve area covers 8.4 million acres in the central section of the range, north of the Arctic Circle. There are no trails or visitor services, but hikers may backpack in from Galbraith Lake. Charter flights also go into the park.

Glacier Bay National Park and Preserve (Alaska)
■ At the height of the Pleistocene epoch, virtually all of the Glacier Bay region, save for a few peaks and headlands, was covered by a continental ice sheet. When Captain George Vancouver arrived in 1784, a single glacier filled the bay.

By the time JOHN MUIR came to investigate in 1879, it had moved out 30 miles and split into two tributary glaciers. The ice continued to retreat rapidly, further opening the bay, and now several glaciers fed by the Brady Icefield, including the Hugh Miller, Reid, and Lamplugh, clog the upper inlets. West of the bay, the La-Perouse Glacier is the only tidewater glacier that flows into the open sea.

Glacier National Park (Montana)
■ Several relatively new (a few thousand years old) small alpine glaciers spot the mountains in a dramatic landscape distinguished by exposed layers of relatively unaltered sedimentary geological formations of Proterozoic age that were deposited between 800 million and 1.6 billion years ago.

Juneau Icefield (Alaska)
■ About 100 feet of snow falls annually on Alaska's largest ice field (1,500 square miles), extending between the Skagway and Taku Rivers and containing about 40 major and 100 minor glaciers. The most accessible glacier in the area is the Mendenhall Glacier, the only drive-up glacier in the state (about 13 miles from Juneau by road); it can also be viewed by flightseeing trip and from the West Glacier trail. 🖥 www.snowcrest.net/geography/field/mendenhall

Katmai National Park and Preserve (Alaska)
■ This park and preserve covering about 4 million acres at the head of the Alaska Peninsula contains active glaciers but offers only two maintained trails and one campsite (Brooks Camp). Visitors may backpack into the park or explore by canoe or kayak. Access to the coast is available by air taxi and boat tour. The primary focus is the Brooks River, a congregating spot for Alaskan brown BEARS.

Kenai Fjords National Park (Alaska)
■ The drawing card of this snow-clad park is the 300-square-mile Harding Icefield, discovered in the last century when surveyors realized that several coastal glaciers were actually part of the same huge system. Eight tidewater glaciers reach the sea, calving icebergs into the fjords.

Mount Rainier National Park (Washington)
■ Nisqually Glacier, which retreated and advanced three times between 1965 and 1992, is one of the most accessible glaciers on Mount Rainier, easily viewed from special vista points near the Paradise visitor facilities. Cowlitz-Ingraham Glacier is best seen from the upper slopes of the mountain. Emmons Glacier, on the eastern slope, has the largest surface area (4.3 square miles) of any glacier outside Alaska and can be viewed from a vista point or a trail. Carbon Glacier is best viewed via a 4-mile trail from Ipsut Creek Campground on the north side of Mount Rainier.

North Cascades National Park (Washington)
■ The 318 glaciers within this park account for more than half of the total glacier-covered area in the lower forty-eight states. Many waterfalls in the northern peaks of the CASCADE MOUNTAINS flow constantly because of their meltoff.

Small alpine glaciers, a feature of Glacier National Park in Montana, can be seen from a transmountain highway on the Lake McDonald side. A park ranger posed here in 1932 to show the scale of the stone parapet.

The end of the Cascade River Road and Schrieber's Meadow on the southern flank of Mount Baker offer closeup views. Hanging glaciers on the northern face of Johannesburg Peak (at work on creating an *arête*) can be seen from the Cascade Pass parking lot.

Olympic National Park (Washington)

■ The Olympic peaks are crowned by more than 260 slow-moving glaciers in a region where an excess of 220 inches of snow falls annually. The most prominent complex covers about 10 square miles on Mount Olympus; glaciers also exist on Mount Carrie, Mount Christie, and Mount Anderson and in the Bailey Range. All of the Olympic glaciers have retreated significantly since the late 1800s. Hiking trails and cross-country ski routes provide access. The Blue and Anderson Glaciers are the most frequently visited. From the Hoh Rain Forest, the upriver hiking trail leads to the snout of Blue Glacier (18 miles). Anderson Glacier can be reached by hiking the Dosewallips River Trail (11 miles) or from the west side by the east fork of the Quinault River (16 miles).

Wrangell–St. Elias National Park and Preserve (Alaska)

■ The largest unit in the NATIONAL PARK SYSTEM, this 13.2-million-acre park in south-central Alaska contains numerous active glaciers, most notably in Chitistone Canyon. The Bering Glacier alone is larger than Rhode Island. No trails are maintained, but visitors can hike, backpack, and ski into the park.

Grand Canyon

There is a story about the Grand Canyon that goes something like this: A Texas cowhand once took a job herding cattle in Arizona. One day, having no inkling whatsoever of the canyon's existence, the out-of-towner and his horse found themselves at the south rim, staring abruptly into the 6,000-foot-deep chasm of buttes, gorges, and ravines cut through by the Colorado River. One can only imagine what the horse thought, but the cowboy is supposed to have paused for a long, astonished swig from his canteen before remarking, "My God! Something has happened here!"

Because several critical links are missing in the geological chain—including a mysterious 450-million-year gap in the rock stratification—what exactly did happen to make the Grand Canyon the most profound example of erosion in the world has yet to be fully explained. Existing evidence indicates that the dramatic formations are the combined results of continental drift, volcanic activity, a series of advancing and retreating oceans, and an inexorable wearing-down process by wind, ice, and river and rain water.

Located entirely in Arizona, the canyon is 1.1 miles deep and varies in width from 0.1 to 18.0 miles, following the course of the Colorado River about 277 miles from Lees Ferry, near the northern Arizona line, to Grand Wash cliffs, near the Nevada border. The schist in the innermost gorge is at least 1.7 billion years old (about one-third the age of the planet), layered under rock strata from the Proterozoic and Paleozoic eras and more recent sheets of black lava. The uppermost rock layer, Kaibob limestone, is about 250 million years old and composed mostly of soft limestone deposited by a now-vanished ocean. Pushing 500,000 tons of sediment daily though the gorges (in pre-dam days), the Colorado River established its present course at least six million years ago, forming the canyon.

The Echo of Human Steps

Paleo-Indian cultures probably inhabited the canyon as long ago as 10,000 years, and evidence puts ancestral pueblan (Anasazi) peoples there as recently as 900 years ago. Five sovereign Indian nations—Hualapai, Havasupai, Navajo, Hopi, and Kaibab Paiute—still live in the greater region. Hopi guides led the first Europeans, members of the Coronado expedition, to the canyon in 1540. To the Spanish it was merely an annoying, if scenic, detour-necessitating hole in the landscape. The first exploration of the canyon was not completed until 1869, when the one-armed geologist and ethnologist John Wesley Powell (1834–1902) made a harrowing journey by boat through the gorge during a geological survey of the Colorado River commissioned by the Smithsonian Institution. Powell detailed the journey in his *Exploration of the Colorado River of the West* (1875) and later publications. These writings, plus the moody pictures of Timothy O'Sullivan (☞ PHOTOGRAPHERS), the first photographer to visit the canyon (1871), and early western landscape paintings such as Thomas Moran's *Chasm of the Colorado* (1873), are said to have dispelled the last real mystery of the western frontier (☞ ROCKY MOUNTAIN SCHOOL ARTISTS).

In a way, however, the canyon's mystery has never truly

The German-born survey photographer John K. Hillers made this image of the Grand Canyon while part of Major John Wesley Powell's exploration of the Colorado River through the gorge in 1871–72. Later in the expedition Hillers was made photographer-in-charge, and when Powell created the Bureau of Ethnology in 1879, Hillers was named its official photographer.

dissipated. The abyss remains a frontier in that no words, camera, or paintbrush can adequately or accurately describe it. "No matter how far you have wandered hitherto," wrote JOHN MUIR, "or how many famous gorges and valleys you have seen, this one, the Grand Canyon of the Colorado, will seem as novel to you, as unearthly in the color and grandeur and quantity of its architecture, as if you found it after death, on some other star."

Legislative efforts to preserve this unearthly national treasure began years before Arizona earned statehood in 1912. Senator Benjamin Harrison introduced the first bill to make the canyon a national park in 1882, and in 1893, as president, he established the Grand Canyon Forest Reserve. In the early 1890s a later series of heroic Grand Canyon scenes by Thomas Moran were shown in highly publicized single-painting exhibits to a fascinated eastern public. Tourists began arriving at the Grandview Hotel in 1895, and the Atchison, Topeka and Santa Fe put the first train line into the south rim in 1901. By the time the railroad's El Tovar Hotel opened in 1905, tourism was in full swing. President THEODORE ROOSEVELT created the Grand Canyon Game Preserve in 1906 and the Grand Canyon National Monument in 1908 (☞ NATIONAL MONUMENTS). The Grand Canyon National Park (☞ NATIONAL PARK SYSTEM) was finally established by act of Congress in 1918. The Marble Canyon National Monument was created in 1969. In 1975 President Gerald Ford signed the Grand Canyon National Park Enlargement Act, absorbing both the Grand Canyon and the Marble Canyon National Monuments into the park, which now covers 1.2 million acres and encompasses the length of the Colorado River from Lake Powell to Lake Mead.

Dam Projects

While nature gets credit for the colossal geological changes in the canyon over the last two billion years or so, it took the hand of man to make the most dramatic recent alteration to the landscape. In January 1963 the gates of the Glen Canyon Dam, built upstream on the Colorado River, closed for the first time, reducing the flow of the once-wild Colorado to its present trickle. That same year a BUREAU OF RECLAMATION plan backed by President Lyndon Johnson to divert water from the Pacific Northwest to the arid Colorado River basin proposed two dams within the national park, at the Bridge and Marble Canyons, using a loophole in the 1918 park legislation permitting reclamation projects.

The battle over the Pacific Southwest Water Plan was one of the era's most intense environmental conflicts, waged in part with print ads sponsored by the Sierra Club (☞ ADVOCATES). At one point the U.S. DEPARTMENT OF THE INTERIOR and Bureau of Reclamation suggested solving the annoying problem of having to deal with land in a national monument by proposing to abolish the Grand Canyon National Monument altogether. In large part because of the united front of national environmental groups, the reclamation project ultimately failed. Only days after Congress passed the 1968 Central Arizona Bill to make all dam building between the existing Hoover and Glen Canyon Dams illegal, President Johnson signed the bill creating the NATIONAL WILD AND SCENIC RIVERS SYSTEM. The national park was made a WORLD HERITAGE SITE in 1979.

Contacts

Grand Canyon National Park ✉ P.O. Box 129, Grand Canyon, AZ 86023. ☎ 520-638-7888. ⌨ www.nps.gov/grca
■ The park encompasses 277 miles of the Colorado River and the connecting uplands.

Grand Canyon National Park Foundation ✉ 23 East Fine Avenue, Flagstaff, AZ 86001. ☎ 520-774-1760. ⌨ www.grandcanyonfund.org
■ This private, nonprofit organization works under agreement with the National Park Service to raise funds to preserve and protect Grand Canyon National Park.

Grand Canyon Pioneers Society ✉ P.O. Box 2372, Flagstaff, AZ 86003-6022.
⌨ www.grand-canyon.az.us/gcps/gc_gcps
■ The society is concerned with the preservation of historic sites, photographs, and artifacts and supports the restoration of sites and buildings in the national park. It sponsors programs and excursions and has established a collection of letters, papers, and photographs at Northern Arizona University's Cline Library in Flagstaff.

Grand Canyon Trust ✉ 2601 North Fort Valley Road, Flagstaff, AZ 86001.
✆ 520-774-7488. ⌨ www.grandcanyontrust.org
■ This advocacy group creates coalitions to work on conservation issues affecting major landscapes within the Colorado Plateau. The trust's Grand Canyon Forests Foundation works with the U.S. Forest Service on the Canyon Forests Partnership, whose ten-year goal is to develop community-based forest ecosystem restoration.

📕 François Leydet, *Time and the River Flowing: Grand Canyon* (1964). 📕 Barbara J. Morehouse, *A Place Called Grand Canyon: Contested Geographies* (1996). 📕 Stephen Pyne, *How the Canyon Became Grand: A Short History* (1998).

Reading

Great Camps

"I never saw anything like it! There's not a foot of land on that lake for sale this minute, and there's not a man in it but what's a millionaire, and some of them ten times over. . . . I tell you if there's a spot on the face of the earth where the millionaires go to play at house keeping in the log cabins and tents as they do here, I have yet to hear about it."

Paul Smith, Adirondack hotel proprietor,
quoted in *Forest and Stream* (1890)

No one may have been more qualified to comment on the excesses of America's Gilded Age wilderness culture than Paul Smith, a hunting guide and former Erie Canal boatman who in 1858 opened on lower Saint Regis Lake what would become the ADIRONDACK PARK's most famous hotel. Competing with the best seaside resorts such as Newport, the eponymous Paul Smiths comprised five hundred rooms and 40,000 acres, setting the scale for the hundreds of private woodland pleasure palaces to follow—many built by Smith's former guests.

When Smith described upper Saint Regis Lake for a *Field and Stream* reporter in 1890, land there was already selling for $4,000 an acre, but he had seen nothing yet. Adolph Lewisohn's camp on nearby upper Saranac Lake cost $2 million in 1903; among the rustic appointments of the complex of twenty-eight bark-sheathed buildings were some forty wastebaskets made of hollow tree stumps clutched by stuffed bear cubs. Topridge (since dubbed "Over the Topridge"), the upper Saint Regis Lake camp remodeled in 1923 by the cereal heiress Marjorie Merriweather Post (then Mrs. E. F. Hutton), featured eighteen guest cottages fitted with color-coordinated fly swatters, a Russian dacha, and a rustic projection room for 35 mm movies (the ladies wore "bat hats" during screenings). Post's service staff numbered eighty-five.

Log Cabin Communities

Typically used for just a few weeks of the summer season, the "log cabins" in which America's barons of industry played at woodland housekeeping were often communities unto themselves, complete with a working farm, plumbing, electricity and central heating, a billiards hall, a taxidermy studio, a boathouse, an ice house, a tea house, floating dining platforms, laundry facilities, an occasional bark replica of the Parthenon, and a staff that might include a private chess tutor or a chef from Delmonico's. The largest of these follies were dubbed Great Camps by preservationists in the 1970s, but in their glory days (from the post–Civil War era to the pre-income-tax 1920s) they were known simply as "camps"—as misleading a moniker as "cottage" was for a Newport mansion.

A defining characteristic of the Great Camp was the use of separate buildings for separate functions (a main lodge, dining room, sleeping cabin, and the like), with a network of boardwalks, paths, and covered passages connecting the buildings and porches that served as outdoor rooms. This layout was heir to the semipermanent tent camp of the ADIRONDACK MOUNTAINS backcountry, in which hunters and their guides pitched a series of tents, set on individual platforms designed to keep out damp (a practice that continued even as the more permanent and elaborate camps were built).

The widely recognized father of the Adirondack Great Camp is William West Durant (1850–1934). The son of the

Modeled after the European alpine chalet, William West Durant's Sagamore in the Adirondacks hosted guests in both summer and winter. The camp was sold to Alfred G. Vanderbilt in 1901.

railroad developer Thomas Durant, he remodeled and built a series of camps in the western Adirondacks from the late 1870s to the turn of the century, selling them in succession to Collis P. Huntington, J. P. Morgan, and Alfred G. Vanderbilt. Durant's camps were distinguished by their deliberately rustic treatment. Buildings were clad in log and bark (☞ BARK-CRAFT, LOG CABINS), trimmed with twigs and tree limbs of spruce and tamarack, papered in birch bark, and furnished with everything from game trophies to SNOWSHOES (☞ FURNITURE). More a matter of image than a style, the rustic conceit incorporated elements of all the fashionable Victorian modes, including the Arts and Crafts, Colonial Revival, and chalet styles. The look was perfectly suited to woodland locations and a prevailing Victorian taste for the exotic, and it was quickly adopted by architects working throughout the region. Not everyone approved of the new fashion, however. In 1904 concerned members of the Adirondack League Club issued a report entitled "The Evil Results of Rustic Architecture," in which the practice of cutting the necessary evergreens was compared to King Herod's slaughter.

An Idea for All Regions

Despite its association with the Adirondacks, the camp phenomenon was not limited to New York State. In the post–Civil War boom economy, camps and lodges began to proliferate in almost every region where steamboats and railroads put the backwoods within reasonable traveling distance of urban centers. A private resort camp named Cottage Grove built on an old logging site on Michigan's Higgins Lake by a group of businessmen from Bay City and Saginaw in 1877—before Durant's first camp—consisted of individual cabins and a central dining hall. Beginning in 1885 Henry Bacon (formerly of the architectural firm McKim, Mead and White) designed a lodge, cottages, a chapel, and a train station all sheathed in rough chestnut bark for the village of Linville, a North Carolina mountain resort.

The GREAT LAKES wilderness was another setting for elaborate camps. Owned by a group of Toledo industrialists, Wa Wa Sum, a private fishing retreat on the Au Sable River in Michigan, included separate log cabins, a boathouse, a barn, and a "bullpen"' where the men played poker. Greeted at the train station at 4:30 on a Friday morning, the owners would have a private guide paddle them 17 miles upstream so they could fish their way down to camp in time for a late breakfast.

Reading

📖 Harvey H. Kaiser, *Great Camps of the Adirondacks* (1982). 📖 Craig Gilborn, *Durant: The Fortunes and Woodland Camps of a Family in the Adirondacks* (1990). 📖 Craig Gilborn, *Adirondack Camps: Homes Away from Home, 1850–1950* (2000).

Great Lakes

Few places in America are as wild as the "midwestern outback" unfolding north of the invisible demographic line connecting Madison, Wisconsin, and Ottawa, Ontario. In a mid-nineteenth-century speech, Henry Clay declared it "a place beyond the remotest extent of the United States, if not the moon." Perhaps remotest of all is the Keweenaw Peninsula, whose jagged finger extends into Lake Superior from Michigan's Upper Peninsula, home to one of the last surviving stands of virgin pine, the Estivant Pines Sanctuary. The pines are an apt symbol of the story of the Great Lakes region, where history is defined by the sheer age and magnitude of the wilderness and the geological landscape is an essay in staggering statistics. There is small doubt that humans lived here at the close of the last Ice Age: pictographs colored with ferrous oxide—some 5,000 years old—depict animal tracks, heron, trout, caribou, and bark CANOES.

"Beautiful Beyond Any Thing"

The five Great Lakes, formed about 12,000 years ago in the wake of the last glacial retreat (☞ GLACIERS), contain one-fifth of the earth's surface fresh water. Lakes in name only, these prodigious bodies of water are more oceanic in character, with tides, surf, and a propensity for weather conditions so harrowing that Herman Melville (1819–91) used his own tortuous nineteenth-century Lake Erie sailing experience as the basis for Town-Ho's story in *Moby-Dick* (1851). At 7,550 square miles, Lake Superior (larger than its four sisters combined) is the biggest in the world.

The landscape is strewn with glacial calling cards: gravely eskers, fields of drumlins, cone-shaped kames, moraines hundreds of miles long, and countless smaller kettle-hole lakes (10,000 on the Michigan-Wisconsin border alone). The world's largest extensive freshwater dune system edges the eastern side of Lake Michigan. At the time of the first European exploration, a swath of the dense coniferous and hardwood forest sweeping from the APPALACHIAN MOUNTAINS west to the plains covered 90 percent of the region, constituting three forest types: the coniferous boreal forest to the north, the central hardwood forest of the Upper Peninsula, and the transition forest of the North Woods, stocked with straight-grained first-growth pines more than 100 feet tall. Ten million beavers inhabited the waterways, and sturgeon—now extinct in Lake Ontario—were still so plentiful in the mid-1800s that they were used to fuel steamboat furnaces.

Samuel de Champlain (1567–1635) first saw Lake Huron in 1615, imagining that it was an ocean with the Indies just beyond; Sault Ste. Marie was founded before Philadelphia. By the 1660s Jesuit missionaries had spread a network of bark

chapels to the far shores of Lakes Michigan and Superior. The Great Lakes basin was the center of the continental fur trade, with French posts located as far west as the lower Missouri River and Lake Winnipeg by the 1730s. The Grand Portage on Lake Superior was the meeting point for canoe-steering *voyageurs* bearing trade goods from Montreal and the winter's fur harvest from the north.

Gained by the British in 1760, control of the lakes passed to the United States at the end of the Revolution. They were known for years after as the English Seas and were the site of many of the battles of the War of 1812. Settlement of the lakeshores began in the early 1800s, causing word of the region's wild beauty to fill the travel columns of the New York and Boston papers. Sent on a western tour by the *New York American* in 1833, the writer Charles Fenno Hoffman (1806–84) tantalized readers with a letter describing his emergence from a stage after the arduous ride from Pittsburgh to Cleveland, to gaze upon Lake Erie "like one who has come out of a pent-up chamber into the full and free air of heaven." After an 1846 canoe trip with Indians and French Canadian *voyageurs* along the Lake Superior shore, Charles Lanman, author of *Adventures in the Wilds of the United States* (1856), described the primeval forest as a "wild and silent wilderness." It was, said the librarian-turned-writer-and-explorer, "beautiful beyond any thing I had imagined to exist in any country on the globe."

The natural legacy of these apparently endless resources was the temptation to exploit them. Pollution commenced with the early-nineteenth-century population of the lakeshores, as forest clearing caused erosion and runoff and as sawdust

Among the early Great Lakes explorers were the French pair Radisson and Groselliers. Of Frederic Remington's series of eleven oil paintings celebrating great explorers, only *Radisson and Groselliers* (1905) is extant.

Boundless Room for Exploitation

from lumber mills clogged waterways. Wetlands were filled, and watercourses were straightened and dredged at the expense of the waterfowl and spawning fish whose habitats were further compromised by industrial runoff. The market for whitefish in Lake Michigan had extinguished many of the fishing grounds by as early as 1860, and the subsequently intense harvesting of lake trout there over the next century had made that population completely extinct by 1957. Bypass canals for Niagara Falls introduced such predator species as the lamprey eel, which has decimated the trout population. The water-clogging zebra mussel, which procreates in mind-boggling exponents, has made its way into every lake since it arrived in 1986. Exotic species are thought to enter the lakes at the rate of one per year, and one hundred-plus species of flora and fauna in the Great Lakes basin are now threatened or endangered (☞ ENDANGERED SPECIES).

The Great Lakes region provides habitat for numerous species of flora and fauna. A bull moose feeds in a beaver pond in Isle Royale National Park in Michigan.

Perhaps the most drastic landscape alterations came with the timber industry (☞ CLEAR-CUTTING, FORESTS). In the half century after 1848, logging of the region's virgin timber yielded $4 billion in profits, far surpassing the value of gold extracted from California in the same era. Begun around 1835, the logging phenomenon known as the "Big Cut" produced eight hundred lumber camps and stripped nearly all the forests from Ohio, Michigan, Indiana, and Wisconsin, which in 1900–5 led the country in timber production. Clear-cuts, covering entire townships, totaled about 50 million acres. The Lake Huron mill town of Alpena produced 200 million board feet of pine in 1889. White pine boards paved the mill road from Saginaw to Flint, Michigan. A huge mound of sawdust collecting in Cheboygan measured almost a mile in circumference. Today, however, Michigan's second-growth forests are a testament to replanting efforts. Trees cover more than 90 percent of the Upper Peninsula, and the state claims the largest state forest system outside ALASKA.

Pollutant buildups are a particular problem in the five Great Lakes, a result of heavy population (the watershed supports 38 million people), development, and the closed nature of the system. The long water-retention periods of Lakes Superior, Michigan, and Huron make them particularly susceptible to

POLLUTION: almost two centuries are required for water entering Lake Superior to flush out again, for example, as opposed to about two and a half years for Lake Erie. The primary effort to confront water pollution issues is the state-run Great Lakes Water Initiative, issued in 1995 under the guidance of the ENVIRONMENTAL PROTECTION AGENCY. This established water-quality criteria for twenty-nine pollutants to provide a consistent level of protection for the human, aquatic, and wildlife populations of the lakes region. Costs and questions over the scientific soundness of EPA's research have made the initiative a subject of considerable controversy. ☞ *also* NATIONAL LAKESHORES, QUETICO-SUPERIOR REGION

Contacts

Michigan Land Use Institute ⊠ P.O. Box 228, Benonia, MI 49616. ☏ 231-882-4723. 🖳 www.mlui.org

■ Efforts of this independent nonprofit research organization, the state's largest environmental advocacy group, focus on land stewardship, resource protection, and environmental and economic policy. Publications include *Great Lakes Bulletin*.

Superior Hiking Trail Association ⊠ P.O. Box 4, Two Harbors, MN 55616. 🖳 www.shta.org

■ This nonprofit supports the Superior Hiking Trail, a long-distance footpath modeled after the Appalachian National Scenic Trail that winds along the edge of Lake Superior in northeastern Minnesota.

Great Smoky Mountains

In 1904, when the historian and woodsman Horace Kephart prepared for his first sojourn to the Great Smoky Mountains—the master chain of the southern APPALACHIAN MOUNTAINS straddling the North Carolina–Tennessee border—he wrote that he was dismayed to find not a single guide or literary work showing an intimate knowledge of the region. At the time, Kephart later noted in *Our Southern Highlanders* (1913), his beautifully unsentimental commentary on life and ways in the Smokies, Americans were far more familiar with the Alps, Pyrenees, and Rockies. "It is true that summer tourists flock to Asheville and Toxaway, Linville and Highlands, passing their time at modern hotels and motoring along a few macadamed roads, but what do they see of the billowy wilderness that conceals most of the native homes? Glimpses from afar. What do they learn of the true mountaineer? Hearsay."

It is more than hearsay that the Great Smoky Mountains are old, part of an Appalachian system that began folding upward perhaps 200 million years ago. Other statistics: The Smokies contain about as many native tree species (130) as are found in all of Europe. There are four thousand plant

Enshrouding mists give the Great Smoky Mountains their distinctive look. This photograph of the mountains in North Carolina, taken from the east end of Mount Collins, was made a century ago.

species, including the region's famed flame azalea and gargantuan mountain laurel, fifteen hundred wildflower types, about two hundred bird types, more than sixty mammal types, two thousand fungi, fifty moss types, seventy kinds of fish, and eighty reptiles and amphibians—including more types (twenty-five) than anywhere in the world of the most ancient land vertebrate, the salamander. One of the odder natural features is the presence of unexplained balds (grass- or heath-covered pates bare of trees), which are thought to account for only about .01 percent of the Smoky territory but contain almost 30 percent of its flora. Hiking from the base of a Smoky mountain to its peak is equivalent to passing through the same levels of biological life as you would encounter if you walked 1,250 miles north.

From Trail of Tears to Biosphere Reserve

The Cherokee Indians, the most numerous peoples of the Southeast at the time of European contact, named these velvety mountains Sha-ci-na-qe ("Place of Blue Smoke"). Partly by means of a fraudulent treaty negotiated with a tribal minority, about sixteen thousand Cherokees were forced westward from the Appalachian lowlands over the Trail of Tears in 1838.

A small faction persevered in the North Carolina Appalachians and acquired a tract of land known as the Qualla Boundary Reservation. The tribal center is in Cherokee, North Carolina, near the southern entrance to the 800-square-mile Great Smoky Mountains National Park, the most-visited national park in America (☞ NATIONAL PARK SYSTEM).

Authorized in 1926, the park was established in 1934, primarily through the purchase of private lands with state funds and donations matched by John D. Rockefeller Jr., but not before three-fourths of the virgin forest had been logged. Much of the local support came from politicians who never actually thought the national park would become a reality but were interested in the associated project of an improved road between Knoxville, Tennessee, and Asheville, North Carolina. The Smokies' extraordinarily rich variety of life has earned the national park designation as both an INTERNATIONAL BIOSPHERE RESERVE and a WORLD HERITAGE SITE.

Friends of Great Smoky Mountains National Park ⊠ 134 Court Avenue, *Contacts*
Sevierville, TN 37862. ☏ 865-453-6231. ▯ www.smokymtnmall.com/mall/
fgsmnp1.html
■ This nonprofit organization operates under agreement with the National Park Service to help restore and protect the park, provide better facilities, and reconstruct trails.

Great Smoky Mountains Institute ⊠ 9275 Tremont Road, Townsend, TN 37882. ☏ 615-448-6709
■ This education center offers workshops and programs for grade-school children, elderhostel groups, and teachers. Programs include hiking, mountain music, living history, and wildlife demonstrations.

Great Smoky Mountains National Park ⊠ 107 Park Headquarters Road, Gatlinburg, TN 37738. ☏ 423-436-1200. ▯ www.nps.gov/grsm
■ The park attracts 10.2 million visitors annually.

Smoky Mountain Field School ⊠ University Outreach and Continuing Education, University of Tennessee, 1534 White Avenue, Knoxville, TN 37996-1526. ☏ 423-974-0150. ▯ www.outreach.utk.edu
■ The school offers workshops, hikes, and wilderness adventures. In cooperation with the National Park Service and the University of Tennessee, experts on Smoky Mountain plants, wildlife, and history lead programs.

📙 Horace Kephart, *Our Southern Highlanders* (1913, 1998). 📙 Harry L. Moore, *A* *Reading* *Roadside Guide to the Geology of the Great Smoky Mountains National Park* (1988). 📙 C. Hodge Mathes, *In the Shadow of Old Smoky: Stories of the Mountains and Their People* (1994). 📙 H. Lea Lawrence, *The Fly Fisherman's Guide to the Great Smoky Mountains National Park* (1998).

Green Mountains

When the French explorer Samuel de Champlain (1567–1635) first laid eyes on the evergreen-covered peaks of this section of the APPALACHIAN MOUNTAINS in 1604, he is supposed to have shouted, "*Voila! Les monts verts!*" From the French words for green mountains came the name *Vermont*. The mountains running a central north-south course through the state retained the name, in English translation, of Green Mountains. The location of numerous ski resorts, this 250-mile-long range rises to the highest point at Mount Mansfield (4,393 feet). Hikers can walk the crest of the range on the 270-mile Long Trail, which extends from Massachusetts to the Canadian border, overlapping a portion of the APPALACHIAN NATIONAL SCENIC TRAIL. The Green Mountain National Forest (550 square miles) was established in 1932 (☞ NATIONAL FORESTS).

Greenways

A greenway is a ribbon of open space that is protected for conservation or recreational purposes and is usually intended to provide a link to a larger network of natural spaces. An urban greenway might be a riverside bike path; rural greenways are often established to preserve wildlife migration routes or planned as natural corridors to link parks, forests, wildlife refuges, and existing scenic and historic trails into a larger whole. Greenways may be publicly or privately owned or established as public-private partnerships. The idea is to protect environmentally significant lands, waterways, plants, and wildlife while raising consciousness and enticing people into the natural world by getting them onto alternative transportation routes. ☞ *also* NATIONAL TRAILS SYSTEM

Contacts

American Greenways ✉ 800 North Kent Street, Suite 1120, Arlington, VA 22209-2156. ✆ 703-525-6300. ▭ www.conservationfund.org/conservation/amgreen/index

■ Managed by the Conservation Fund, American Greenways is the primary program dedicated to creating a national greenway system. An information clearinghouse, it consults with government agencies, nonprofits, and corporations to plan urban and rural greenway projects. Educational materials and seed grants are provided.

East Coast Greenway Alliance ✉ 135 Main Sreet, Wakefield, RI 02879. ✆ 401-789-4265

■ The alliance is working on a greenway network of hiking, cycling, horseback riding, and other nonmotorized uses intended to connect cities from Maine to Florida by linking existing and proposed trails and greenways. These would be locally owned and managed section by section, much like the Appalachian National Scenic Trail.

Four the nineteenth-century sportsman, no figure better personified a fundamental kinship with the wilderness than the backwoodsman, and no backwoodsman personified it better than the guide-for-hire. A necessary institution of any backcountry hunting or angling expedition, this grizzled high priest of woodland wisdom—part servant, part father figure—not only knew the location of every good portage and fishing hole in a given region but could also find them by instinct. Although guides were often characterized as rude and illiterate, a good one could row a boat 30 miles, set up camp, build a lean-to, and have dinner cooking over the fire before nightfall. Most of the best knew their territory so well because they had lived their entire lives in the woods ("borned in the kentry and ain't never been out o' hit"). The traveler from town and city might have money and manners, but it was the guide whose affinity with nature seemed to put him that much closer to God.

The common theme running through the many accounts of nineteenth-century camping adventures in deep-woods Maine, the ADIRONDACK MOUNTAINS, and other largely unmapped areas in America's wilderness is how leveling the experience was. Conventions receded, pretensions were shed, fellowship emerged, and patrons and their guides—the oddest of bedfellows in any other setting—developed strong bonds that lasted for years. Hunters, fishermen, and other backwoods wanderers depended on their guides for their safety and comfort. They also admired them for primal instincts that had long since been cultivated out of their own genetic makeup by the "artificial" culture of city life.

Years after his legendary 1858 camping trip with a group of scientists and authors in the Adirondacks, the writer and artist William James Stillman (1828–1901) noted in his essay "The Philosophers' Camp" how his friend RALPH WALDO EMERSON became fascinated with the astonishing physical and intuitive abilities of their guides, whose innate connection to nature was something the campers could never expect to have. "This he had never seen—the man at his simplest terms, unsophisticated and, to him the nearest approach to the primitive savage he would ever be able to examine. . . ."

The archetype of guide as primal sage had deep roots in America, where white settlers depended on the skills of native guides from the earliest forays of the Spanish explorer Francisco Vásquez Coronado (1510–54) well into the 1800s. The guide as folk hero began to take on mythical proportions as early as 1761, when DANIEL BOONE started leading hunting parties from Pennsylvania and Virginia west across the BLUE RIDGE

Guides

"I believe that Adam in paradise was not so favorably situated on the whole as is the backwoodsman in America."

Henry David Thoreau

Archetype
of Primitive Man
(and Woman)

MOUNTAINS into the Watauga region, an area then utterly unpen-
etrated except by a few British and French Indian traders. The
first mountain guides to wittingly capitalize on the romance
of the rough-hewn image from a tourism standpoint were
probably the famous Crawford family of New Hampshire.
Skilled pathmakers and mountain guides, two generations of
Crawfords ran a series of three travelers' inns in the WHITE
MOUNTAINS beginning in the 1790s. Among the attractions was
the well-known fact that the Crawford boys kept wild animals, including wolves and elk, as pets. Two of Maine's best-
known fly-fishing guides were women, another novelty.

In 1837 the editor Charles Fenno Hoffman (1806–84) published a serialized account of an Adirondacks trip in his
weekly, the *New York Mirror*, proclaiming his own guide, John
Cheney, to be the human incarnation of JAMES FENIMORE COOPER'S
fictional woodland scout-hero, Natty Bumppo. By midcentury
the guides themselves were fully aware of the image, and some
capitalized on it. One was Orson "Old Mountain" Phelps, a
compatriot of Cheney, who sported colored pants and a mat-
ted beard; according to the writer Charles Dudley Warner
(1829–1900), his yellow hair grew out of a frayed felt hat "like
some nameless fern out of a pot." A sought-after guide, the
aromatic Phelps supplemented his income by selling his own
line of guidebooks, maps, a "Phelps" fly-fishing rod, and
copies of his photograph. For her part, the six-foot-tall Cor-
nelia "Fly Rod" Crosby, one of the women Maine guides, had
her own exhibit, including a log cabin (☞ LOG CABINS) furnished with mounted fish at the first annual Sportsman Show
at Madison Square Garden in New York City. Crosby dressed
for the occasion in a green leather dress from Paris; she later
took a job as Maine's first professional publicity agent.

One of the first priorities for any hiker is to keep hydrated and well fueled by drinking plenty of liquids and nibbling on snacks, energy bars, and trail mix frequently to satisfy the craving for carbohydrates and salt. The typical adult male requires an average of 4,000 calories per day, and the typical woman 3,000 calories to sustain adequate energy while hiking. In addition to good snacks, a handbook on wilderness first aid is also essential in your pack. This will provide advice on handling potential problems such as blisters, abrasions, burns, puncture wounds, sprains, broken bones, bites and stings, rashes, infections, and other hazards that one might encounter in the wilds. Always heed posted warnings and weather reports and use your common sense. Carry a first-aid kit, available prepacked from any good sports outfitter, and consider taking a course in first aid. Anyone with asthma, serious allergies, or diabetes should wear an identification bracelet.

The following afflictions are almost always preventable—never even think about setting foot on a trail without educating yourself about them. (For more information on emergencies involving any of these conditions and their profound stages, consult a reputable guide to wilderness first aid.)

☞ *also* CLOTHING, DESERT HIKING, HIKING, ICE SAFETY, MOUNTAINEERING, SNAKES, SNOW CAMPING, SURVIVAL STRATEGIES

Health and First Aid

As this 1914 sightseer at the rim of the Grand Canyon may have realized, altitude sickness strikes indiscriminately, regardless of how fit one might be.

Altitude Sickness

As altitude increases, the air's oxygen content diminishes. Altitude sickness, also known as acute mountain sickness (☞ MOUNTAINEERING), occurs when the air becomes too thin to supply sufficient oxygen to the blood stream. The onset of this hypoxic condition seems to bear no relation to age, sex, fitness, or expertise.

■ **Causes.** Fast ascents, overexertion, high sleeping altitudes (if camping), extended periods of exposure at a high altitude, high-fat and high-protein diets, dehydration.

■ **Symptoms.** Dull headache, lethargy, shortness of breath, dizziness, nausea, loss of appetite, insomnia, staggering, and irrational behavior. Mild symptoms usually disappear after a day of rest. In extreme cases, acute mountain sickness can escalate into high-altitude pulmonary edema and, more rarely, high-altitude cerebral edema. Both of these dangerous conditions require evacuation.

■ **Treatment.** Stop climbing and take time to acclimate. Treat mild symptoms with pain relievers such as asparin or ibuprofin. If necessary, descend to the last level where you felt comfortable. Avoid sedatives.

■ **Prevention.** Acclimatize gradually to height changes. Drink plenty of fluids; adhere to a high-carbohydrate diet; avoid caffeine, alcohol, salt, and heavy meals before and during an ascent.

Dehydration

Water, which accounts for 60 percent of total body weight, helps carry oxygen and nutrients and regulate body temperature and metabolism. Dehydration—simply put, the lack of enough water—can bring on a host of problems, including heat stroke, hypothermia, and altitude sickness. Dehydration can catch you unaware because most people tend to underestimate their fluid requirements (☞ DESERT HIKING). Drink even when you don't feel thirsty.

- **Cause.** Insufficient fluid intake.
- **Symptoms.** Headache, fatigue, insatiable late-night thirst, cloudy or dark urine, muscle cramps.
- **Treatment.** Rest and water.
- **Prevention.** Drink plenty of water before starting out, and then drink water or sports drinks constantly throughout the day. Avoid caffeine, alcohol, and other diuretics. Avoid antihistamines, which can inhibit sweating. Take frequent rest stops and water breaks.

Frostbite

Frostbite occurs in subfreezing temperatures when tissue is damaged by cell dehydration and diminished blood circulation (☞ SNOW CAMPING). It affects cheeks, fingers, toes, and ears first.

- **Causes.** Wind chill; contact with cold objects and materials, especially metal; constricting clothing and boots; confined body position; dehydration.
- **Symptoms.** The mildest form, called frostnip, results in white, waxy, or gray (pink or red in dark-skinned people), mottled skin. Superficial frostbite, which penetrates the skin, may look much the same, but the skin will feel hard on the surface and soft underneath; blisters typically form within a day of warming. Deep frostbite penetrates underlying tissue and muscle; the frostbitten area feels hard, is white or bluish in color, and experiences a complete loss of sensation.
- **Treatment.** Immediate warming by total immersion in warm water. (Frostnipped areas can be rewarmed simply by being covered.) Elevate to reduce swelling. Because complete thawing and constant water temperature are necessary, a severe frostbite injury should be kept frozen until it can be properly thawed—which almost always means in a hospital. A freeze-thaw-freeze sequence can cause permanent damage. Never rub frostbite with snow or anything else.
- **Prevention.** Dress properly from the start. At the first sign of chill, warm your cold extremities using mittened hands or the warmth of armpits. Carry heat packs that you can pop into your mittens.

Ansel Adams's 1933 view of an apple orchard in Yosemite Park reveals the silent beauty of a winter landscape, but prolonged exposure in such conditions is dangerous. Frostbite begins with superficial damage and then works its way deeper into tissues.

Giardiasis

Giardia lamblia and other microscopic organisms, often spread by animal feces, may be present in streams, rivers, and lakes, even if the natural waters look and smell fresh and seem to be running clean. Giardiasis is easily transmitted—between people and between people and their dogs.

- **Cause.** Drinking untreated water.
- **Symptoms.** Diarrhea, gas, loss of appetite, stomach cramps, fatigue, nausea, weight loss, all of which may occur days or weeks after drinking.
- **Treatment.** See a doctor.
- **Prevention.** Never drink untreated water. Boil water for 10 minutes (add one minute for each 1,000 feet above sea level). Or use a chemical disinfectant, such as iodine, which comes in tablet or tincture form for this purpose; special water purifiers and microfilters are also available from camping-supply stores.

Heat Exhaustion

Heat exhaustion occurs when the body's heat-regulating system breaks down because it cannot dispose of enough of the heat it manufactures or absorbs from the environment (☞ DESERT HIKING).

- **Causes.** Usually the inability to sweat enough as well as dehydration and lack of shade.
- **Symptoms.** Lightheadedness, cramps, heavy sweating, exhaustion, weakness, nausea, headache, cramps, dry skin, confusion, escalating body temperature, rapid pulse, clammy, cold, or flushed skin. The profound stage is heat stroke, a life-threatening condition in which the body's core temperature can exceed 105 degrees Fahrenheit.
- **Treatment.** Loosen clothes and rest in the shade with feet elevated about 10 inches higher than the head. Cool the body with a damp sponge or cloth. Drink

Heat exhaustion and dehydration are two primary concerns when hiking in dry or desert conditions. Because mapped water sources can dry up and disappear, drinking water should be cached in places along the route.

half a glass of cool water every 15 minutes for about an hour. In case of heat stroke, rapidly cool the victim by wetting the skin or immsersing in water and having him or her drink cool water. Evacuation is necessary for heat stroke.

■ **Prevention.** Adequate hydration, pacing, and shade breaks. Wear a hat and don't hike in extremely hot, humid conditions.

This is the most common of all wilderness health problems and the primary cause of death in the outdoors. It occurs when body heat is lost faster than it is produced, causing the temperature of vital organs to fall dangerously low. Onset is caused by cold and exposure, but it is not limited to winter. In fact, most cases occur in a remarkably mild temperature range of 30 to 50 degrees Fahrenheit. Victims are often fair-weather hikers who are unprepared for the sudden temperature drops, chilling squalls, and hail that commonly occur above the treeline, even in the middle of summer.

Hypothermia

■ **Causes.** Exposure to cold weather, immersion in cold water, the refrigerating effect of wind on cooling sweat and wet clothes.

■ **Symptoms.** Prolonged, and eventually violent, shivering; fatigue; sluggishness; clumsiness; slurred speech; disorientation. In the profound stages, shivering stops and muscles go rigid, skin turns blue and pupils dilate; the ultimate stages are loss of consciousness, erratic heartbeat, coma, and death.

■ **Treatment.** Find shelter or create a windbreak; remove wet clothes and warm up immediately with dry ones (body heat escapes from a wet body two hundred times faster); get into a SLEEPING BAG or wrap up in a blanket; drink warm fluids; stay awake; and eat foods containing simple sugars. A severely hypothermic victim will need help from a companion and extremely gentle handling. Never offer alcohol or let the victim fall asleep. Using a hot-water bottle or heat pack, warm the victim at vital points—groin, neck, armpit—to get heat to vital organs before warming extremities. Apply mild heat only and evacuate for controlled rewarming.

■ **Prevention.** Always carry rain gear, gloves, a hat, and extra layers of CLOTHING; stay dry; evenly pace a hike or a climb to avoid overexertion. Pausing for frequent rest breaks usually makes you feel colder. If you suspect that you or a member of your hiking party is overly chilled, err on the side of caution. Never hike or let a companion insist on continuing to hike (pride can be deadly) without first warming up adequately. Cold-weather hikers should always carry self-activating heat packs that can be popped into gloves and boots.

This nonfreezing cold condition, also known as trench foot, usually occurs in temperatures of 30 to 40 degrees Fahrenheit. It can also affect the hands.

Immersion Foot

■ **Causes.** Prolonged exposure to cold and wet; wearing hip waders, vapor-barrier footwear, and ill-fitting footwear.

■ **Symptoms.** Cold, mottled skin; blue or gray tinge; numbness; tingling; pain and pulsing upon warming. In severe cases, cracked skin and blisters occur.

Treatment. Air dry, preferably at room temperature. Elevate feet to prevent swelling. Avoid rapid warming.

Prevention. Keep feet dry; wear warm, dry socks and change them frequently.

Plant Poisoning

The most common poisonous plants that cause toxic skin reactions in the wild are poison ivy, sumac, and oak. All contain the irritating oil known as urushiol, to which an estimated three-fourths of humans react allergically.

■ **Causes.** Contact with the plant (even brief) or with the oil (on your dog, for example).

■ **Symptoms.** Itchy red rash and blisters.

■ **Treatment.** Wash area immediately with cold water, but avoid harsh soaps, which can cause more irritation. Apply topical lotions. See a doctor if the condition persists. If you have eaten a plant that you think might be poisonous, drink water, induce vomiting, and get medical attention immediately.

■ **Prevention.** Know how to recognze the cuplrits. Poison ivy and oak are relatively easy to identify because they have leaf clusters in threes. Wear long sleeves and pants when possible and avoid touching your face or eyes with a bare hand, which may inadvertantly spread a rash. Never eat any plant that you cannot identify with absolute certainty; avoid all mushrooms.

Snowblindness

This is usually a temporary condition, but it can be quite painful.

■ **Cause.** Sunburned cornea.

■ **Symptoms.** Irritation and the need to squint; swelling and pain set in a few hours after the sunburn occurs.

■ **Treatment.** Put on sunglasses or tape glasses or goggles so that only a narrow slit remains open. In severe cases, use cold compresses and rest in complete darkness.

■ **Prevention.** UV-blocking sunglasses and a brimmed hat.

Sunburn

Protection from the sun's damaging ultraviolet rays is necessary even on cloudy or overcast days. The sun is strongest between 10 A.M. and 3 P.M. The higher you go, the less the sun's rays are filtered; skin burns twice as fast at 6,000 feet as it does at sea level. A good tan or overcast skies do not provide protection.

■ **Cause.** Too much unprotected exposure. As reflectors, snow, water, rocks, and sand exacerbate the problem.

■ **Symptoms.** Redness, soreness, swelling, or, in severe cases, blistering, chills, fever.

■ **Treatment.** Aloe vera, topical lotions, cool dressings. And of course, get out of the sun.

■ **Prevention.** A good, frequently applied sunscreen rated SPF 15 or above; apply an hour before sun exposure. Hat, neckerchief, sunglasses.

American Red Cross ✉ 431 Eighteenth Street, NW, Washington, DC 20006.
☎ 202-639-3520. 🖳 www.redcross.org
■ Your local Red Cross chapter is a source of training courses in first aid and CPR.

Wilderness Medicine Institute ✉ P.O. Box 9, Pitkin, CO 81241. ☎ 970-641-3572, 970-641-0882. 🖳 www.wmi.nols.edu
■ This division of the National Outdoor Leadership School offers intensive courses in wilderness EMT (emergency medical trauma) and first aid; some courses are designed specifically for outdoor professionals.

📖 Paul Gill Jr., *Simon and Schuster Pocket Guide to Wilderness Medicine* (1991). 📖 Kathleen Handal, M.D., Kathleen A. Handal, and Elizabeth H. Dole, *The American Red Cross First Aid and Safety Handbook* (1993). 📖 Jeff Isaac et al., *The Outward Bound Wilderness First-Aid Handbook* (1998). 📖 William Forgey, *Basic Essentials: Wilderness First Aid* (1999). 📖 Tilton and Frank Hubbell, *Medicine for the Backcountry* (1999). 📖 Tod Schimelpfenig et al., *National Outdoor Leadership School Wilderness First Aid* (2000).

Hiking

A good hiking trip is a safe and comfortable hiking trip. The essentials: the right clothes and footwear (☞ CLOTHING), plenty of water, conditioning, preparedness (☞ HEALTH AND FIRST AID, MAPS AND NAVIGATION, SURVIVAL STRATEGIES), an understanding of where you are going, a spirit of adventure, and, above all, a good sense of humor. Detailed trail guides are usually available for popular hiking regions. The state and federal agencies (☞ FEDERAL GOVERNMENT *and specific federal agencies*) responsible for parks, refuges, forests, and wilderness areas can also provide useful information on the regions under their management. If you are hiking in a national forest (☞ NATIONAL FOREST SYSTEM), for example, stop in at the local ranger's office for maps, suggestions, and weather tips. If you persist, you can even get material and maps on wilder destinations that are off the beaten path. Inexperienced hikers, however, should stick to accessible, well-traveled terrain. Check in advance to find out if you need a fire or camping permit. ☞ *also* BACKPACKS, CAMPING, DESERT HIKING, MOUNTAINEERING, SLEEPING BAGS, SNOW CAMPING, TENTS

Planning

Hiking shouldn't be a competition for racking up miles. Nevertheless, you need to have some sense of distance in order to plan well for the trip. As a guideline the average, fit hiker should be able to cover 10 to 12 miles a day over moderate terrain, but this varies depending on the elevation, temperature, and size and weight of the walker. Consult a reputable guidebook for a detailed description of the trail, accurate distances, and estimated "book" time. Many guides figure the average pace at 2 miles per hour plus one hour for each 1,000 feet of elevation gain. Thus, a 4-mile hike up a 3,000-foot vertical gain would figure at five hours. Then you need to factor in load and what will be underfoot (slow-going bog, fords, puncheons, or slippery rock faces, for instance). Distance doesn't mean everything. Interestingly, many trails in the ADIRONDACK, CATSKILL, and APPALACHIAN MOUNTAINS, where peaks may range from 3,000 to 4,000 feet, are harder climbs than switchback pack trails in the West. For overnight hikes, you will need to plan distances to get you to the desired camping area, which means that you will have to give some consideration in advance to the location of those camps. If you are not using established camping areas, check a good topographical map to be sure that there are level areas for camping.

Pacing

The goal is to maintain a constant level of exertion, and that necessitates adjusting your stride to hills and difficult underfoot conditions, such as scree (loose rock debris) or slippery rocks, to avoid excessive fatigue. Working your muscles hard produces lactic acid, which counteracts the muscle performance; to keep that acid level down you must stop for periodic rests or shorten your gait. The main trick is to find a good rhythm for energy output, or "sustained endurance." You don't want to stop and start so much that you use up even more energy, but it is better to pause long enough for a refreshing drink and some trail mix than to force yourself on to a point of exhaustion just to keep up the pace. In tough territory you will want to slow to a pace that you can keep up comfortably, which may mean taking 6-inch steps on a really steep grade (up or down). For steep slopes, experienced hikers recommend the "rest" step, which involves letting the back leg go completely limp for a half second or so before taking the next step.

Start any hike slowly to ration energy needed later in the day. The ideal gait differs from person to person, so it is best to hike with companions of similar speed habits. If capabilities vary significantly, the slower hikers should start out sooner, or the faster people should move on ahead and wait at an assigned meeting point. (Everyone should know this is the plan.) Men can usually carry more weight than women, so couples who want to keep the same pace should think about redistributing their loads.

Trail Etiquette

■ Decent behavior in hotels, stores, and towns in the vicinity does much to foster good will toward hikers in general. Keep voices low on the trail.

■ Don't litter. Pack it in, pack it out. If you encounter trash, carry out as much of it as possible.

■ Pack animals and horses have the right-of-way; move several yards out of the

way, preferably downslope, and let the animals pass. Always ask a faster group of hikers behind you if they wish to pass. The usual courtesy is for upward-bound hikers to step aside for downhill walkers when hikers meet head on.

■ If your party includes more than five or six members, break down into smaller groups and pace yourself a bit apart. Passing a big cluster of hikers can ruin the experience for other walkers, and large groups tend to have heavy impact on the trail.

■ Established camping sites and shelters along the trail are intended for everyone to use, so trail etiquette dictates sharing them. This is usually necessary in popular areas where fire rings are scarce (☞ CAMPFIRES, COOKING). If you are already using a shelter and more hikers arrive, welcome them in. If you expect to arrive at a given shelter after people are likely to be asleep or to leave it early in the morning, pitch a tent for that night instead.

■ Stay on the trail as much as possible to avoid erosion and degradation. Don't deviate to explore. Trekking poles should be planted inside the trail.

■ Where dogs are allowed, keep them leashed on the trail and safely tied when in camp.

Hikers who set out for overnight treks, such as these in California's Sierra Nevada Range, must take into account added pack weight when estimating travel time and the distance to be covered in a day. Everything packed into a campsite must always be packed out again.

Trail Safety

■ The first rule of hiking is don't go alone. Also, always advise someone of your plans before leaving; sign in at the trailhead as well.

■ Check the weather report and prepare accordingly for it.

■ Know when the hunting season is open and wear blaze orange during those times.

■ Never respond to taunts or harassment, and be cordial but circumspect in any exchange with strangers. Cut a wide berth around anyone who acts aggressively, oddly, or high on liquor or drugs, and don't discuss your itinerary with anyone you don't trust. If you feel threatened, say that you are part of a large group, even if that's not the case.

■ The closer you are to the road, the higher the chances of theft. Don't leave any valuables locked in your car, and never leave your pack unattended.

■ Never take a dog into an area where there are wolves or grizzlies. In grizzly country, a minimum of three hikers in a party is a good idea (☞ BEARS).

Contacts

American Alpine Club ✉ 710 Tenth Street, Suite 100, Golden, CO 80401. ☎ 303-384-0110. 🖥 www.americanalpineclub.org

■ Founded in 1902, the club promotes education about mountains and mountaineering, the conservation of climbing areas, and exploration and scientific study throughout the world. The American Alpine Club Library, established in 1916, is the oldest alpine research facility in the country and is available for research on any subject that falls within the scope of mountaineering and climbing interests. The club also offers climbing and exploration grants.

American Hiking Society ✉ 1422 Fenwick Lane, Silver Spring, MD 20910. ☎ 301-565-6704. 🖥 www.americanhiking.org

Even in the days before high-tech gear and equipment, an intrepid party of hikers in 1932 was game for a ranger-led sunrise nature walk in Washington's Mount Rainier National Park.

■ This recreation-based conservation organization is committed to establishing, maintaining, and protecting foot trails. It maintains the Hiker's Information Center (a state-by-state guide to hikes, trail events, trail guides, and work projects), promotes National Trails Day, posts news releases on legislative actions affecting trail conservation and use, and offers information on equipment and trail safety. Publications include *American Hiker Magazine*, *Pathways across America*, *Trails Today*, and *Hikers' Journal*. Internships and volunteer vacations are also offered.

Appalachian Mountain Club ✉ 5 Joy Street, Boston, MA 02108. ☎ 617-523-0636. 🖥 www.outdoors.org

■ The club promotes responsible recreational use of mountains, rivers, and trails. Twelve local chapters sponsor guided hikes, canoe outings, outdoor skills training, and outdoor adventure workshops and are responsible for maintaining 1,400 miles of trails with volunteers. The club publishes several respected hiking and camping guides and a journal that includes trip and gear reports.

Leave No Trace ✉ P.O. Box 997, Boulder, CO 80306. ☎ 800-332-4100. 🖥 www.lnt.org

■ Leave No Trace builds awareness and respect for public places of recreation, emphasizing low-impact camping and wilderness ethics. Training courses are offered in conjunction with the National Outdoor Leadership School.

The Mountaineers ✉ 300 Third Avenue West, Seattle, WA 98119. ☎ 800-573-8484. 🖥 www.mountaineers.org

■ An advocate for trail and park conservation, the organization is also a recreational club focusing on wilderness exploration and outdoor activities such as hiking and climbing, as well as skiing, biking, travel, sea kayaking, and snowshoeing. Courses are offered in outdoor skills and wilderness first aid. The club sponsors a Forest Watch Committee and alerts members to legislative issues concerning the environment. Publications include *The Mountaineer*.

The Illinois WPA Art Project encouraged healthful hiking in 1939 with this poster of a city dweller in a park.

National Outdoor Leadership School ✉ 288 Main Street, Lander, WY 82520-3140. ☎ 307-332-5300. 🖥 www.nols.edu

■ NOLS specializes in all aspects of wilderness education, stressing safety, leadership, teamwork, outdoor skills, and environmental studies. The school has nine branches.

Outward Bound ✉ 100 Mystery Point Road, Garrison, NY 10524. ☎ 888-882-6863. 🖥 www.outwardbound.org

■ This noted training organization maintains five wilderness schools in the United States. Its emphasis is on "expeditionary learning," wilderness skills training, and environmental stewardship.

Web sites devoted to hiking and backpacking offer chat rooms, book and gear reviews, online shopping, state-by-state trail news, articles, classifieds, and information on health, safety, trails, hiking clubs, and adventure travel. Some of the best:

Web Sites

Adventure Network 🖥 www.adventurenetwork.com

Backpacking and Hiking Trailhead 🖥 www.geocities.com/Yosemite/Falls/9200/backpacking_and_hiking.html

Basecamp.Com 🖥 www.backpacker.com

Escaping to Nature ⊟ www.outdoorphoto.com/hiking

Great Outdoors.Com ⊟ www.greatoutdoors.com

Great Outdoor Recreation Pages ⊟ www.gorp.com/gorp/activity/hiking.htm

The Lightweight Backpacker ⊟ www.backpacking.net

Mtnhike ⊟ www.mtnhike.com

Peak to Peak ⊟ www.peaktopeak.net

The Sight ⊟ www.win.net/ ~ sydwdn/backpack/backpack.htm

Hudson River School Artists

"Untamed nature everywhere asserts her claim on us, and the recognition of this claim constitutes an essential part of our Art."   *The Crayon* (1855)

"The great distinction between American and European scenery, as a whole, is to be found in the greater want of finish in the former than in the latter, and to the greater superfluity of works in art in the old world than in the new."
    Washington Irving, *The Sketch-Book of Geoffrey Crayon, Gent.* (1819–20)

The loosely knit group of painters known as the Hudson River School is considered the country's first native school of landscape artists. Associated primarily with large-scale canvases expressing the majesty of the American wilderness (jagged chasms, billowing clouds), the movement emerged in the 1820s under the leadership of Thomas Cole (1801-48), flourished until the 1870s, and eclipsed contemporary movements in portrait and FRONTIER GENRE PAINTING. The leading figures—including Cole, Asher B. Durand (1796–1896), Frederick Edwin Church (1826–1900), John Kensett (1816–72), and the great colorist Jasper Cropsey (1823–1900)—rejected the fashion for historical allegories and looked instead to the "noble" beauty of the wilderness landscapes that inspired their work. Their destinations included not only the Hudson River valley but also the ADIRONDACK and CATSKILL MOUNTAINS of New York; the WHITE MOUNTAINS of New Hampshire; the Berkshires of Massachusetts; and Maine's Mount Desert Isle. The ROCKY MOUNTAINS and California were also a magnet for such Hudson River painters as Sanford Gifford (1823–80), Worthington Whittredge (1820–1910), Albert Bierstadt (1830–1902), and Thomas Moran (1837–1926) (☞ ROCKY MOUNTAIN SCHOOL ARTISTS).

The early rise of the Hudson River painters coincided with the opening of the 363-mile-long Erie Canal (1835), which ran through a nearly unbroken course of wilderness from Albany, New York, on the Hudson River to Buffalo on Lake Erie and put the state on the map as a cultural and financial center. Among the canal's backers were the author JAMES FENI-MORE COOPER and the New York governor DeWitt Clinton, a patron of the American Academy of Fine Arts who promoted the dramatic canvases of Cole and others as the ideal means of capturing nature's "operations on a grand scale." Thomas Cole, singled out by Philip Hone, another canal patron, made his artistic debut in New York the same year the canal opened; Hone bought two of his works.

Kindred Spirits (1849) by Asher B. Durand shows Thomas Cole, father of the Hudson River School, standing with his friend the poet and editor William Cullen Bryant. Painted as a tribute to Cole a year after his death, the work is considered a portrait, although the Catskill Mountains scenery is really the focus of the composition.

Canvas Evangelists

In a sense, the Hudson River painters were evangelists with paint and brush. Many were pantheists who identified nature and the universe with God and God with the universe and nature. Their belief was that the natural landscape was the physical manifestation of God, and their gospel was to record it with fidelity, although some details were in fact contrived in the studio for overall dramatic effect. In particular, the English-born Cole, a poet-philosopher who settled in the Catskills in the 1820s, also saw an essential relationship between painting and other arts. Wandering in the woods, he might pause before an inspiring scene to play his flute or write down bits of poetry to later serve as a reference while he worked on a painting.

Particularly close ties formed between the Hudson River School and the works of such contemporary literary figures as Nathaniel Hawthorne, WASHINGTON IRVING, WILLIAM CULLEN BRYANT, and JAMES FENIMORE COOPER (☞ WRITERS (NINETEENTH CENTURY)). Cole himself was strongly influenced by Cooper and was a close friend of the poet Bryant. The two shared a deep reverence for the outdoors and frequently "tramped" together in the wilds. Collaborations were a natural manifestation of such close bonds. *Kindred Spirits* (1849), perhaps Durand's most famous painting, shows Bryant and Cole overlooking a panoramic vale in the Catskills: bit players in a drama whose main character was the magnificent scenery.

In the universe of these artists, nature itself was considered a superior teacher to academic training. Most believed that only after the artist had immersed himself sufficiently in the experience of nature and let it inspire his own individual artistic signature might he possibly benefit from the formal instruction that would otherwise foster homogeneity. Some of the Hudson River painters also developed strong views on the environment, and their standing among society's elite gave them louder voices for the cause than might have otherwise been heard. Moved by the beauty of Niagara Falls, Frederick Edwin Church, one of Cole's last students, worked with the landscape architect Frederick Law Olmsted (1822–1903) to fight developers and establish an American-Canadian international park at the falls in 1885. Cole's own response to the wilderness, however, was conflicted: for him, nature embodied an element of both fear and enjoyment, but taken apart from the human emotion of love, he said, nature could not be a completely sustaining force.

Contact **Metropolitan Museum of Art** ⊠ 1000 Fifth Avenue (at East Eighty-second Street), New York, NY 10028. ✆ 212-535-7710. ▯ www.metmuseum.org
■ The Met has a substantial collection of the works of Hudson River School painters.

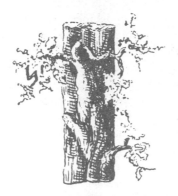

Anyone who has had the somewhat dubious pleasure of fishing through freshwater ice in subarctic temperatures or a raging snowstorm probably won't have any trouble believing that such primitive conditions are associated with a prehistoric practice. Barbs, wood decoys, and spears carved of bone and tusk surviving from before the Ice Age indicate that ice fishing was spread by NATIVE AMERICANS from present-day ALASKA through Canada into the North Woods and New England.

Early methods involved luring one's quarry—typically perch, walleye, northern pike, pickerel, crappie, and bluegill— with a weighted decoy tied to a pole and lowered through a hole cut in the ice. Sheltered from daylight so that the decoy could be seen and tracked in the water, fishermen speared the fish attracted to the decoy. European settlers adopted the native technique, and by the nineteenth century ice fishing had become a large-scale commercial enterprise in regions such as Saginaw Bay, Michigan, where clusters of ice-fishing shelters formed semipermanent communities on the ice throughout the winter. Buyers transversed the frozen surface by wagon to buy the day's catch directly from the ice.

By its nature, the sport of ice fishing comes with weather conditions about which nothing can be done. Numerous amenities, however, may frequently be spotted on the ice

The master ice fisher-
man Oscar Peterson of
Cadillac, Michigan,
made thousands of fish
carvings and detailed
decoys in the mid-1900s.

these days, including heated shacks, automatic fishing "tip-ups" for lines, powered augurs for cutting holes, and even electronic wireless pages ("You've got fish"). In lieu of spears, modern ice fishing is usually done with a variety of bait: grubs and worms for bluegill, crappie, perch, and rock bass, and minnows, chub, and shiners for crappie, perch, bass, pike, and walleye. Artificial lures are also used but usually in combination with bait.

The real trick to ice fishing is figuring out where the fish are. Because particular species prefer particular water levels, the key lies in determining depth. Anglers do this by a range of means, from reading clues in the surrounding terrain to using electronic depth finders that can read through clear ice. The tried-and-true method: look for a group of fishermen who are busily hauling in a catch, and then set up shop in the same vicinity.

As in all types of fishing, all those who want to fish in the ice should get the proper permits and educate themselves about size limits; catch-and-release rules apply year-round. Derbies and championships take place annually in all the major ice-fishing regions. Check the Internet for regional events, camps and lodges, and a listing of hut operators who lease shelters. Portable huts and kits are also available. ☞ *also* ANGLING

Reading

📖 Jim Capossela, *Ice Fishing: A Complete Guide* (1992). 📖 Tom Gruenwald, *Hooked on Ice Fishing: Secrets to Catching Winter Fish* (1995). 📖 In Fishe et al., *Ice Fishing Secrets* (1998). 📖 Noel Vick, *Fishing on Ice* (1999).

Ice Safety

Short of having an augur, an ice ax, or a drill on hand, you can't always accurately test ice thickness, but you can always be aware of signs of soft ice. These include any patch of frozen water that animals have clearly avoided, depressions and discolored or slushy snow, and milky or honeycombed ice. Clear blue ice is the sturdiest and preferred type; 4 to 5 inches is the minimum thickness for supporting a single person on foot. Slush ice is about half as strong as clear ice.

Ice Safety Tips

■ Avoid traveling on ice in spring conditions.

■ Always tap ahead with a ski pole or a hiking stick.

■ Never travel alone on ice, but always spread out from companions to distribute weight.

■ Keep your backpack unbuckled so that you can unload it quickly in the event of a breakthrough.

■ Never venture onto tributaries or feeder streams, and avoid ice around stones, logs, and tree trunks.

- If you fall in, spread your arms out on the ice and kick your feet hard to throw your body up and over the ice.
- Once out, you should roll away from the hole rather than stand up.
- If you can't heave yourself out, draw your knees and arms to your chest to minimize heat loss and call for help.
- If a companion falls through, offer the victim any logical item you can think of (a belt, a tree bough, a ski pole, or jumper cables, for example) as a handhold.
- Lie flat on the ice and extend the handhold, but do not move up to the hole yourself.
- Warmly wrap the rescued person, get him or her out of the wind, and call for immediate medical help. Do not offer the victim alcohol to drink.

"Thick and blue, tried and true.
Thin and crispy, way too risky."

American proverb

Iditarod

The Iditarod originated as a network of supply trails during the approximately thirty major gold strikes that fueled the economy of ALASKA between the 1880s and 1914. In 1910 the federal government responded to the growing demand for year-round service to interior mining camps and boomtown settlements to the west by establishing a dogsled trail from Seward to Nome for use when winter weather precluded riverboat access. The Iditarod trail began about 50 miles north of Seward at the terminus of the Alaska Central Railway and led through wilderness to the trading post of Knik, west through the ALASKA RANGE to the Kuskokwim River valley, still onward to the town of Iditarod, then up a frozen expanse of the Yukon River to Kaltag, where the route followed the 90-mile Kaltag portage, an ancient pass through coastal mountains to the Bering Sea. From Unalakleet the trail followed the shore of the Seward Peninsula through a series of Inupiat villages to Nome.

The practice of dogsledding was adapted from the region's native peoples, who bred various dog types—the malamute among them—suited to specific terrains and purposes. A team of sled dogs had the advantage over a team of horses: the dogs did not require special feed, were light enough to run over deep-drifting snow without sinking into it, and yet could haul cargo weighing up to half a ton. Moreover, stronger in the long haul, sled dogs outpower horses because they are able to sustain average speeds of about 10 miles per hour over distances of several hundred miles with intermittent rest stops about a day's sledding apart.

The trip from Seward to Nome took a musher and twenty dogs three weeks. As many as 120 sleds might make the trip monthly from the coast westward, going in with supplies and mail and coming out with gold. Most of the 2,450-mile trail is passable only during the winter, when the rivers and tundra are completely frozen; from spring through fall it is impassable.

The supply trail was used regularly into the 1920s and partially into the 1940s, until the bush plane started to make dog travel obsolete. Local and short-distance mushing was still common well after World War II, but the snowmobile finally put the practice to rest in the 1960s. The Iditarod, which is administered by the U.S. DEPARTMENT OF THE INTERIOR'S BUREAU OF LAND MANAGEMENT, was designated a National Historic Trail (☞ NATIONAL TRAILS SYSTEM) in 1978.

The trail's revival has come in the form of the Iditarod Sled Dog Race, first held in full form in 1973, which keeps the spirit of the supply route alive even though it passes through several towns that were not on the original trail. The yearly 1,150-mile race takes place in March and follows a meandering path from Anchorage to Nome. A path taken in even years follows a northern route designed to include several villages along the Yukon. Teams are limited to sixteen dogs, and although some of the best mushers finish in less than ten days, the trip can take three weeks or more of grueling travel through a wilderness of coastline and desolate tundra. In the long hours of darkness, temperatures drop to minus 60 degrees Fahrenheit. Almost half of the stringent fifty-seven race rules govern the care and protection of the dogs, and veterinarians volunteer at the checkpoints. No special breed of dog is required, and most sled dogs are the generic Alaskan husky.

A newer Iditasport race has also been created for skiers, mountain bikers, and snowshoers (☞ SNOWSHOES). Other major Alaskan dogsled races include the grueling 1,000-mile

Before bush planes and snowmobiles made them obsolete, dog sleds were the necessary means of winter travel in interior Alaska. This Yukon dog team was photographed near Juneau about 1898. The Iditarod Sled Dog Race, following parts of an old mail route, draws about fifty teams and drivers a year.

Yukon Quest, the Kobuk 440, the Kusko 300, the Klondike 300, and the Copper Basin 300. Among the races in the lower forty-eight states are the John Beargrease Race in Minnesota, Big Sky in Montana, and Upper Peninsula 200 in Michigan.

Web Sites

Iditarod National Historic Trail. Offers information on trail history and management. 🖳 www.anchorage.ak.blm.gov/inhthome.html

Iditarod Race. Provides race updates, rules, and policies. 🖳 www.iditarod.com

International Biosphere Reserves

International Biosphere Reserves are those natural areas on the World Heritage List (☞ WORLD HERITAGE SITES) that have been recognized under UNESCO's Man and the Biosphere Program as having worldwide significance. Such reserves must have a legally protected core area subject to little or no human activity and a low-intensity buffer zone. Biosphere reserves are nominated by the country in which they are situated and can be removed from the list by a request from that country. The goal is to promote comparative studies of ecosystems around the world without destroying their essential properties in the research process. The forty-seven U.S. biosphere reserves—located in areas such as the California coast ranges, OLYMPIC MOUNTAINS, YELLOWSTONE, EVERGLADES and Dry Tortugas, southern APPLACHIAN MOUNTAINS, Mammoth Cave, Hawaiian Islands, and Glacier Bay in ALASKA—are part of a global network of more than 390 such areas in about ninety-four countries worldwide.

Washington Irving

The broad body of work by Washington Irving (1783–1859), American author and diplomat, includes satire, fiction, plays, and literary travel writing. A life divided between Europe and the United States not only helped make Irving a success on both sides of the Atlantic but also underscored the writer's particular comparison of America's majestic scenery (the heritage of a new country of "youthful promise") with a Europe "rich in the accumulated treasures of age." His first international success was a collection of essays and tales entitled *The Sketch-Book* (written under the pen name Geoffrey Crayon). Among other tall tales, this volume contained the darkly romantic "Rip Van Winkle" and "The Legend of Sleepy Hollow," both set in the wilds of the CATSKILL MOUNTAINS.

Irving made his first frontier journey through upper New York and into Canada in 1804. In 1832, after a seventeen-year interval spent in England and Spain, he joined a group of U.S. Rangers on an Indian reconnaissance mission in the

"... never need an American look beyond his own country for the sublime and beautiful of natural scenery."

The Sketch-Book of Geoffrey Crayon, Gent. (1819–20)

Kansas and Oklahoma Territories with the express intent of experiencing the American frontier before progress destroyed it. In *A Tour on the Prairies* (1835), Irving acknowledged the power of the American landscape to define character, declaring that a journey west was an experience sure to produce "that manliness, simplicity, and self-dependence most in unison with our political institutions." Ignited by his own travels on the frontier, Irving's imagination was also captured by the exploits of swaggering frontier figures like John Jacob Astor (1763–1848). In *Astoria* (1836, with Pierre Irving), he recounts Astor's attempt to establish a fur-trading empire on the Pacific Coast. *The Adventures of Captain Bonneville, U.S.A.* (1837) is a romanticized version of the journal of Benjamin Louis Eulalie de Bonneville (1796–1878), the American army officer who led a trade expedition to the Green River and took the first wagon train across the South Pass of the ROCKY MOUNTAINS. ☞ *also* WRITERS (NINETEENTH CENTURY)

Selected Works

📖 *Letters of Jonathan Oldstyle* (1802). *Salamagundi* (1807), with William I. and J. K. Paulding. *A History of New York, by Dietrich Knickerbocker* (1809). *The Sketch-Book of Geoffrey Crayon, Gent.* (1819–20). *Bracebridge Hall* (1822). *Tales of a Traveller* (1824). *The Alhambra* (1832). *A Tour on the Prairies* (1835). *Astoria* (1836). *The Adventures of Captain Bonneville, U.S.A.* (1837).

Contact

Sunnyside ✉ West Sunnyside Lane, Tarrytown, NY 10591. ☏ 914-631-8200 ■ Irving's Hudson River valley house and its landscaping are preserved as a museum site.

An 1848 engraving shows a dapper Washington Irving relaxing at Sunnyside, his Hudson River home. A faithful dog was the requisite companion for outings in the nearby woods.

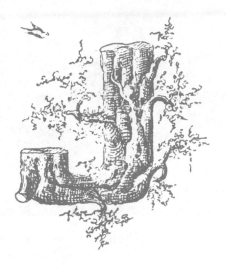

William Henry Jackson (1843–1942) is regarded as the greatest pioneer landscape photographer of the American West—for both the quality of his work and his success in publicizing the historic and picturesque sites in which he specialized. Born in New York's ADIRONDACK MOUNTAINS, Jackson set out for California in 1866, traveling part of the way as an ox-team driver in a Mormon wagon train. He later settled in Omaha, where he opened a studio with his brother Edward. In 1870 a photographic commission came from the U.S. Geological and Geographical Survey under Ferdinand V. Hayden (1829–87). Jackson spent the next decade with the Hayden Survey. That explorer's expeditions into the Yellowstone River valley (☞ SURVEYS, YELLOWSTONE NATIONAL PARK) produced a famous Jackson portfolio of large-plate images published as *Yellowstone's Scenic Wonders* (1871). The impact of Jackson's pictures was so strong that they no doubt had a major part in the area's designation as a national park in 1872.

Jackson's work for Hayden also produced the first images of the future Grand Teton and Mesa Verde National Parks (☞ NATIONAL PARK SYSTEM, TETON MOUNTAINS). In 1880 he opened a studio in Denver and soon took on a commission from the Denver and Rio Grande Railway. His already popular work was mass marketed in postcard form by the Detroit

William Henry Jackson

In 1878 William Henry Jackson made this view of stalactite basins, known as "hot pots," at Mammoth Hot Springs in Yellowstone National Park.

Publishing Company, which used a photolithographic process to make color images from black-and-white photos. Jackson was named president of the firm in 1924 and added a large stock of negatives to its files. In his early nineties he turned to landscape painting and completed a set of murals of the Old West for the new headquarters of the U.S. DEPARTMENT OF THE INTERIOR in Washington, D.C. ☞ *also* PHOTOGRAPHERS

Thomas Jefferson

Thomas Jefferson's presidency (1801–9) was responsible for many policies critical to the development of the new republic, but the master stroke of his administration was the 1803 purchase of Louisiana from France. Acquisition of the roughly 800,000-square-mile tract, which extended north to the British possessions in Canada, west to the CONTINENTAL DIVIDE, and southwest to Spanish claims, was the pivotal piece in a program of western territorial expansion. By acquiring the western Mississippi drainage, Jefferson (1743–1826) both doubled the national domain and secured America's foothold in the trans-Mississippi West.

The historian Stephen Ambrose maintains in his biography of Meriwether Lewis (1774–1809), *Undaunted Courage* (1997), that mapping the West was the important first step in satisfying Jefferson's dream to create "a peaceable kingdom through persuasion and trade." Indeed, Jefferson had been promoting exploration of the trans-Mississippi since Captain Robert Gray (1755–1806) had discovered the Pacific outlet of the Columbia River in 1792 (in present-day Oregon) and precisely recorded the country's western limits for the first time. In addition to commissioning the Lewis and Clark expedition into the Louisiana Territory (☞ CORPS OF DISCOVERY), Jefferson also promoted explorations of the Mississippi and Arkansas Rivers and the ROCKY MOUNTAINS. Moreover, he was so keen to find a trade route to the Pacific that he had persuaded Congress to secretly appropriate the $2,500 for the Lewis and Clark expedition ($38,000 was actually spent) months before he even knew that the nation would be able to acquire the territory.

A prime vision of Jefferson's presidency was in fact a unified nation extending from the Atlantic to the Pacific. In his imagination the Great Plains would serve as a kind of gigantic reservation for Indians, who would be taught to drop their guns and tomahawks and farm. White pioneers could settle across the northern territories of Ohio, Indiana, and Illinois (conveniently emptied of Indians), ensuring the neat, inexorable progression of the frontier West while forging a harmonious national whole.

Despite the bargain price of $15 million for Louisiana, Jefferson was widely criticized for the purchase. His political foes, the anti-West Federalists, accused him of abusing his executive power and derided the folly of paying hard cash for land no one knew anything about. The *Columbian Centinel and Massachusetts Federalist* argued that America had bought "an immense wilderness for the purpose of cultivating it with the labor of slaves." That wilderness may have literally constituted the western half of the Mississippi drainage, but Ambrose points out that possessing those 600 million acres ultimately endowed the new republic with the entire country west to the Pacific. This is partly because the Louisiana Purchase forced the colonization of Texas and by extension the Texas-Mexico border disputes, ultimately leading to the acquisition of California. Claiming a stake in the Pacific Northwest, the Lewis and Clark expedition into the territory via the upper Missouri and Columbia Rivers in turn opened the way for the Oregon Trail. With the territory also came millions of acres of fertile farmland and an unimaginable storehouse of natural resources. The collective result was a country so strengthened materially and strategically that it was in a position to become an international power.

Avalon Project, Yale Law School ✉ 127 Wall Street, New Haven, CT 06511. ☏ 203-432-1600. ▢ www.yale.edu/lawweb/avalon/avalon.htm

Major Collections of Jefferson Papers

Jefferson National Expansion Memorial ✉ Library and Archives, 11 North Fourth Street, St. Louis, MO 63102. ☏ 314-655-1600. ▢ www.nps.gov/jeff/lib-title.htm

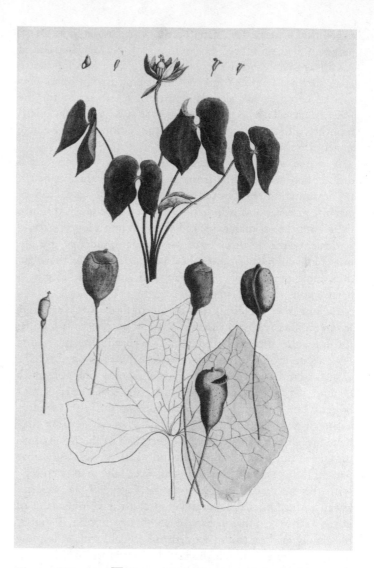

A botanical sketch, possibly by Pierre Turpin, illustrates *Jeffersonia diphylla*, a plant named by Benjamin Smith Barton in honor of Thomas Jefferson.

Library of Congress ✉ Manuscript Division, James Madison Building, Room LM 101, 101 Independence Avenue, SE, Washington, DC 20540-4680. ☎ 202-707-5387. ⌨ memory.loc.gov/ammem/mtjhtml/mtjhome.html

University of Virginia ✉ Alderman Library, Special Collections Department, Charlottesville, VA 22903. ☎ 804-924-3021. ⌨ www.lib.virginia.edu/speccol/tj/tjpapers.html

Williams Research Center, Historic New Orleans Collection ✉ 410 Chartres Street, New Orleans, LA 70130. ☎ 504-598-7171. ⌨ www.hnoc.org/willcent.htm

The kayak ("hunter's boat" in Inuit) is the traditional hunting boat of the Arctic peoples, who crafted the fast, maneuverable boats by lashing a narrow whalebone frame with sinew and sheathing the whole with sealskin. These silent, streamlined hunting vessels defined by low deck profiles were deepwater seagoing craft propelled by a double-bladed paddle for economy of motion. Regional designs evolved to suit the waters around Greenland, Baffin Island, the Aleutian Islands, and the Bering Strait. The hulls could be rounded or V shaped and the bows pointed or upswept in a curve. Ballast of up to 60 pounds increased seaworthiness.

Because the skin-covered Arctic kayak was probably devised by the Aleuts as early as 7000 B.C., it has been argued that the kayak, rather than the canoe, is the oldest and purest form of watercraft used by NATIVE AMERICANS. In a way it is a moot point: the kayak is technically defined as a type of canoe.

The first sport kayak was patented by a German architecture student, Alfred Heurich, around 1905 in Germany, where by the 1930s at least eighty manufacturers existed. Perceived as a daredevil activity limited to the most intrepid of outdoor adventurers, kayaking made its debut as an Olympic sport in 1936, but it took many decades before it gained a broad popular following on both fresh and salt water. Sport models of

Developed by Arctic peoples for hunting, the silent, deepwater kayak was usually designed to hold only one or two people—no deterrent to these young Inuit boys in Grantley Harbor, Teller, Alaska, about 1915.

the 1950s were first made of fiberglass, which was eventually superceded by lightweight polyethylene, the dominant kayak material by the 1980s. The first official sea kayaking meet was the 1981 Sea Kayaking Symposium in Damariscotta, Maine.
☞ *also* CANOES

Reading

📕 Steven M. Krauzer, *Kayaking: Whitewater and Touring Basics* (1995). 📕 Mark B. Solomon, *The Kayak Express!* (1995).

Knots

Knowing how to tie a few trustworthy knots is one of the most useful tools that you can bring along on a camping trip. The best way to learn a particular knot is to practice tying it at home until you know it by heart; then use it frequently.

Square Knot

This good, simple "bend" is used to tie together two lines. Don't use it under heavy loads, however, because it can distort its shape and come undone.

■ Place one line over the other and wrap the top line around front to back to front.
■ Recross the ends, and wrap the top line front to back, pulling the end through the loop and tightening by pulling gently on both ends.

Clove Hitch

Another light-duty knot, this simple hitch is good for tying a light item to a pack or for tethering a dog leash. It consists of two loops snug side by side.

■ Loop the end of the line around or through the object you are tying it to front to back to front.
■ Loop it again in the same direction, tucking the end under the crossover and snugly cinching it.

A more complex version of the clove hitch, this variation is often used to tighten slackened guylines, allowing you to do so without moving your tent anchors.

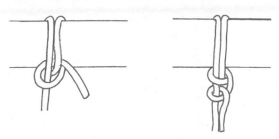

■ Pass the end of the line around or through the object you are tying it to and make a long loop.
■ Pass the end over the inert (standing part) of the line, turn twice, then pass the end up through the long loop.
■ Make one final turn around the standing part and snugly cinch it.

This compact hitch is a simple, strong, load-bearing knot and works well on slick synthetic lines. It is preferred for anything but the most extreme loads.

Buntline Hitch

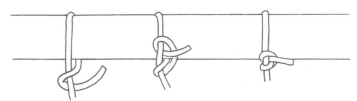

■ Pass the end of the line around or through the object you are tying it to, and then make a turn front to back around the standing part.
■ Bring the end above the turn and make a second loop front to back, snugly cinching it. Slide together the two turns.

This sailor's knot is one of the most reliable ways to make a large, secure loop.

Bowline

■ Form a small loop in the standing part, leaving a length of line to the end equal to twice the size of the large loop desired.
■ Pass the end up through the small loop and then around the standing part back to front to create a large loop.
■ Pull the end back down through the small loop and tightly cinch it.

Learned Societies

earned societies are devoted to scholarly study, preservation of materials and artifacts, and dissemination of research. Membership is usually—but not always—by election and based on distinction in a given field or profession. Members typically include scholars and academics, independent researchers, and museum curators. Some societies also offer institutional membership to libraries, archives, and similar institutions. They usually sponsor lectures, workshops, and seminars; fellowships are often given to visiting researchers and scholars. Despite membership restrictions, society libraries are generally open to researchers with legitimate credentials. This may involve presenting a letter of introduction or information about the research project in question.

American Academy of Arts and Sciences

Chartered in 1780 to "cultivate every art and science which tend to advance the interest, honor, dignity, and happiness of a free, independent, and virtuous people," the American Academy of Arts and Sciences counts among its members leading scientists, scholars, artists, and public leaders. Publications include *Daedelus*. Regional centers are located at the University of Chicago and University of California.

✉ Norton's Woods, 136 Irving Street, Cambridge, MA 02138. ☎ 617-576-5039.
🖳 www.amacad.org

Founded in 1812, the American Antiquarian Society preserves the largest single collection of printed materials—including books, almanacs, maps, newspapers, stereoscopic views, and postcards—relating to the history, literature, and culture of the country's first 250 years. The society is also the chief repository of American newspapers.

American Antiquarian Society

✉ 185 Salisbury Street, Worcester, MA 01609. (508-755-5221. 🖥 www.americanantiquarian.org

A research institution and think tank known for pioneering cartography and aerial photography standards, the American Geographical Society was founded in 1851 to produce and disseminate current, accurate geographical data and analysis. The oldest professional geographical organization in the country, it has sponsored expeditions to polar regions and compiled a leading library and collection of maps, charts, and instruments. By 1870 the library was recognized as the largest and most valuable of its type in the United States and is now housed at the Golda Meir Library of the University of Wisconsin–Milwaukee. Publications include *Geographical Review, Focus Magazine,* and *Ubique.*

American Geographical Society

✉ 120 Wall Street, Suite 100, New York, NY 10005. (212-422-5456. 🖥 www.amergeog.org

The American Historical Association was founded in 1884 and incorporated by Congress in 1889 "for the promotion of historical studies, the collection and preservation of historical manuscripts and for kindred purposes in the interest of American history and of history in America." A leader in the preservation of government records, the association was influential in the establishment of the National Archives. Publications include *Perspectives* and *American Historical Review.*

American Historical Association

✉ 400 A Street, SE, Washington, DC 20003. (202-544-2422. 🖥 www.theaha.org

The country's first learned society, this organization was founded in 1743 by Benjamin Franklin as an association "of the most ingenious and curious men." A cosponsor with the federal government of the Lewis and Clark expedition (☞ CORPS OF DISCOVERY), the society oversees a vast and significant assemblage of books, manuscripts (more than seven million), maps, and graphic materials relating to the history of science and early North American history, exploration, and culture.

American Philosophical Society

A sketch of a bobcat by Titian Ramsay Peale made in 1819 is among the holdings of the American Philosophical Society, founded in 1743 by Benjamin Franklin as the country's first learned society.

THOMAS JEFFERSON, an early society president, made it the unofficial national repository of scientific, museum, and library collections. Key holdings include Lewis and Clark journals and Jefferson papers; the collection is also strong in materials relating to NATIVE AMERICAN languages and ethnohistory and the scientific exploration of the American West (☞ SURVEYS). Publications include the journal *Proceedings.*

✉ Independence Mall East, 104 South Fifth Street, Philadelphia, PA 19106. ℂ 215-440-3400. ▯ www.amphilsoc.org

Organization of American Historians

The Organization of American Historians is the largest learned society devoted to promoting the study and teaching of the American past. Members include scholars, teachers, archivists, museum curators, and institutional subscribers. The organization provides guest speakers to the public through its lecture program and sponsors discussion of historical questions and controversies. Publications include the *Journal of American History.*

✉ 112 North Bryan Avenue, Bloomington, IN 47408. ℂ 812-855-7311. ▯ www.oah.org

Legislation

American legislative efforts to protect the environment have evolved over the years from statutes designed to save watersheds and provide recreational parks to laws directed more specifically at preserving wilderness in an untouched state and controlling pollutants, an issue that came to the fore in the 1960s. Western legislators have historically supported fewer federal restrictions on the use of PUBLIC LANDS because the majority of those lands are in the West.

Land Ordinance. To prepare for the sale of public lands, provided that the Northwest Territories be surveyed in six-mile-square townships along east-west and north-south survey lines. *1785*

Northwest Ordinance. Provided for a representative legislature in and division of the Northwest Territories; also forbade slavery and religious persecution. *1787*

Swamp and Overflowed Lands Act. Conveyed the whole of Florida's swamp-lands and Everglades to the state. *1850*

Homestead Act. Allowed citizens to claim 160 acres of land for $10 and receive full title after five years in exchange for cultivating it. *1862*

Yosemite Land Grant Bill. Granted the Yosemite Valley and Mariposa Big Tree Grove to California for preservation as a public park. *1864*

Mineral Land Act. Offered free land to spur development of mineral wealth. *1866*

Yellowstone Act. Established Yellowstone National Park as the first national park in the world, setting aside federal lands for public enjoyment. *1872*

Timber Culture Act. Allowed settlers to apply for an additional 160 acres if 40 acres were planted with trees within five years. *1873*

Desert Land Act. Allocated 640 acres to settlers in the Southwest at 25 cents an acre; title was contingent on irrigation and an additional $1. *1877*

Timber and Stone Act. Facilitated the purchase of nonmineral land at low prices so that miners and settlers could obtain timber and building materials from supplementary wildlands for construction on their sites. *1878*

Yosemite Act. Created Yosemite National Park. *1890*

Creative Act (Forest Reserve Act). Authorized the president to set apart forests "wholly or in part covered with timber or undergrowth, whether of commercial value or not, as public reservations." *1891*

Yellowstone Park Protection Act. Made illegal the killing of wildlife in Yellowstone National Park. *1894*

Forest Management Act (Forest Reserve Organic Administration Act). Outlined protection and development of forests, regulated cutting, and gave the president the power to modify executive orders regarding national forests. *1897*

Scripper Act (Lieu-Land Clause, Forest Management Act). Provided that patented claims within forest reserves and Indian reservations could be exchanged for an equal area of vacant public domain elsewhere.

Water reclamation to aid settlement of the arid western states was authorized by the 1902 Reclamation Act. One of the most famous Bureau of Reclamation projects is the Hoover Dam (1935) (seen from its crest), located downstream from the Grand Canyon on the Colorado River. To ensure a "damless" Grand Canyon, a 1968 statute precluded dams on the Colorado River between the Hoover and the controversial Glen Canyon Dam (1963).

1900   **Lacey Act.** The first federal law protecting game; supported state laws against commercial hunting of wildlife.

1902   **Newlands Act.** Withdrew areas of water supply from future settlement.

Reclamation Act. Authorized the secretary of the interior to administer a reclamation program to provide year-round irrigation water to seventeen western states.

1906   **Antiquities Act.** Authorized presidential designation of national monuments and established an archaeological excavation and research program.

1910   **Pickett Act.** Permitted the president to temporarily withdraw any public lands from settlement, sale, or entry to allow classification for other public purposes.

1911   **Weeks Forest Purchase Act.** Gave the federal government its first power to expand the National Forest System by acquiring private forest lands in the eastern headwaters of navigable streams to protect watersheds.

1913   **Weeks-McLean Act.** Assigned responsibility for migratory game birds to the federal government, providing the basis for legislation to protect waterfowl and shorebirds.

Migratory Bird Act. Gave the secretary of agriculture the authority to adopt regulations for closed seasons.

National Park Service Organic Act. Created the National Park Service to con-   *1916*
serve the scenery, natural and historic objects, and wildlife in national parks.

Migratory Bird Treaty Act. Mandated bag limits and hunting seasons for   *1918*
migratory birds and made it unlawful to trade in migratory birds, feathers, parts,
nests, or eggs.

Mineral Leasing Act. Provided for the lease of lands for exploration and pro-   *1920*
curement of certain minerals, including oil and gas.

Clarke-McNary Act. Amended the Weeks Act (1911) to permit federal purchase   *1924*
of land valuable for timber production and watershed protection; authorized federal assistance for state and private forestry.

Migratory Bird Conservation Act. Established a national system of waterfowl   *1929*
refuges.

Reorganization Act. Transferred national memorials, parks, and monuments to   *1933*
the National Park Service, virtually doubling the size of the agency.

Indian Reorganization Act (Wheeler-Howard Act). Conserved Indian lands   *1934*
and returned surplus lands to tribal ownership with certain provisions; established a credit system for Native Americans and extended to them the right to
form businesses; granted certain rights of home rule; and provided for vocational
education.

Taylor Grazing Act. Established the first regulations for grazing on public
lands through use of permits; gave the U.S. Department of the Interior responsibility for management of the nonreserved public domain for grazing and related
purposes.

When Edward S. Curtis
published *Custer's
Crow Scouts* about 1907,
the country was still
a generation away from
major legislation to
protect Native American
interests. The Indian
Reorganization Act con-
serving Indian lands
was passed in 1934.

1934	**Duck Stamp Act.** Raised revenues for the purchase of migratory bird habitats.
	Fish and Wildlife Coordination Act. Authorized federal water agencies to purchase lands associated with water-use projects to enhance wildlife and fish habitats.
1935	**Historic Sites, Buildings, and Antiquities Act.** Declared a national preservation policy and established a national landmarks program.
1936	**Park, Parkway, and Recreation Area Study Act.** Enabled the National Park Service to coordinate parkways and facilities at federal, state, and local levels.
1937	**Federal Aid in Wildlife Restoration Act (Pittman-Robertson Act).** Provided aid to states for wildlife management and research as well as land acquisition.
1940	**Bankhead-Jones Farm Tenant Act.** Allowed certain lands to be designated by executive order for management as wildlife refuges.
	Bald Eagle Protection Act. Prohibited the import, export, taking, selling, purchase, and barter of bald eagles.
1949	**National Trust Act.** Chartered the private National Trust for Historic Preservation.
1955	**Air Pollution Control Act.** Identified air pollution as a national problem.
1956	**Fish and Wildlife Act.** Set a comprehensive national fish and wildlife policy and broadened the authority to develop refuges.
1959	**Wild Horse Annie Bill.** Made illegal the use of airplanes to hunt wild horses on federal land.
1960	**Multiple Use Sustained Yield Act.** Established multiple use as the National Forest System management policy and directed the secretary of agriculture to promote logging up to the level of sustained yield; redefined the purpose of the national forests to include recreation, wildlife, fishing, hunting, and soil conservation.
	Bald and Golden Eagle Protection Act. Extended protection to golden eagles.
1963	**Clean Air Act.** Set emission standards for power plants and steel mills.
	National Outdoor Recreation Act. Declared a national policy to support recreation activities in a public-private partnership under National Park Service leadership.
1964	**Wilderness Act.** Established the National Wilderness Preservation System as an overlay designated by Congress that can be applied to any qualified federal public land; laid the foundation for the system with 9.1 million acres within the national forests, to be supplemented with lands from national parks and wildlife refuges.

Major federal legislation concerning national forest land began with the 1897 Forest Management Act. National policy favors commercial interests in all national forests, including Oregon's Willamette, photographed in 1942 by Russell Lee for the Farm Security Administration. Wilderness areas located within the National Forest System are designated under the 1964 Wilderness Act.

Land and Water Conservation Fund Act. Authorized federal recreation and land-management agencies to acquire land for outdoor recreation and created a fund to aid federal and state purchases of park lands and their conservation in perpetuity.

1965

Endangered Species Act. Provided for the federal protection of endangered and threatened species on a discretionary basis only.

1966

National Historic Preservation Act. Established the Advisory Council on Historic Preservation to advise the government on historic preservation issues; required federal agencies to consider the effects of their actions on historic properties.

National Wildlife Refuge System Administration Act. Established the National Wildlife Refuge System.

National Trails System Act. Established the National Trails System.

1968

National Wild and Scenic Rivers Act. Established the National Wild and Scenic Rivers System.

National Environmental Policy Act. Required systematic analysis of major federal actions, including consideration of all reasonable alternatives and description of impacts; also called for a Council on Environmental Quality.

1969

1969   **Endangered Species Conservation Act.** Amended the Endangered Species Act (1966) to prohibit importation of species threatened with extinction worldwide.

1970   **Clean Air Act.** Tightened standards for auto emissions.

Environmental Education Act. Created the Office of Environmental Education to develop education curricula and train teachers (eliminated in the 1980s).

Environmental Quality Improvement Act. Ensured that federal public works agencies follow existing law; created the Office of Environmental Quality to provide professional and administrative staff for the Council on Environmental Quality.

General Authorities Act. Consolidated all areas administered by the National Park Service into one National Park System.

1971   **Alaska Native Claims Settlement Act.** Withdrew "national interest" lands earmarked for future preservation and called for a $1 billion appropriation and a 44-million-acre allotment to Alaska natives to settle aboriginal land claims.

Wild Free-Roaming Horse and Burro Act. Mandated the management and humane care of wild horses and burros on public lands.

1972   **Clean Water Act.** Set objectives for restoring and maintaining the chemical, physical, and biological integrity of the nation's waters.

Great Lakes Water Quality Agreement. Authorized cleanup of the Great Lakes.

Marine Mammal Protection Act. Stopped the taking and importing of marine mammals such as polar bears, sea otters, manatees, whales, porpoises, seals, and sea lions.

Water Pollution Control Act. Regulated pollutant discharges into U.S. waters, allowing the Environmental Protection Agency to set standards on an industry basis.

The 1862 Homestead Act inadvertently led to oversettlement of the prairies. Some fifty-five grassland species are listed as endangered or threatened under the 1966, 1969, and 1973 Endangered Species Acts, including prairie dogs, depicted in their ecosystem by Alfred Sully.

Endangered Species Act. Enhanced the protection, restoration, and propagation of threatened plants, fish, and other wildlife; their habitats; and their ecosystems.   *1973*

Forest and Rangeland Renewable Resources Planning Act. Provided for periodic assessment by the secretary of agriculture of forest and rangeland resources; required updating every ten years after 1979.   *1974*

Archaeological and Historic Preservation Act. Mandated that federal construction projects and federally licensed activities protect archaeological relics.

Eastern Wilderness Areas Act. Added sixteen areas east of the 100th meridian to the National Wilderness Preservation System; also allowed condemnation of private lands and authorized funding to purchase private property.   *1975*

Federal Land Policy and Management Act. Provided that public lands be retained in federal ownership unless disposal of a parcel will serve the national interest; mandated the management of public rangelands; and allowed the removal of wild free-roaming horses and burros that pose a threat to themselves and their habitat.   *1976*

National Forest Management Act. Required that the U.S. Forest Service issue a comprehensive management plan every ten to fifteen years for each national forest.

Homestead Act (1862) repealed.

Clean Water Act. Amended the Water Pollution Control Act (1972), focusing on toxic pollutants.   *1977*

Amendments to Clean Air Act (1970). Targeted air quality and visibility in national parks and wilderness areas.

Archaeological Resources Protection Act. Supplemented the Antiquities Act (1906) with clearer definitions and penalties; secured protection for archaeological resources and sites on public and Indian lands; and fostered information exchange.   *1979*

Alaska National Interest Lands Conservation Act. Designated more than 100 million acres of parks, wildlife refuges, and wilderness areas.   *1980*

Comprehensive Environmental Response, Compensation, and Liability Act (Superfund). Created a tax on the chemical and petroleum industries; broadened federal authority to respond to hazards endangering health or the environment.

Endangered Species Act. Required federal agencies to ensure that their actions do not jeopardize endangered or threatened species or adversely affect critical habitat.   *1983*

1990   **Clean Air Act.** Built on previous legislation to establish a nationwide program to control air pollution and established National Ambient Air Quality Standards.

Oil Pollution Act. Strengthened the Environmental Protection Agency's ability to prevent and respond to catastrophic oil spills.

National Environmental Education Act. Reestablished an Office of Environmental Education as part of the Environmental Protection Agency.

Pollution Prevention Act. Encouraged pollutant reduction at the point of origin and set up an Office of Pollution Prevention at the Environmental Protection Agency.

Great Lakes Critical Programs Act. Amended the Clean Water Act (1977) by establishing pollution limits and cleanup deadlines for the Great Lakes.

1992   **Wild Bird Conservation Act.** Addressed problems concerning the international trade in wild birds.

1994   **California Desert Protection Act.** Brought the National Wilderness Preservation System to 104.7 million acres; established the Mojave National Preserve.

1997   **National Wildlife Refuge System Improvement Act.** Amended the National Wildlife Refuge System Administration Act (1966); set wildlife conservation as the top priority; and provided for more science-based management and long-term planning.

Aldo Leopold

Aldo Leopold (1887–1948) began to develop his philosophy of ecological conscience while working as a forest assistant in the desert Southwest after graduating from Yale Forestry School in 1909. He was the first champion of the preservation of ROADLESS AREAS in the New Mexico and Arizona Territories, where he identified six enormous regions of primitive wilderness (more than half a million acres each) for preservation as game refuges; only the GILA NATIONAL WILDERNESS AREA remains today in any substantial size. During his long career in forestry and refuge management, Leopold served as a cofounder of the Wilderness Society (☞ ADVOCATES) and in 1933 was appointed professor at the University of Wisconsin, where he taught the nation's first graduate course in game management.

Like FREDERICK JACKSON TURNER, Leopold identified being American with the character-building pioneer experience, and he failed to see the wisdom of preserving our cultural institutions without preserving the wildness that produced this "indigenous part of our Americanism." His great literary

legacy is *A Sand County Almanac*, a compendium of essays written for such periodicals as *American Forests*, *Journal of Forestry*, and *Journal of Wildlife Management* that was published posthumously in 1949. The central thesis of this body of work is Leopold's "land ethic," which tests the importance of wilderness according to ecological principles that recognize the complexity of natural systems and humankind's place in them. "The land ethic simply enlarges the boundaries of the community to include soils, waters, plants, and animals, or collectively: the Land," wrote Leopold. "We abuse land because we regard it as a commodity belonging to us. When we see land as a community to which we belong, we may begin to use it with love and respect."

Aldo Leopold, seen at work outdoors on a bench-desk of his own design, believed that the "richest values of wilderness lie not in the days of Daniel Boone, nor even in the present, but rather in the future."

📖 *Game Management* (1933). *A Sand County Almanac, and Sketches Here and There* (1949). *Aldo Leopold's Wilderness: Selected Early Writings* (1993).

Selected Works

Libraries

Public and university libraries house significant collections concerning American settlement, arts and letters, environmental studies, and westward expansion. Academic libraries may require permission to use their collections but are usually open to legitimate researchers.

Beinecke Library

Mark Catesby's *Natural History of Carolina, Florida, and the Bahama Islands* (1731–43). with this drawing of a flying squirrel, is preserved at Yale University's Beinecke Library.

The celebrated Yale Collection of Western Americana consists of some 40,000 printed works, 2,000 manuscripts, thousands of photographs, and hundreds of artworks related to European exploration, history and culture of NATIVE AMERICANS, and settlement of the trans-Mississippi West. The collection includes a notable archive of American western art and photography (☞ PHOTOGRAPHERS). Native American materials are strong in early Indian grammars and texts. It also covers early Spanish exploration in America, includes the field notes and field maps of Lewis and Clark (☞ CORPS OF DISCOVERY), and contains records of the great western surveys (☞ SURVEYS), railroad development, travel history, DIME NOVELS, and manuscripts by JAMES FENIMORE COOPER, Vardis Fisher, and A. B. Guthrie.

✉ Yale University, 121 Wall Street, New Haven, CT 06511. ☏ 203-432-2972. 🖳 www.library.yale.edu/beinecke/blgwa

Boston Public Library

The library houses a significant collection of photographs by Carleton Watkins (especially his views of YOSEMITE VALLEY), Eadweard Muybridge, Alexander Gardner, Timothy O'Sullivan, and William Bell (photographer for the Wheeler Survey, 1871–74), Andrew Joseph Russell, WILLIAM HENRY JACKSON, and John K. Hillers (☞ PHOTOGRAPHERS, SURVEYS). The John A. Lewis Library of Americana contains rare books relating to colonial settlement and maps and atlases of the Americas from the sixteenth to the twentieth centuries. The vast Picture Research Collection contains 200,000 prints, engravings, and chromolithographs. The Walt Whitman Collection (Rare Books and Manuscripts) contains more than 300 volumes by and relating to WALT WHITMAN.

✉ 700 Boylston Street, Copley Square, Boston, MA 02117. ☏ 617-536-5400. 🖳 www.bpl.org

Environmental Science and Public Policy Archives

Collections at Harvard University include the Environmental Science and Public Policy Archives, which document the evolution of the environmental science and public policy movement from the mid-1960s to the present.

✉ Harvard University, Science Center, One Oxford Street, Cambridge, MA 02138. ☏ 617-496-6158. 🖳 hcl.harvard.edu/environment

Holdings cover forestry, ecology, environmental science, hydrology, plant physiology, and soil science.

✉ Harvard University, 324 North Main Street, Petersham, MA 01366. ☎ 978-724-3302. 🖥 Internet.edu/hfr

Harvard Forest Library

Some 5 million books, manuscripts, prints, maps, and other materials make this library one of the most complete archives in the country relating to Anglo-American civilization, beginning with the explorations of Columbus. Collections include papers of THOMAS JEFFERSON, concentrate on Indian history (☞ NATIVE AMERICANS), and serve as major repositories of material on westward expansion, the Mormons, Spanish settlement, and the history of the Pacific Northwest.

✉ 1151 Oxford Road, San Marino, CA 91108. ☎ 626-405-2100. 🖥 www.huntington.org

Huntington Library

The Library of Congress houses the largest and most comprehensive "accumulation of human expression" ever assembled. Chartered by an act of Congress in 1800, it has built a collection of 115 million items. Its holdings of maps, photographs, and print materials are probably the largest in the world; newspapers and gazettes are another strength. The Rare Book and Special Collections Division is built around THOMAS JEFFERSON's personal library, which was purchased by Congress in 1814. Other holdings in this division include the Dime Novel Collection (☞ DIME NOVELS), Henry Harisse Collection, materials concerning early American exploration, and Walt Whitman Collection (☞ WALT WHITMAN).

✉ 101 Independence Avenue, SE, Washington, DC 20540. ☎ 202-707-5000. 🖥 www.loc.gov

Library of Congress

Holdings cover western art, firearms, Indian history (☞ NATIVE AMERICANS), and natural history of the northern Rockies and Great Plains and include the Buffalo Bill Cody (☞ BUFFALO BILL) and Annie Oakley Collections, Cowboy Songs and Range Ballads Collection, and Yale Western Americana Series (7,000 volumes) on microfilm.

✉ Buffalo Bill Historical Center, 720 Sheriden Avenue, Cody, WY 82414. ☎ 307-587-4771. 🖥 www.bbhc.org

McCracken Research Library

Covering the history of the Louisiana Purchase and the American West, this 80,000–item archive is strong in western travel, exploration and river transportation, the American fur

Missouri Historical Society Research Collections

trade, Native American history (☞ NATIVE AMERICANS), and western art. Some 1,800 manuscript collections preserve papers of Lewis and Clark (☞ CORPS OF DISCOVERY) and THOMAS JEFFERSON, records of the American fur trade, and Missouri French and Spanish colonial archives. The Photographs and Prints Collection includes more than 430,000 images. There are also extensive ethnographic artifacts of the prehistoric Mississippi mound builders as well as artifacts of the Lewis and Clark expedition.

✉ 225 South Skinker Boulevard, St. Louis, MO 63105. ☎ 314-746-4599. 🖳 www. mohistory.org

Montana Historical Society

The Montana Historical Society, founded in 1865, is the oldest historical organization in the West. This official state archives has the largest collection of books, newspapers, and magazines relating to Montana, including the Teakle Collection of Ranching Literature. It also maintains a Charles Russell (☞ WESTERN ILLUSTRATORS) art gallery. Publications include *The Magazine of Western History*.

✉ 225 North Roberts, Helena, MT 59620. ☎ 406-444-2694. 🖳 www.his.state. mt.us

National Archives and Records Administration

An independent federal agency responsible for all federal records, this national strongbox consists of thirty-three facilities and national branches, including the main branch in Washington, D.C. Together they preserve more than 4 billion paper documents; 5.3 million still photographs; 5 million maps, charts, and architectural drawings; 2,000 sound recordings; 91 million feet of motion picture film; and 7,600 computer data sets. Among the holdings are the papers of the Continental Congress, historical correspondence, congressional records, and records of federal agencies deemed to be of "enduring value."

✉ 700 Pennsylvania Avenue, NW, Washington, DC 20408. ☎ 202-501-5000. 🖳 www.nara.gov

National Museum of American History Library

This library, a branch of several Smithsonian libraries, houses more than 120,000 books and 45,000 volumes of bound serials on the history of science and technology in America.

✉ Smithsonian Institution, Fourteenth Street and Constitution Avenue, NW, Washington, DC 20560. ☎ 202-357-2700. 🖳 www.sil.si.edu/Branches/nmah-hp.htm

Established in 1999, the library holds works in natural history disciplines. A major strength is its collection of nineteenth-century publications resulting from voyages and expeditions.

Natural History Rare Book Library

✉ National Museum of Natural History, Smithsonian Institution, Tenth Street and Constitution Avenue, NW, Washington, DC 20560. ☎ 202-357-2700. 🖥 www.mnh.si.edu

The New York Public Library's holdings include an 1854–55 report to Congress on a railroad survey through California and Oregon. J. S. Newberry's *Manzanita* illustrated one botanical species described as "among the most magnificent in the world."

The I. N. Phelps Stokes Collection of American Historical Prints comprises more than 800 prints and drawings of town views and historical scenes. The Rare Book Division is particularly strong in Americana before 1801, including eighteenth-century newspapers and periodicals, notable collections of Isaak Walton's *Compleat Angler*, the Oscar Lion Collection of Walt Whitman (☞ WALT WHITMAN), and the Beadle and Adams Collections of DIME NOVELS. More than 3,000 collections in the Manuscripts and Archives Division preserve the papers of WASHINGTON IRVING, WILLIAM CULLEN BRYANT, and Nathaniel Hawthorne; the Henry E. and Albert A. Berg Collection of English and American Literature is one of the country's best collections of manuscripts, rare books, and letters, representing RALPH WALDO EMERSON and HENRY DAVID THOREAU, as well as Irving, Whitman, and Hawthorne.

New York Public Library

✉ Forty-second Street and Fifth Avenue, New York, NY 10018. ☎ 212-930-0830. 🖥 www.nypl.org/research/chss/spe/rbk/mss.html

The Everett T. Graff Collection of Western Americana makes the Newberry one of the world's premier libraries for the study of the American West. Another outstanding archive is the Edward E. Ayer Collection, which contains more than 130,000 volumes, 2,000 maps, 500 atlases, 6,000 photographs,

Newberry Library

and 3,500 photographs and paintings documenting Native American history and culture (☞ NATIVE AMERICANS). The D'Arcy McNickle Center for American Indian History, founded in 1972, encourages use of the Newberry collections on Indians and offers fellowships and colloquia.

✉ 60 Walton Street, Chicago, IL 60610. ☎ 312-943-9090. 💻 www. newberry.org

St. Louis Mercantile Library

Founded in 1846, the St. Louis Mercantile Library is the oldest library west of the Mississippi River. This major repository of western Americana houses archives relating to the Mississippi River valley and its exploration, rail transportation, the fur trade, and major collections of western art representing such artists as Karl Bodmer, George Caleb Bingham, George Catlin, Charles Russell, and Frederic Remington (☞ FRONTIER GENRE PAINTERS, WESTERN ILLUSTRATORS). The Norbury Wayman Collection is an exceptional resource for maps, guidebooks, and ephemera concerning the United States.

✉ University of Missouri–St. Louis, 8001 Natural Bridge Road, St. Louis, MO 63121. ☎ 314-516-7240. 💻 www.library.wustl.edu.units/spec/archives/aslaa/directory/mercantile.htm

Stephen H. Hart Library

This library contains more than 45,000 books and manuscripts covering major western topics.

✉ Colorado Historical Society, 1300 Broadway, Denver, CO 80203. ☎ 303-866-3682. 💻 www.history.state.co.us/home.htm

Wisconsin State Historical Society Library

Wisconsin's historical society, established in 1846, has received continuous public funding longer than any other state historical society. It is charged with advancing research on the trans-Allegheny West; the collection is strong in U.S. Census material and pre-1850 American periodicals and books and contains one of the country's largest newspaper archives (including Indian papers) (☞ NATIVE AMERICANS).

✉ 816 State Street, Madison, WI 53706. ☎ 607-264-6400. 💻 www.shsw.wisc.edu/library

Contact

National Library for the Environment ✉ National Council for Science and the Environment, 1725 K Street, NW, Suite 212, Washington, DC 20006. 💻 www.cnie.org
■ The library offers a comprehensive online library cataloguing information on environmental legislation, which includes a directory of educational resources, journals, and publications and an environmental yellow pages.

"After I married we moved across the valley westwards where we had to tough it. I had toughed it at my father's and now I had to tough it here. Only a half acre was cleared. There we lived for five years without a stove or fireplace. We absolutely had no chimney. We burned wood right against the logs of the cabin and when they got afire we put it out."

Mrs. Adolphus Sheldon, quoted in
Home Sketches of Essex County (N.Y.) (1858)

"It is a sturdy structure that can be either primitive or pretentious without losing its frontier feeling. The ax, the auger, and the saw are the simple tools with which it is built and furnished. Its timbers sprang from the soil on which it stands and of which it remains a part."

William Bruette, ed., *Log Camps and Cabins: How to Build and Furnish Them (By Practical Campers and Woodsmen)* (1934)

Log Cabins

The log cabin is the only type of domestic architecture to span every generation of American history—an icon of design democracy that transcended class and economic lines to become a universally understood paradigm of frontier values and perhaps of American culture itself. Conventional log cabin construction, in which the logs are laid up horizontally and notched at the corners, is both a Swedish and a German legacy. Introduced independently to the Atlantic seaboard by settlers of both nationalities, this was one of the first construction techniques used by Europeans on the coast. The Swedes brought the log cabin to the

A symbol of frontier life, the log cabin became a universally recognized icon of wilderness resourcefulness. *An American Log-house* appeared in Georges Henri Victor Collot's *Voyage dans l'Amérique septentrionale ...* (1826).

Delaware River area in the 1630s, while German-speaking settlers in the Mid-Atlantic were using traditional building methods from such forested regions in Germany as Schwarzwald and Odenwald. Adapting the technique from the Swedes and Germans, the Scots-Irish were the first English-speaking immigrants to use log construction extensively in the colonies, spreading the type south and west. Their low-slung "improvement cabins" were devised to lay claim to property and amounted to nothing more than a sleeping shelter.

Saddlebags, Dog-trots, and More

Log cabin types, chinking and notching techniques, and timbers (usually oak, black ash, spruce, or chestnut) developed according to climate, location, and cultural patterns. The essential form was usually a variation on the single-room, or pen, unit, because the dimensions of that room were necessarily dictated by the length of the logs. In a true log cabin, constructed without upright support posts, the horizontal timbers are locked into place by the notched ends and bear the full weight of construction, and the length of the logs dictates the room measurements. That same principle limits the size of window and door openings: a large opening would not provide the necessary support for the logs laid above it.

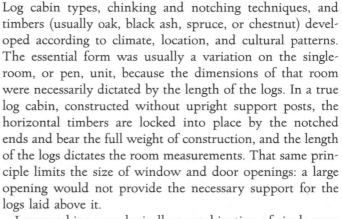

Larger cabins were logically a combination of single pens joined as units. Two pens flanking a chimney makes a "saddlebag," while two pens flanking a breezeway form a "dog-trot" or a "possum-trot": a ventilated southern form that originated in southeastern Tennessee and spread to Florida, west to Texas, and along the Tennessee River into western Kentucky, Missouri, Arkansas, and eventually on to Ohio, Indiana, and Illinois. The Swedish-Finnish form of the upper Midwest was a triple-pen variant. In the Finnish model, skillfully dressed and squared logs were often laid so tightly flush that no chinking was used. Cabins of dressed logs are better survivors of the frontier period than those of bark-covered round logs because the bark hastened timber deterioration.

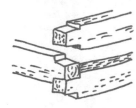

The saddle notch (above) permits round timbers to fit snugly, while the square notch (below) was designed for dressed timbers. Logs were held in place by their own weight.

Log construction, also used for farm outbuildings and saunas, was not limited to backwoods settlements or to these basic forms, however. Quite sophisticated 2½-story houses in the classic hall-and-parlor plan were built of squared-and-chinked logs, with the rooms divided by batten partitions.

Symbol of the American Frontier

Part of the log cabin's unique position in American history lies in its transition from a building form used by necessity to one used by choice. As frontier symbol, it signified courage and determination in the face of hardship. As early as 1840, Daniel Webster was apologizing for *not* being born in one; DANIEL BOONE and Honest Abe had better luck. The log cabin figured prominently in the presidential campaigns of William Henry Harrison (1840), Abraham Lincoln (1860), and James Garfield (1880). By the late 1800s a string of presidential biographies known as the Log Cabin Series established the cabin in the national consciousness as the proper birthplace for the upstanding American. County histories, which were particularly popular in the Midwest in the late nineteenth century, spread the iconography with lavish illustrations in which the log cabin was shown as the foundation for expanding farmsteads.

During the same period, the emerging popularity of hunting and ANGLING endowed the cabin with a new role as a backwoods retreat. Forerunners of elaborate GREAT CAMPS, hunting and fishing cabins were built as early as the 1840s in the eastern woodlands. From the post–Civil War period through the 1930s, pattern books made simple plans for woodland cabins and furnishings widely available to the public. The federal government also published manuals on rustic cabin building (☞ PARK ARCHITECTURE) to promote the sale of timber offered at cheap stumpage rates. During the Great Depression the log cabin image tarnished somewhat as the building type became a symbol of poverty, associated with the run-down sharecroppers' cabin of the American South and with Appalachia's backwoods poor. Nevertheless, the association with good values and frontier spirit ran deeper. Promoters of the building type extolled it as a refuge from encroaching urbanization. "The cabin in the forest, on the banks of a quiet lake or buried in the wilderness back of beyond," claimed one pattern book of the 1930s, "is an expression of man's desire to escape the exactins of civilization and secure rest and seclusion by a return to the primitive."

📖 Harold R. Shurtleff, *The Log Cabin Myth: A Study of the Early Dwellings of the English Colonists in North America* (1939, 1967). 📖 Clinton A. Weslager, *The Log Cabin in America: From Pioneer Days to the Present* (1969). 📖 Terry G. Jordan, *American Log Buildings: An Old World Heritage* (1985).

Reading

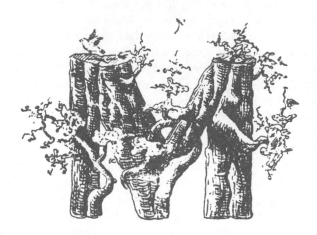

Maps and Navigation

"Maps—Draw these on tracing linen which will stand wear. Use Indian waterproof ink, as otherwise, if the map gets wet, very serious results may follow, especially if the route is through uninhabited country."

James Edmund Jones, *Camping and Canoeing: What to Take, How to Travel, How to Cook, Where to Go* (1903)

Opposite: This map showing the Columbia River valley was used in the frontispiece of Meriwether Lewis's 1814 *History of the Expedition*. . . . Lewis and William Clark were such skilled navigators that they could separate for days at a time and then reconvene at another location in territory never before traveled by them— or any other white man.

The basic tools of navigation are a map and a compass; the basic rule is to practice with these tools before setting out into the wilds. Study a good manual to learn how to calculate magnetic declination, determine bearings, and plot routes. You might even consider taking a course; many hiking clubs offer weekend seminars. Maps are available at the local forest ranger's office and in published trail guides. Guidebooks to a particular region can be found in local bookstores and at camping retailers. Overnight trips or hikes in DESERTS (☞ DESERT HIKING) and any areas without well-marked trails require topographical maps, which are available from the U.S. GEOLOGICAL SURVEY. Most USGS "topo" maps, which come in sheets, use a scale of 1:24,000; these so-called 7.5-minute maps cover an area of about 6-by-8 miles, which means a lot of them are needed if you are hiking over a large area. (ALASKA is mapped in a larger 15-minute scale.) However, be aware that many USGS maps have not been updated in the last twenty-five years; while the actual topography in a given area likely hasn't changed much, the trail roads and magnetic declination often have. ☞ *also* HIKING, SURVIVAL STRATEGIES

■ No matter where you are, stay aware of your surroundings, watch diligently for the markers known as trail blazes, and note landmarks such as unusual trees and boulders.

■ If you start to doubt the trail or your bearings, don't keep marching onward and get yourself into a bigger mess. Stop immediately and sort out the situation.

■ If you do get lost, don't panic. Stay put and confer with your hiking partners. Look around and assess the terrain. Then check your map and trail guide to determine where you were when you last knew for sure where you were. Thinking through what you've done since then will often get you unlost.

*Keeping
Your Bearings*

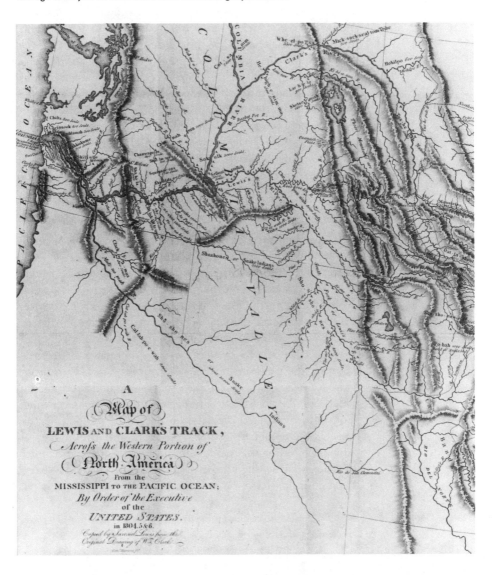

A
Map of
LEWIS AND CLARK'S TRACK,
Across the Western Portion of
North America
From the
MISSISSIPPI TO THE PACIFIC OCEAN;
By Order of the Executive
of the
UNITED STATES,
in 1804.5.&6.
Copied by Samuel Lewis from the
Original Drawing of W. Clark

■ If that doesn't work, mark the spot on the map where you last knew with certainty where you were, estimate the distance you've gone since then, and draw a circle using that as a radius. You are almost surely somewhere within that circle. Try correlating any unusual features around you with those marked on your topographical map so that you can pinpoint your location.

The Compass

No hiker—day hiker or backpacker—should be without a compass. By far the most common type used for hiking is the orienteering card compass, which has a flat rectangular plastic base plate marked on the edges with scales in metric and decimal systems. Look for a durable model with a "floating" liquid-filled housing (to minimize needle jamming), luminous arrows, and a rotating bezel ring. The base card should be as detailed as possible, showing numerous intercardinal directions. Deluxe models come with a mirror split with a sighting line for easier sighting and bearing.

If by some chance you find yourself without a compass and get turned around, use this old woodsman's trick: Set your watch to standard time and aim the hour hand of your watch at the sun. In the Northern Hemisphere, south always lies halfway between the hour hand and 12:00. Before 6 A.M. and after 6 P.M., south lies halfway between the hour hand and 12:00 using the longer way around the clockface. If you have a digital watch, note the time, draw a clock face on the ground with a stick, and then apply this method using the drawing.

Magnetic Declination

Also known as deviation, magnetic declination refers to the difference in degrees between true (polar) north and magnetic north (the point in Canada where magnetic lines of force come together). This means that when the magnetic needle of a compass points north, it is really pointing a bit east or west of true north. You need to account for this difference, because the north marked on most maps is true north. To adjust for this deviation and synchronize your compass and map, you must add or subtract the difference in degrees between the two norths. That difference is noted on topographical maps, although it may not be absolutely accurate on older maps because the magnetic fields can change over time. Consult the magnetic field guide published periodically by the U.S. Geological Survey. Some compasses have an adjustable setting for the deviation, but you must remember to change that setting when you go to a different area because the amount of deviation will change.

Using a Compass

■ To use a compass, first hold it level and turn the dial so that the magnetic needle aligns with the north indicator.

■ To adjust for deviation, turn the dial according to the degrees of magnetic declination indicated on your map. Use a left (counterclockwise) turn of the dial for eastward deviation, a right (clockwise) turn for westward deviation (a good way to remember this is "East is least; West is best"). For example, if the declination is 10 degrees east, move the dial left until the magnetic needle points to 10 degrees. If the declination is 10 degrees west, move the dial right until the magnetic needle points to 350 degrees. Take your bearings with north set at this adjusted setting.

■ To orient the compass with the map, start with an unadjusted compass. Align the bearing arrow on the compass base (indicating direction of travel) with true north on the dial. Place the compass on the map with the bearing arrow aligned with north as marked on the map. Holding the map and compass together, turn them as a unit until the magnetic needle points to the number on the dial that indicates the declination (deviation), or adjustment, for magnetic north. For example, if your map indicates 10 degrees east for declination, stop when the needle points to 10 on the compass. For 10 degrees west declination, stop when the needle points to 350 degrees. The compass, landscape, and the map are now in sync.

■ Be aware that magnetic disturbances can create anomalies in a compass reading. If you suspect this, check to see if something you are wearing, such as a watch, might be the problem. Other possibilities are snowmobiles, cars, radios, and power lines. If the needle starts to act sluggish, a static charge is probably causing the problem; rub a little water over the housing to get rid of the charge. Sometimes bubbles form in high altitudes or at low temperatures, but these should not affect compass function and will disappear when you return to a lower altitude or when the compass warms up.

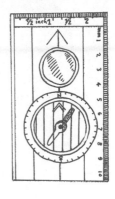

A card compass should show inches and millimeters and an arrow indicating the direction. This line, on the compass base, is used when aligning the compass with a map and for taking bearings.

Waterproofing Maps

Waterproofing maps is still a good idea, but these days there are easier ways to do it than with "Indian waterproof ink." Although commercial plastic map protectors are now available, many people choose the less expensive option of a sealable freezer bag, which can be reinforced along the edges with waterproof tape. Either option allows you to take the map out of the covering to make notations. You can also protect a map with see-through contact paper, as well as with liquid and spray-on varnishes made specifically for this purpose. To make notes, you will need an indelible marker.

Global Positioning System

This network of U.S. military satellites sends signals that can be used to determine accurate bearings. Handheld GPS receivers are designed to pick up signals from a minimum of three satellites, expressing your position as a pair of coordinates. You can also determine the distance and direction (only as the crow flies) to other points. These high-tech gizmos are useful for getting your bearings in conditions of extremely low visibility, such as in the dark of night, in heavy fog or snow, or in an area where topographical information is difficult to read. However, a GPS receiver does not function as a compass and does not read magnetic north. It can be used only to get you to another destination if you have those coordinates. It can supplement a map and compass but should not substitute for them.

Contacts

Earth Science Information Center ⊠ U.S. Geological Survey, 507 National Center, 12201 Sunrise Valley Drive, Reston, VA 20192. ✆ 888-275-8747. 🖳 www.nwi.fws.gov/order_maps.htm
■ The U.S. Fish and Wildlife Service, National Wetlands Inventory, and U.S. Geological Survey's Earth Science Information Center have a cooperative agreement for the sale and distribution of National Wetlands Inventory maps.

National Geologic Map Database ⊠ Information Services Branch, U.S. Geological Survey, Box 25286, Denver Federal Center, Denver, CO 80225. ✆ 303-202-4700. 🖳 ngmdb.usgs.gov
■ This database catalogues paper and digital maps and related data for geology and earth resources, among other subjects. It also offers free state indexes of its detailed topographical maps, also available on CD-ROM.

Tennessee Valley Authority Map Store ⊠ 1101 Market Street, Chattanooga, TN 37402. ✆ 423-751-6277. 🖳 www.tva.gov/river/mapstore/index.htm
■ The central repository for TVA's mapping program offers current topographical maps, navigation charts, state maps, underwater contour maps, archaeological reports, historical records, aerial photographs, cadastral (survey) maps, and information on wildlife and game refuge areas.

U.S. Army Corps of Engineers ⊠ Navigation Data Center, 7701 Telegraph Road, Casey Building, Alexandria, VA 22315. ✆ 703-428-9061. 🖳 www.wrsc.usace.army.mil/ndc
■ The Corps, which is responsible for maintaining the nation's waterway system to ensure safe passage of commercial and recreational vessels, publishes nautical charts showing water depths and other navigation data.

U.S. Forest Service ⊠ U.S. Department of Agriculture, P.O. Box 96090, Washington, DC 20090-6090. ✆ 202-205-8333. 🖳 www.fs.fed.us/links/maps.shtml
■ The Forest Service offers detailed maps of U.S. forests by region: East, South, Southwest, Rocky Mountains, Pacific Northwest, and Pacific Southeast.

Web Sites

Delorme Maps and Eartha Maps. Offers detailed maps of the United States. 🖳 www.delorme.com

Global Positioning System Overview. Provides an overview of the GPS system. 🖳www.colorado.edu/geography/gcraft/notes/gps/gps_f.html

The Living Earth Satellite Views. Furnishes satellite views of the earth. 🖳 www.livingearth.com

Magellan Global Positioning. Sells satellite access products. 🖳 www.magellangps.com

National Geographic Map Machine. Provides a full range of maps. ⊟ www. plasma.nationalgeographic.com/mapmachine

📖 Glenn Randall, *Outward Bound Map and Compass Handbook* (1998). 📖 Bob Burns, *Wilderness Navigation* (1999). 📖 Cliff Jacobson, *Basic Essentials: Map and Compass* (1999). 📖 Calvin Rutstrum, *The Wilderness Route Finder* (2000).

Reading

George Perkins Marsh

Historians consider *Man and Nature: Physical Geography as Modified by Human Action* (1864) the single most important literary influence on the nineteenth-century environmental movement. This carefully reasoned argument by George Perkins Marsh (1801–82) of Woodstock, Vermont, a U.S. congressman from 1843 to 1849, against the indiscriminate abuse of natural resources offered the first systematic demonstration of environmental ethics. At a time when America's resources seemed limitless, Marsh asserted that their destruction presented a cataclysmic threat to the essential natural balance and was harmful to both nature and humans. To support the thesis that nature will keep adapting to its circumstances rather than revert to its original health and condition, he used the model of desertification in the eastern Mediterranean, where he had been an ambassador and where long-term abuse had dried out the once-fertile landscape.

He predicted the same outcome for the ADIRONDACK MOUNTAINS,

An 1888 photo by Seneca Ray Stoddard shows lumbermen at work in the Adirondacks. George Perkins Marsh had that region in mind when he wrote his groundbreaking *Man and Nature* (1864).

Vermont, and other heavily logged regions of America. Although Marsh supported scientific forestry and sustained-yield management (☞ CLEAR-CUTTING, FORESTS), he urged that primitive wilderness be set aside in national parks (☞ NATIONAL PARK SYSTEM). The book proved the main source for an 1873 study by the American Association for the Advancement of Science that eventually contributed to the formation of the NATIONAL FOREST SYSTEM. *Man and Nature* was particularly remarkable in its shift from the then-prevailing viewpoint that humans are somehow exempt from the rules of nature. Marsh did regard people as a higher order but charged them, as intelligent beings, with the moral responsibility for the world they inhabit.

Minerals Management Service

Established in 1982 under the U.S. DEPARTMENT OF THE INTERIOR, this agency manages mineral resources on the Outer Continental Shelf and collects and distributes revenues due the federal government from mineral extraction and mineral leases (on shore and offshore), which constitute one of the largest nontax sources of government income. Outer Continental Shelf production accounts for about 27 percent of the country's natural gas production and 20 percent of U.S. domestic oil production; about $3.5 billion is collected annually from offshore leases alone. In consultation with Congress, the twenty-three coastal states, local governments, environmental groups, and industry, the Minerals Management Service develops five-year oil- and gas-leasing programs and is responsible for follow-up inspections of offshore mineral operations.

Contact

Minerals Management Service ✉ U.S.Department of the Interior, 1849 C Street, NW, Room 4260, MS 4230, Washington, DC 20240-7000. ☎ 202-208-3985. 💻 www.mms.gov

Mountaineering

High altitude:
    8,000 to 14,000 feet
Very high altitude:
    14,000 to 18,000 feet
Extreme altitude:
    18,000 feet and above

The technical ice- and snow-climbing expertise intrinsic to true mountaineering is usually beyond the average hiker's scope, but that doesn't mean that you won't ever confront mountaineering conditions on a normal hike. The basic gear for mountaineering includes an ice ax, a helmet, rope, a harness, heavy boots, and crampons. If you think you might encounter snow fields or ice—both possible at high altitudes even in summer (☞ ICE SAFETY, SNOW CAMPING)—consider bringing some of these items, especially the heavy hiking boots and the toothlike crampons, which make it easier to walk and climb in snow and ice. (Models include in-step and full crampons, with various configurations of teeth, and either frame or strap-on bindings for attaching them to

A mountaineer climbing on the west side of Ensawkwatch Creek in Washington's North Cascades National Park hikes at elevations where jagged quartz mononite is exposed.

boots.) An ice ax is the mountaineer's tool for stopping a sliding fall on an icy slope, but one should never be carried or used without proper instruction first.

Hiking in higher elevations brings its special risks: altitude sickness, hypothermia, frostbite, and dehydration (☞ HEALTH AND FIRST AID). Although altitude sickness can come on at heights as low as 5,000 feet, people generally start to feel the effects of reduced oxygen at around 9,000 or 10,000 feet. At just 6,685 feet, Mount Mitchell in North Carolina, in the Black Mountains (☞ APPALACHIAN MOUNTAINS), is the tallest peak east of the Mississippi River, so chances are that most people hiking or skiing in the East will never experience the symptoms. Winter sports in the ROCKY MOUNTAINS, however, can take people as high as 12,000 feet. Mount Rainier in Washington (☞ CASCADE MOUNTAINS) soars 14,410 feet and is climbed by some six thousand persons a year; according to the National Outdoor Leadership School (☞ HIKING), more than half of those who approach the summit suffer from altitude sickness.

High-Altitude Risks

Every 1,000 feet of elevation gained is the equivalent of traveling 170 miles north. Because people generate body heat when they hike, they often think air temperatures are warmer than they actually are. It is critically important to dress and layer properly (☞ CLOTHING). When you begin to get cold, the

Exposure and Cold

instinctive response is to exercise to keep warm—yet this will tax energy reserves that are already compromised by a reduced blood supply to your extremities. When cold reaches the brain, as it does when hypothermia sets in, your reasoning powers are affected, but you are unaware of this. Loss of hand and body control then occurs, and chilling continues, making it difficult to put on mittens or work buttons and zippers, constantly exacerbating the problem.

Bushwhacking

Another consideration when mountain hiking is that you can lose the trail. This might happen because some higher trails are less traveled or less well maintained or because snow has covered up the route. For this and other good reasons, you should always have a good map, be familiar with orienteering, and understand how to take a bearing and pinpoint your location (☞ MAPS AND NAVIGATION). If you know where you are and what your destination is, you should be able to map a course between the two and get there by traveling cross-country. If you are uncertain where you are, match a prominent natural feature in your vicinity, such as a body of water or a long ridge, with one on your map. Or hike to a feature that you can see in the distance and determine its location on the map. In snowy conditions, check for a telltale depression in the snow, which may indicate the trail underneath. ☞ *also* AVALANCHES, GLACIERS, SURVIVAL STRATEGIES *and specific mountain ranges*

Dressing properly when venturing into high altitudes is critical to survival. This casual backpacker from a generation ago was able to get close to the south ridge of Davis Peak in Washington's North Cascades National Park.

Mountain Rescue Resources ✉ Mountain Rescue Association, P.O. Box 501, *Contact*
Poway, CA 92074. 🖥 www.mra.org

■ Founded in 1958, this volunteer program dedicated to saving lives through mountain-safety education and rescue at no taxpayer cost operates in twelve states: Arizona, California, Colorado, Idaho, Maryland, Nevada, New Mexico, Oregon, Pennsylvania, Utah, Vermont, and Washington. See its Web site for regional contact information.

John Muir

The contribution of the Scottish-born explorer John Muir (1838–1914) to the American environmental movement should not be measured solely by the number of articles (dozens) and books (seven) produced by this prolific spokesman for mountain and tree but also in the strength and eloquence of his personal wilderness philosophy. Although other contemporary writers addressed the subject, Muir can rightly be called the first real public advocate for wilderness preservation. Unlike his mentor RALPH WALDO EMERSON, whom he met in the YOSEMITE VALLEY in 1871, Muir was willing to immerse himself without qualification in the solitary life of the wilderness, and his encounters with earthquakes, bees, BEARS, AVALANCHES, tourists, breeding salmon, meadow larks, lava beds, and blizzards are legendary.

"Why should man value himself as more than a small part of the one great unit of creation?"

John Muir (1867)

Yet however much he wished to shed the "galling harness" of civilization, Muir also emerged from his lone adventures in the Yosemite Valley forests, SIERRA NEVADA RANGE, and ALASKA glacier fields (☞ GLACIERS) to persuade Americans that wilderness was a human necessity. For this he is considered the most important public and political influence in the history of environmentalism. It was Muir's petitioning, both in person and in print, that helped motivate Congress to establish Yosemite, Sequoia, GRAND CANYON, and Petrified National Forest as national parks (☞ NATIONAL PARK SYSTEM). He enjoyed a long friendship with JOHN BURROUGHS and helped their mutual friend THEODORE ROOSEVELT forge his progressive wilderness policy. He lobbied for federal legislation for national forests (☞ NATIONAL FOREST SYSTEM). He was a founder of the Sierra Club (1892) (☞ ADVOCATES) and served as its first president.

Muir's writing was accessible to the general reader because it spoke so plainly and genuinely from observation, thus expressing the inherent worth of whatever he described. His straightforward prose conveys the belief that nature ("lovely, invincible, glad") is the representation of divine harmony: God's work in its most complete and undisturbed form. Rock and tree are the ultimate scripture for her healing powers, and her rhythmic motions evidence of a grand and everlasting spectacle.

John Muir (right) and John Burroughs met in 1893 and became close friends. Their travels together included a trip to Alaska on the Harriman Expedition of 1899, when the two bearded naturalists were photographed out on Muir Glacier.

Selected Works

📖 *Picturesque California and the Region West of the Rocky Mountains, from Alaska to Mexico* (editor, 1888–90). *The Mountains of California* (1894). *Our National Parks* (1901). *Stickeen: The Story of a Dog* (1909). *My First Summer in the Sierra* (1911). *Edward Henry Harriman* (1911). *The Yosemite* (1912). *The Story of My Boyhood and Youth* (1913). *Letters to a Friend* (1915). *Stickeen: An Adventure with a Dog and a Glacier* (abridged version, 1915). *Travels in Alaska* (1915). *A Thousand-Mile Walk to the Gulf* (1916). *The Cruise of the Corwin* (1917). *Steep Trails* (1919). *John of the Mountains* (1938).

Contacts

John Muir National Historic Site ✉ 4202 Alhambra Avenue, Martinez, CA 94553. ☎ 925-228-8860. 🖥 www.nps.gov/jomu
■ This National Park Service site preserves the fruit ranch and adjoining woodlands where Muir lived from 1890 to 1914. It is supported in conjunction with the John Muir Memorial Association (🖥 fly.to/johnmuir).

University of the Pacific ✉ Department of Special Collections, University Library, Stockton, CA 95211. ☎ 209-946-2945. 🖥 jarl.cs.uop.edu/library/deptholmuir.html
■ The library houses a significant collection of Muir papers.

Web Site

The John Muir Exhibit. A comprehensive Sierra Club Web site posting the full texts of Muir's books, biographical information, and related links. 🖥 www.sierraclub.org/john_muir_exhibit.

Accounting for the majority of federal forest land in America, the National Forest System covers more than 191 million acres in forty-four states (a total of 8 percent of U.S. land area), the Virgin Islands, and Puerto Rico. It comprises 155 national forests, 20 NATIONAL GRASSLANDS, and 103 other units, including NATIONAL RECREATION AREAS, special research areas, and NATIONAL MONUMENTS. About one-third of the NATIONAL WILDERNESS PRESERVATION SYSTEM is also designated on national forest land. The entire system is managed by the U.S. FOREST SERVICE under the aegis of the U.S. DEPARTMENT OF AGRICULTURE, and the majority of the land is in the West. Nevertheless, the Forest Service administers more land in the East than all other federal agencies combined.

The National Forest System serves a combination of commercial, recreational, and conservation purposes. Timber production and the associated industries of lumber, plywood, veneer, and pulp and paper products are the main commercial enterprises. Recreation encompasses such activities as camping, fishing, hunting, and off-road vehicle use and snowmobiling, which are permitted in designated areas. Conservation efforts include "utilization" projects and other research areas targeted for soil-erosion studies, wildlife protection, and reforestation projects. The developed areas include campgrounds, swimming and boating facilities, resorts, observation

National Forest System

"Caring for the land and serving people."

U.S. Forest Service motto

areas, and visitor centers. Privately owned commercial concessions—such as gas stations, restaurants, lodgings, and ski resorts—are allowed under special-use permits and leasing arrangements. Regional management plans may also permit construction of private houses and other buildings on existing footprints, which is why such structures are often encountered in a national forest. ☞ *also* FORESTS, TREES

Early History

The first fifteen national forests, covering more than 13 million acres, were established between 1891 and 1893. Then known as forest reserves, these areas were designated by President Benjamin Harrison under the Forest Reserve Act (1891); Grover Cleveland followed with another 21 million acres. Passed largely through the efforts of JOHN MUIR, the Forest Reserve Act, a rider to a watershed protection bill known as the Creative Act, was the first federal legislation to have major implications for the protection of forest land in America by authorizing the president to set aside forests as public reserves even if logging was an option. The statute, however, made no provision for management or use, and the purpose

Despite the economic incentive to harvest trees, in 1994 the Clinton administration prohibited logging on about 4 million acres of old forests on federal lands in northern California, Oregon, and Washington (where this picture of a virgin timber stand was made around 1913). Previous administrations had earmarked about 3 million acres for protection.

of the reserves was unclear. The first federal legislation to establish statutory language providing management guidelines was the Forest Management Act (1897), also known as the Forest Reserve Organic Administration Act. While this law mandated improvement and protection for national forest land, it also called for a continuous supply of timber "for the use and necessity of citizens of the United States."

In 1905 the forest reserves were transferred from the Division of Forests (created in 1881) in the Land Office to the Agriculture Department. The designation was changed to "national forest" in 1907. The Weeks Forest Purchase Act (1911) authorized the government to purchase or trade woodlands to extend national forest land along the headwaters of navigable streams for watershed protection, thus permitting expansion of national forests in the East for the first time.

The forest system had a major growth spurt in this era under the administration of THEODORE ROOSEVELT, when 148 million acres of national forest were established. At the time national forest land was also reserved for buffalo-breeding grounds and other wildlife preserves (☞ BISON, NATIONAL WILDLIFE REFUGE SYSTEM) and for NATIONAL MONUMENTS. In all, twenty-one national monuments were set aside on national forest land before most were transferred to the NATIONAL PARK SYSTEM in 1933.

Forest Management

U.S. forest management policy historically has emphasized the active development of forest land through scientifically planned harvest and replanting programs. This approach was set by the Division of Forests in 1881 and vigorously pursued by the first forestry professionals, including Gifford Pinchot (1865–1946), who served as chief forester from 1898 to 1910. Working in close partnership with Theodore Roosevelt, Pinchot stressed the concept of forest conservation (managed use) as distinct from forest preservation (protection). Under this policy, commercial development of timber, water, grazing, mining, and other income-producing resources for the public benefit were all priorities.

The first official nod to recreational development came in 1915, when Congress authorized the Forest Service to lease forest land to private individuals and enterprises for the construction of vacation houses, resorts and hotels, campgrounds, and concessions. Focus on recreation increased in the 1930s under the leadership of Robert Marshall as head of the Division of Recreation and Lands and as facilities were built as part of the CIVILIAN CONSERVATION CORPS program. The Land and Water Conservation Fund Act (1965) authorized the secretary of agriculture to acquire forest land specifically for

Treacherous geography did not impede a crew of foresters working to get harvested timbers across a deep canyon. This engineering feat, which used an elaborate pully system, was captured by the photographer Darius R. Kinsey in the early 1900s.

recreation. Because recreation on public lands was traditionally the purview of the NATIONAL PARK SERVICE, the increased involvement by the Forest Service exacerbated an already tense rivalry between the two agencies.

Current national forest management policy is shaped largely by the Multiple Use Sustained Yield Act (1960), which permits optimum yield from the major income-producing resources in any given forest. Timber cutting is allowed, for example, if it does not compromise other, subordinate uses and interests (☞ CLEAR-CUTTING). Long-range planning is guided by the Forest and Rangeland Renewable Resources Planning Act (1974) and the National Forest Management Act (1976) and is usually subject to a review under the National Environmental Policy Act (1969).

Federally managed timber harvests are not widely seen as good business. The expense of road maintenance, harvest preparation, and replanting often exceeds the profits. Concerns center on the practice of minimizing costs by removing only the most valuable timbers, which contributes to deteriorating forests and below-cost timber sales. Many advocacy groups (☞ ADVOCATES) also cite the Forest Service for permitting excess logging, high-impact recreation, and the exclusion of pristine wilderness from official inventories of ROADLESS AREAS to allow logging trucks easy access. Road building is another subject of controversy. National forest roads total 378,000 miles, eight times more than the Interstate Highway System crisscrossing the entire United States. Under the Clinton administration (1993–2001), a forest policy shift deemphasized logging and road building and favored increased environmental protection for national forests. About 50 percent of national forest land is now closed to logging (☞ ROADLESS AREAS).

John Muir Project ✉ Earth Island Institute, 726 Seventh Street, SE, Washington, DC 20003. ☎ 202-547-9124. 🖥 www.johnmuirproject.org
■ Committed to preventing commercial exploitation of all federal public forest lands, this nonprofit organization works to end timber sales and redirect timber subsidies into "worker re-training, ecological restoration and reduction of the national debt."

U.S. Forest Service ✉ U.S. Department of Agriculture, P.O. Box 96090, Washington, DC 20090-6090. ☎ 202-205-8333. 🖥 www.fs.fed.us

Contacts

National Forests by State. Presents a state-by-state listing of forests with pertinent data. 🖥 www.fs.fed.us/recreation/states/us.shtml

Web Site

National Grasslands

The twenty national grasslands managed by the U.S. FOREST SERVICE encompass 4.2 million acres of public domain in California, Colorado, Idaho, Kansas, Nebraska, New Mexico, North and South Dakota, Oklahoma, Oregon, Texas, and Wyoming. These grasslands are the remnants of one of the most jeopardized ecosystems in the country. About 70 percent of America's short- and mixed-grass prairies have disappeared, and only about one percent of tallgrass prairie remains in scattered patches, much of it under private ownership.

As part of a U.S. DEPARTMENT OF AGRICULTURE restoration effort, the first national grasslands were formally established in 1960. Administered through local ranger districts and as independent units, they are managed under the same multiple use–sustained yield policy that applies to the NATIONAL FOREST

Homesteaders' farms on the prairie failed when the grasses were plowed under for crops that the punished topsoil could not sustain. Alfred Jacob Miller's view of a settlers' wagon train dates from before 1874.

SYSTEM. Long-term management plans give priority to livestock grazing, oil and gas development, and such recreational uses as mountain biking, off-road vehicle use, fishing, and sport hunting for deer, waterfowl, antelope, and grouse.

Despite efforts to restore grasslands—which are important habitats for big-game species, peregrine falcons, golden eagles, burrowing owls, mountain plovers, prairie chickens, black-footed ferrets, prairie dogs (routinely shot for target practice), and swift foxes—fifty-five grassland species are now classified as endangered or threatened (☞ ENDANGERED SPECIES). According to the National Wildlife Federation, more than seven hundred other grassland species are imperiled.

Contacts

National Wildlife Federation ✉ 11100 Wildlife Center Drive, Reston, VA 20190. ☎ 703-438-6000. ▢ www.nwf.org/natlwild/2000/viewaso.html

■ The National Wildlife Federation sponsors a public education program targeting grassland preservation, which has lagged behind other environmental conservation efforts. Its projects include working with the Inter-Tribal Bison Cooperative to restore free-roaming bison to healthy tribal and public grasslands and fighting to stop decimation of black-tailed prairie dogs and their habitat.

U.S. Forest Service ✉ U.S. Department of Agriculture, P.O. Box 96090, Washington, DC 20090-6090. ☎ 202-205-8333. ▢ www.fs.fed.us

Web Site

List of National Grasslands. A Forest Service site listing grasslands. ▢ www.fs.fed.us/grasslands/loc.htm

National Lakeshores

Authorized by Congress in 1966 and 1977, the four national lakeshores—Pictured Rocks, Apostle Islands, Indiana Dunes, and Sleeping Bear Dunes—are all located on the GREAT LAKES. They are part of the NATIONAL PARK SYSTEM and are open to activities such as hiking, swimming, camping, boating, and cross-country skiing. All preserve exceptional natural features. The first national lakeshore to be designated was Pictured Rocks, which consists of 72,000 acres on Michigan's Upper Peninsula and skirts 42 miles of Lake Superior. It includes sandstone cliffs, kettle lakes, and hardwood forests. Sculpted into natural caves and arches, the "pictured rocks" are a wall of sandstone cliffs that rise directly from the lake to heights of 200 feet for a 15-mile stretch. Some of the national lakeshores include state park lands.

Contact

National Park Service ✉ U.S. Department of the Interior, 1849 C Street, NW, Washington, DC 20240. ☎ 202-208-6843. ▢ www.nps.gov

"I believe there are certain places humankind simply cannot improve upon—places whose beauty and interest no photograph could capture, places you simply have to see for yourself. We must take this time of unparalleled prosperity to ensure [that] people will always be able to see these places as we see them today."   William Jefferson Clinton (2000)

National Monuments

National monuments are sites, structures, and landmarks of historical and cultural value on PUBLIC LANDS that have been designated by the president under the Antiquities Act (1906), the first comprehensive federal preservation legislation to protect historic and archaeological resources. By permitting the chief executive, at his personal discretion, to designate national monuments and to reserve PUBLIC LANDS (or to accept private lands into the public domain), it authorizes remarkable presidential power. The original intent was to protect relatively small national archaeological sites; each monument was supposed to be a man-made wonder or a scenic curiosity, and the land included was technically limited to the smallest area compatible with the site's care and management. Within months of ratification, however, President THEODORE ROOSEVELT exercised his new power to create Devils Tower (Wyoming), Petrified Forest and Montezuma Castle (Arizona), and El Morro (New Mexico) National Monuments, thus establishing large areas of public lands as monuments in and of themselves. Roosevelt further

The 1906 Antiquities Act was intended to protect archaeological ruins but is now used to designate areas of great scenic and environmental import as well. Canyon de Chelly National Monument was created in 1931 to recognize the Indian villages built in wall caves in this part of Arizona between A.D. 350 and 1300.

stretched the act's legal limits in declaring the 800,000-acre Grand Canyon National Monument in 1908 (☞ GRAND CANYON); that designation was upheld by a Supreme Court ruling in 1920.

Today national monuments range in size from 10 acres to 12 million acres and total about 70 million acres. Most are overseen by the NATIONAL PARK SERVICE, although some are administered by the U.S. FOREST SERVICE. The Grand Staircase–Escalante National Monument (Utah), designated in 1996, is the first and only national monument under the aegis of the BUREAU OF LAND MANAGEMENT. A national monument can encompass private land, where owners are permitted to remain and continue existing uses. Grazing, recreation, and sport hunting are permitted if consistent with the area's character. Monument status, however, prohibits the alteration or destruction of sites and objects without permission from the appropriate department secretary. Mining and off-road vehicles are also forbidden.

More than one hundred national monuments have been designated since 1906. Several of the early sites have become national historical parks, and about thirty of them, including the Grand Canyon, Mount Olympus (☞ OLYMPIC MOUNTAINS), and Mukuntuweap (☞ ZION NATIONAL PARK) have been absorbed into or have been redesignated as national parks (☞ NATIONAL PARK SYSTEM). After President Franklin Roosevelt's 1943 designation of the Jackson Hole National Monument (Wyoming) was bitterly challenged in a congressional session, Roosevelt's successor, Harry Truman, signed a provision exempting Wyoming from the Antiquities Act as part of the deal to meld the Jackson Hole National Monument into the Grand Teton National Park (☞ TETON MOUNTAINS) in 1950.

Because designation is purely discretionary, monuments are often declared by lame-duck presidents trying to wield some last-minute power. No system of review or public participation in the creation of the monuments is required, and at present a designation can be overturned only by an act of Congress. The process thus has engendered long-standing opposition, mostly from Republican leaders in the rural West, where the majority of public lands are located. In 1978 President Jimmy Carter declared seventeen national monuments in ALASKA in a single day when Congress failed to pass an Alaskan lands bill. By the end of his term in 2001, President Bill Clinton had set aside more national monuments in the contiguous forty-eight states—3.6 million acres in eleven new or expanded monuments—than any previous president. No national monuments were created by Clinton's Republican predecessors, Ronald Reagan and George H. Bush.

A key component of the U.S. DEPARTMENT OF THE INTERIOR, the National Park Service was created in 1916 as one of the federal government's chief wilderness-protection agencies. Its fundamental role is to conserve the scenery, natural and historic objects, and wildlife within the various units of the NATIONAL PARK SYSTEM, including national parks, NATIONAL MONUMENTS, NATIONAL PRESERVES, NATIONAL LAKESHORES and SEASHORES, NATIONAL RECREATION AREAS, selected trails in the NATIONAL TRAILS SYSTEM, selected rivers in the NATIONAL WILD AND SCENIC RIVERS SYSTEM, and certain historic sites that are of such national significance as to justify special protection and recognition by various acts of Congress. As the official custodian of the national parks, the Park Service operates campgrounds and other visitor facilities including lodging (☞ PARK ARCHITECTURE) and concessions and oversees outdoor recreation planning on state and federal levels.

The agency is also the primary U.S. contact for UNESCO's WORLD HERITAGE SITES in this country, and it oversees the National Register of Historic Places, Historic American Buildings Survey and Historic American Engineering Record, interagency archaeological services, and the state portion of the Land and Water Conservation Fund (☞ ENVIRONMENTAL FUNDS). Its mandate further includes the protection of species that are listed as endangered by the states (☞ ENDANGERED SPECIES).

National Park Service

National Park Service ✉ U.S. Department of the Interior, 1849 C Street, NW, Washington, DC 20240. ☎ 202-208-6843. 🖥 www.nps.gov

Contact

The conservation responsibilities of the National Park Service extend to fauna and flora, including ferns in Montana's Glacier National Park, photographed by Ansel Adams on behalf of the agency. Plant restoration ranges from minor soil preparation and seeding to major grading, soil replacement, and planting.

National Park System

The 83.4-million-acre National Park System consists of 379 units—parks, monuments, battlefields, lakeshores, forts, parkways, historic sites, memorials, and the like—established by a patchwork of legislative acts, presidential proclamations, and department orders over the years and brought together under a single banner in 1970. The unifying qualification for all national park units is an unspoiled natural, ecological, cultural, historic, or recreational feature that is so unique as to be of national importance and merits preservation for future generations. The system is represented in all states but Delaware as well as in American Samoa, Guam, Puerto Rico, the Northern Mariana Islands, and the Virgin Islands. Most units are now added to the system by acts of Congress, although the president may declare NATIONAL MONUMENTS on Park System land. Most of the system (about 77 million acres) falls on federal land, but a national park unit may also incorporate state and private land. The administering agency is the NATIONAL PARK SERVICE.

"Beautiful and Thrilling" Specimens

Unlike the NATIONAL WILDERNESS PRESERVATION SYSTEM, the National Park System was not created by a single piece of legislation. The first designated sites now in the system were the national capital parks, National Mall, and White House, which were included with the authorization of the District of Columbia in 1790. As early as 1832 the artist George Catlin (☞ FRONTIER GENRE PAINTERS) called on the federal government to create a "nation's park" that would be "a beautiful and thrilling specimen for America to preserve and hold up to the view of her refined citizens and the world." That effort failed, but that same year the first public reserve on federal lands was set aside as the Hot Springs Reservation in Arkansas—the first unit of an emerging national park system located outside the nation's capital. Thirty-two years passed before the first federal legislation preserved federal lands for public recreation and the general "benefit of mankind" with the transfer of YOSEMITE VALLEY to California in 1864. The first national park, YELLOWSTONE NATIONAL PARK, was created by an act of Congress in 1872. Yellowstone was followed by Mackinac National Park in Michigan in 1873 and Sequoia and General Grant National Parks in California in 1890.

When the National Park Service was formed in 1916, it was made responsible for the parks, reservations, and monuments then under the U.S. DEPARTMENT OF THE INTERIOR. The Park Service was a long time forming in part because of resistance from the rival U.S. FOREST SERVICE, which correctly predicted the future requisition of public parks from national forest land (☞ NATIONAL FOREST SYSTEM). The first Park Service director, Stephen T. Mather, promoted the idea of a formal administrative body by

Established in 1940, Kings Canyon National Park in the southern Sierra Nevada Range is now administered jointly with Sequoia National Park; both are designated International Biosphere Reserves. The granite dome in the distance provided a focal point in 1892 for John K. Hillers.

stressing the potential of parks as tourist destinations. Although the Park Service was charged with preserving the parks in essentially their natural state, recreation was a priority, and automobile traffic, camps, hotels (☞ PARK ARCHITECTURE), natural history museums, and all manner of sports activity were permitted in the national parks early on.

Consolidation efforts started in earnest in 1933 with an executive order by President Franklin Roosevelt that transferred the national capital parks, national military parks, and a number of national monuments from various managing agencies to the Park Service. The General Authorities Act (1970) created a single park system for the various units. The system was roughly doubled in size by the Alaska National Interest Lands Conservation Act (1980) (☞ ALASKA); the California Desert Protection Act (1994) transferred about 3 million acres from the Bureau of Public Lands to the system (☞ DESERTS).

There are now some twenty classifications within the system. The term *national park* generally applies to the largest, most impressive scenic areas. Other units include NATIONAL TRAILS,

Twenty Classifications

NATIONAL RECREATION AREAS, NATIONAL WILD AND SCENIC RIVERS, NATIONAL LAKESHORES, NATIONAL PRESERVES, NATIONAL SEASHORES, as well as NATIONAL MONUMENTS. National wilderness areas (☞ NATIONAL WILDERNESS PRESERVATION SYSTEM) also encompass land in the system. Some classifications—national park, for example—are unique to the National Park System. Others—national recreation areas, trails, monuments, and rivers—are also found in systems administered by other agencies. Except for national monuments, additions to the National Park System are usually made by an act of Congress, typically as recommended by the secretary of the interior, who is required by law to submit an annual list of areas recommended for study as future park units.

Park units are administered according to the legislation or administrative order that created them. Accordingly, livestock grazing, sport hunting, trapping, and fishing are allowed in certain instances. In 2000 the Park Service announced a ban on recreational use of snowmobiles in all national parks except those in ALASKA and Glacier National Park (☞ GLACIERS). Grand Teton (☞ TETON MOUNTAINS) and YELLOWSTONE NATIONAL PARK, two of the country's most popular national parks for snowmobiling, began phasing out recreational use of the vehicles in 2001. Plans also called for banning personal watercraft by September 2002.

The health and well-being of national parks are jeopardized primarily by overcrowding, POLLUTION, and infringing development. Among the ten most threatened parks in various stages of decay cited by the National Parks Conservation Association are Yellowstone (the winter recreation season brings a thousand snowmobiles daily); Joshua Tree in California (what would be the nation's largest dump is proposed within 1.5 miles of the

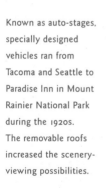

Known as auto-stages, specially designed vehicles ran from Tacoma and Seattle to Paradise Inn in Mount Rainier National Park during the 1920s. The removable roofs increased the scenery-viewing possibilities.

park); Haleakala in Hawaii (alien species are on the attack); and Petrified National Forest in Arizona (visitors steal an estimated 12 tons of fossilized wood a year). ☞ *also* PARK ARCHITECTURE

National Park Service ✉ U.S. Department of the Interior, 1849 C Street, NW, Washington, DC 20240. ☎ 202-208-6843. 🖥 www.nps.gov

Contacts

National Parks Conservation Association ✉ 1300 Nineteenth Street, NW, Suite 300, Washington, DC 20036. ☎ 800-NAT-PARKS. 🖥 www.npca.org

List of National Park Units. Presents a listing of all national parks. 🖥 www. nps.gov/parks.html

Web Site

National Preserves

A national preserve is a unit of the NATIONAL PARK SYSTEM that has been designated for its scenic, historical, or environmental value; many of the preserves contain important watersheds. A national preserve generally has the same characteristics as a national park, but sport hunting, trapping, and oil and gas exploration and extraction are generally permitted. Ten of the sixteen national preserves are located in ALASKA.

National Recreation Areas

National recreation areas are places that merit recognition and protection but do not necessarily qualify for other designations with more stringent use restrictions. This is often because of an existing precedent for recreation that would be unpopular to reverse and because many are man-made reservoirs or natural areas that do not meet the standards of national parks (☞ NATIONAL PARK SYSTEM). They are usually more than 20,000 acres in size and within 250 miles or so of a metropolitan area and are administered according to the provisions of individual legislation by the NATIONAL PARK SERVICE, U.S. FOREST SERVICE, or BUREAU OF LAND MANAGEMENT. The Park Service, which formally adopted the category in 1964, manages the majority.

The first national recreation area was the Boulder Dam National Recreation Area (Arizona and Nevada) on Lake Mead, created by the 1935 Boulder Dam (later Hoover Dam) on the Colorado River. The Park Service began managing recreation activities here in 1936. Renamed the Lake Mead National Recreation Area in 1947, it now incorporates Lake Mojave, created by the 1952 Davis Dam, and totals 1.5 million acres.

A more recent designation is the Oregon Dunes National Recreation Area (1972), which is part of the Siuslaw National Forest (☞ NATIONAL FOREST SYSTEM) and thus administered by the

Forest Service. The vast 32,000-acre dune area on the Oregon coast includes several towns and is a popular spot for all-terrain vehicles. The recreation area designation was applied as an alternative to the stricter designation for NATIONAL SEASHORES, which likely would have precluded the all-terrain vehicles.

National Seashores

In 1934 a survey of the Atlantic and Gulf Coasts identified twelve significant areas deserving federal protection. Three years later Congress authorized the first national seashore: Cape Hatteras (North Carolina), a 100-mile chain of barrier islands and beaches. Following were Cape Cod (Massachusetts) in 1961; Point Reyes (California) and Padre Island (Gulf of Mexico) in 1962; Fire Island (New York) in 1964; Assateague Island (Maryland and Virginia) in 1965; Cape Lookout (North Carolina) in 1966; Gulf Islands (Gulf Coast) in 1971; Cumberland Island (Georgia) in 1972; and Cape Canaveral (Florida) in 1975.

All of the national seashores have been established by congressional act and are part of the NATIONAL PARK SYSTEM, although some include state parks and are administered in conjunction with other agencies. This is done according to individual plans and legal requirements outlined by the statutes that created them. The primary administrative goal is to protect particular coastal features while providing recreational opportunities such as camping, swimming, boating, hunting, and fishing in accordance with federal and state laws. The level of development depends in part on state coastal development law and on what was there before the national seashore designation was made. The Fire Island National Seashore, for example, encompasses 3,800 businesses and properties, and building on the dunes is permitted. Some national seashores, including Assateague, Gulf Islands, and Cape Lookout, have been lightly developed for recreation. Cape Canaveral's legislation limits new development to what is necessary for safety and administration.

The 1961 designation of the Cape Cod National Seashore, a 40-mile stretch of dunes and salt marshes, marked the first time that Congress appropriated funding to acquire a large natural recreation area as a reserve in conjunction with the designation. Legislation specifically called for cooperation between local agencies and the federal government, precluding Interior Department condemnation of private improved property within the seashore after zoning regulations designed to work within the reserve were set. This "Cape Cod formula" has served as the model for future seashore designations. The strictest regulations apply to Cumberland Island, where the seashore must be permanently preserved in its primitive state,

Cape Hatteras in North Carolina was established by Congress as the first national seashore in 1937. Restrictions on use and development vary from seashore to seashore.

no development incompatible with the preservation of the flora and fauna is allowed, and no roads or causeways connecting this barrier beach to the mainland can ever be built.

Coast Alliance ✉ 600 Pennsylvania Avenue, SE, Suite 340, Washington, D.C. 20003. 📞 202-546-9554. 🖥 www.coastalliance.org
■ This alliance and information clearinghouse leads a network of about 500 conservation organizations concerned with preservation of the Pacific, Atlantic, Gulf, and Great Lakes coasts. Efforts focus on shoreline conservation, pollution issues, and coastal development.

Contacts

National Park Service ✉ U.S. Department of the Interior, 1849 C Street, NW, Washington, DC 20240. 📞 202-208-6843. 🖥 www.nps.gov

National Trails System

Covering 40,000 miles, the National Trails System comprises twenty trails that fall under the auspices of federal agencies but are administered cooperatively with state and private partner agencies and such nonprofit hiking and trail organizations as the Appalachian Trail Conference. There are two primary federal trail types—scenic and historic—and these may be designated only by congressional act. Scenic trails are limited to hikers on foot and are intended to preserve and highlight exceptional corridors of scenic, cultural, or historical value. They usually pass through several states, with side trails branching out to towns along the way. Historic trails follow and commemorate historically significant routes: those of transcontinental explorations, military campaigns, early pioneers, traders, or forced Indian resettlement. These thematic trails are not necessarily continuous and sometimes incorporate segments of water, marked highways paralleling the trail, and linked historic sites. As such, historic trails are open to both foot and auto traffic.

The National Trails System was established by the National Trails System Act (1968), which created and provided funding for the first two scenic trails: the APPALACHIAN NATIONAL SCENIC TRAIL, administered by the secretary of the interior, and the PACIFIC CREST NATIONAL SCENIC TRAIL, administered by the secretary of agriculture. Their genesis was to provide recreation for the expanding American population and to promote access to historic and wilderness areas. An important proviso was that the trails be accessible from metropolitan areas. The statute was amended in 1978 to include the new category of national historic trail. That year the National Parks and Recreation Act designated four historic trails with more than 9,000 miles and a third scenic trail along the CONTINENTAL DIVIDE. Eight national scenic trails and twelve national historic trails have been created so

National scenic trails permit foot travel only. A careful hiking pace protects foliage from damage, preserving the kind of natural detail that caught the eye of Ansel Adams.

far. The NATIONAL PARK SERVICE administers fifteen of these trails, the U.S. FOREST SERVICE four, and the BUREAU OF LAND MANAGEMENT one.

A third classification—national recreation trail—refers to established trails in or near urban areas that are recognized by the National Park Service as integral to the national system although they are not technically part of the federal system. About eight hundred national recreation trails exist. These are open to hikers, bikers, horseback riders, and cross-country skiers and provide handicapped access. A fourth classification—connecting or side trail—refers to those pathways offering access to or connections among the other trail classes.

With the exception of the first two national scenic trails, the National Trails System Act does not provide for sustained funding for operating and maintaining the federal trails or authorize dedicated funds for their expansion and protection. National recreation trails may be established by the secretaries of interior or agriculture on land wholly or partly within their jurisdiction with the consent of the involved states and other land managing agencies, if any. The secretaries are permitted by law to acquire land for the system through cooperative agreement, donation, purchase with donated or appropriated funds, trade, or condemnation (within limited authority). They must encourage states to administer the nonfederal lands through agreements with landowners and private organizations for the rights-of-way.

National Wild and Scenic Rivers System

Established by the National Wild and Scenic Rivers Act (1968), this national system is intended to preserve a network of rivers and river segments in free-flowing condition and to protect their immediate environments and wildlife. The system includes three classes: wild, scenic, and recreational rivers. Wild rivers, the most primitive, are free of dams and other impoundments and can generally be reached only by foot trail. The most developed type, the recreational rivers, are easily accessible and may include previously existing impoundments and some shoreline development.

Passed to recognize waterways with outstanding scenic, recreational, geological, fish and wildlife, historic, or cultural resources, the 1968 act immediately identified 789 miles in eight rivers and adjacent land corridors in nine states. Several rivers were added in the 1970s, and the system was more than doubled in size by the Alaska National Interest Lands Conservation Act (1980) (☞ ALASKA). By the late 1980s the national rivers totaled nineteen and protected about 1,600 miles of waterway, including forty-six river segments in Oregon. More recent additions include the Niobrara National Scenic River

(Nebraska) in 1991 and Great Egg Harbor Scenic and Recreational River (New Jersey) in 1992. By 1995 the system comprised 150 rivers flowing 10,734 miles through thirty-four states.

The National Wild and Scenic Rivers System was modeled on the NATIONAL WILDERNESS PRESERVATION SYSTEM in that it represents an effort to balance protection of the nation's wilderness resources with pressure to develop their resources (all rivers are potential hydropower sources). Indeed, the Wild and Scenic Rivers Act was a direct reaction to the proliferation of dam and hydroelectric projects on America's waterways and mandates specifically that "the established national policy of dam and other construction at appropriate sections of rivers in the United States needs to be complemented by a policy that would preserve other selected rivers. . . ." A few states have passed legislation establishing wild and scenic rivers that are managed under state jurisdiction as well. State-classified rivers can be included in the national system by approval of the secretary of the interior if the river is to be administered permanently by the state agency.

The areas along the rivers within the national system are managed variously by the NATIONAL PARK SERVICE, U.S. FOREST SERVICE, U.S. FISH AND WILDLIFE SERVICE, BUREAU OF LAND MANAGEMENT, U.S. Army Corps of Engineers, or one or more states. A river may be designated by an act of Congress or through nomination by a state with approval of the secretary of the interior. Classification does not typically provide the same level of protection as national wilderness designation and does not necessarily curtail development because Congress directed that other land uses not be limited unless they "substantially interfere with public use and enjoyment" of the values protected by designation.

The frontispiece of a U.S. Geological Survey report shows Fort Benton on the Missouri River in 1863. A 149-mile segment running downriver from the fort was designated as part of the National Wild and Scenic Rivers System in 1976. This is the only major portion to be protected in its natural, free-flowing state and is part of the Lewis and Clark National Historic Trail.

National Wilderness Preservation System

Land set aside as national wilderness areas by Congress under the Wilderness Act (1964) and subsequent related bills makes up the National Wilderness Preservation System. As of 2000 the system included 628 wilderness areas in thirty-eight states and totaled more than 104 million acres (about 4.5 percent of the land area of the United States).

The idea of protecting wilderness as a national policy has its roots in two sets of discretionary regulations—L-30 (1929) and U (1939)—that protected large areas of primitive forest land from logging, road building, motorboat and seaplane use, and construction of camps, lodges, and other amenities. About 14 million acres were set aside in national forests as "primitive areas" by 1939. The U regulations allowed wilderness classification, on the U.S. FOREST SERVICE's recommendation, of primitive areas (100,000 acres or more); wild areas (5,000 to 100,000 acres); and canoe areas, such as the Boundary Waters Canoe Area Wilderness (☞ QUETICO-SUPERIOR REGION). Permanent protection, however, was not guaranteed by law.

The Wilderness Act

Conrad Schwering's *Safe Haven* (1983) pictures the wilds as a place untrammeled by humans—one definition in the Wilderness Act.

The Wilderness Act, passed in 1964 under the Johnson administration, mandated the establishment of a National Wilderness Preservation System to be composed of public lands designated by Congress for preservation in a "wilderness condition." The culmination of an eight-year effort, the act was the first federal statute to provide for the designation of PUBLIC LANDS primarily to keep them in a primitive state. It was also the first to provide a legal definition of wilderness, which it recognized under somewhat general guidelines,

rather than specific dictates, as an area that retains its primeval character, shows little or no sign of human presence, and offers outstanding opportunities for solitude. As specified by the act, a wilderness area must contain a minimum of 5,000 acres or be of sufficient size to make practicable its preservation and use in an unimpaired condition. By putting the matter in the hands of Congress, the statute signaled the end of the public's reliance on the Forest Service to designate wilderness. It acknowledged that discretion alone did not provide sufficient protection for wilderness, giving federal backbone to designations that before were made only on an administrative basis.

Under the Wilderness Act, fifty-five primitive wilderness areas that were already set aside on 9.1 million acres of Forest Service land received instant federal protection as part of the National Wilderness Preservation System. Most of these areas became known as national wilderness areas (only the Blue Range Primitive Area in the Apache-Sitgreaves National Forest of Arizona retains the original designation). Subsequent acts have added millions of acres, the largest designation coming under the Alaska National Interest Lands Conservation Act (1980) (☞ ALASKA), which preserved 56.4 million acres. Twenty-one wilderness laws enacted in 1984 designated 8.6 million acres in twenty-one states. The California Desert Protection Act (1994) (☞ DESERTS) designated 7.7 million acres of wilderness. Four wilderness areas, all in Alaska, cover more than 5 million acres each.

National Wilderness Areas

Preserving the wilderness character of the designated areas falls under the jurisdiction of the department or agency responsible for that land immediately before designation. Management of the entire 104-million-acre system is thus shared by the NATIONAL PARK SERVICE (42 percent, about 42 million acres), U.S. Forest Service (33 percent, about 35 million acres), U.S. FISH AND WILDLIFE SERVICE (20 percent, about 22 million acres), and BUREAU OF LAND MANAGEMENT (5 percent, about 5 million acres). A single wilderness area may overlap state borders and can spread into more than one forest or park unit. The 8,000-acre Big Frog National Wilderness Area, for example, is located partly in the Chattahoochee National Forest in northern Georgia and partly in the Cherokee National Forest in eastern Tennessee. The wilderness system may also include state as well as privately owned land, which can be acquired by the secretary of agriculture under certain conditions.

Designated for its intrinsic scenic and environmental value, a national wilderness area is intended to be protected in its primitive state for the purposes of recreation, scientific research, education, and conservation. Wilderness designation offers the highest level of protection of any federal designation on public lands in America. In principle, a wilderness area is exempt from resource exploitation, motor traffic, mining, and any other activity incompatible with its wilderness character. Visitors are welcome, but unlike in a national monument, national forest, or national park (NATIONAL MONUMENTS, NATIONAL FOREST SYSTEM, NATIONAL PARK SYSTEM), they must hike, ride a horse, or paddle in. In theory, no administrative structures, campgrounds, or visitor centers are permitted; road building is limited to the minimum required for administration and fire prevention; and commercial use is restricted to outfitter and guide services specifically for recreational use of the wilderness.

Lumbering, grazing, and road building, however, do occur in some national wilderness areas because of various exemptions and provisions for preexisting uses. If a wilderness area contains state or private land, access to this is permitted as well. Motorboats and aircraft landings are also allowed where these uses were already established. In some cases subsequent laws authorize nonconforming uses, such as mechanized portage equipment, motorized access for maintenance and fire prevention, and rights-of-way for military access.

Within the National Wilderness Preservation System are research natural areas, which are set aside as gene pools for rare and endangered species and as examples of significant ecosystems. Unlike national wilderness areas, research natural areas do not typically accommodate recreational use.

The secretary of agriculture is authorized to acquire privately owned land within the perimeter of any designated national wilderness area if the owner concurs or the acquisition is specifically authorized by Congress. Land may also be acquired through condemnation under the Eastern Wilderness Areas Act (1975). The secretary may accept gifts and bequests of land within or adjacent to wilderness areas for preservation as wilderness. New wilderness areas must be approved by an act of Congress, which can also mandate review of potential sites.

Congress may designate wilderness study areas for review by the appropriate federal agency for potential inclusion in the National Wilderness Preservation System. During the prescribed review period, the land is supposed to be managed in a manner that will protect its primitive character and will not disqualify it for future inclusion in the system until Congress has made a final determination. Because of the Wilderness Act's somewhat ambivalent guidelines for defining wilderness, the administering agencies often adopt loose interpretations that can nevertheless lead to activities like mining and logging. The Wilderness Society is among the advocacy groups (☞ ADVOCATES) that focus on the status of these areas while the review process is under way.

U.S. Forest Service ✉ U.S. Department of Agriculture, P.O. Box 96090, Washington, DC 20090-6090. ☎ 202-205-8333. 🖳 www.fs.fed.us

Contact

National Wilderness Areas. Presents a comprehensive listing of national wilderness areas. 🖳 www.wilderness.net/nwps

Web Site

President Theodore Roosevelt created the first federal wildlife refuge, located on Pelican Island in Florida. The primary beneficiaries of this designation were brown pelicans.

Created in 1966, the National Wildlife Refuge System provides a national network of land and water refuges for the preservation, restoration, and management of threatened and endangered species and the perpetuation of migratory bird populations. Administered by the U.S. FISH AND WILDLIFE SERVICE, the 93.5-million-acre system of land and water comprises 525 national wildlife refuges, as well as about 150 waterfowl production areas (on about 1.9 million acres) and about fifty wildlife coordination areas. Refuges are located in all fifty states, American Samoa, Puerto Rico, the Virgin Islands, Johnson Atoll, Midway Atoll, and several other Pacific islands, although 83 percent (all but 15 million acres) are in ALASKA. About 20.6 million acres of refuge lands are part of the NATIONAL WILDERNESS PRESERVATION SYSTEM. All but the coordination areas, which are managed by state wildlife agencies under cooperative agreement with the Fish and Wildlife Service, are defined as refuges, even though a number of research centers, administrative sites, and more than eighty fish hatcheries run by the

National Wildlife Refuge System

A page from an 1868 edition of *Harper's Weekly* enumerated scenes from the *Life of a Trapper*, whose catch included bison, elk, cougar, and wolves. Most early legislation was enacted to protect such game species, in part to preserve them for sport hunting.

service are not technically part of the national system. The cornerstone of the system is the sixteen Alaskan refuges, which are home to grizzly, black, and polar BEARS, musk ox, wolves, moose, Dall's sheep, lynx, martins, Pacific walrus, beluga and baleen whales, seals, the threatened Stellar's sea lion, and more than three hundred bird species. Refuges are usually created by congressional act or executive order. Land may be reserved from the public domain or acquired from private or state owners by purchase, long-term lease, or easement.

Beginning with Fish and Game

This vast and complex system is the result of a long chain of federal acts, administrative decisions, and executive orders confined to no single type of federal land. The sequence began with the 1864 transfer of YOSEMITE VALLEY from the public domain to the State of California with the proviso that all fish and game within the reservation be protected from wanton destruction and capture for sale and profit. Supported in large part by sportsmen's organizations, most early wildlife legislation targeted game species—sought for feathers and furs—by regulating hunting and commerce. The first federal lands reserved specifically for wildlife protection were the Pribilof Islands in Alaska, set aside in 1868 by President Ulysses S. Grant as a preserve for the northern fur seal. By 1885 bag limits and other hunting laws had been passed in all states and territories. The federal government followed with the Yellowstone Park Protection Act (1894) (☞ YELLOWSTONE NATIONAL PARK) and a series of migratory bird statutes designed to control plume hunting and other activities affecting birds whose migration patterns made state statutes more or less meaningless (☞ BIRDS). In 1903 by executive order President THEODORE ROOSEVELT established Pelican Island in Florida as the first true wildlife refuge on federal lands. Before leaving office Roosevelt designated fifty-one bird reservations; several wildlife reserves were also created on national forest land in the next few years.

Efforts to acquire land for bird conservation began in the 1920s. The Migratory Bird Conservation Act (1929) established the first national refuge system; supported by congressional appropriation, this was specifically designed for waterfowl. The Duck Stamp Act and the Fish and Wildlife Coordination Act (both 1934) targeted revenue for more acquisitions. The Fish and Wildlife Act (1956) established the first comprehensive national fish and wildlife policy. Recreation in wildlife refuges was authorized in 1962, and management directives were finally set in 1966 by the National Wildlife Refuge System Administration Act. By 1999 fifty-six refuges had been added to the system under the Endangered Species Act (1973) (☞ ENDANGERED SPECIES) and 53.7 million acres had been acquired under the Alaska National Interest Lands Conservation Act (1980) (☞ ALASKA), which added nine refuges and expanded seven.

State and Federal Cooperation

Within the national refuge system, the states have the principal management responsibility for resident species, including controlling fishing and hunting, for example, while the U.S. Fish and Wildlife Service is responsible for the habitats. The system is administered through seven regional Fish and Wildlife Service offices. The legislation or administrative order establishing a refuge typically identifies its primary purpose, which is usually concerned with habitat or species preservation. Management of endangered species involves captive propagation, predator control, population monitoring, and law enforcement and is dictated largely by recommendations in species recovery plans under the Endangered Species Act. Timber harvesting and grazing are permitted in national wildlife refuges if they are determined by the regional director to be compatible with the refuge's primary purpose. Powerboat recreation, birdwatching, swimming, camping, and hiking are other possible activities.

In general conformance with state regulations, hunting has been allowed in certain refuges since 1924, when Congress established the Upper Mississippi River Wild Life and Fish Refuge, contingent on the continuance of the traditional practice of hunting there. Although subject to a review process, hunting remains a controversial issue. Proponents argue that it can be used to control wildlife populations in refuges that are in fact supported by the sale of duck stamps (hunting permits); detractors point to the absurdity of killing animals in any habitat designated as a refuge. Another issue is oil drilling; a proposal to extract oil and other resources from the 19.6-million-acre Arctic National Wildlife Refuge—larger than the states of Massachusetts, Rhode Island, Connecticut, Delaware, Hawaii, and New Jersey combined—has been hotly debated over the last two decades.

Waterfowl Production Areas

A 1958 amendment to the Duck Stamp Act (1934) permitted federal acquisition of wetlands for wildlife protection and authorized waterfowl production areas, federally designated grasslands or wetlands deemed critical as breeding habitat for migratory waterfowl and other wildlife. Averaging about 226 acres in size, the waterfowl production areas cover 1.9 million acres, primarily in the prairie wetlands, or "potholes," of the Dakotas, Minnesota, and Montana, with a scattering in Maine, Idaho, Michigan, Nebraska, and Iowa. Together with the wetlands of the Canadian prairies and Alaska, this habitat constitutes the bulk of the breeding grounds for North American waterfowl. The production areas are managed as part of a system of wetland management districts created in 1962 under an accelerated duck stamp sales program. Some of the wetlands and waterfowl production areas are designated on public lands and some on land acquired from private owners through easements purchased to provide grassland cover and prevent draining and filling projects. The latter are operated under agreement with the farmers and ranchers who own the land.

Contacts

Wildlife Refuge Campaign ✉ National Audubon Society, 1901 Pennsylvania Avenue, NW, Suite 1100, Washington, DC 20006 ☎ 202-861-2242. 🖳 www.audubon.org/campaign/refuge

■ This campaign focuses on raising awareness of the refuge system, targeting such threats as incompatible uses and development-oriented legislation. Initiatives include Arctic Refuge Keepers (ARK) and Earth Stewards, a neighborhood school program.

U.S. Fish and Wildlife Service ✉ U.S. Department of the Interior, 1849 C Street NW, Washington, DC 20240. ☎ 202-208-5634; 800-344-WILD (Refuge System Visitors Guide). 🖥 www.fws.gov

National Wildlife Refuges and U.S. Fish and Wildlife Databases. Offers a complete list of refuges as well as wildlife databases. 🖥 bluegoose.arw. r9.fws.gov

Web Site

The first photographs of Indians were daguerreotypes made in the 1840s. Photography remained a primary means of recording information about Native Americans, including their dwellings. The tipi was a portable shelter used by the Cree, Blackfeet, Crow, Cheyenne, and other Plains Indians.

Native Americans

In 1492 there were an estimated 840,000 Indians in tribal societies in North America. The Association of American Indian Affairs puts the current population of American Indians and Alaska natives at more than two million, about half of whom live in or near reservations and native villages. The federal government recognizes about 771 sovereign tribes, which are subject to federal and tribal laws but not to the laws of the state where they are located. As trustee of Indian assets, the BUREAU OF INDIAN AFFAIRS is responsible for protecting tribal property, ensuring the right to self-government, and providing services guaranteed by treaties.

From the time of the earliest European settlement, native peoples were regarded as living links to prehistory in America, and ancient Indian earthworks and midden and burial mounds elicited widespread interest. The first systematic scientific study and recording of sites, customs, and linguistics did not occur until the nineteenth century; leaders in this effort were the American Philosophical Society, American Antiquarian Society (☞ LEARNED SOCIETIES), and Smithsonian Institution. At the same time public interest in Indian artifacts began to grow as collections went on display at museums, world's fairs, and other expositions and Indian furnishings were made available as souvenirs by railroad and hotel concessionaires. By the end of the 1800s, looting of native archaeological sites (☞ ARCHAEOLOGICAL PARKS) was a problem and became the major impetus behind the Antiquities Act (1906) (☞ NATIONAL MONUMENTS).

Advocacy for Indians

The federal government's forced assimilation efforts and manipulative policies toward native populations, corresponding with all phases of western expansion, have been widely documented. In the nineteenth century a largely missionary-based movement coalesced, beginning with the American Society for Promoting Civilization and General Improvement of the Indian Tribes, founded in 1820. In the post–Civil War era, about twenty so-called reformer groups, run primarily by women, formed a loose advocacy network devoted to improving the "Indian plight." Like all Indian reform efforts in America up to this point, these were based in the East and focused on Christianity as the key to "civilizing" native peoples, who might otherwise be lost to their own savage ways. Many private reform efforts were met with federal resistance. In 1828 the Board for the Emigration, Preservation, and Improvement of the Aborigines was formed to subvert opposition to President Andrew Jackson's forced relocation of southeastern tribes along the Trail of Tears; it continued to fragment the influence of reformer groups in the following decades. Federal abuses were covered in the popular press and in such books as Helen Jackson's *Century of Dishonor: A Sketch of the United States Government's Dealings with Some of the Indian Tribes* (1881).

This evocative image of warriors entitled *An Indian Horse Dance* was included in a book on Sioux Indian painting compiled by Hartley Burr Alexander and published in France in 1938. Images made by the natives themselves were published less often than depictions by white European and American artists.

The first national initiative established by Native Americans for Native Americans was the Society of American Indians, an all-Indian advocacy group formed in 1911. The first national intertribal organization, the National Congress of American Indians, was not created until 1944. Many of the federally funded legal service programs established as part of the mid-1960s War on Poverty initiative under the Office of Economic Opportunity were located on or near Indian reservations. A National Council on Indian Opportunity was created by executive order of President Lyndon Johnson in 1968 and ratified in 1970 in response to pressure for tribal participation in national policy formation. Chaired by the vice president, the council was to include several cabinet members, including the secretaries of the interior and agriculture as well as six Indian representatives selected by the president. The purpose was to ensure that Indians received proper benefits from federal programs and to facilitate relations between tribal and government agencies; Indian participation in federal policy making was a high priority. However, the full council rarely if ever assembled and had no real direct access to the president.

Today the National Congress of American Indians is the foremost advocacy group for tribal interests. Among many concerns is preventing the use of sacred sites for hiking and rock climbing and their promotion as tourist attractions.

Contacts

Association on American Indian Affairs ✉ Box 268, Sisseton, SD 57262. 📞 605-698-3998. 🖥 www.indian-affairs.org
■ This organization had its genesis in a 1922 reform group of non-Indians opposed to a controversial bill favoring non-Indian claims to Pueblo lands. Its then-novel approach was to encourage rather than subvert pride of race and cultural traditions with a focus on health care and artistic and craft heritage. In 1937 the association joined with the American Indian Defense Association to promote the welfare of the American Indian "by creating an enlightened public opinion, by assisting and protecting him against encroachment of his constitutional rights, and by promoting suitable legislation and enforcement of law." Reestablished in South Dakota in 1995 with Indian administrators, the group offers scholarships and emphasizes the preservation of sacred sites. Extensive archives are housed at Princeton University.

Bureau of Indian Affairs ✉ U.S. Department of the Interior, 1849 C Street, NW, Washington, DC 20240. 📞 202-208-3710. 🖥 www.doi.gov/bureau-indian-affairs.html
■ The bureau, through the American Indian Trust Office, acts as trustee of the Indian assets held in trust by the federal government. The Tribal Enrollment Office provides information on tracing Indian ancestry and requirements to qualify for membership in a federally recognized Indian tribe.

National Archives and Records Administration ✉ 700 Pennsylvania Avenue, NW, Washington, DC 20408. 📞 202-501-5000. 🖥 www.nara.gov
■ The archives house census rolls and other Indian records identified by tribe, band, or tribal group and dating from 1830 to 1940. It will search the records according to individual English and Indian names and the names of tribal groups and provide information on other sources for genealogical research.

National Congress of American Indians ✉ 1301 Connecticut Avenue, NW, Suite 200, Washington, DC 20036. 📞 202-466-7767. 🖥 www.ncai.org
■ The congress, formed in 1944, was the first national Indian group to unify tribal representatives and bring them together with national policy makers, bypassing the Bureau of Indian Affairs. It has defended tribal sovereignty and treaty and civil rights and worked to preserve cultural traditions. A major goal is public education about the government rights of American Indians and Alaska natives. Programs focus on social issues, environmental protection, natural resource management, preservation of Indian cultural resources, and religious freedom.

National Indian Policy Center ✉ The George Washington University, 2021 K Street, NW, Suite 211, Washington, DC 20006. ☏ 202-973-7667. 🖳 www.hfni. gsehd.gwu.edu/ ~ eaceast/corpcap/indian.html

■ An information clearinghouse, this center was established by Congress in 1990 and operates under a planning committee composed of tribal leaders and representatives of major Indian organizations. It sponsors forums and research, monitors policy issues, and disseminates information on Indian policy issues relating to education, tribal governance, natural resource management, health, cultural rights and resources, law, and economic development. It also operates an electronic database.

Museums and
Historical Societies

Colorado Historical Society ✉ 1300 Broadway, Denver, CO 80203. ☏ 303-866-3682. 🖳 www.history.state.co.us/home.htm

■ The collection includes 20,000 items relating to the ancient ancestral pueblan cultures of southwestern Colorado and an ethnographic archive of artifacts from the peoples of the Great Plains, Great Basin, and Southeast, including the Ute, Cheyenne, Sioux, Arapaho, Navajo, Apache, Shoshone, and Pueblo tribes.

A 1953 political rally at the statehouse in Montpelier, Vermont, brought out Chief Poking Fire of the Mohawk Indians. Although the tipi was used by Plains Indians rather than northeastern tribes, it strikes a symbolic chord.

Eiteljorg Museum of American Indians and Western Art ✉ 500 West Washington Street, Indianapolis, IN 46204. ☏ 317-636-9378. 🖳 www. eiteljorg.org

■ The museum absorbed the collections of the Museum of Indian Heritage in 1989, amassing thousands of Native American artifacts including pottery, jewelry, ceremonial garments, baskets, totems, and tipis. The entire country is represented, with an emphasis on native peoples of the Great Plains and Southwest.

Heard Museum ✉ 2301 North Central Avenue, Phoenix, AZ 85004. ☏ 602-252-8840. 🖳 www. Heard.org

■ Founded in 1929, the Heard Museum houses a private collection of art and artifacts emphasizing native cultures of the Southwest. A learning center is devoted to Arizona's twenty-one federally recognized tribes.

Joslyn Art Museum ✉ 2200 Dodge Street, Omaha, NE 68102. ☏ 402-342-3300. 🖳 www.josyln.org

■ This extensive collection encompasses drawings, prints, and decorated objects made by the native peoples of North America.

National Gallery of Art ✉ Sixth Street and Constitution Avenue, NW, Washington, DC 20565. ☏ 202-737-4215. 🖳 www.nga.gov

■ Containing some 800 Indian portraits, the gallery has a significant number of prints by Karl Bodmer and more than 300 paintings by George Catlin.

National Museum of the American Indian ✉ George Gustav Heye Center, Alexander Hamilton U.S. Custom House, One Bowling Green, New York, NY 10004. ☎ 212-514-3700. 🖥 www.si.edu/nmai

■ A branch of the Smithsonian Institution devoted to the languages, literature, history, and arts of Native Americans, this museum was established by an act of Congress in 1989. The Heye Center, opened in October 1994, displays masks, weapons, clothing, musical instruments, pottery, and other artifacts from pre-history to the present. Programs on music, dance, theater, and storytelling are also offered. A new sister museum is in Washington, D.C.

The Plains Indian Museum ✉ Buffalo Bill Historical Center, 720 Sheridan Avenue, Cody, WY 82414. ☎ 307-587-4771. 🖥 www.bbhc.org

■ Emphasizing the early reservation period, from the 1880s to the present, the collection relates primarily to northern Plains tribes, including the Sioux, Crow, Arapaho, Shoshone, and Cheyenne.

Web Sites

National Congress of American Indians. Provides a directory of tribes in the contiguous forty-eight states. 🖥 www.ncai.org/TribalDirectory/Lower48 Tribes/lower48tribes.htm

Native American Consultation Database. A joint project between the National Park Service's Archeology and Ethnography Program and the U.S. Air Force's Center for Environmental Excellence providing information on tribal leaders and organizations for all 771 federally recognized Indian tribes (including Alaska native villages), Alaska native corporations, and native Hawaiian organizations. 🖥 www.cast.uark.edu/other/nps/nacd

Smithsonian Institution Native American History and Culture. An excellent selection of links to sites hosted by its museums and organizations, including folkways, music, American Indian biographies, exhibitions, and a tribal museum directory. 🖥 www.si.edu/resource/faq/nmai/start.htm

Naturalists

The New World could not claim Europe's ancient ruins or its centuries-old cultural heritage, but it surpassed both with its natural riches: an exotica of rhododendron, hydrangea, Venus flytrap, aster, camellia, bison, turtle doves, jaguars, sturgeon, prairie dogs, and countless other previously unknown species. The first accounts of these marvels were supplied as early as the 1540s by the Spanish conquistadors and Jesuit missionaries. More systematic studies were primarily English efforts, often detailed in the descriptive accounts of early surveyors and colonial administrators. One of the first comprehensive volumes about American wildlife was the *New English Canaan* (1637) by Thomas Morton, a British trader. Sir Hans Sloane (1660–1753), the English naturalist whose extensive collection of books, manuscripts, and botanical specimens became the foundation of the British Museum, actively encouraged the collection of seeds and specimens in the New World.

The next generation of naturalists to investigate and record American flora and fauna was often as colorful as their subjects—from Mark Catesby, who cultivated a garden of poison ivy, to the foppish JOHN JAMES AUDUBON, who entertained in British drawing rooms by imitating bird calls and eating corn on the cob. Although the scientific accuracy of these men was sometimes challenged, their field descriptions provided some of the first and best accounts of migration habits and now-extinct species; many, Audubon and William Bartram among them, were also serious students of Indian peoples and keen observers of native agriculture and settlement patterns.

Mark Catesby (1682–1749), the noted British plant collector and ornithologist, made his first trip to the colonies for the Royal Society as early as 1712, sending back specimens embalmed in bottles of rum. An expert in bird migration, Catesby was also a gifted scientific illustrator and the first naturalist of the era to combine that talent with authoritative text descriptions in a single published volume. *The Natural History of Carolina, Florida, and the Bahama Islands* (1731) was among the most advanced scientific chronicles of the time.

The first American naturalist of significant accomplishment was the Pennsylvania-born John Bartram (1699–1777). Although he had no formal training, Bartram was a highly skilled field botanist whose pioneering trips into the wilds of the Allegheny Mountains, CATSKILL MOUNTAINS, the Carolinas, and Florida produced detailed records of hundreds of new species and supplied European scientists with more than three hundred plant samples. His name is commemorated in a genus of mosses, *Bartramia.*

Bartram's son William (1739–1823) was a field scientist of equal if not greater merit. Together, father and son traveled 400 miles by canoe along Florida's St. John River, sold seeds to THOMAS JEFFERSON, and maintained the first experimental botanical garden in America, near Philadelphia. William Bartram, appointed royal botanist to George II in 1765, was the first American naturalist to follow in Catesby's tradition of illustrated scientific research. His *Travels* (1791), a compendium of text descriptions supplemented by illustrations printed from copper plates, records his explorations deep into the American South and West into largely uncharted Indian territory. The entries on 215 American birds made up the most thorough account of the subject to date. *Travels* was issued in nine European editions and translated into six languages; its evocative descriptions of nature are said to have influenced a

The English naturalist Mark Catesby made two visits to America, in 1712–19 and 1722–25, and is considered one of the most important plant collectors of the century. His detailed renderings, including this one of a bullfrog, always showed flora and fauna in their proper ecological context.

number of England's great romantic poets, including Coleridge, Wordsworth, and Shelley.

William Bartram's work also had a strong impact on the Scottish-born Alexander Wilson (1766–1813), who discovered thirty-nine bird species on his American travels. In 1807 Meriwether Lewis commissioned him to illustrate specimens collected during the CORPS OF DISCOVERY expedition for the publication of the explorer's journals. Wilson's *American Ornithology* (1808–14) established the standard for the next generation of naturalists, in particular Audubon, whom Wilson had met during his wilderness field studies. ☞ *also* BIRDS, BISON

📖 Thomas Morton, *New English Canaan* (1637). 📖 Robert Beverly, *The History and Present State of Virginia* (1705). 📖 John Lawson, *A New Voyage to Carolina* (1709). 📖 Mark Catesby, *The Natural History of Carolina, Florida, and the Bahama Islands* (1731). 📖 John Bartram, *Observations* (1751). 📖 Peter Kahn, *Travels in North America* (1753). 📖 John Bartram, *Account of East Florida* (1767). 📖 Thomas Jefferson, *Notes on the State of Virginia* (1788). 📖 William Bartram, *Travels* (1791). 📖 Alexander Wilson, *American Ornithology* (1808–14). 📖 Henry Marie Breckenridge, *Views of Louisiana* (1814). 📖 John Bradbury, *Travels in the Interior of America* (1817). 📖 Thomas Nuttall, *Genera of North American Plants* (1818).
Reading

New York State Forest Preserve

Created in 1885, the New York State Forest Preserve is the oldest state forest preserve in the United States. Its primary purpose was to protect the New York City watershed by setting aside state-owned forest land in the ADIRONDACK and CATSKILL MOUNTAINS. Rather than a single tract, the New York forest preserve comprises a patchwork of noncontiguous parcels of FORESTS (primarily hardwood) ranging from less than 10 acres to 300 acres in size—for a current total of about 2.7 million scattered acres in the Adirondack Forest Preserve and 287,000 acres in the Catskill Forest Preserve.

The preserve was created under a two-part piece of New York state legislation (1885 and 1894) requiring that the forest be "forever kept as wild forest lands," with no possibility for sale, lease, or cutting or removal of trees. This legislation was the first state ruling to protect a wilderness area in the United States, and it remains the most restrictive in the entire country, offering far more protection than the federally mandated NATIONAL WILDERNESS PRESERVATION SYSTEM. Changing the "forever wild" status would require an amendment to the state constitution that would have to be passed by two consecutive legislative sessions and ratified by voters in a public referendum.

"If the Adirondacks are cleared, the Hudson River will dry up."

Forest and Stream (1883)

New York State Department of Environmental Conservation ✉ 50 Wolf Road, Albany, NY 12233. ☎ 518-485-8940. 🖥 www.dec.state.ny.us

Contact

Office of Surface Mining Reclamation and Enforcement

Established in the U.S. DEPARTMENT OF THE INTERIOR by the Surface Mining Control and Reclamation Act (1977), this office operates nationwide to ensure that surface coal mining follows environmental protection measures. The agency oversees state mining regulatory and abandoned-mine reclamation programs and regulates mining and reclamation activities on federal and Indian lands. The agency also coordinates the public-private Appalachian clean streams initiative, undertaken to clean up streams and rivers polluted by acid mine drainage (☞ APPLACHIAN MOUNTAINS).

Contact **Office of Surface Mining Reclamation and Enforcement** ⊠ U.S. Department of the Interior, 1849 C Street, NW, Washington, DC 20240. ☎ 202-208-2719. 🖥 www.osmre.gov

Olympic Mountains

Part of the coastal ranges of the Pacific Northwest, the Olympic Mountains thrust upward almost from the water's edge, running a rugged course along the Olympic Peninsula south of the Juan de Fuca Strait and west of Puget Sound in Washington. The mountains are part of an ancient sea floor forced skyward by heaving geological pressure. At last count 266 GLACIERS were at work reshaping the peaks and the range's defining profile of lake basins, U-shaped

valentes, and jagged summits, the highest of which is Mount Olympus (7,965 feet). The moist Pacific climate is responsible not only for the area's astounding forest growth in lower elevations but also the glaciers at the highest levels. Part of the Olympic forests were declared a national forest reserve by President Grover Cleveland as early as 1897 (☞ FORESTS, NATIONAL FOREST SYSTEM). THEODORE ROOSEVELT followed by declaring part of the region a NATIONAL MONUMENT in 1909; this area is now incorporated in Mount Olympus National Park (☞ NATIONAL PARK SYSTEM). About 96 percent of the park was designated for inclusion in the NATIONAL WILDERNESS PRESERVATION SYSTEM in 1988.

A 1913 image showing glaciated peaks in the Olympic Mountains of Washington records the range as a striking backdrop for a view of the Skokemesh River near Lake Cushman.

Olympic National Park ✉ 600 East Park Avenue, Port Angeles, WA 98362. ☏ 360-565-3130. ▯ www.nps.gov/olym

Contact

■ The park embraces three ecosystems: mountain/glacier, Pacific coastline, and temperate rain forest.

Ozark Mountains

These heavily wooded highlands, also known as the Ozark Plateau, likely derive their name from that of an eighteenth-century trading post—Aux Arc—run by French trappers in the region. The Ozarks ramble south from St. Louis to the Arkansas River, unfolding into eastern Oklahoma, Missouri, southern Illinois, Kansas, and northern

Canoeists paddle in the Current River, part of the Ozark Rivers National Scenic Riverway in Missouri. In 1964 this and the Jacks Fork River were the first two American rivers so designated, and in 1968 they became part of the National Wild and Scenic Rivers System.

Arkansas to cover about 50,000 square miles. Along with the neighboring Ouachitas to the south, the gradually sloping plateau accounts for the only significantly mountainous terrain between the APPALACHIAN MOUNTAINS and the ROCKY MOUNTAINS. The highest Ozark peaks, rising to about 2,400 feet, are located in the Boston Mountains. Steep ridges and gorges, dense forests, and numerous springs and streams shape a distinctive landscape where the fall foliage is said to rival that of New England. Of the many waterways draining the region, the Current and Jacks Fork Rivers of southeastern Missouri were designated the first national scenic riverway; the 140-mile stretch authorized by Congress in 1964 became part of the NATIONAL WILD AND SCENIC RIVERS SYSTEM created in 1968. The Ozark region was first popularized as a tourist destination in Harold Bell Wright's novel *The Shepherd of the Hills* (1907) and now ranks among the fastest developing rural areas in the United States.

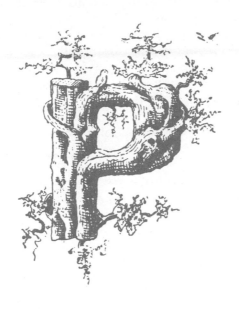

One of the two original national scenic trails authorized by Congress in 1968 as part of the NATIONAL TRAILS SYSTEM was the Pacific Crest Trail. Open to hikers and equestrians, this scenic corridor begins near Campo, California, not far from the Mexican border, and ends at the Canadian border east of Ross Lake, Washington. Over its 2,650-mile course it rides the shoulders of the SIERRA NEVADA RANGE and CASCADE MOUNTAINS, traversing three states (California, Oregon, and Washington), approximately one hundred mountain peaks, thirty-three national wilderness areas, twenty-four national forests, eight named passes higher than 11,000 feet, seven national parks, several state parks, and even a few highways. To hike the entire route (about sixty people do so annually) is to pass through a changing landscape of desert, canyon, snow field, volcanic soil, glacier, meadow, ponderosa pine, and alpine lake. The highest point is the Forester Pass (13,180 feet) in central California.

The idea for the trail is generally credited to Clinton Clarke, who organized the Pacific Coast Trail System Conference in 1932 using a concept similar to that of the APPALACHIAN NATIONAL SCENIC TRAIL. The initial route was scouted by YMCA hikers and first fell into place as a series of shorter, unconnected trails; the complete trail was not dedicated until 1993. The BUREAU OF LAND MANAGEMENT is responsible

Pacific Crest National Scenic Trail

for 115 miles of the trail in California, while the Oregon and Washington segments are administered by the U.S. FOREST SERVICE. Because several areas traversed by the trail require hiking permits, the Pacific Crest Trail Association has put together a single permit and made it available to through-hikers traveling 500 or more miles in a single trip. Numerous day hikes are also possible.

Contact

Pacific Crest Trail Association ⊠ 5325 Elkhorn Boulevard, Sacramento, CA 95842. (916-349-2109. ▯ www.pcta.org

■ The federal government's primary partner for the trail, this nonprofit membership group works to protect the route from abuse and commercial encroachment. It also maintains a Web site with a detailed state-by-state description of trail segments and access points and sponsors cleanups and other volunteer maintenance efforts.

Park Architecture

The concept of a cohesive architecture for the nation's parks dates to the 1916 creation of the NATIONAL PARK SERVICE. Experimentation with rustic designs had begun years before, but because designated wilderness areas were administered by so many agencies, no clear design guidelines for the scattered tent camps, lodges, and auxiliary structures being built in the nation's parks had ever been drawn up. However, Stephen T. Mather, the first director, was determined that park buildings conform to the natural landscape and made planning for them a priority. Supported by the American Civic Association and the American Society of Landscape Architects, Mather committed the new agency to unobtrusive roads and structures and called for a staff of professionals "with a proper appreciation of the aesthetic value of park lands." Part of the agenda was to cultivate popular support for existing and future parks by ensuring a pleasurable tourist experience in a wilderness landscape unspoiled by unsympathetic development. This strategy was rigorously pursued until World War II and resulted in a woodlands aesthetic that has become so instantly identifiable with the nation's parks that it is now known affectionately as "parkitecture."

The National Park Service's 1935 "parkitecture" manual showed this rustic spring house in Boyle State Park, Arkansas, with cedar shingles and a stone base.

"Sprung from the Soil"

The major era of construction in American parks occurred during the Works Progress Administration work-relief programs of the 1930s, which put thousands of Americans to work on park projects throughout the country (☞ CIVILIAN CONSERVATION CORPS). The 1933 consolidation of parks and monuments under the Park Service helped centralize administrative efforts, and it became the supervising agency for building projects in national, state, and community parks under the Emergency Conservation Work Program the same year.

In 1935 the Park Service published an instruction manual for designing and building park architecture. Noting architects' lack of experience in meeting the "special needs" of park design, *Park Structures and Facilities* offered photographs and detailed specifications for all manner of accoutrements, from bridges and overlooks to barbecues, boathouses, swimming pools, and sleeping cabins. The introspective text began with a remarkable "Apologia": if the creation of the world had failed to provide the appropriate picnic tables and kiosks, then it was up to the National Park Service to do so—even if this meant playing the role of "jester in Nature's unspoiled places." Design guidelines dictated a harmonizing color palette, attention to textures, irregular rooflines, and natural foundation plantings to bring to each building "that agreeable look of having sprung from the soil." The stated objective was to minimize the impact of man-made intrusions by blending them into the landscape and creating a sense of history suited to the broader park plan.

The allure of the Grand Canyon's El Tovar resort was enhanced by an ensemble of structures designed by Mary Elizabeth Jane Colter and built between 1905 and 1932. Recalling ancient pueblan structures, her stone Desert View Watchtower blended into the precipice.

Ahwahnee, a Miwok Indian word that roughly translates as "deep, grassy valley," is an aptly fanciful name for Gilbert Stanley Underwood's 1927 hotel set against a granite buttress in California's Yosemite National Park. The $1.5 million fire-proof structure was built of concrete stained to resemble redwood.

Hotels and Resorts

The first resorts in America were the post-Revolution destinations of the Mid-Atlantic plantation gentry—the Tidewater region of Virginia, Maryland, and the Carolinas. These consisted primarily of health springs, at least one of which, Warm Springs, Virginia, has been in continuous operation for about 250 years. By the early 1800s mountain lodges had begun appearing along stage lines in such nascent tourist areas as the WHITE MOUNTAINS and CATSKILL MOUNTAINS. Rustic decorations were an early theme. For example, fir trees and hemlock boughs bedecked the reception rooms of the Mountain House, a popular Catskills lodge built in Pine Orchard, New York, in 1823.

The nineteenth-century proliferation of lodges and retreats for leisure and recreation in backwoods destinations corresponded with the development of steamer and railroad lines. Well before the transcontinental railroad was completed in 1869, competing rail companies were establishing "fishing lines" into lake regions and speculating in tourist developments. More hotels and resorts were opened in the four decades following the Civil War than in any other era. Rail companies were responsible for the first significant hotel and concession development in the wilderness parks and consistently lobbied Congress for the creation of additional national parks. Protecting company interests in its rail line into Montana, the Great Northern Railway strongly promoted Glacier National Park, established by Congress in 1910.

Park accommodations ranged from tent camps and rustic chalets to rambling hotels designed in all the popular Victorian styles. The era of the great wilderness hotels associated with rustic design, however, began in 1904 with Yellowstone Park's Old Faithful Inn and essentially ended with the fabulous Timberline Lodge, a 1938 WPA project undertaken by the U.S. FOREST SERVICE in Oregon's Mount Hood National Forest (☞ NATIONAL FOREST SYSTEM). The theatrical designs were perfectly suited to the high drama of the landscape. The Grand Canyon's jewel was the 1905 El Tovar in Arizona, sited just 20 feet from the canyon's rim. The hotel incorporated ersatz Pueblo outbuildings as well as "art rooms" embellished with paintings by the successful landscape artist Thomas Moran (☞ HUDSON RIVER SCHOOL ARTISTS, ROCKY MOUNTAIN SCHOOL ARTISTS).

The grande dame of them all, however, remained the Old Faithful Inn, a Disneyland-like extravaganza conceived by the Northern Pacific Railway as a showcase resort for the Upper Geyser Basin in Wyoming. The inspired design deliberately played on the exaggerated scale of the Yellowstone scenery by incorporating giant timbers and boulders. The centerpiece was the 92-foot-high lobby, where staggered log staircases and balconies of burled lodgepole pine encouraged guests to pause for views at various levels as they climbed and descended, much in the same manner as hikers stop for vistas in the park itself. To complete the exotic woodland effect, the original hotel furnishings, which cost a staggering $28,000 in 1904, included "Indian" throw rugs, hickory rockers, and studded leather-top tables. ☞ also FURNITURE, NATIONAL PARK SYSTEM

The gnarled timbers and stone fireplace in the lobby of the Old Faithful Inn project a wilderness image that captures the magic of the landscape and pays homage to the scale of the scenery. The novel hotel, which was designed by Robert Reamer for Yellowstone National Park, caused excitement as soon as it opened in 1904 and has proven almost as much a curiosity as the park's hydrothermal wonders.

■ **Old Faithful Inn, Yellowstone National Park, Wyoming.** Opened 1904. Architect: Robert C. Reamer. Early concessionaires: Northern Pacific Railway and Yellowstone Park Association.

■ **El Tovar, Grand Canyon National Park, Arizona.** Opened 1905. Architects: Charles Whittlesey and Mary Elizabeth Jane Colter. Early concessionaires: Atchison, Topeka and Santa Fe Railway and Fred Harvey Company.

■ **Glacier Park Lodge, Glacier National Park, Montana.** Opened 1913. Architects: S. L. Bartlett and Thomas McMahon. Early concessionaires: Great Northern Railway and Glacier Park Hotel Company.

■ **Lake McDonald Lodge (originally Lewis Glacier Hotel), Glacier National Park, Montana.** Opened 1914. Architect: Kirtland Cutter. Early concessionaires: John Lewis, Great Northern Railway, and Glacier Park Hotel Company.

■ **Many Glacier Hotel, Glacier National Park, Montana.** Opened 1915. Architect: Thomas McMahon. Early concessionaire: Great Northern Railway.

■ **Crater Lake Lodge, Crater Lake National Park, Oregon.** Opened 1915. Architect: Raymond Hockenberry. Early concessionaire: Crater Lake Company.

■ **Paradise Inn, Mount Rainier National Park, Washington.** Opened 1917. Architects: Heath, Grove, and Bell. Early concessionaire: Rainier National Park Company.

■ **Bryce Canyon Lodge, Bryce Canyon National Park, Utah.** Opened 1925. Architect: Gilbert Stanley Underwood. Early concessionaire: Union Pacific Railway.

■ **The Ahwahnee, Yosemite National Park, California.** Opened 1927. Architect: Gilbert Stanley Underwood. Early concessionaire: Yosemite Park and Curry Company.

■ **Grand Canyon Lodge, Grand Canyon National Park, Arizona.** Opened 1928 (burned 1932; rebuilt 1937). Architect (original): Gilbert Stanley Underwood. Early concessionaire: Union Pacific Railway.

■ **Oregon Caves Chateau, Oregon Caves National Monument, Oregon.** Opened 1934. Architect: Gust Lium. Early concessionaire: Oregon Caves Company.

■ **Timberline Lodge, Mount Hood National Forest, Oregon.** Opened 1938. Architects: W. I.Turner, Linn Forrest, Howard Gifford, Dean Wright (U.S. Forest Service architects); Gilbert Stanley Underwood, consultant. Early concessionaires: U.S. Forest Service and Timberline Lodge.

■ **Painted Desert Inn, Petrified Forest National Park, Arizona.** Opened 1940. Architect: Thomas C. Vint. Early concessionaire: Fred Harvey Company.

Photographers

Photography's evolution in America as both a documentary and an art form coincided with frontier expansion and advancements in the medium itself. Photographs made during the era of western exploration could be almost as laborious to produce as a painting, yet the finished products offered an indisputably real record of time and place that a painting could not. Their reality and their mystery had a tremendous impact on public interest in the wilderness and in some cases helped garner support for national parks and monuments (☞ NATIONAL MONUMENTS, NATIONAL PARK SYSTEM).

Almost as soon as the daguerreotype process was introduced from France in the 1840s, American photographers began using it and adopted the more advanced wet photography (collodion solution) and gelatin dry-plate negative as soon as they were available. The possibility of producing high-quality pictures in multiple prints using the enormous dry-plate negative (introduced in 1880) opened new opportunities for sale and publication of images and made possible successful careers for such wilderness image makers as WILLIAM HENRY JACKSON and EDWARD S. CURTIS.

In the early 1840s J. H. Fitzgibbon's St. Louis gallery was exhibiting daguerreotypes of riverboats and Indian chiefs, the first frontier subjects recorded on film. The gold rush inspired the first significant wave of western photography, and California boomtowns attracted numerous professional photographers by the early 1850s. Immediately after the Civil War, the western railroad and geological mapping SURVEYS resumed in earnest, and these expeditions produced the first systematic photodocumentation of the frontier and some of the very first photographic images of American Indians. The

Documenting the Frontier

An apprentice of the photographer Mathew Brady (1823–96), Timothy O'Sullivan took his camera from the Civil War battleground to penetrate some of the most remote regions of America. In 1873–74 he made pictures of the prehistoric Indian villages at Canyon de Chelly in Arizona. The stark southwestern landscapes endow O'Sullivan's work with a detached, abstract quality that contributes to their graphic impact.

Civil War painter and photographer Captain Andrew J. Russell (1830–1902) was the most prolific railroad photographer of the West. Russell was hired by the Union Pacific Railway to document completion of the transcontinental rail line, which pushed through the ROCKY MOUNTAINS and finally joined the Central Pacific line at Promontory Point in Utah in 1869. In the process he captured vast panoramas along the Union Pacific route, scenes of various engineering feats, and natural oddities such as Skull Rock, which became popular landmarks for travelers on the line.

In 1867 the noted photographer Timothy O'Sullivan (1840–82) joined the Clarence King Survey, traveling from what is now northern Utah to southern Wyoming, on to the Great Salt Lake basin, and into the Rockies in Colorado. The German-born John K. Hillers (1843–1925) developed a lasting association with the GRAND CANYON explorer John Wesley Powell (1834–1902) and in 1873 accompanied Powell and the painter Thomas Moran (☞ HUDSON RIVER SCHOOL ARTISTS, ROCKY MOUNTAIN SCHOOL ARTISTS) on his Utah expedition to what is now the site of ZION NATIONAL PARK. Later in the same trip he traveled to the Grand Canyon and also photographed Paiute Indians in the Kanab Canyon region after Moran arranged their clothes and positioned them in artful groupings.

From the gold rush days onward, California remained a center for the art of photography. The first successful independent landscape photographer of the West was Carleton Watkins (1829–1916), the well-known documenter of YOSEMITE VALLEY and

Old Faithful Geyser (above) at Yellowstone National Park erupted on schedule for William Henry Jackson in 1883. Eight years earlier, John K. Hillers photographed the Green River (below) from a cave in Split Mountain Canyon at Dinosaur National Monument in Colorado.

pioneer in the use of large-plate negative printing to create stunning images for exhibition. In 1861 Watkins made the first of eight trips to Yosemite, and his California views showed a landscape of monumental beauty untarnished by humankind and thus all the more awe inspiring. The English-born Eadweard Muybridge (1830–1904) followed Watkins to Yosemite and from 1868 to 1872 was his major competitor. In 1868 Muybridge's large-plate images provided the first illustrations for a guidebook to the area, *Yosemite: Its Wonders and Beauties*, by John S. Hittell.

In addition to the noted ANSEL ADAMS, early-twentieth-century contributors to the field included Edward Weston (1886–1958), known for his stunningly pure images of rocks and trees. An Illinois native, Weston went to California after the 1906 earthquake there to work as a surveyor for the San Pedro, Los Angeles, and Salt Lake Railway. A 1937 Guggenheim fellowship—the first ever awarded to a photographer—allowed him to continue exploring western subjects and resulted in the publication of *California and the West* in 1940. He set out the following year to illustrate a new edition of *Leaves of Grass* (1855) by WALT WHITMAN.

In 1872 E. O. Beamon, a colleague of John K. Hillers, turned his camera on members of his western survey party. John F. Steward posed in Glen Canyon, Colorado, with field equipment and a gun.

Cecil Green Library ✉ Department of Special Collections, Stanford University, Stanford, CA 94305. ☎ 650-723-2300. ▯ www.sul.stanford.edu/depts/spc
■ The library preserves the papers of Ansel Adams and photographic collections of Eadweard Muybridge and Carleton Watkins.

Contacts

Colorado Historical Society ✉ 1300 Broadway, Denver, CO 80203. ☎ 303-866-3682. ▯ www.history.state.co.us/home.htm
■ Photographic holdings here include more than 500,000 images with specific Colorado connections. A highlight is the William Henry Jackson collection of 20,000 glass-plate prints and negatives documenting the first extensive exploration of Yellowstone and development of the western railroads. The archive also contains Detroit Publishing Company materials relating to the trans-Mississippi West.

Library of Congress ✉ Prints and Photographs Division, 101 Independence Avenue, SE, Washington, DC 20540. ☎ 202-707-6394. ▯ www.loc.gov.lcweb. loc.gov/rr/print/202_detr.html
■ The division's Detroit Publishing Company archive contains most of the company's prints and negatives relating to the trans-Mississippi West. It also houses 1,600 original Edward S. Curtis prints representing each of the regions documented in *The North American Indian*.

Los Angeles County Museum of Art ✉ 5905 Wilshire Boulevard, Los Angeles, CA 90036. ☎ 323-857-6000. ⌨ www.lacma.org/art/perm_col/permcol.htm
■ Modern masters include Edward Weston as well as Berenice Abbott, Ansel Adams, Walker Evans, Lisette Model, Alfred Stieglitz, and Minor White.

Museum of Modern Art ✉ 11 West Fifty-third Street, New York, NY 10019. ☎ 212-708-9750. ⌨ www.moma.org
■ An archive of more than 25,000 photographic works dating from about 1840 to the present endows this museum with one of the most comprehensive photograph archives in the world.

Society of California Pioneers ✉ 300 Fourth Street, San Francisco, CA 94107. ☎ 415-957-1849. ⌨ www.californiapioneers.org
■ The collection features a substantial number of photographs by Carleton Watkins and the San Francisco firm of Lawrence and Houseworth, as well as views by other photographers of San Francisco, Yosemite, and the Central Pacific Railway.

Pollution

As the United States becomes more populated and as more people use national parks, forests, and backcountry areas for recreation, pollutants of all types pose an increasing threat to the American wilderness. Water pollutants may be the most insidious because they are not always evident to the eye. Anyone who has scaled a peak in the GREAT SMOKY MOUNTAINS or gained the edge of the GRAND CANYON, however, cannot deny the impact of smog and haze on his or her wilderness experience. The buzz of all-terrain vehicles and snowmobiles, a more recent subject for debate, is not only annoying to people but is also believed to be harmful to wild animals, which alter their grazing and feeding patterns in response

Clean Air and Water

The first piece of federal legislation to identify air pollution as a national problem was the Air Pollution Control Act (1955). The Clean Air Act of 1963 set emission standards for power plants and steel mills and was followed by a series of amendments in that decade authorizing expansion of local controls and auto emission standards, which were significantly tightened by the Clean Air Act of 1970.

The Clean Air Act of 1990 focuses on five major issues: air quality standards, motor vehicle emissions and alternative fuels, toxic air pollutants, acid rain, and stratospheric ozone depletion. The act delegates to the states much of the work of air pollution control. The ENVIRONMENTAL PROTECTION AGENCY sets limits on how much of a pollutant is allowable in the air anywhere in the country. Individual states may strengthen their pollution controls but may not weaken them below the national standards.

The Air Resources Division of the NATIONAL PARK SERVICE works in partnership with the Air Quality Branch of the U.S. FISH AND WILDLIFE SERVICE to protect the air quality of parks and wildlife refuges. Areas of concern include visibility, flora, fauna, soil, water, and virtually all resources affected by air quality. The air monitoring program IMPROVE tracks visibility changes to fulfill the 1977 visibility provisions added to the Clean Air Act, specifically to protect the views the public expects to see when visiting parks and wilderness areas.

The Clean Water Act (1972) was the first comprehensive national legislation to address the problem of water pollution and the first to protect the country's lakes, rivers, coastal areas, aquifers, wetlands, and aquatic habitats. At that time only one-third of American waters were considered safe for fishing and swimming. Three years earlier the Cuyahoga River in Cleveland, Ohio, was so filled with trash and toxic spills that it had erupted in fire. In addition to sewage and industrial waste, another major concern was agricultural runoff, which was eroding millions of tons of soil and depositing dangerous amounts of nitrogen and phosphorous into waters.

Air quality has been legislated by federal statutes in America since 1955. Pollution quotients are set by the Environmental Protection Agency.

The act requires industries to meet federal pollution-control standards and mandates that states and tribal nations set standards and develop programs to meet them. In the last three decades the legislation has resulted in significant surface improvement but has not done much to help aquatic habitats. Aquatic species remain the most ENDANGERED SPECIES in America.

Controlling Pollution at the Source

The Pollution Prevention Act (1990) established the federal policy of preventing or reducing pollution at its source and mandates that polluting materials that cannot be prevented be disposed of in an environmentally safe manner. The statute is significant in that it shifted the approach of pollution control from dealing with the problem at the point of release into the environment to attempting to control it at its point of origin. This strategy—source reduction—is considered the preferred approach to environmental protection because it reduces raw-material costs for industries as well as liability and public health risks. This watchdog legislation mandated that the EPA create an Office of Pollution Prevention to develop a source-reduction strategy and models and require manufacturers to annually account for their source reduction and recycling programs.

Acid Rain ☎ 202-564-9620

Clean Air Technology ☎ 919-541-0800

EPA Information Resources Center ☎ 202-260-5922

Hazardous Waste Ombudsman ☎ 800-262-7937

Pesticides ☎ 800-858-7378

Pollution Prevention Information Clearinghouse ☎ 202-260-1023

Radon ☎ 800-767-7236

Safe Drinking Water ☎ 800-426-4791

Stratospheric Ozone Information (CFCs) ☎ 800-296-1996

Web Site

Clean Air Act Information Network. Presents a fact sheet and access to the document library. 💻 www.envinfo.com/caalead.html

A 1929 horseback riding party makes its way along the East Rim Trail in Zion National Park in Utah, one of hundreds of units in the public domain overseen by the National Park Service. The Bureau of Land Management, also part of the U.S. Department of the Interior, administers the great majority of U.S. public lands.

Public Lands

Federal public lands—owned equally by all Americans—constitute about 28 percent, or about 650 million acres, of the nation's 2.3 billion acres. Almost all of this public domain is west of the APPALACHIAN MOUNTAINS.

The Articles of Confederation (1781), adopted after the Revolution, superseded speculative claims and provided that the western territories be divided into distinct states and admitted to the Union on equal terms with the first thirteen as soon as the free population in each equaled that of any of the original states. In preparation for land sales to individuals,

Congress passed the Land Ordinance (1785), which provided for the survey of the Northwest Territory into townships six miles square along a grid running east-west and north-south and encouraged the establishment of land offices to speed up sales. The Northwest Ordinance (1787) dictated that the region be divided into no fewer than three or no more than five territories while providing for representation, freedom of religion, and antislavery measures, thus setting a precedent for western territorial expansion for the rest of the next century.

By 1802 cessions to the Union had endowed the new Republic with 236.8 million acres of public lands, including the territories of present-day Ohio, Indiana, Illinois, Michigan, and Wisconsin; the portion of Minnesota situated east of the Mississippi; and the sections of Alabama and Mississippi located north of the 31st parallel. The balance of public domain was acquired primarily through a combination of purchases, annexation, war spoils, and cessions beginning with the 1803 Louisiana Purchase (☞ CORPS OF DISCOVERY, THOMAS JEFFERSON). Two major land settlements of the mid-1800s involved the acquisition of Oregon to the 49th parallel in 1846 and the 1848 Treaty of Guadalupe Hidalgo, which gained for the United States the future states of California and New Mexico and established the Rio Grande boundary with Mexico.

Early on, Congress recognized the western domain as a source of fast cash for the federal government, which the founders had envisioned as only a short-term steward of public lands. This territory was routinely surveyed and put up for sale to raise revenues. Designed to encourage western settlement, nineteenth-century homestead laws accounted for a significant portion of divestiture. One-fifth of the public domain, totaling 287.5 million acres, passed into private hands under the Homestead Act (1862) before that statute was repealed in 1976. Large tracts also went to land-grant companies and to railroads as rights-of-way.

No land was actually reserved from the public domain for such uses as national parks, refuges, and reclamation until after 1849, when the U.S. DEPARTMENT OF THE INTERIOR was created to oversee public land management. At that time the federal government's role began to shift toward acquisition rather than disposal. This change in policy was solidified by the Weeks Forest Purchase Act (1911), which allowed the federal government to enlarge the NATIONAL FOREST SYSTEM through outright purchase of property. During Franklin D. Roosevelt's administration, large tracts of barren land were purchased for the public domain under emergency recovery acts, while the

Taylor Grazing Act (1934) permitted the secretary of the interior to withdraw unappropriated public lands for grazing leases. In the mid-1930s President Roosevelt used the authority of the Pickett Act (1910) to reserve from sale the major portion of public domain outside the Alaska territory pending a decision on its permanent use.

Management of the Public Domain

About 98 percent of public land is administered by one of four federal agencies: the NATIONAL PARK SERVICE, U.S. FOREST SERVICE, U.S. FISH AND WILDLIFE SERVICE, or BUREAU OF LAND MANAGEMENT (the remainder is administered primarily by the U.S. Department of Defense). Of these agencies, the BLM has exclusive jurisdiction over the majority—226 million acres, or about 41 percent—of the federal domain, about one-third of which is in ALASKA. Most of the more than $1 billion in annual revenues derived from BLM lands comes from mineral extraction, timber product sales, grazing fees (90 percent of BLM land outside Alaska is used for grazing and is classified as rangeland), and recreation fees, in that order. Because federal property is generally exempt from state and local taxes, revenues are typically shared with state and local governments. For example, each of the contiguous forty-eight states receives 50 percent of mineral leasing revenues from public domain lands within its boundaries.

The Forest Service manages 191 million acres of public domain (about 29 percent), the Fish and Wildlife Service about 91.6 million acres (about 13 percent), and the National Park Service about 78 million acres (12 percent). The property under Defense Department jurisdiction consists primarily of military lands used for training and testing. Although land management is not a Defense Department mandate, military property often remains in a natural condition and can provide habitats for threatened and ENDANGERED SPECIES.

Public lands may be classified by the administering agency according to three categories: single use, dominant use, and multiple use. Dominant use—for example, timber harvesting in a national forest or recreation in a national park—is the norm. Additional land for the public domain may be acquired for commercial and conservation purposes through exchange, purchase, donation, and easement. The Federal Land Policy and Management Act (1976) permits the disposal of public lands that are determined to be better suited to private ownership or the sale of which will serve a public need such as community expansion or economic development. The predominant eastern view has been that public lands should remain in the national domain, while the western view advocates management on a state and local level. ☞ also FEDERAL GOVERNMENT and entries from NATIONAL FOREST SYSTEM to NATIONAL WILDLIFE REFUGE SYSTEM

This 14,000-square-mile region of lakes and portages straddling the Ontario-Minnesota border is the largest international area set aside for wilderness recreation in the
world. In addition to the Boundary Waters Canoe Area
Wilderness in the Superior National Forest, Voyageurs National
Park, and the Grand Portage National Monument, all in Minnesota, the region encompasses the 1.2-million-acre Quetico
Provincial Park, the second largest wilderness area in Ontario.

The Indian word *Quetico* is a Cree name for a benevolent
spirit whose presence infuses any area of extraordinary
beauty. As early as 7500 B.C., archaeologists believe, prehistoric
cultures inhabited the region, which preserves numerous
ancient pictographs on ancient bedrock outcroppings; painted
near water level, these may have been done by Indians working from their CANOES. The first documented French exploration in the waters west of Lake Superior was in 1688.
French missionaries were followed by prospectors and
traders, and by the eighteenth century the region was a center of fur-trading competition for the Hudson's Bay, American Fur, and Northwest Companies. The region—territory of
the Sioux and later the Chippewa—was an important link in
the fur trade route known as the Voyageurs' Highway, which
connected Lake of the Woods with Lake Superior (☞ GREAT
LAKES). There the settlement of Grand Portage in northeast

Quetico-Superior Region

Minnesota served as an important fur-trading post until the early 1800s.

Border disputes based on the location of the various customary fur-trade canoe-and-portage routes flared in the early nineteenth century. The British Crown claimed a border that would have put all of the present Quetico-Superior region in what would become Canada under the British North America Act (1867). The United States argued for a national boundary running along a trade route used by the Northwest Company until 1821. The Webster-Ashburton Treaty (1842) settled the matter by setting the border between the two, following the Grand Portage route. In 1909 the Canadian government set aside more than one million acres northwest of Lake Superior for wilderness recreation in the future Quetico Park. President Franklin Roosevelt established the Quetico-Superior Committee to study the area in 1934, and the Boundary Waters Canoe Area was charted by the U.S. FOREST SERVICE five years later.

Boundary Waters Canoe Area Wilderness

A one-million-acre web of lakes, peninsulas, islands, and portages in northern Minnesota, north and west of Lake Superior, the Boundary Waters Canoe Area, a national wilderness area (☞ NATIONAL WILDERNESS PRESERVATION SYSTEM) adjoining the Quetico Provincial Park, was designated in 1978. On the American side of the border, it falls partly in the Superior National Forest (☞ NATIONAL FOREST SYSTEM). Some 1,200 miles of canoe routes and 70 miles of hiking trails contribute to its rank as the most heavily used national wilderness area.

The area's recent history serves as a template for the competing interests that shape battles over wilderness designation: recreation, highway and resource development, preservation, and government regulation. Conflict began almost as soon as loggers began cutting large pines in the border lakes country in 1895. The present-day boundaries of the wilderness area follow roughly those of the Superior Roadless Primitive Area, which was designated by the Forest Service in 1926 to eliminate the private development that was allowed by earlier homesteading and prospecting laws.

Among the most bitterly contested plans for the area was a proposal for a series of power-generating dams across the Rainy Lake watershed (finally defeated in 1941), which would have submerged islands, streams, and waterfalls under four enormous reservoirs. After lodges, fishing camps, and commercial resorts were established on pockets of private land in the Quetico-Superior country in the 1940s, the area was increasingly subject to motorboat, snowmobile, and hydroplane use. After World War II, fly-ins to private

lodges became so intrusive that the Isaak Walton League (☞ ADVOCATES) mounted a protest that produced a 1949 executive order banning aircraft below 4,000 feet. On behalf of the Forest Service, the league established a fund to purchase some of the private lands. This effort was supplemented by a $500,000 congressional appropriation to acquire resorts, cabins, and private lands in the future wilderness area.

Despite conservation efforts, sections of the region were opened to logging as timber interests pressed for and received contracts from the Forest Service to build logging roads and harvest virgin timber within the area (☞ CLEAR-CUTTING, FORESTS). Battles also erupted over mining rights and the use of motorboats and snowmobiles. In 1974 a mining ban was overthrown, and the Forest Service issued a management plan continuing logging and the use of motorboats. Since then, a continuous series of legal rulings banning logging and mining, and their many reversals, has underscored the lack of lasting consensus on these issues.

A leading voice in the fight to bar roads and dams from the Quetico-Superior country was the Minnesota writer and conservationist Sigurd Olson (1899–1982). Beginning in the 1940s, when he led the effort to ban airplanes, Olson devoted his professional life to the national conservation movement. He served as wilderness ecologist for the Izaak Walton League, a leader of the National Parks Association and the Wilderness Society (☞ ADVOCATES), and an adviser to the NATIONAL PARK SERVICE and

On the Canadian side of the border, Quetico Provincial Park covers 1.2 million acres, most of which is accessible only by canoe or kayak. Cliff faces here and in the Great Lakes preserve prehistoric pictographs that may have been painted from canoes.

Sigurd Olson: The Voice of Conservation

the secretary of the interior. He also helped draft the Wilderness Act (1964) and helped identify and recommend Alaskan lands preserved under the Alaska National Interest Lands Conservation Act (1980) (☞ ALASKA).

Selected Works

📖 *The Singing Wilderness* (1956). *Listening Point* (1958). *The Lonely Land* (1961). *Runes of the North* (1963). *Open Horizons* (1969). *The Hidden Forest* (1969). *Wilderness Days* (1972). *Reflections from the North Country* (1976). *Of Time and Place* (1982). *Songs of the North*, edited by Howard Frank Mosher (1987).

Contacts

Friends of Quetico Park ✉ P.O. Box 1959, Atikokan, Ontario, Canada P0T 1C0. (807-929-2571; 807-274-4870
■ Publications on Quetico are disseminated by this nonprofit organization.

Grand Portage National Monument ✉ P.O. Box 660, Grand Marais, MN 55604. (218-387-2780. 🖳 www.nps.gov/grpo/home.htm
■ Designated as a national historic site in 1951 and redesignated as a national monument in 1958, this site consists of the Northwest Company's Lake Superior trading post; the route of the 9-mile portage connecting it to Fort Charlotte; and the site of Fort Charlotte itself.

Ontario Parks ✉ P.O. Box 7000, Peterborough, Ontario, Canada K9J 8M5. (800-669-1940. 🖳 www.OntarioParks.com
■ This nonprofit group provides information about Ontario's wilderness-class parks and other provincial parks.

The Quetico Foundation ✉ 48 Yonge Street, Suite 610, Toronto, Ontario, Canada M5E 1G6. (416-941-9388. 🖳 www.queticofoundation.org
■ Focusing on northern boreal forest areas, the foundation supports wilderness protection in the Quetico-Superior region and other wilderness-class provincial parks in Ontario. It also produces and sells Quetico park canoe route maps.

Quetico Provincial Park ✉ Ministry of Natural Resources, Atikokan, Ontario, Canada P0T 1C0. (807-597-2735. 🖳 www.mnr.gov.on.ca/MNR/parks/quet.html
■ This 1.2-million-acre Canadian wilderness is primarily a canoe-based park.

Superior National Forest ✉ Forest Supervisors' Office, 8901 Grand Avenue Place, Duluth, MN 55808. (218-626-4300. 🖳 www.snf.superiorbroadband.com
■ This national forest was established by President Theodore Roosevelt in 1909 as part of a conservation effort in the larger Quetico-Superior region.

Voyageurs National Park ✉ 3131 Highway 53 South, International Falls, MN 56649. (218-286-5261. 🖳 www.nps.gov/voya
■ The water-based Voyageurs National Park was created by Congress in 1975.

Web Site

Boundary Waters Canoe Area Wilderness. Provides information about the area and how to obtain permits. 🖳 www.bwcaw.org

Federal roadless areas exist on land administered by the U.S. FOREST SERVICE, NATIONAL PARK SERVICE, and BUREAU OF LAND MANAGEMENT. These wildlands are particularly important as watershed protectors, wildlife habitats, and research and recreation areas, but they also contain minerals and timber—potential targets for resource development. When controversy arises over roadless areas, it is almost always over those in the NATIONAL FOREST SYSTEM, the vast majority of which are administered by the Forest Service; commercial activity such as mining and lumbering is usually not an issue within the less commercially oriented NATIONAL PARK SYSTEM.

The Forest Service must keep an inventory of roadless areas and review them periodically for management concerns and potential inclusion in the NATIONAL WILDERNESS PRESERVATION SYSTEM. Inventoried roadless areas usually consist of tracts of a minimum of 5,000 acres. Two extensive national inventories of roadless areas, RARE I and RARE II, took place in the 1970s, and Forest Service management plans in the 1980s called for development of many of these areas. As development means logging and road building, the term *roadless* itself is something of a misnomer: it technically refers to federally owned wilderness that contains no roads into or across it, but in actuality some so-called roadless areas do have roads.

One of President Bill Clinton's last administrative acts was to

Roadless Areas

A mountain stream cascades over moss-covered rocks in the 34,000-acre Eagle Rock Roadless Area in Washington's Mount Baker–Snoqualmie National Forest. Despite their name, these supposedly pristine wilderness areas are often targeted for logging or mining.

issue an executive order in January 2001 protecting 58.5 million acres of inventoried roadless areas within the National Forest System (in both national forests and NATIONAL GRASSLANDS), totalling more than one-third of the nation's forest lands; the act banned logging and road building to gain access to mineral and gas extraction sites in previously unleased areas. (Exceptions may be made for limited stewardship activities, such as fighting and preventing wildfires; preapproved timber sales may also proceed.) One of President George W. Bush's first administrative acts was to modify the Clinton regulations by permitting the rules to be amended on a case-by-case basis. Included in the overall ban are 42.2 million existing inventoried roadless areas; "specially designated areas," such as NATIONAL RECREATION AREAS (where road building was previously allowed); and, effective after after 2003, roadless areas in the Tongass National Forest, a 17-million-acre coastal rain forest in ALASKA.

Web Site

U.S. Forest Service. Provides information on issues concerning roadless area conservation. ▢ www.roadless.fs.fed.us

Rocky Mountains

"I am delighted with the scenery. The mountains are very fine; as seen from the plains, they resemble very much of the Bernese Alps, one of the finest ranges of mountains in Europe, if not the world. They are of a granite formation, the same as the Swiss mountains and their jagged summits, covered with snow and mingling with the clouds, present a scene which every lover of landscape would gaze upon with unqualified delight."

Albert Bierstadt, *The Crayon* (1859)

For what is the most formidable and consistently high cordillera in the contiguous forty-eight states, the name *Rocky* seems an understatement. Forming the CONTINENTAL DIVIDE, these mountains are in fact the backbone of the great upland system of western North America. The range ignores state and national limits to extend from northwestern ALASKA (encompassing the BROOKS RANGE), through Canada's Yukon territory, down into Washington, Idaho, Montana, Utah, Wyoming, and Colorado, and finally terminating in northern New Mexico. Along the way the Rockies measure anywhere from 70 to 400 miles across as they rise from the Great Plains on the east and fall to the Basin and Range region to the west. Mount Elbert (14,442 feet) in Colorado is the highest point in the American Rockies.

The system was called a variety of names—Stoney Mountains, Mountains of Bright Stones, Shining Mountains—before it appeared as the Rocky Mountains on late-eighteenth-century maps. It consists of a series of uplifts and tilting fault blocks fractured out of the continental crust as it underwent massive compression about 40 to 80 million years ago. Augmented by volcanic and glacial activity (☞ GLACIERS), subsequent stretching and heaving created alpine plateaus and wide, flat valleys at high elevations (from 5,000 to 7,000 feet). Among the many resulting mountain chains within the greater Rocky Mountains system are the TETON, UINTA, and WASATCH MOUNTAINS; the Absaroka, Bighorn, Bitterroot, Gallatin, Laramie, Salmon River, and Sawtooth Mountains; the Front, Medicine Bow, Park, San Juan, Sangre de Cristo, and Wind River Ranges; and many smaller groups.

After the APPALACHIAN MOUNTAINS had been crossed, the Rockies presented the major obstacle to western migration—once they were discovered. The Spanish, who began exploring north of Mexico in the 1500s, were the first Europeans to encounter the Rocky Mountains, which sustained numerous NATIVE AMERICAN tribes, including the Shoshone, Paiute, Crow, and Blackfeet. The Scottish-born fur trader Sir Alexander Mackenzie (ca. 1764–1820) made the first transcontinental journey north of Mexico, crossing the Continental Divide in the Canadian Rockies and arriving at the Pacific Ocean in 1793. For Lewis and Clark, the mountains were hard proof that no continuous water route from the upper Missouri River to the Pacific could possibly exist; their CORPS OF DISCOVERY expedition (1804–6), following Indian trails, crossed the Rockies over the Lehmi and Lomo Passes.

In 1806 Lieutenant Zebulon Pike (1779–1813) led a detachment of twenty-three men through the Spanish Southwest,

Barrier to the West

exploring as far as the South Platte River and the Sangre de Cristo Range in Colorado. Pikes Peak bears his name, although the explorer actually never scaled the mountain and later ended up under Spanish arrest in Santa Fe. Major Stephen H. Long (1784–1864) failed to establish a fort on the Yellowstone River during an 1819-20 army expedition but did explore much of the Front Range and climbed several mountains, including what is now known as Long's Peak.

The first real knowledge of the Rockies came during the era of the mountain men, which began with the pioneering fur expeditions of William Ashley (1778–1838) from St. Louis into the Yellowstone region in the 1820s and continued with successive fur-trading ventures until the beaver trade collapsed in the 1840s. During this period an extended band of scouts worked deep into the Rockies, where such legendary figures as John Colter (1775–1813), Jedediah Smith (1799–1831), Jim Bridger (1804–81), and Kit Carson (1809–68) became familiar with existing Indian routes and began to break new trails to California and the

In the 1890s Balanced Rock on Pikes Peak Trail in the Colorado Rockies was bought by a father-and-son team, Paul and Curt Goerke, who made a living taking pictures of tourists, often seated atop supplied burros. By 1905 it was "the most photographed object in the United States."

Pacific Northwest. Their explorations eventually opened up routes for the major survey expeditions through the Rockies and the western settlement that followed (☞ SURVEYS). Settlers initially bypassed the formidable Rockies: California and Oregon gained statehood in 1850 and 1859, respectively, years before any territory in the mountains. When Colorado was admitted to the Union in 1876, easterners saw the new state as "nothing more than Denver, the Kansas Pacific Railway and the scenery."

The Rockies are the setting for the largest concentration of federally designated parks, monuments, and wilderness areas outside Alaska. ☞ *also* YELLOWSTONE NATIONAL PARK

Parks, Monuments, and Wilderness Areas

■ **Colorado.** National parks: Mesa Verde, Rocky Mountain. National monuments: Black Canyon of the Gunnison, Florissant Fossil Beds, Great Sand Dunes, Yucca House. Wilderness areas: more than 60 (for a complete listing, see ▣ www.wilderness.net/nwps).

■ **Colorado and Utah.** National monuments: Dinosaur, Hovenweep.

- **Idaho, Wyoming, and Montana.** National Park: Yellowstone.
- **Montana.** National Park: Glacier. Wilderness areas: Black Elk, Bob Marshall, Cabinet Mountains, Gates of the Mountains, Great Bear, Lee Metcalf, Medicine Lake, North Absaroka, Rattlesnake, Red Rock Lakes, Selway-Bitterroot.
- **New Mexico.** National monument: Aztec Ruins.
- **Wyoming.** National park: Grand Teton. National monuments: Devil's Tower, Fossil Butte. Wilderness areas: Absaroka, Black Elk, Bridger, Cloud Peak, Encampment River, Fitzpatrick, Gros Ventre, Mount Zirkel, Platte River, Popo Agie, Rawah, Teton, Vinegar Hole, Washakie.

Contacts

Alliance for the Wild Rockies ✉ P.O. Box 8731, Missoula, MT 59807. ☎ 406-721-5420. 🖥 www.wildrockiesalliance.org
- This group spearheads grassroots campaigns to protect and restore a wild Rockies bioregion encompassing Idaho, Wyoming, Montana, and eastern Washington and Oregon, as well as the Canadian provinces of British Columbia and Alberta.

American Wildlands ✉ 40 East Main, Suite 2, Bozeman, MT 59715. ☎ 406-586-8175. 🖥 www.wildlands.org
- Concentrating on wilderness legislation and natural resource conservation in the West, this advocacy group works to "promote, protect and restore biodiversity and advocate for sustainable management of the West's wildlands, watersheds, and wildlife, with special attention to the Northern Rocky Mountain region." It also sponsors the Corridors of Life Project, which identifies for preservation conduits of wildlife movement in the northern Rockies.

Museum of the Mountain Man. ✉ P.O. Box 909, Pinedale, WY 82941. ☎ 877-686-6266. 🖥 www.museumofthemountainman.com
- Holdings focus on the Rocky Mountain fur trade, western exploration, Plains Indians, and settlement of western Wyoming. The research library has a strong collection of western literature.

Museum of the Rockies ✉ Montana State University, 600 West Kagy Boulevard, Bozeman, MT 59717-2730. ☎ 406-994-2251. 🖥 www.montana.edu/wwwmor
- This natural history museum specializes in paleontology research and dinosaur exhibits.

Southern Rockies Watershed Network ✉ P.O. Box 1351, Boulder, CO 80306. ☎ 720-849-6412. 🖥 www.earthisland.org/srrp/srrp.html
- Promotion of sustainable management of watersheds in Colorado and northern New Mexico is the focus of this network.

Auto travel increased visitation to wilderness regions. Containing road maps of every state, the 1920 edition of *Clason's Touring Atlas* featured a Rocky Mountain scene on its cover. A benevolent Indian chief appears to welcome such progress.

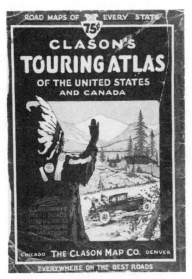

Reading

📖 Francis Parkman, *California and Oregon Trail: Being Sketches of Prairie and Rocky Mountain Life* (1849). 📖 Francis Parkman, *Discovery of the Great West* (1869). 📖 Scott Elias, *The Ice-Age History of National Parks in the Rocky Mountains* (1996). 📖 Thomas Schmidt, *The Rockies* (1996). 📖 William Bueller, *Roof of the Rockies: A History of Colorado Mountaineering* (2000).

Rocky Mountain School Artists

"There is no phase of landscape in which we are not richer, more varied and interesting than any country in the world."

Thomas Moran

Nineteenth-century painters lured to the western territories by accounts of majestic scenery were a melting pot of the art world. From Europe and America they came as trailblazers and artist-explorers, poets and academics, opportunists and ideal seekers, working independently or for government SURVEYS after the 1869 completion of the transcontinental railroad. Following the first generation of western painters (☞ FRONTIER GENRE PAINTERS) was a second wave of panoramic landscape artists, given to grandiose interpretations of the ROCKY MOUNTAINS and points beyond and known collectively as the Rocky Mountain School. Their epic scenes captured the wonder of the western wilderness just as they satisfied a public curiosity about its primitive and sensual features. Gazing on the theatrically lighted sunsets, snow-covered peaks, and semiclad Indians doomed to extinction—all rendered in a slightly lurid palette—verged on voyeurism.

Most Rocky Mountain School painters exhibited widely and cultivated a clientele from East Coast and European society whose private galleries were not complete without a Rocky Mountain landscape, which could range in price from $3,000 to as much as $35,000. Among the successful landscapists of the era were Worthington Whittredge (1820–1910) and John Kensett (1816–72), two HUDSON RIVER SCHOOL ARTISTS who worked extensively in the Colorado Rockies; Thomas Hill (1829–1908), an English-born painter who built a successful trade in YOSEMITE VALLEY views; and the American impressionist John Twachtman (1852–1902), commissioned in 1895 by a private collector to paint scenes in the area of YELLOWSTONE NATIONAL PARK.

The leaders of the Rocky Mountain School included two other followers of the Hudson River painters: Albert Bierstadt (1830–1902), a German-American who studied in Düsseldorf, and Thomas Moran (1837–1926), painter of scenic views in the TETON MOUNTAINS, Yellowstone Valley, GRAND CANYON, and SIERRA NEVADA RANGE. Bierstadt was the first major landscape artist to travel west. In 1859 he joined the Pacific expedition of Colonel Frederick Lander (1821–62) to the Wind River country of the Wyoming plains, possibly after hearing a lecture by Bayard Taylor, the popular author of *Eldorado* (1856). He returned west in 1863, inspired by a New York exhibition of Carleton Watkins's Yosemite views (☞ PHOTOGRAPHERS) in New York, and eventually moved to San Francisco so that he could paint in California.

Bierstadt worked primarily with sketches and stereopticon photographs made in the field and constructed his compositions later in the studio, a contrivance necessitated in part by the gigantic size of his canvases. Because he never traveled very far into the Rockies and thus never observed them at

close range, it has been inferred that he incorporated studies from his alpine travels into his lush American panoramas, in which atmospheric effect invariably superseded geographic accuracy. No matter: Bierstadt's first major work, *The Rocky Mountains, Landers Peak* (1863), which measured 6 by 10 feet, caused a sensation, sold for $25,000, and made him the only real rival of Frederick Church (1826–1900), his Hudson River School contemporary.

Thomas Moran was the first landscape artist to visit the GREAT LAKES wilderness in 1860, but it was his western work, much of it done in connection with geological surveys, that gained him fame. The artist joined Ferdinand V. Hayden's 1871 Yellowstone survey, which included the photographer WILLIAM HENRY JACKSON. The combined impact of Moran's watercolor illustrations, published in *Harper's Weekly*, and Jackson's photographs is believed to have influenced Congress's designation of Yellowstone National Park in 1872. That same year Moran exhibited his first major Yellowstone painting, *The Grand Canyon of the Yellowstone*, which measured 7 by 12 feet. Congress appropriated $10,000 to purchase the work, and after a national tour it was mounted in the Senate lobby of the U.S. Capitol. Moran was so utterly entranced by the Rocky Mountains that he earned the nickname "Yellowstone" and began signing his paintings "TYM" (Tom "Yellowstone" Moran).

In 1873 Moran joined John Wesley Powell (1834–1902) on a survey of the Colorado River through the Grand Canyon in Arizona and later returned many times to the region. The Santa Fe Railway, which offered the only rail travel to the canyon rim, routinely used Moran's paintings to illustrate

Thomas Moran helped establish the western wilderness as a central subject for American art with canvases like his *Grand Canyon of the Yellowstone* (1872). The painting was completed in his eastern studio with the help of his own sketches and photographs by William Henry Jackson. It was the first landscape bought for display in the U.S. Capitol.

travel brochures. So stunning were his later Grand Canyon pictures that they were presented as autonomous exhibits rather than as a part of larger shows. Congress also acquired Moran's second major landscape, *Chasm of the Colorado* (1873). The third canvas of this triptych, *Mountain of the Holy Cross* (1875), was finished after Moran rejoined the Hayden Survey. He hoped to exhibit all three at the 1876 Philadelphia centennial, but Congress refused to lend its two.

Contacts

Haggin Museum ⊠ 1201 North Pershing Avenue, Stockton, CA 95203. ☎ 209-940-6300. 🖳 www.hagginmuseum.org

■ The museum's strong holdings include paintings by Thomas Hill and Thomas Moran and a significant collection of Albert Bierstadt's later works.

Stark Museum of Art ⊠ 712 Green Avenue, Orange, TX 77630. ☎ 409-883-6661. 🖳 www.starkmuseum of art.org

■ Albert Bierstadt, Thomas Moran, John James Audubon, Frederic Remington, and Charles Russell are represented here along with southwestern paintings featuring the Taos Society of Artists. Indian arts include baskets, clothing, rugs, and pottery from the Great Plains, Southwest, eastern woodlands, and Pacific Northwest.

Theodore Roosevelt

Assuming the U.S. presidency in 1901 at the age of forty-two, Theodore Roosevelt (1858–1919) was a figure of inexhaustible vitality whose well-known adventures hunting, birding, and camping in the wilds coincided with a deep appreciation for nature and its "masterful virtues." Roosevelt's personal connection to ranch life and the wilderness was underscored by the conviction that America's resources were a public trust that should not be auctioned off to the highest financial or political bidder. The first national leader to join the debate over resource preservation, he adroitly used his presidency to further the cause. An 1897 camping trip with JOHN MUIR in the SIERRA NEVADA RANGE opened Roosevelt's mind to Muir's proposal that YOSEMITE VALLEY be attached to the existing national park, an achievement of his presidency in 1906. Roosevelt established millions of acres of western woodlands as national forests; signed the Antiquities Act (1906) and used it freely to establish America's first eighteen NATIONAL MONUMENTS, among them the 800,000-acre GRAND CANYON; and established the National Conservation Commission to compile the first inventory of national resources.

Roosevelt was a great admirer of JOHN BURROUGHS and shared his contempt for the work of "imitation" nature writers such as Ernest Thompson Seton's popular *Biography of a Grizzly* (1900) and William Long's *School of the Woods* (1902). Attacking Long and Jack London in a 1905 magazine interview, Roosevelt dubbed them "nature fakers," a term quickly recoined as "nature fakirs." He didn't believe for a minute, he said, that "some of these nature writers know the heart of a wild thing." In response, Roosevelt was duly castigated for his well-known proclivity for killing wild game in the big hunt.

A prolific writer in his own right, Roosevelt covered history, politics, the environment, and his favorite subject: life on the frontier. Much of his early work was inspired by life at Elk Horn, one of two ranches he owned in the Little Missouri Badlands. His compendium of Elk Horn stories entitled *Ranch Life and the Hunting Trail* (1888) is an affectionate if wistful ode to cattle roundups, barroom brawls, stampedes, and horse thieves. These, of course, were the necessary ingredients of a manly, life-sustaining experience in the wilds—summed up in Roosevelt's choice of a verse by Robert Browning (1812–89) for the frontispiece: "Oh, our manhood's prime vigor! . . . Oh, the wild joys of living!" Yet even in 1888 Roosevelt saw the primitive existence he associated with the "great free ranches" and the primeval forest as doomed. Americans will not only regret its passing "for our own sakes," he wrote, "but must also feel real sorrow that those who come after us are not to see, as we have seen, what is perhaps the pleasantest, healthiest, and most exciting phase of American existence."

📖 *Hunting Trips of a Ranchman* (1885). *Thomas Hart Benton* (1887). *Ranch Life and the Hunting Trail* (1888). *The Winning of the West*, vols. I and II (1889). *The Wilderness Hunter* (1893). *The Winning of the West*, vols. III and IV (1894). *American Ideals* (1897). *Trail and Campfire*, with George Bird Grinnell (1897). *The Rough Riders* (1899). *Outdoor Pastimes of an American Hunter* (1905). *Good Hunting* (1907). *Autobiography* (1913). *History as Literature* (1913). *The Great Adventure* (1918).

Selected Works

Among Teddy Roosevelt's many camping companions was John Burroughs, seen standing with the "Conservation President" on a 1903 trip to Yellowstone Valley. Roosevelt went so far as to borrow the name Rough Riders, from the title of one of Buffalo Bill Cody's Wild West Shows, for the first U.S. Volunteer Cavalry.

Sierra Nevada Range

California's major inland mountain range runs about 430 miles, from Tehachapi Pass near the Mojave Desert in the south to Lassen Peak in the north. The system's rugged eastern front oversteps the Nevada state line near Lake Tahoe; the western flank unfolds more gently into the Sacramento and San Joaquin River valleys. Peak height varies from about 11,000 feet to 14,000 feet, rising to 14,495 feet atop Mount Whitney, the tallest mountain in the contiguous forty-eight states.

The Sierras were formed by a massive uplift that occurred primarily within the last two million years. The system's spectacular moraines, valleys, and alpine lakes (Lake Tahoe, at 1,640 feet, is one of the deepest in the country) are the result of massive glacial activity during the Pleistocene epoch, a subject of much research and speculation by the great nineteenth-century environmentalist JOHN MUIR (☞ GLACIERS). Home to the Yokut, Sierra Miwok, Miadu, Mono, and Washo Indians, the region was opened to some minor Spanish missionary activity and early-nineteenth-century fur trade but remained relatively unexplored until the 1848 discovery of gold nuggets in the American River. The ensuing gold rush brought a staggering fifty thousand miners to the mountains within two years.

Although there is no year-round pass through the wild central section of the Sierra Nevada, other portions of the range betray the impact of human activities ranging from logging and water reclamation to mining and tourism. The range has been a leading California timber area; the U.S. FOREST SERVICE has long made commercial logging a priority in its eleven national forests (☞ NATIONAL FOREST SYSTEM), many set aside in the early 1900s by THEODORE ROOSEVELT. An estimated 80 percent of old-growth forests outside national parks in the Sierras has been harvested. Under the Clinton administration (1993–2001), however, logging there was significantly curtailed.

In 2000 the Forest Service released plans for the Sierra Nevada Framework Project, which would further reduce logging and end old-growth harvest on PUBLIC LANDS in the Sierras over the next two decades. The plan also calls for new limits on mining, grazing, and road use and shifts emphasis to recreation and conservation of fish and wildlife habitat. In 2000 President Clinton sat at the base of a giant sequoia in Sequoia National Forest and signed a directive creating the Grand Sequoia National Monument (☞ NATIONAL MONUMENTS), providing federal protection for thirty-four groves of the ancient trees in the Sierra Nevada. The designation added further clout to a 1992 directive by President George H. Bush banning logging within 1,000 feet of a sequoia (☞ TREES). Among other public reserves in the Sierra Nevada are three national parks: Yosemite (☞ YOSEMITE VALLEY); Sequoia, designated in 1890 as the second national park in America; and Kings Canyon, set aside in 1940. The latter two parks, located in the southern Sierras near Three Rivers, are now managed as one and are both designated INTERNATIONAL BIOSPHERE RESERVES.

Around 1901 William Henry Jackson's lens captured a seemingly endless view across the High Sierras and Tenaya Canyon from Glacier Point in Yosemite Valley.

Friends of the River ✉ 915 Twentieth Street, Sacramento, CA 95814. ☎ 916-442-3155. ▣ www.friendsoftheriver.org

■ This statewide conservation organization for California rivers helped spearhead the Sierra Nevada Forest Protection Campaign. It also has a rafting chapter with more than 350 trained guides.

Information Center for the Environment ✉ College of Agricultural and Environmental Sciences, University of California, Davis, CA 95616. ☎ 530-752-0532. ▣ ice.ucdavis.edu

■ This cooperative effort of environmental scientists includes collaborators from more than thirty private, state, federal, and international environmental protection organizations. Its database include maps, models and reports, and the official species database systems for all U.S. national parks and California state parks. It has also developed integrated inventory and monitoring programs for the U.S. Man and the Biosphere program, National Park Service, and California state parks.

Sierra Nevada Alliance ✉ P.O. Box 7989, South Lake Tahoe, CA 96158. ☎ 530-542-4546. ▣ www.sierranevadaalliance.org

■ An umbrella coalition of grassroots and regional groups, this organization attempts to forge alliances among activists, elected officials, and community leaders. It was formed after the Pulitzer Prize–winning series "The Sierra in Peril" was published in the *Sacramento Bee* in 1991.

Sierra Nevada Ecosystem Project ✉ Centers for Water and Wildland Resources, One Shields Avenue, University of California, Davis, CA 95616. ☎ 530-752-7992. ▣ www.ceres.ca.gov/snep

■ This project was the result of a 1992 congressional order mandating a scientific evaluation of the entire Sierra Nevada ecoregion, including forests, important watersheds, and all significant natural areas on public land to enable future management of these systems at sustainable levels. The final report was submitted to Congress in 1996.

Sleeping Bags

One perfectly good reason why so many people hate to camp is that they don't want to go to sleep cold or wake up cold. In his popular camping guide *Wildwood Wisdom* (1945), Ellsworth Jaeger assured his readers that this would never be the case if they simply followed the North Woods Indian practice of making a blanket from woven strips of dried rabbit skins (directions conveniently included). Short of that, the author advised a heavyweight eiderdown robe ("it will see you through any kind of cold weather") or a waterproof canvas tarpaulin.

Thanks to the many advancements in shell design and fills since Jaeger's time, the newest sleeping bags can perform well even in an arctic blast, although efficiency will vary depend-

A Maine camper beds down in 1888 in an animal-hide sleeping bag that had previously done duty on Adolphus Washington Greely's treacherous Arctic expedition of 1881; it apparently came back with one of the few survivors. These days, goose down or a light synthetic fill does the job.

ing on clothing, body size, metabolism, and fitness, as well as humidity, wind chill, and even what you had for dinner.

How to choose? The good news is that sleeping bags come with a temperature rating. The bad news is that the ratings have little meaning, are not standardized, and, experts say, help only as a starting point and a measure of comparison with other bags. Clearly, you want to err on the warm side, but you also don't want a bag that is going to be too hot. The rule is to buy for the condition in which you are camping most often. Rather than buying for the most extreme weather you might encounter, choose a bag for nights that might be somewhat below the expected average. And remember that sleeping in your bag inside a tent or a bivouac sack (a bag overcoat) will increase your bag's warming power. ☞ *also* BACKPACKS, CAMPING, SNOW CAMPING, TENTS

■ **Summer Bag.** These are the least expensive bags, designed for temperatures down to about 40 degrees Fahrenheit and generally made of polyester fleece, with a rectangular profile and a side zipper.

■ **Three-Season Bag.** Effective to about 20 degrees Fahrenheit and good for cool spring and fall nights, these are lightweight (no more than 3½ pounds) and insulated with waterfowl down or synthetic fill. The classic is a down-filled mummy bag, tapered at the feet.

■ **Winter Bag.** These bear a temperature rating of zero or below and come with two zipper flaps.

Sleeping Bag Types

Layering

As in clothes dressing (☞ CLOTHING), layering for sleeping outdoors is a sound concept, although you will want to avoid gimmicky all-in-one systems in favor of well-chosen individual layers. Among these is the bivouac sack, a kind of sleeping bag overcoat that serves as a miniature tent (☞ TENTS) and adds about 5 to 10 degrees of warmth. Because of its small size in relation to a regular tent, the bivi sack reacts directly to the amount of moisture you generate when inside it. Moisture buildup can be problem, potentially soaking the bag and turning to ice in very cold temperatures. You can also add about 20 degrees of warmth with reflective liners designed to slip inside or outside the primary bag. Another option is the vapor barrier liner (VBL), an impermeable waterproof liner designed to go close to your skin. The one obligatory layer is an inexpensive ground cloth of nylon or vinyl topped by a pad to provide insulation between you and the bag and to compensate for bag compression under the weight of your body. One option is a foam pad or an inflatable air mattress.

Materials

Most sleeping-bag shells are made from a tightly woven windproof or waterproof synthetic such as polyester or a durable polyester-nylon blend, such as ripstop, with a durable water-repellent (DWR) finish. There are two types of fills (usually channeled or baffled): synthetic (almost always a form of short-fiber polyester) and waterfowl down. The polyester fills are made under a variety of trademark names and are constantly being improved. The less expensive polyesters are light (but not as light as down) and compressible; however, they are less durable and will eventually break down and lose their loft with continued use. They are better for wet, cold conditions because they dry much faster than down. The loftier down is a superior insulator for its weight and compresses to a tiny volume for packing. Good down, however, is far more expensive than polyester, needs airing after each use to wick away dampness, and is a disaster when it gets wet.

Sizes and Shapes

Size also relates to warmth. Dead space is not an asset. Extra size means extra weight to carry. Moreover, the more room, the more your body has to work to heat the dead space. A properly sized sleeping bag should have just enough extra room at top and bottom to accommodate a full body stretch. The narrower the bag, the more efficient it will be, but a too-tight fit will cause the fill to compress and loose its effectiveness. Mummy bags, which taper from the shoulders down to follow the body's shape, are considered by many to be the most efficient because they offer the most warmth for the least fill (and thus weight). A rectangular design is less confining and leaves room for you to put on extra clothes, but more heat can escape from the larger opening at top. A compromise is a barrel-shape bag or a semirectangular silhouette, which has a tapered foot but is roomier than a mummy bag.

Finer Features

All but the most basic summer bags usually offer many critical efficiency-boosting features. One is a draft tube running parallel to the main zipper. This should be a seamless feature rather than stitched through the bag's lining and shell, because cold air will come in through the stitch holes. The zipper itself should zip in both directions. A top fastener will prevent it from coming loose as you move and working its way open. Three-season and cold-weather bags have an attached drawstring hood with an insulated collar to provide extra insulation in the neck area. Some bags come with built-in radiant-heat barriers.

Pads

A pad or a mattress increases both comfort and the bag's warming capacity. One common type is a durable, waterproof pad made of closed-cell foam, open-cell foam, or a combination. These come in various thicknesses and lengths; a shorter pad is easier to pack and fine for moderate temperatures, but a full-length pad is necessary for cold weather. The alternative is the more expensive and popular foam-filled self-inflating air mattress. When deflated, these mattresses are surprisingly compact, but they are vulnerable to leaks.

Choosing a
Sleeping Bag

■ Shaking the bag will tell you if the fill is evenly distributed; it should stay in place. If it is not adequately channeled or baffled in place, it will probably migrate away from your body, which is not what you want.

■ Bits of feathers or leaking polyester fill indicate that the shell's weave may not be sufficiently tight.

■ Tie on the hood and make sure that it doesn't choke you when you roll on your side.

■ Pluck up a section of the shell fabric and blow through it: if you can feel the air, this means that cold can get through too.

■ Open the bag and scrutinize the stitching and detailing, looking for tight double stitching and strong bar tacking in stress areas.

■ Be sure that the stuff sack is waterproof.

■ Look for hanging loops.

■ Once you have a candidate, spread it out and try it on for size.

Caring for a
Sleeping Bag

■ Store your bag by hanging it or folding it loosely in a cool, dry place rather than keeping it in the stuff sack, which will wear out the loft by compressing it for extended time periods.

- A quick run through the clothes dryer before a camping trip will fluff out the loft and ensure dryness.
- Before you use the bag, snap it out a few times to puff it up to full size, but never twist it or yank on it.
- If weather permits while camping, air it every morning on a bush or sun-warmed rocks, but long periods in the sun will damage the synthetic shell.
- Never dry-clean a sleeping bag. Wash it according to the manufacturer's directions in a bathtub or a washing machine and tumble dry.

Snakes

Snakes feel about people the way most people feel about them, so they will usually stay out of the way. Bites tend to occur when you surprise one by reaching for a handhold in a rocky area or step on one in tall grass. Fortunately, of the many snakes found slithering through America's major wilderness areas—forty-five species live in Florida alone—only four types and their various subspecies are venomous: the rattlesnake, which ranges through the contiguous forty-eight states, although seldom in Maine; the copperhead, found from the Florida panhandle north to Massachusetts and west to Nebraska; the coral snake, which courses from the Florida Keys north to North Carolina and west to eastern Texas; and the cottonmouth, or water moccasin, found from southern Virginia down to the Florida Keys and west to Illinois, Missouri, Oklahoma, and Texas.

Rattlesnakes, cottonmouths, and copperheads are known rather alarmingly as pit vipers because of the deep pits found between eye and nostril. The head is flat and much wider than the neck and patterned with blotches or cross bands. The coral snake, a member of the cobra family, is distinguished by red, yellow, and black stripes. Unless a snake you come across is rattling at you, however, chances are that you can't know for sure what kind it is. Never touch one unless you do know, and never pick up a dead snake, because its reflexes can still cause it to deliver venom. Venomous bites can be treated effectively by a doctor with antivenin, although its value is compromised with each passing hour. Even a nonpoisonous bite can induce an allergic reaction or infection, so medical help should always be sought. ☞ *also* HEALTH AND FIRST AID

The Texas diamondback rattlesnake is one of several U.S. varieties of pit viper. The "pit," or valley, between the snake's eyes is a heat sensor for finding prey.

*First Aid
for Snake Bites*

- Wash the bite with soap and water.
- Keep the bitten area immobilized and below heart level.
- Opinions are divided over tourniquet use. Some experts cautiously recommend a bandage tied 2 to 4 inches above the bite, knotted loosely enough so that a finger can slip under. The danger is that a tight tourniquet can cut blood flow to an extremity, putting you in danger of losing it.

The cottonmouth, or water moccasin, ranges south from Virginia to Florida and west to Missouri, Oklahoma, Texas, and parts of Illinois. Characteristic of pit vipers, it has a some-what flattened head and mottled markings.

■ Don't treat the bite with ice or cool it in any way.

■ Don't make an incision or try to suck out the venom by mouth. However, a multipurpose venom extractor (also good for insect stings), available from camp-ing-supply sources, can be used.

Snow Camping

Yes, people do camp willingly in the snow. In fact, many people actually favor winter CAMPING as an alternative to the oft-crowded recreational sites of summer wilderness destinations because of the peace and quiet it affords. Snow camping, however, is recommended only for experi-enced and physically fit outdoors people. Novices should try a few weekends in the backyard, followed by a trip with an experienced snow camper before venturing out on one's own. Camping in the cold is much harder on body and soul in every way than camping in the milder seasons.

For one thing, snow makes it difficult to see and follow trails. Moreover, most snow camping involves traveling by SNOWSHOES or cross-country skis, which not only saps more energy than HIKING but also makes you work up a potentially chilling sweat. You also need to carry much more: warm gar-ments for inactive periods, a heavier tent, a heavier sleeping bag, plenty of food, and a stove. Bad weather can force you to use your cookstove inside the tent, which is never the ideal choice. Changing snow conditions also make it hard to gauge travel time. And—it's cold.

Before embarking, check the weather forecast and avalanche conditions. Carry a first-aid kit, personal identification, a pocketknife, signaling items, candles and waterproof matches, sunglasses or goggles, extra clothing, and emergency food

Snow camping conditions are often windy, which requires that the tent and all equipment be securely anchored. Campers in Alaska around 1930 found shelter for their campsite in the lee of a low-lying tree. Their dogs braved the elements.

such as instant soups, as well as a compass and a Global Positioning System receiver. ☞ *also* HEALTH AND FIRST AID, ICE SAFETY, MAPS AND NAVIGATION, MOUNTAINEERING, SURVIVAL STRATEGIES

Avalanches

■ Always check with a ranger, a local land agency, or the National Ski Patrol for avalanche alerts, which are especially likely in the spring or after periods of several cold nights followed by warm days.

■ Never walk on or under an ice slope if avalanche conditions prevail.

■ Avoid any obvious snow or ice chutes; these are the areas where slides tend to occur repeatedly from year to year.

■ Treeless slopes with a relatively gentle incline (about 33 degrees) are another risk area. ☞ *also* AVALANCHES

Clothing

■ Never wear cotton, which retains water from sweat and snow and produces a chilling effect when that wetness evaporates.

■ Layer your clothes with a wicking layer (starting with synthetic long underwear), one or two middle insulating layers of polar fleece and synthetic lofting fibers, and the last layer of protective outerwear in a water-resistant but breathable fabric.

■ Try to repeat the same layers on your head and extremities. ☞ *also* CLOTHING

- Use an internal-frame backpack, which will fit snugly on your back and help keep you better balanced.
- Use a four-season sleeping bag rated to zero degrees Fahrenheit or colder.
- Synthetic fill is heavier but possibly better for extended snow trips because of its water resistance.
- Down is lighter and loftier but more adversely affected by water. A down bag should have a minimum of 550 fill power (the more loft, the more warmth).
- ☞ also BACKPACKS, COOKING, SLEEPING BAGS

Gear and Equipment

- Use a four-season model with a good, strong frame and rain fly.
- Pack special snow stakes to hold down tent lines.
- Also take a good liner such as a quilted space blanket to go under your sleeping bag.
- You may need to build a snow wall outside as a wind barrier. ☞ also TENTS

Tents

National Ski Patrol. The National Ski Patrol is a federally chartered nonprofit membership association serving the public and the mountain recreation industry by providing education services about emergency care and safety. 🖥 www.nsp.org

National Weather Service. Allows visitors to click on maps for current watches, warnings, and advisories. 🖥 www.wrh.noaa.gov

Web Sites

📕 Chris Townsend, *Wilderness Skiing and Winter Camping* (1994). 📕 Stephen Gorman, *Winter Camping* (1999). 📕 Calvin Rutstrum, *Paradise below Zero: The Classic Guide to Winter Camping* (2000).

Reading

Snowshoes

Fashionable footwear for the ancient aboriginal set, the snowshoe is believed to have originated in central Asia around 4000 B.C. and was a factor in the northern migration into what is now Scandinavia and Siberia. Although there is no hard evidence to prove it, archaeologists speculate

Essential footwear for native cultures living in cold climates, the snowshoe also found its way into ritual dances, such as the one recorded here by George Catlin. The ethnographer-artist resided with the Plains Indians during the years 1832–40.

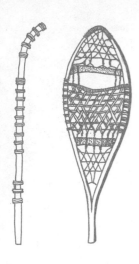

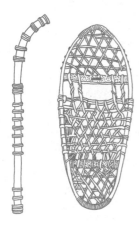

The Maine, or Michigan, snowshoe (above), is similar to the Algonquin. The broader bear-paw style (below) turns more easily, with no tail drag.

that this practical method for snow travel was brought across the Bering land bridge by the predecessors of NATIVE AMERICANS. Eventually, the ski was adopted in Europe and northern Asia, whereas the snowshoe was developed by North American natives in the forested temperate zones. Individual tribes perfected designs to suit regional snow conditions. The Ojibwa and Cree of the Lake Superior basin, for example, used a narrow, upturned shoe with relatively loose lacing, designed to track across a dense, crusted snow cover. The Algonquins of the Ottawa and St. Lawrence River valley regions developed a rounder "bear paw" with numerous adaptations for use in loose, deep snow.

The Indian snowshoe, made with a flexible wood frame and sinew or rawhide lacing, was adopted and modified by French-Canadian trappers in the seventeenth century and became requisite military equipment in Canada and the northern New England colonies. Military training drills and competitions led to the formation of snowshoe clubs, which helped make snowshoeing a popular recreational sport in the mid- to late 1800s. While colorful uniforms and a drum and bugle corps perpetuated the military spirit, the clubs were primarily social institutions. Snowshoe activities favored both fierce competition and good fellowship: meets, moonlight supper treks, picnics, and parties were the custom.

The French-Canadian club tradition filtered from Quebec and Montreal into the northern U.S. snowbelt, where fashionable institutions like the Chinato Snowshoeing Club of St. Paul staged winter carnivals to persuade skeptical easterners that it was actually possible to survive a Minnesota winter. Large-scale commercial manufacture of snowshoes began in Maine in 1862; in the 1920s and 1930s snowshoe hikes were a particularly popular New England pastime. Post–World War II technology introduced the lightweight aluminum snowshoe frame. Among recent innovations are molded polyurethane models designed for backpacking and racing. Classic wood snowshoes are still made commercially as well.

Traditional Styles

■ **Algonquin.** This shoe, a teardrop design with a tapered tail and a slightly upturned nose, is good for trails and open country.

■ **Green Mountain (also called Bear Paw).** Designed for repeated turning, this elongated oval design is recommended for woodland treks.

■ **Maine (also called Michigan).** This is another teardrop design good for trails and open areas.

■ **Ojibwa.** Designed with a pointed nose and tail, this Canadian deep-snow model is suitable for trails and open country.

■ **Yukon (also called Pickerel or Alaskan).** A deep-snow adaptation of the Algonquin, this very elongated oval shoe has a tapered tail and an upturned snout.

- Never snowshoe alone, and always advise someone at home of your plans.
- For backcountry trips, consult maps and familiarize yourself with terrain and weather patterns before setting out; carry a compass.
- Snowshoes can tear up ski trails; if you plan to snowshoe on Nordic (cross-country) ski trails, check the rules of the park or resort in advance.
- Step to the side and make way for passing skiers.
- Pack out whatever you pack in.

Reading

📕 William Osgood and Leslie Hurley, *The Snowshoe Book* (1975). 📕 Marianne Zwosta, *The Essential Snowshoer: A Step-by-Step Guide* (1997). 📕 Gil Gilpatrick, *Building Snowshoes* (1998). 📕 Larry Olmsted, *Snowshoeing: A Trailside Guide* (1998). 📕 Gene Prater, *Snowshoeing*, 4th ed. (1998).

Surveys

Exploratory ventures into the western territories following Lewis and Clark's CORPS OF DISCOVERY mission centered around fur trade and army expeditions. Beginning in 1817 the army engineer Stephen H. Long (1784–1864) led several government-sponsored missions to the upper Missouri River, GREAT LAKES, and ROCKY MOUNTAINS. John Charles Frémont (1813–90) was the preeminent American explorer of the pre–Civil War era. In the early and mid-1840s, Frémont commanded survey expeditions into the Rockies and Oregon with Kit Carson (1809–68) as a guide and also crossed the SIERRA NEVADA RANGE into California.

The Hayden Survey of the "Yellow Stone" region began in 1871, when the party was photographed on the shores of Yellowstone Lake in Wyoming.

Army and Railroad Surveys

In the period of the Mexican War (1846–48), the U.S. Army assigned topographical engineers to the important field commands to map boundaries and secure territorial rights over Mexico. As of 1849 only five states had been laid out west of the Mississippi—Texas, Louisiana, Arkansas, Missouri, and Iowa—and not one mile of railroad track. To determine the best route to the West Coast and thereby open up commerce and settlement, the Pacific Railway Survey Act (1852) launched six surveys into the western territories in the mid-1850s.

Led by military escort, these expeditions were conducted by the Army Corps of Topographical Engineers, the federal agency in charge of exploring and mapping the West, and they invariably consisted of civil engineers and topographers educated at West Point. The surveys fixed the location of prominent mountain peaks; measured rivers; discovered GLACIERS; mapped rivers, trails, and wagon routes; and set boundaries. The mandate to record a huge range of data— mineral resources, NATIVE AMERICANS, flora, fauna, and natural history—required an equally broad personnel roster that also included geologists, botanists, zoologists, and natural scientists from America's top academic institutions and LEARNED SOCIETIES. Among other survey members were physicians, astronomers, and meteorologists; blacksmiths, carpenters, and cooks; and reporters and photographers. Eleven painters and engravers traveled with the Pacific Railway Survey; this and other postwar surveys brought national recognition to a generation of photographers and landscape painters.

Geological surveys were critical to construction and extension of rail lines, which required complicated systems of bridges and overpasses in the West's mountain and canyon regions. An 1885 photograph shows a Santa Fe Railway bridge spanning Canyon Diablo in Arizona.

The last four major western surveys—by King, Wheeler, Powell, and Hayden—began after the Civil War and were completed by 1879, when the U.S. GEOLOGICAL SURVEY was formed to unify the disparate efforts. This period of topographical study emphasized potential natural resource development and ethnology, two areas of study deemed essential to political and economic domination of the West. Geological studies as they related to God, Creation, and the world's place in the universe were also matters of intense interest.

The Yale-trained geologist Clarence King (1842–1901) was a particularly passionate proponent of catastrophism, which held that all nature was the perfect work of God, who created the universe with sporadic bursts of geological enthusiasm. King secured congressional funds to survey the 40th parallel between the 105th and 120th meridians. The endeavor took his team in a 100-mile-wide swath across the Basin and Range region: from Denver through what is now Utah and Nevada to the crest of the Sierras near Virginia City. Encompassing the intended route of the Central Pacific Railway, the survey charted the Great Salt Lake basin and explored the Ruby, WASATCH, and UINTA MOUNTAINS. George Montague Wheeler (1842–1905) also worked west of the 100th meridian, beginning with an 1869 exploration south from Nevada into Mormon country near Las Vegas.

Both Clarence King and Major John Wesley Powell (1834–1902) helped organize the U.S. Geological Survey; King served as its first director, followed by Powell in 1881. Powell was commissioned by the Smithsonian Institution to make an expedition down the upper Colorado River, and with that 1869 boat journey he became the first official explorer of Arizona's GRAND CANYON. Powell's studies of western Indian nations and his pioneering classification of Native American vocabularies made him an advocate for responsible Indian reservation policies that promoted education and self-reliance. In 1879 he became the first director of the federal Bureau of American Ethnology.

The geologist-paleontologist Ferdinand Vandeveer Hayden (1829–87) led the first scientific reconnaissance of what is now Colorado and New Mexico and documented the ruins of Mesa Verde, but he is best known for his first venture into the Yellowstone basin in 1871. As head of the U.S. Geological Survey of the Territories, Hayden secured a $40,000 appropriation from Congress that year under the Sundry Civil Act to undertake an expedition to the Idaho and Wyoming Territories in the "Yellow Stone" region. The secretary of the interior's directive required him to make instrumental observations to construct an accurate map of the district and to

The Hayden expedition included two cooks, the artists Sanford Gifford and H. W. Elliott, two meteorologists, an agriculturist, a mineralogist, a photographer, a hunter, and a few assistants and guests. Hayden, the geologist-in-charge, sits third from the left at the table in the dark jacket. William Henry Jackson, the photographer, stands at the far right.

gather as much information as possible on the geological, mineralogical, zoological, botanical, and agricultural resources and Indian tribes of that unknown country.

The Union Pacific and Central Pacific Railways offered to carry the expedition and supplies free of expense to Hayden's first base camp near Ogden, Utah. Jay Cooke, financier of the Northern Pacific, provided Hayden with his introduction to the artist Thomas Moran (☞ ROCKY MOUNTAIN SCHOOL ARTISTS). Intending to explore the sources of the Yellowstone, Green, Missouri, and Columbia Rivers, the party undertook a thorough study of the region's lakes, springs, and geysers, finding all the existing maps, official and otherwise, "utterly inadequate to travel by."

Hayden's findings excited immediate press coverage. A *New York Times* article likening such discoveries to exploring the sources of the Nile reflected the romance and curiosity associated with the expedition to Yellowstone, which the *Times* dubbed "The New Wonderland." Hayden's lobbying was a strong influence in Congress's designation of YELLOWSTONE NATIONAL PARK as the first national park in 1872. The final Hayden Survey returned to Wyoming and Idaho in the area of Yellowstone in 1878. ☞ *also* PHOTOGRAPHERS

Reading

📖 William H. Goetzman. *Exploration and Empire: The Explorer and the Scientist in the Winning of the American West* (1978). 📖 Herman J. Viola, *Exploring the West* (1987). 📖 Roger L. Nichols and Patrick L. Halley, *Stephen Long and American Fron-*

tier Exploration (1995). 📕 Edward C. Carter, ed., *Surveying the Record: North American Scientific Exploration to 1930* (1999). 📕 Marlene Deahl Merrill, *Yellowstone and the Great West: Journals, Letters, and Images from the 1871 Hayden Expedition* (1999). 📕 James G. Cassidy, *Ferdinand V. Hayden: Entrepreneur of Science* (2000).

Survival Strategies

Anyone contemplating anything more than an occasional day hike in a well-traveled area should enroll in a wilderness emergency training course. Helpful techniques to learn include mouth-to-mouth breathing and cardiopulmonary resuscitation (CPR); treatment for shock, panic, choking, poisoning, and lightning strikes; and the proper use of bandages, tourniquets, and splints. Offered by many outing clubs and wilderness organizations, such courses also prepare hikers for emergencies by covering backcountry evacuation and rescue techniques. Special programs on survival techniques teach how to obtain food and water, how to make an emergency camp, how to improvise a litter, and standard procedures for signaling for help.

Pack an emergency kit containing a whistle, a mirror, flares, and an orange cloth for signaling as well as waterproof and windproof matches and candle stubs for starting a fire. Don't forget fishhooks and line, a notebook and pencil, safety pins, duct tape, a rolled saw blade, a reflecting space blanket, a folding pocketknife, a lightweight twist-on flashlight, cord, an extra compass, extra prescription glasses or lenses, and a paperback guide to edible plants. Carry change for a pay phone; a cell phone can be useful, but you cannot count on getting a signal or 911 in many wilderness areas.

In addition to exposure and temperature extremes, fear and loneliness are particular threats in emergency and survival situations. Stay busy by tackling a small, practical (and necessary) task to stave off boredom and keep up morale. ☞ *also* DESERT HIKING, DESERTS, HEALTH AND FIRST AID, HIKING, ICE SAFETY, MAPS AND NAVIGATION, MOUNTAINEERING, SNOW CAMPING

Evacuation

■ Any injured person who is able to hike out should do so, even if splints or other supports are needed.

■ Severe neck, back, head, and leg injuries, however, may require evacuation.

■ If there is any doubt, don't move an injured companion. Stabilize the person and keep him or her warm, comfortable, and informed of what you are doing to get help.

■ A victim should not be left alone if at all possible. Ideally, two members of the hiking party should go back down the trail in search of trained rescue personnel while someone remains with the injured person.

■ Never bushwhack off the trail when you are looking for help. This is dangerous and will likely get you lost.

■ Anyone hiking out for help should be sure to know how to describe the location where help is needed.

■ Take the bearings from a map as best you can and write them down so that you can pass them on to a would-be rescuer.

Signaling

■ The universal distress call is three signals made with a cloth, flashlight, mirror, noise, or anything else that seems to make sense.

■ The universal semaphore is an orange-colored cloth.

■ Two signals in kind indicate an answer.

■ If possible, signal from an area that is visible from all directions.

■ If you are truly stranded, build a triangle of smoky fires.

■ If you are unable to hike out, stay put, keep warm, and signal at regular intervals.

Fatigue

■ If you are stranded for an extended period, get as much rest as you can.

■ The more tired you are, the greater likelihood there is of injuries and poor decisions.

Thirst

■ To minimize the need for fluid intake, try to minimize exertion.

■ Avoid smoking and alcohol and stay hydrated; the human body can go much longer without food than without fluids.

■ Sodas and prepared sports drinks should be diluted because sugar inhibits absorption.

■ Look for a natural water source at the base of an incline; an area of lush vegetation can also be an indicator.

■ Like rain, clean snow is a good source of pure water and does not require the filtering needed for most other natural water sources, including ice from ponds, lakes, and streams, which may carry giardiasis.

Survival country: the hottest temperatures in the United States are routinely posted in California's Death Valley, which at 282 feet below sea level is the lowest point in the nation. A record high of 134 degrees Fahrenheit was recorded in 1913, and the ground temperature has reached 201 degrees Fahrenheit.

- Avoid complicated traps for snaring animals in favor of foraging for fruit, nuts, and edible plants.
- Many nourishing natural foods are found in the wilderness, including rose hips, chicory, dandelions, lamb's-quarter, nettles, cacti, mosses, and tree bark, but they won't do you much good if you can't identify them.
- Familiarize yourself with the edible plants of the region before starting out on a backcountry trip, and pack along an identification guide.
- Worms, grubs, insects, minnows, and crayfish all work as fishing bait. Use a penknife to whittle a hook from a large twig; a partially open knife can also serve as a hook.

Hunger

- A poncho, tarpaulin, or space blanket can be improvised as an emergency shelter against cold and wet.
- Wrapping yourself in a large plastic garbage bag can also provide protection.
- If you are caught in a rainstorm or a sudden snow squall, try to set up your tent.

Shelter

- In extreme conditions a snow cave may be necessary—and can be surprisingly warm.
- Look for soft snow on the downwind side of logs and rocks, where it tends to drift the most, and mound more if necessary. You will need to start with a snow pile about 5 feet deep if possible.
- After piling snow, try to let it sit undisturbed for about an hour so that the snow crystals can stabilize. The cave base should be flat and stable.
- Dig an entrance into the downwind side, and then hollow out a dome-shaped compartment big enough to fit into with extra air space. The entry can be closed off with a backpack.
- If you have enough time, tunnel your entrance in a few feet, then angle it upward before digging out the cavity. This will trap warmer air and route colder air down and out.
- The shelter walls and roof should be at least one foot thick, with a fist-sized vent hole punched in the roof.
- Line the floor with pine boughs for insulation.
- Place an emergency signal, such as an orange semaphore or crossed skies, outside.

Emergency Shelter

Stretching a tarp over an overturned canoe is one good way to improvise when a tent is not available. Secure the canoe with lines and tip the bottom to windward.

Roger Tory Peterson, *Field Guide to Edible Wild Plants* (1982). Tom Brown Jr., *Tom Brown's Field Guide to Wilderness Survival* (1989). Thomas S. Elias and Peter A. Dykeman, *Edible Wild Plants: A North American Field Guide* (1990). Ernest Wilkinson, *Snow Caves for Fun and Survival* (1992). Paul Tawrell, *Camping and Wilderness Survival: The Ultimate Outdoors Book* (1996). Gregory J. Davenport, *Wilderness Survival* (1998). Bradford Angier, *How to Stay Alive in the Woods* (1998). Eric Weiss, *Wilderness 911: A Step-by-Step Guide for Medical Emergencies and Improvised Care in the Backcountry* (1999).

Reading

Tents

A good tent will provide many seasons of leakless nights and storm protection. Consider it an investment in your safety and survival, and choose the very best your budget will allow. Also consider renting a sample tent or setup before committing to purchase one.

If a simple roof is all you want, a water-repellent tarpaulin of urethane-coated nylon may be sufficient. A good 10-by-12-foot tarp weighs about 2 to 3 pounds and can be strung up to tree branches using cord through its grommets.

The next step up is a true tent. Backpacking models range from lightweight summer mesh designs to heavy-duty mountaineering models intended for severe winter conditions. Somewhere in the middle is the so-called three-season tent, a kind of all-in-one spring-through-fall model that is fine for most moderate trips. A good three-season tent should be able to withstand heavy rain and strong winds. In drenching downpours the tent can be used in tandem with a tarp, strung above the tent roof and slanted slightly to slough off the water. ☞ *also* BACKPACKS, CAMPING, SLEEPING BAGS

Shapes and Sizes

Tents come in several configurations, but the majority are some incarnation of a dome—framed with flexible arcing poles—because of the extra head room provided by this

rounded design. Manufacturers tend to overestimate size, implying that they hold more than a sleeping body. According to the Sierra Club's *Walking Softly in the Wilderness* (1998) by John Hart, any tent offering less than 27 square feet of floor area (or measuring about 4 by 7 feet) should be regarded strictly as a solo shelter; 32 square feet of floor area will snugly accommodate two sleepers, while 40 square feet provides room for three. Other considerations include head room, adequate space for a full stretch in your sleeping bag, how much time you plan to spend inside, and room to stow gear.

When these trail builders camped in Rocky Mountain National Park in 1916, heavy canvas was the standard tent material. Today's alternative is a lightweight water-repellent synthetic tent.

Weight

Walk a few yards up an incline with a tent in your pack and you will understand why weight is an important consideration. The larger the tent the heavier it is, so don't buy more tent than necessary. A solo tent should weigh no more than 2 to 3 pounds, a double or triple a maximum of 4 to 9 pounds. For family camping the tradeoff of a little more weight for extra space may be worth it.

Materials

Three-season backpacking tents are usually made of nylon taffeta, ripstop nylon, polyester, or a nylon-polyester blend; all are strong and lightweight. Coated polyester and cotton-poplin canvas, which is often used to manufacture family tents, is heavier and really practical only for car camping. The tent floor should be treated on the upper (interior) side with a urethane coating that continues up the tent sides and door bases for several inches to create a waterproof sill.

Ventilation and Weatherproofing

As is true of all camping gear, the main goal is to provide a barrier against rain and wind while encouraging the escape of interior moisture from breathing and perspiration. The need for ventilation is one good reason why the tent should not be entirely treated with urethane weatherproofing. Moisture from normal breathing causes condensation, which collects under sleeping bags and pads.

A traditional double-wall tent design allows air circulation. To protect the untreated, permeable walls, a second layer of material (called a rain fly) extends down over the tent walls without ever actually touching them (and can also be completely removed). This 2- or 3-inch layer of air sandwich inside works on a wicking principle similar to that used for outdoor apparel (☞ CLOTHING).

A single-wall tent does the job with one layer of waterproof yet breathable material. It is lighter and less bulky but also much more expensive than the double-wall version and can be risky because the technology is not foolproof. Single-wall tents are generally considered worthy investments only for serious mountaineers camping in more severe cold-weather conditions (☞ SNOW CAMPING).

Some tents have a double roof designed on the same two-layer principle to help prevent condensation and dripping from above. The tent fly may also extend out to create a small floorless "porch," thereby creating a handy entry vestibule. This extra space outside the tent proper can be used for storing gear and cooking. In addition to a door or doors, a tent should be equipped with at least one vent. Tents made entirely of insect-proof mesh are a logical option for the arid Southwest (☞ DESERT HIKING), but in most other regions a three-season tent is the usual choice.

Doors

The type and placement of tent doors affect both convenience and ventilation. Doors are designed to open and close by zipper and can open sideways, like a regular door, or downwards (from the top). Doors that open sideways are less convenient in a two-person tent but are usually larger and offer more air circulation; however, the waterproof rim at the bottom can be a constant trip-up. Doors that open from the top zip down on both sides and thus flop further down the more they are unzipped, which can be handy for creating an extra window; however, when the door is open all the way, the door panel itself has nowhere to go but on the floor. For warm-weather camping, tent doors should be equipped with zip-out panels over mesh inserts.

Brilliant orange and other high-visibility neon colors are the standard safety hues for potential emergency situations, but the truth is that most camping takes place in designated campsites where extreme search-and-rescue situations are rare. Nonetheless, a bright color is easy to spot if you get lost on your way back to a campsite and offers a bright interior for gloomy rain-bound days. Many people, however, find bright colors to be a visual blight. A background-blending gray, green, blue, or buff fits into the landscape and helps filter glare on the tent interior.

Colors

Most poles these days come in elasticized shock-cord-threaded segments designed to snap into place for quick rigging and to unsnap easily for take-down. The choices are aluminum, tempered aluminum, and fiberglass. Aluminum is usually more expensive but is rainproof and has the best strength-to-weight ratio. Fiberglass is more susceptible to sun and rain and can splinter; however, it is also more flexible and breaks down to pole segments in a more packable size. Carbon fiberglass is a stronger and more expensive alternative, but its flexibility can be a liability in high winds. A frame in which all the poles are the same length is an advantage when setting up in the dark.

Poles and Stakes

Stakes may or may not come as part of the tent package. Choices are steel (strong but heavy), aluminum (strong but less durable), and plastic (the lightest). Have an assortment on hand to accommodate a variety of ground and weather conditions.

A simple sheet of vinyl or coated nylon is necessary as a ground cloth to protect the tent bottom from dampness and snagging. Some tents come with ground cloths sized exactly to the floor dimension. If not, make sure that the cloth's edges are tucked in under the tent bottom to prevent it from collecting water in a rain storm.

Ground Cloths

■ Shop for a tent in a camping store where several models are displayed. Crawl inside, stretch out, and move around to test the space and head room.
■ Ask a salesperson how hard the tent is to pitch.
■ Examine the frame's sturdiness.
■ Look for lap-felled (doubled-over) seams at the floor joints.
■ Check for stability; the taller the tent, the less stable it is likely to be.
■ The seam selvages on the tent body should be taped to prevent raveling. Many tents require application of a liquid seam sealer; find out if this is the case.

Choosing a Tent

- Look for secure, corrosion-proof grommets of aluminum or brass; stress points—where the stake-out loop is attached, for example—should be reinforced with bar tacking or double stitching.
- Be sure that essentials—an ample-sized rain fly and vestibule and enough ventilators, for example—have not been sacrificed to reduce the tent's weight.
- Bring along your backpack and test the packed tent and poles inside for weight and bulk.

Caring for a Tent

- Gear experts are divided over whether to pack a tent in its storage sack by rolling it around the bundled poles or by stuffing it first and then packing the poles on the side. Some go by this mandate: roll when wet and stuff when dry.
- Avoid pitching the tent in direct sunlight, which will break down the fibers.
- Before packing the tent after use, clean off any sap and dirt if possible.
- To wash, hose down the tent and dry it in the shade.

Teton Mountains

The first explorer to set eyes on the spectacular craggy peaks of this segment of the ROCKY MOUNTAINS is believed to have been the trapper and guide John Colter (1775–1813), a former member of the Lewis and Clark expedition (☞ CORPS OF DISCOVERY) who set off on a return trip to the wilderness immediately on discharge from his duties in 1806. Two years later a reconnaissance mission to the Crow Indians brought Colter to the southern part of what is now YELLOWSTONE NATIONAL PARK, where the Tetons begin their

Ansel Adams, whose focus on turbulent skies and silhouetted mountains created compelling images, found an apt subject in the Teton Mountains for this 1942 silver print. Winding in the foreground is the Snake River, which rises in northwest Wyoming and flows into Idaho.

40-mile southern course through northwest Wyoming. French trappers later named the three most prominent peaks *les trois tétons* (the three breasts), hence the English derivation.

The Tetons are the youngest mountains in the Rockies. The range was formed about 6 to 9 million years ago as two blocks of continental crust heaved in opposite directions along the 40-mile Teton fault. The fault block on one side thrust upward to create the mountains; the block on the other side worked its way down to form the aptly named valley of Jackson Hole. A dozen Teton peaks measure higher than 12,000 feet and support as many GLACIERS. The highest point in the range is Grand Teton (13,766 feet above sea level), which rises 7,000 feet above Jackson Hole to its east. This is the centerpiece of Grand Teton National Park (☞ NATIONAL PARK SYSTEM), which was established in 1929 and expanded in 1950 to embrace most of the Jackson Hole National Monument (☞ NATIONAL MONUMENTS). The Teton and Targee National Forests (☞ NATIONAL FOREST SYSTEM) also fall within the range.

Grand Teton National Park ✉ P.O. Drawer 170, Moose, WY 83012. ☎ 307-739-3300. 🖳 www.nps.gov/gte

■ Twelve Teton peaks in the park rise above 12,000 feet.

Contact

"The tops of mountains are among the unfinished parts of the globe, whither it is a slight insult to the gods to climb and pry into their secrets, and try their effect on our humanity. Only daring and insolent men, perchance, go there."
Henry David Thoreau, "Ktaadn" (1848)

Henry David Thoreau

Among other less lofty pursuits, the author Henry David Thoreau (1817–62) was something of a peak bagger. Beginning in 1839 with Mount Washington (☞ WHITE MOUNTAINS) in New Hampshire, he answered the call of the wild by making some twenty ascents of New England mountains before 1860—Greylock and Wachusetts in Massachusetts; Lafayette, Monadnock, Red Hill, Temple, Uncanoonuc, and Wantiastiquet in New Hampshire; and Kineo in Maine. In August 1846 Thoreau left his cabin on Walden Pond near Concord, Massachusetts, on the first of three trips to Maine, in part to make an ethnological study of the Abenaki Indians. A humbling attempt to climb Mount Katahdin left him lost in a sopping fog with a sprained ankle but produced the lyrical essay "Ktaadn" (later published in *The Maine Woods* in 1864). In it Thoreau reflects that life is harder on a mountain than at his Massachusetts cabin. Personifying nature as a force of dark power with no

Walden, Henry David Thoreau's most famous nature treatise, was published in 1854.

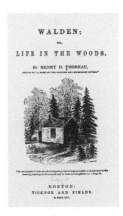

WALDEN;
or,
LIFE IN THE WOODS.
By HENRY D. THOREAU,

BOSTON:
TICKNOR AND FIELDS.

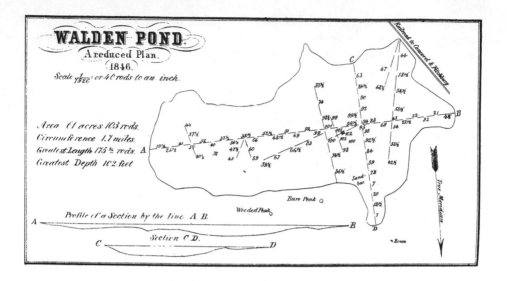

WALDEN POND.
A reduced Plan.
1846.

Scale 1/1920 or 40 rods to an inch.

Area 61 acres 103 rods.
Circumference 1.7 miles.
Greatest Length 175 ½ rods.
Greatest Depth 102 feet

Profile of a Section by the line A B.

Section C D.

Railroad to Concord & Fitchburg

Bare Peak

Wooded Peak

True Meridian

Sand bar

House

In 1845 Henry David Thoreau retreated to his cabin on Walden Pond in Concord, Massachusetts, and spent about two years there. Long afterward, he wrote that he still felt the periodic need to "go off to some wilderness where I can have a better opportunity to play life."

small measure of contempt for climbers like himself, he writes that she seemed to ask sternly, "Why seek me where I have not called thee, and then complain because you find me but a stepmother."

Shocked by his encounters with a Maine landscape badly scarred from logging, Thoreau made one of the country's first calls for wilderness preserves. In his essay "Chesuncook" he warns against beating the rugged Maine forests into submission along the model already established in Massachusetts. "We seem to think that the earth must go through the ordeal of sheep-pasturage before it is habitable by man," Thoreau chastised. This essay was also remarkable for these lines: "It is the living spirit of the tree, not its spirit of turpentine, with which I sympathize, and which heals my cuts.... It is immortal as I am, and perchance will go to as high a heaven, there to tower over me still." Deemed too shocking to print, the words were reportedly edited out by James Russell Lowell (1819–91) before he ran the piece in *Atlantic Monthly* in 1854.

For Thoreau the soul provided the potential tool to transcend the material world through a connection to nature, allowing humans to build their own relationship with the divine. Acknowledging that nature and all her plant and animal creatures had intrinsic worth, he moved from transcendentalism toward the doctrine of pantheism, which held that neither humanity nor nature is entirely separate and distinct from God. Indeed, Thoreau contended, humans are governed by the same forces and principles as the entire universe, and wilderness—their source of strength—provides the "rawmaterial" of life. ☞ *also* WRITERS (NINETEENTH CENTURY)

📖 "Civil Disobedience" (1848). *A Week on the Concord and Merrimack Rivers* (1849). *Walden* (1854). *Excursions* (1863). *The Maine Woods* (1864). *Cape Cod* (1865). *A Yankee in Canada* (1866). *Early Spring in Massachusetts* (1881). *Summer* (1884). *Winter* (1888). *Autumn* (1892).

Selected Works

Walden Pond State Reservation ✉ 915 Walden Street, Concord. MA 01742. ☏ 978-369-3254. 🖥 www.state.ma.us/dem/parks/wldn.htm

■ This national historic landmark includes Thoreau's cabin and 333 acres of woods around Walden Pond.

Contact

Trees

For a country easily impressed by statistics, America's trees deliver some especially gratifying numbers. The aristocrat of the eastern forests is the eastern white pine (*Pinus strobus*), Maine's state tree, which ranges from Newfoundland as far south as Georgia and west to Iowa. This, the largest of all northeastern conifers, is distinguished by a supremely straight grain and typically grows to 100 feet, although the first-growth white pines that so impressed tree-deprived settlers from Europe were at least twice that tall. The British Crown coveted the species and its naturally tapering trunk for use as ships' masts for the expanding

Americans have shown their affection for monumental trees—like this venerable live oak in Bay St. Louis, Mississippi—with everything from plaques to platforms.

royal naval fleet in the eighteenth century. Each timber is said to have brought 100 pounds sterling, and appropriation of virgin stands under the White Pine Acts was one of the incendiary measures that helped fuel the American Revolution.

The paragon of the American West is the sequoia, which refers to either of two types of enormous coniferous evergreens of the *Sequoia* genus of bald cypress. One is the so-called big tree, or giant sequoia *(Sequoiadendron giganteum)*, found in the western SIERRA NEVADA RANGE. The other is the redwood *(Sequoia sempervirens)*, native to the coast of California and southern Oregon. These two are the only sequoia species that remain of the once-diverse sequoia forests that spread over the globe before the Ice Age. Giant sequoias are among the oldest trees in the world, living as long as 3,000 to 4,000 years and typically growing as high as a 26-story building. Their long life is partially attributed to their thick fire- and

A giant sequoia dwarfs two visitors to what is now Sequoia and Kings Canyon National Park in California about 1903. Once widespread in the Northern Hemisphere's temperate regions before a series of ice ages, the big tree sequoia propagates naturally only on the western slopes of California's Sierra Nevada. Trial plots of the species are being planted in Europe, but new growth is susceptible to acid rain.

disease-resistant bark, and they also contain a natural wood preservative. Redwood trees routinely grow more than 300 feet high and are thought to be the tallest trees in the world. Other western species ranking close behind the sequoia are the Sitka spruce (*Picea sitchensis*), western hemlock (*Tsuga heterophylla*), and Douglas fir (*Pseudotsuga menzieseii*), which can also shoot 300 feet high in its Pacific Coast territory.

According to the National Register of Big Trees, the largest tree in America in overall size is a giant sequoia in Sequoia National Park (California) that measures 998 feet around and 275 feet high. The tallest registered tree is a coast redwood, 321 feet high, in Jedediah Smith State Park (California), and the oldest is a 4,000-year-old western juniper in Stanislaus National Forest (California). The tallest recorded tree east of the Mississippi is a white pine measuring 207 feet in the GREAT SMOKY MOUNTAINS. The oldest tree in the East may be a 1,400-year-old live oak on John's Island, South Carolina, although some equally old trees have recently been discovered in North Carolina. The largest tree in crown spread, at 159 feet, is a pecan tree in Weatherford, Texas.

One of the saddest American tree stories is that of the American chestnut, which once accounted for about 30 percent of the tree canopy in the APPALACHIAN MOUNTAINS. Virtually all of the wild chestnuts in America have been wiped out by a blight, begun in New York City in 1904, which does not actually kill the trees but nips new growth in the early stages so that they never reach maturity. In their former glory, chestnuts reached 100 feet high and as broad as 4 feet in diameter. They were often cut down simply to make it easier to get at the nuts. ☞ *also* CLEAR-CUTTING, FORESTS, NATIONAL FOREST SYSTEM

Tree Statistics

- **Balsam fir** (*Abies balsamea*). The only native fir that grows in the Northeast.
- **Black cherry** (*Prunus serotina*). The largest native cherry; one of the first American trees introduced to England.
- **Black spruce** (*Picea mariana*). One of the most widespread conifers in North America.
- **Fraser fir** (*Abies fraseri*). The only fir native to the Southeast.
- **Longleaf pine** (*Pinus palustris*). The world's principal producer of pitch, turpentine, and other naval stores.
- **Noble fir** (*Abies procera*). The largest true native fir in America.
- **Quaking aspen** (*Populus tremuloides*). The North American tree with the broadest-ranging habitat.
- **Sitka spruce** (*Picea sitchenis*). The world's largest spruce tree.
- **Table mountain pine** (*Pinus pungens*). The only Appalachian pine that does not grow elsewhere.
- **Yellow birch** (*Betula alleghaniensis*). One of the largest hardwoods in the Northeast.

National Arbor Day Foundation ✉ 211 North Twelfth Street, Suite 501, Lincoln, NE 68508. (402-474-5655. ⌨ www.arborday.org
■ Established in 1972 to promote Arbor Day and encourage the planting and care of trees, the foundation annually provides more than 8 million trees for planting. "What Tree Is That?" is an excellent online tree identification guide.

National Register of Big Trees ✉ American Forests, P.O. Box 2000, Washington, DC 20001. (202-955-4500. ⌨ www.americanforests.org/big_trees
■ American Forests has maintained an official register of "champion" trees with respect to height, size, and weight since 1940. The group also keeps track of famous and historic trees, offers authentic saplings for sale online, and provides standards and instructions for measuring big trees.

Save the Redwoods League ✉ 114 Sansome Street, Room 1200, San Francisco, CA 94104-3823. (415-362-2352. ⌨ www.savetheredwoods.org
■ The league buys redwood forest land through private subscription and gives it to public parks and preserves. Founded in 1918 after discovering that none of the great coast redwoods was owned by a public agency or protected, it acquired the first memorial grove in 1921 and spurred creation of Redwood National Park in 1968.

Eastern Native Tree Society. A cyberspace interest group devoted to the celebration of trees of the eastern United States through art, poetry, music, science, mythology, medicine, and wood crafts. It maintains an ancient forests bibliography and a database of big and tall trees in the East. ⌨ www.uark.edu/misc/ents

Giant Sequoia. An American Museum of Natural History site offering a visit to a piece of a 1,300-year-old giant sequoia felled in the Sierra Nevada by lumberjacks in 1891. ⌨ www.amnh.org/Exhibition/Expedition/Treasures/Giant_Sequoia/sequoia.html

📕 *National Audubon Society Field Guide to North American Trees: Eastern Region* (1995); *Western Region* (1998).

Frederick Jackson Turner

First presented to a meeting of the American Historical Association in 1893, Frederick Jackson Turner's so-called frontier thesis is arguably one of the most influential and provocative theories of American development ever debated among historians. Turner (1861–1932) was thirty-two years old and a professor of history at the University of Wisconsin when he delivered his now-famous address, "The Significance of the Frontier in American History," to colleagues at the World's Columbian Exposition in Chicago. Noting that the 1890 U.S. Census had declared the end of a line of clear demarcation for the American frontier, the young historian proposed that this official conclusion marked the end of "a great historic movement."

Turner's thesis argued three primary points: that the American West represented an unparalleled gift of riches, individuality, and freedom of opportunity; that the constantly evolving frontier experience—reborn and redefined with each line of contact across the primitive wilderness—had more impact on shaping the country's democratic institutions than any European or Puritan influence; and that the unique frontier work ethic produced the confidence and sense of independence that make Americans American. The historian's address was published three years later in *Atlantic Monthly*, and the essay was reprinted with a collection of his papers in *The Frontier in American History* in 1920.

Turner taught at the University of Wisconsin until 1910 and then at Harvard from 1910 to 1924. By the time of his death, his frontier thesis was increasingly criticized as overly simplistic. Challengers cited his failure to recognize such defining influences on American culture as the southern agrarian movement, eastern industrialism, and European immigration. Another criticism was the inability to adequately reconcile the implications of a new age of industrial wealth and its concomitant ethics with the frontier character that had made possible such capital progress. Notwithstanding, Turner's thesis has never been entirely dismissed, and its ambiguities have contributed to the ongoing debate over its validity.

Fanny Palmer's Across the Continent: Westward the Course of Empire Takes Its Way (1868) foreshadowed Turner's frontier thesis.

📖 *The Rise of the New West, 1819–29* (1906). *The Frontier in American History* (1920). *The Significance of Sections in American History* (1932). *The United States, 1830–1850: The Nation and Its Sections* (1935).

Selected Works

Uinta Mountains

With a dozen summits measuring more than 13,000 feet high, the Uintas are Utah's tallest mountain range and include the highest point in the state: Kings Peak (13,528 feet). The mountains, a middle range of the ROCKY MOUNTAINS, run south of the Wyoming border, covering about 150 miles between Kamas and Flaming Gorge, Utah, and making this one of North America's few large east-west ranges. The system seldom dips below 10,000 feet and encompasses scores of high-altitude glacial lakes and alpine basins as well as the largest tracts of ROADLESS AREAS found in Utah's NATIONAL FOREST SYSTEM. The Uintas harbor a diverse range of fauna, including Canada lynx, cougar, black bear, wolverine, golden eagle, moose, elk, and Rocky Mountain bighorn sheep. The 460,000-acre High Uintas Wilderness Area was designated by Congress in 1984 as part of the NATIONAL WILDERNESS PRESERVATION SYSTEM. The Bear, Weber, Provo, and Duchesne Rivers all rise in the Uintas, while the Green River slices a 3,000-foot-deep canyon through the northeast segment of the range, located in the Flaming Gorge National Recreation Area.

Contact

High Uintas Preservation Council ⊠ P.O. Box 72, Hyrum, UT 84319. ▯ www.hupc.org

■ Committed to preserving the High Uintas ecosystem, this group also works to establish additional wilderness areas in the backcountry lake district.

Created by an act of Congress in 1862, the U.S. Department of Agriculture was made an executive department in 1889. The agency works to improve farm income, develops international markets for agricultural products, and maintains inspection and grading standards. Key programs focus on rural development, forest and soil management (☞ FORESTS, NATIONAL FOREST SYSTEM), and agricultural marketing and transportation. The department also runs the Animal and Plant Health Inspection Service, various food safety and nutrition services, and crop insurance and agricultural research programs. The department's Foreign Agricultural Service, through its Forest and Fishery Products Division, promotes the export of U.S. wood products, including lumber, plywood, veneer, and glue-laminated timbers. Its primary agency concerned with wilderness administration is the U.S. FOREST SERVICE.

The Agriculture Department's conservation arm is the Natural Resources Conservation Service, formerly the Soil Conservation Service, which helps farmers and ranchers voluntarily protect natural resources. Programs focus on technical assistance in preventing soil erosion, conserving wetlands, enhancing fish and wildlife habitats (☞ NATIONAL WILDLIFE REFUGE SYSTEM), forecasting snow and water supply, surveying river basins, providing emergency watershed protection, and preventing floods. Under the Wetlands Reserve Program, the service purchases easements for agricultural landowners who agree to restore and protect wetlands. At some two dozen plant material centers across the country, the National Resources Conservation Service also tests and makes available plants for erosion reduction, streambank protection, coastal dune stabilization, and wetland restoration.

U.S. Department of Agriculture

Natural Resources Conservation Service ✉ U.S. Department of Agriculture, P.O. Box 2890, Washington, DC 20013. ☎ 202-720-3210. ⌨ www.nrcs.usda.gov

Contacts

U.S. Department of Agriculture ✉ Fourteenth Street and Independence Avenue, SW, Washington, DC 20250. ☎ 202-720-2791. ⌨ www.usda.gov

The U.S. Department of the Interior, established by an act of Congress in 1849 to take charge of the nation's internal development, was initially responsible for Indian affairs (☞ NATIVE AMERICANS), exploration of the West (☞ SURVEYS), regulation of territorial governments, and management of public parks. In the ensuing century and a half, the department's role has shifted from housekeeper of general domestic affairs to custodian of the nation's PUBLIC LANDS and mineral resources, national parks (☞ NATIONAL PARK SYSTEM),

U.S. Department of the Interior

wildlife refuges (☞ NATIONAL WILDLIFE REFUGE SYSTEM), and western water resources. The secretary of the interior is responsible for providing general guidelines for all federal archaeological activities (☞ ARCHAEOLOGICAL PARKS). Other areas of responsibility include migratory wildlife conservation, historic preservation, protection of endangered plant and animal species and their habitats (☞ ENDANGERED SPECIES), protection and restoration of surface-mined lands, and mapping. The department also oversees the trust resources of Native Americans and native tribes in ALASKA. ☞ also BUREAU OF INDIAN AFFAIRS, BUREAU OF LAND MANAGEMENT, BUREAU OF RECLAMATION, MINERALS MANAGEMENT SERVICE, NATIONAL PARK SERVICE, OFFICE OF SURFACE MINING RECLAMATION AND ENFORCEMENT, U.S. FISH AND WILDLIFE SERVICE, U.S. GEOLOGICAL SURVEY, *and specific programs*

Contact **U.S. Department of the Interior** ✉ 1849 C Street, NW, Washington, DC 20240. ☎ 202-208-3100. 🖳 www.doi.gov

U.S. Fish and Wildlife Service

William Brewster was an early bird advocate. The U.S. Fish and Wildlife Service is now responsible for managing migratory bird populations.

Responsibility for conserving and protecting fish, wildlife, and plants and their habitats falls to this federal agency, part of the U.S. DEPARTMENT OF THE INTERIOR. In addition to acting as chief administrator of the Endangered Species Act (☞ ENDANGERED SPECIES), it oversees the 94-million-acre NATIONAL WILDLIFE REFUGE SYSTEM and is the lead federal agency for managing and protecting migratory bird populations (☞ BIRDS). The agency enforces federal wildlife laws and also oversees the Federal Aid Program, which distributes to state wildlife agencies funds raised from excise taxes on fishing and hunting equipment and sets state limits for season length and bag limits for migratory game-bird hunting. It operates numerous national fish hatcheries, fish and wildlife management assistance offices, and ecological services field stations. The overall mandate is to develop an environmental stewardship ethic based on sound scientific research, while balancing demands for recreational hunting and fishing (☞ ANGLING). Responsibilities include the surveillance of pesticide use and effects and environmental impact assessment of such developments as hydroelectric dams and nuclear power sites. Funding for many projects comes from excise taxes on arms and fishing equipment levied on states and territories.

The Fish and Wildlife Service's National Conservation Training Center provides training and education services to government employees as well as conservation professionals from nonprofit organizations and corporate sectors. Courses cover natural resource damage assessment, habitat conservation planning, and environmental negotiation. ☞ also NATIONAL PARK SERVICE, PUBLIC LANDS, *and specific programs*

National Conservation Training Center ✉ Shepherd Grade Road, Shepherdstown, WV 25443. ✆ 304-876-7263. ▢ www.training.fws.gov

U.S. Fish and Wildlife Service ✉ U.S. Department of the Interior, 1849 C Street, NW, Washington, DC 20240. ✆ 202-208-5634. ▢ www.fws.gov

The 1.6-million-acre Willamette National Forest stretches for 110 miles along the Cascades in Oregon and encompasses numerous volcanic peaks and waterways. The Tamolitsh Falls are located on the MacKenzie River.

U.S. Forest Service

Established in 1905, the U.S. Forest Service, an agency of the U.S. DEPARTMENT OF AGRICULTURE, is the only important federal land-management agency outside the U.S. DEPARTMENT OF THE INTERIOR. It has comparable responsibility in the major areas of land management and has significant autonomy within the federal bureaucracy. There are three main arms: the dominant branch is responsible for the NATIONAL FOREST SYSTEM; the second overseas research and experimentation; and the third and smallest is a cooperative program providing federal assistance to state and private forestry efforts. Grazing and timber sales are two priorities; more than nine thousand farmers and ranchers buy permits to graze livestock on National Forest System land. The service also administers NATIONAL GRASSLANDS and NATIONAL RECREATION AREAS and is in the business of managing scenic parkways, picnic and camping facilities, and ski resorts. Most work is delegated to ten regional field offices and nine experiment stations. ☞ *also* CLEAR-CUTTING, FORESTS, PUBLIC LANDS

U.S. Forest Service ✉ U.S. Department of Agriculture, P.O. Box 96090, Washington, DC 20090-6090. ✆ 202-205-8333. ▢ www.fs.fed.us

A member of the U.S. Geological Survey climbs a pinnacle of lava at Hannegan Pass on Ruth Mountain in Washington's North Cascades National Park. The USGS was established in 1879.

U.S. Geological Survey

The mission of the U.S. Geological Survey, created in 1879, is to undertake and disseminate reliable research relating to the earth sciences; minimize losses to such natural disasters as volcanoes, landslides, earthquakes, floods, and droughts; research and manage water, biological, energy, and mineral resources; and maintain cartographic, geologic, and geographic databases. An agency of the U.S. DEPARTMENT OF THE INTERIOR, the survey was established to assess the resources of PUBLIC LANDS and take charge of chemical and physical research and detailed topographical mapping in the United States. Responsibility for gauging streams and determining the national water supply was added in 1894. The agency manages the National Geological Mapping Program and Database for long-term global environmental monitoring, and it is the lead agency for the Federal Water Information Coordination Program. ☞ also SURVEYS

Contact

U.S. Geological Survey ✉ U.S. Department of the Interior, 12201 Sunrise Valley Drive, Reston, VA 20192. ☏ 703-648-4000. 🖥 www.usgs.gov

O pportunities to volunteer for wilderness and environ-mental organizations are almost as plentiful as the organizations themselves. Many hiking associations and environmental groups—local and national alike—depend on volunteer aid to maintain trails and help with political action projects, congressional lobbying efforts, research, communications, and jobs within their mission. Almost any advocacy group (☞ ADVOCATES) welcomes inquiries about volunteer help, and many offer paid student internships. A good way to start is to check the Web site of the group or agency that interests you.

Most of the agencies of the FEDERAL GOVERNMENT involved with administering the country's wild areas accept volunteers of all ages and backgrounds, and many run organized volunteer and internship programs. Training is often provided.

Numerous opportunities exist for students and volunteers to become involved in archaeological fieldwork (☞ ARCHAEO-LOGICAL PARKS). The NATIONAL PARK SERVICE's *Fieldwork Opportunities Bulletin* and *Passport in Time* newsletter list volunteer jobs, field schools, and workshops across the country. Interested per-sons can also contact the anthropology department of any university or search the Electronic Cultural Resource Train-ing Directory (💾 tps.cr.nps.gov/directory).

Volunteer Opportunities and Internships

Selected Volunteer Programs

American Hiking Society ✉ 1422 Fenwick Lane, Silver Spring, MD 20910. ☎ 301-565-6704. 💻 www.americanhiking.org
■ This group offers one- and two-week "volunteer vacations" into America's "most remote places."

Bureau of Land Management ✉ Environmental Education and Volunteers Group, 1849 C Street, NW, Room 406 LS, Washington DC 20240. ☎ 202-452-5125. 💻 www.blm.gov/volunteer/index.html
■ Volunteers work as river rangers, campground hosts, hiking and interpretive guides, tree planters, fossil excavators, and fence builders. They also assist with wild horse adoption, mapping petroglyphs, computerizing databases, and monitoring wilderness study areas.

Earthwatch Institute ✉ 3 Clock Tower Place, Suite 100, Maynard, MA 01754. ☎ 978-461-0081. 💻 www.earthwatch.org
■ Field research and conservation and education programs are carried out through organized expeditions worldwide staffed with volunteers; participants are charged housing and travel fees (sometimes subsidized). Internships are also available.

Landmark Volunteers ✉ P.O. Box 455, Sheffield, MA 01257. ☎ 413-229-2050. 💻 www.volunteers.com
■ This youth volunteer program focuses on historical, cultural, environmental, and social service institutions in twenty states.

League of Conservation Voters ✉ 1920 L Street, NW, Suite 800, Washington, DC 20036. ☎ 202-785-868. 💻 www.lcv.org
■ Six-month political action and communications internships are available.

Wildlife researchers count royal terns on Fisherman's Island in Virginia, a type of activity that attracts committed volunteers.

Natural Resources Conservation Service ✉ U.S. Department of Agriculture, 7515 N.E. Ankeny Road, Ankeny, IA 50021. ☏ 888-LANDCARE. ⌨ www.ftw.nrcs. usda.gov/volunteer.html
■ Volunteers who join the Earth Team work side by side with U.S. Department of Agriculture professionals on soil and water conservation projects.

Save America's Forests ✉ 4 Library Court, SE, Washington, DC 20003. ☏ 202-544-9219. ⌨ www.saveamericasforests.org
■ Semester-long internships are offered to students with a background in ecology, forest protection, and politics.

University of California Research Expeditions Program ✉ One Shields Avenue, Davis, CA 95616. ☏ 530-752-0692. ⌨ urep.ucdavis.edu
■ Volunteer expeditions in archaeology, animal studies, geology, arts and culture, the environment, and conservation welcome participants who contribute an equal share of costs (tax deductible) to cover project expenses.

U.S. Fish and Wildlife Service ✉ U.S. Department of the Interior, 1849 C Street, NW, Washington, DC 20240. ☏ 202-208-5634. ⌨ volunteers.fws.gov
■ Volunteers conduct fish and wildlife population surveys, lead tours, assist in laboratory research, participate in bird banding and habitat modification projects, and work on photography and computer projects.

U.S. Forest Service ✉ U.S. Department of Agriculture, P.O. Box 96090, Washington, DC 20090-6090. ☏ 202-205-8333. ⌨ www.fs.fed.us
■ Short- and long-term assignments are made in photography, visitor services, computer technology, tree planting and seeding, fence and nest-box building, and campground hosting. The Touch America Project is a youth volunteer project for ages 14–17 (call your local U.S. Forest Service office). Volunteers for Peace sponsors short-term projects for volunteers around the world (⌨ www.vfp.org).

Volunteers-in-Parks ✉ U.S. Department of the Interior, 1849 C Street, NW, Washington, DC 20240. ☏ 202-565-1050. ⌨ www.nps.gov/volunteer
■ More than 120,000 people volunteer each year in national parks, helping with docent services, visitor information, computer and library technology, trail maintenance, campground hosting, bird monitoring, site interpretation, gardening, ranger assistance, plant inventory, and archaeology.

Wilderness Volunteers ✉ P.O. Box 22292, Flagstaff, AZ 86002. ☏ 520-556-0038. ⌨ www.wildernessvolunteers.org
■ Volunteers can enroll in one-week outdoor or camping projects for such public land agencies as the National Park Service, U.S. Fish and Wildlife Service, and U.S. Forest Service.

Service Leader. Provides information about outdoor volunteer opportunities and wilderness areas. ⌨ www.serviceleader.org/advice/outdoors.html   *Web Site*

Wasatch Mountains

A chromolithograph of Thomas Moran's *The Great Salt Lake of Utah* was published in Ferdinand Hayden's 1876 report of his geological survey of Yellowstone and the "mountain portions" of Idaho, Nevada, Colorado, and Utah. The shallow body of briny water lies west of the Wasatch Range.

Rising abruptly from the eastern edge of Utah's Great Basin, this segment of the ROCKY MOUNTAINS shelters valleys that support more than two-thirds of the state's population. Mormon settlers arrived in 1847 and used the water from the Wasatch streams to irrigate the arid bottomlands. The range extends from the Bear River in southern Idaho down to Mount Nebo in north-central Utah, covering about 250 miles and rising to its highest point at Mount Timpanogos (12,008 feet) near Provo, Utah. The other best known peaks are Ben

Lomond, Mount Olympus, and Lone and Boxelder Peaks. The Wasatch range—which encompasses the Cache, Uinta, and Wasatch National Forests and the Timpanogos Cave National Monument—is a popular destination for mountaineering, hiking, and alpine and cross-country skiing. ☞ also NATIONAL FOREST SYSTEM, NATIONAL MONUMENTS, UINTA MOUNTAINS

Water Trails

Water trails consist of a long-distance network of coastal and inland waterways served by campsites and other overnight accommodations (bed and breakfasts, for instance). The actual trail is not so much a physical trail as a route on paper, typically mapped by the group or agency overseeing the trail and marked on charts available to users. Access to the waters, which are frequently shallow, is often limited to environmentally friendly watercraft powered by paddle or wind, although small motorboats are sometimes permitted. Water trails may cross and connect private and PUBLIC LANDS, and some are recommended for experienced canoe campers only. Fees may be charged for camping and access, and reservations are required for campsites. Many routes can take ten days to two weeks to complete, based on an average travel time of 10 to 12 miles per day. Water trails are located all over the country. New trails are being plotted, and some are already mapped with planned campsites. ☞ also CANOES, KAYAKS, NATIONAL WILD AND SCENIC RIVERS SYSTEM

Selected Water Trails

Allagash Wilderness Waterway ✉ Maine Department of Conservation, Bureau of Parks and Lands, 106 Hogan Road, Bangor, ME 04401. ☏ 207-941-4014. 🖥 www.state.me.us/doc/dochome.htm
■ Surrounded by a private forest, this 92-mile north-south inland water trail connects ponds, rivers, streams, and several large areas of public lands. Eighty rudimentary campsites are located at intervals.

Everglades National Park Wilderness Waterway ✉ 40001 State Road 9336, Homestead, FL 33034 ☏ 941-695-3311 (Gulf Coast Visitor Center); 941-695-2945 (Flamingo Visitor Center). 🖥 www.nps.gov/ever/visit/canoe-ww.htm
■ Running along the west side of Everglades National Park, this 99-mile stretch of water connects Flamingo, on the Gulf Coast, and Everglades City. Most canoeists allow at least eight days for the trip, which winds through mangrove islands and involves such ominously named destinations as Alligator Creek and the Nightmare.

Les Cheneaux Water Trail ✉ Les Cheneaux Islands Area Tourist Association, P.O. Box 422, Cedarville, MI 49719. ☏ 888-364-7526. 🖥 www.lescheneaux.org
■ Canoes, kayaks, and small motorboats are permitted on this 75-mile-long water trail, which winds along the north shore of Lake Huron through the thirty-six islands known as Les Cheneaux (channels) near Michigan's Upper Peninsula.

V. G. Audubon's *Land-scape along the Hudson* portrays the mighty river as it looked in 1842. Paddlers can now explore it via one of the many water trails being mapped for waterways throughout the nation.

Lower Tomol Trail ⊠ Santa Monica Mountains Trail Council, P.O. Box 345, Agoura Hills, CA 91376. ☏ 818-222-4531
■ The paddling corridor followed by the Chumash Indians in their tomols (plank boats), this route runs through the channel islands along the Pacific coast north of Santa Monica, California. Kayakers are welcome at two campsites.

Maine Island Water Trail ⊠ Maine Island Trail Association, P.O. Box C, Rockland, ME 04841. ☏ 207-596-6456. ▱ www.mita.org
■ This 325-mile-long waterway winds over shallow waters from Casco to Machias Bay and is intended specifically for small motor, sail, and self-propelled watercraft such as canoes and kayaks. A hundred islands along the trail are ideal for camping.

Web Site

Hudson River Watertrail. Sponsored by the Hudson River Watertrail Association, this trails runs 140 miles from the mouth of the Hudson River to the Great Lakes and the St. Lawrence Seaway via the Erie and Champlain Canals. Guidebooks are available to association members. ▱ www.hrwt.org

Western Fiction

One of the most distinctive of all American genres, the western novel may also be the subject of the most debate over its merits. Its substance is judged in terms of the true West, interpreted through the nuance of the local landscape and vernacular, versus a West of myth and escapism told through pasteurized tales of chase and capture, in which good triumphs over evil and the rough-and-ready cowboy always gets the sweetest girl. The truth is that myth is an essential element in all western novels: the western wilderness looms large in the American imagination, and the images of cowpunch, cactus, and corral are indelible national icons. In addition, the overwhelming vastness of the landscape—sometimes so impossible to comprehend—is itself an inevitable storehouse for dreams and fantasy.

The West's first literary center was San Francisco, which early on attracted a coterie of such literary carpetbaggers as Samuel Clemens (Mark Twain) (1835–1910), drawn to its lawless frontier aspect. Among the first to establish a reputation as a western literary figure was the writer and poet Bret Harte (1836–1902), whose stories drawn from a stint in local goldmining camps earned him a national following. As the first editor of *Overland Monthly*, from 1868 to 1870, Harte helped establish something of a bohemian literary circle in San Francisco. This included the poet and actress Adah Menken (ca. 1835–68) and the journalist Ada Clare (ca. 1836–74), both of whom went west to broaden their perspective at the urging of their friend WALT WHITMAN. Another important figure was the poet Ina Coolbrith (1841–1928), an *Overland* contributor who arrived by way of the Beckwourth Pass in a covered wagon.

In addition to the national *Overland Monthly*, San Francisco supported such regional publications as the *Californian*, *Golden Era*, and *San Francisco Bulletin*, which also helped create a following for tales of the California frontier by writers like Clemens and Harte. By the 1890s such national magazines as *Outlook*, *Scribner's*, *Harper's Monthly*, *The Saturday Evening Post*, and *Atlantic Monthly*, all based in the East, were courting such great storytellers as Owen Wister (1860–1938), the best-selling author of *The Virginian* (1902), and Jack London (1876–1916), who embellished his own biography with a fictional lineage of trappers and scouts.

The work of these two writers represents the two primary landscapes of western fiction: the frontier range of the cowboy and the backwoods wilderness of the scout and mountain man. The rise of the cowboy as a fictional hero coincided directly with his fading role in real life at the turn of the twentieth century and the waning popularity of DIME NOVELS, which had whetted a taste for melodramatic plots. The cowboy of fiction is brave, handsome, and well mannered; he takes off his hat indoors and does not swear or drink. Like Wister's Virginian, he is "a courageous loner who follows his private code of honor while prevailing over the forces of evil." His woodlands counterpart, the trapper and scout, learns from the land and lives by his wits. Shaped by their respective wilderness experiences, both figures live fast and die well.

"My name is Lester Langdon, and I am but a poor cowboy."

"You are a brave one and a gentleman, be your calling what it may."

Prentiss Ingraham,
*Crimson Kate,
the Girl Trailer;
or, the Cowboy's
Triumph* (1881)

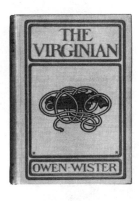

A lasso rope and a holstered pistol adorned the cover of the first edition of Owen Wister's *Virginian* (1902), dedicated to Theodore Roosevelt.

Rustic Heroes: Cowboys and Mountain Men

They are the essence of loyalty, honor, and dignity, ennobled by their role as misfits in a civilized world and their choice of living close to the land instead of exploiting it.

Despite the shadow of the popular pulp westerns that proliferated throughout the first decades of the twentieth century, such serious students of the West as Vardis Fisher (1895–1968), Harvey Fergusson (1890–1971), Frederick Manfred (1912–94), Struthers Burt (1882–1954), and A. B. Guthrie Jr. (1901–91) strove for scrupulous authenticity, a dictate that also shapes the work of more contemporary authors such as Cormac McCarthy (b. 1933) and Larry McMurtry (b. 1936). The trapper's legend has lost its romance in Fergusson's *Wolf Song* (1927), Guthrie's epic *The Big Sky* (1947), and Manfred's *Lord Grizzly* (1954), based on the famous true survival story of a bear-mauled trapper left for dead—nor do the heroes' quests come to tidy resolutions.

Indeed, the most introspective western fiction of the period was an ethical critique that elicited respect for wilderness, wild animals, and Indians alike and confronted the inevitability of change. Manfred, Conrad Richter, Mary Hunter Austin (1868–1934), and Frank Waters (1902–95) were among the notable authors who made NATIVE AMERICANS a serious subject; Richter's *Light in the Forest* (1953) is an attempt to portray the Indian from a native perspective. The Nebraska-born Willa Cather (1873–1947) made nature and the land—of the Great Plains and the ancestral pueblans—the core of stories and novels that quietly lament the frontier's passing. Nature's indifference to the fate of humanity is another theme, found, for example, in the North Woods fiction of Jack London. Of London's some fifty books, the best known is *The Call of the Wild* (1903), in which the protagonist is an animal (part dog, part wolf) that triumphs as the leader of a wild wolf pack.

A part-time hobo and Alaska adventurer, Jack London dressed for a mock "Klondike" scene in Truckee, California. When both *Overland Monthly* and *Atlantic Monthly* accepted his wilderness stories in 1898 and 1899, London was encouraged to keep on writing.

Writers of the Purple Sage

For many writers the West offered an escape from conventional lives and a cure for wanderlust, both temporary and permanent. The Princeton-educated Struthers Burt was a transplanted Wyoming dude wrangler who lobbied for establishment of Grand Teton National Park, which now incorporates land from Burt's ranch (☞ TETON MOUNTAINS). Zane Grey (1872–1939) was a frustrated dentist and semiprofessional baseball player whose life was transformed by his first sight of the GRAND CANYON in 1907. Exploring the impact on the human spirit of the West's wild frontier, Grey's books, including *Spirit of the Plain* (1906) and *Riders of the Purple Sage* (1912), made him one of the best-selling western authors ever. His only real competition came from Louis L'Amour (1909–

88). During a thirty-year career, that North Dakota resident wrote more than one hundred novels, many influenced by tales passed down by a grandfather who fought in the Indian wars. More than 225 million copies of L'Amour westerns are currently in print.

Owen Wister and the artist and writer Frederic Remington (1861–1909) both initially went west for health reasons. Remington, who had ridden with the U.S. Cavalry trailing the Apache raiders of Geronimo, illustrated his own tales and wrote for a number of periodicals, including *Century Magazine, Harper's, Collier's,* and *Cosmopolitan.* The artist (☞ WESTERN ILLUSTRATORS) also provided drawings for Wister's stories in *Harper's* before he became incensed over the success of *The Virginian,* which Wister had dedicated to his friend and Harvard classmate THEODORE ROOSEVELT. As in his art Remington was not interested in pretty pictures, and he considered the book sentimental pap. Remington, who as a child had avidly read the journals of George Catlin (1796–1872) and Lewis and Clark (☞ CORPS OF DISCOVERY), responded with his own novel, *John Ermine of Yellowstone* (1902). In it, the main character, a white man raised by Indians, is tortured by a hunchback hermit and finally murdered by an Indian whom he had the exceedingly poor judgment to insult. The book was not a critical success, although it did inspire a Boston theater production. For its part, *The Virginian* sold 50,000 copies in the first two months and may be the most widely read American novel ever published.

☞ *also* WRITERS (CONTEMPORARY), WRITERS (NINETEENTH CENTURY)

Mary Hunter Austin. 📗 *The Land of Little Rain* (nonfiction) (1903). *The Flock* (1906). *Lost Borders* (1909). *Starry Adventure* (1931).

Selected Works

Struthers Burt. 📗 *The Diary of a Dude Wrangler* (1924). *Malice in Blunderland* (1935). *Let 'er Buck* (1938). *Powder River* (1938).

Willa Cather. 📗 *O Pioneers!* (1913). *My Antonia* (1918). *Death Comes for the Archbishop* (1927).

Walter Van Tilburg Clark. 📗 *The Ox-Bow Incident* (1940). *Track of the Cat* (1949). *Big Sky* (1969).

Stephen Crane. 📗 "The Blue Hotel" (1898). "The Bride Comes to Yellow Sky" (1898).

Frederick Faust (Max Brand). 📗 *The Untamed* (1919). *Riders of the Plains* (1940). *Ride the Wild Trail* (1966). *The Gentle Desperado* (1985). *Slumber Mountain* (1998).

Harvey Fergusson. 📖 *Wolf Song* (1927). *In Those Days* (1929). *Grant of Kingdom* (1950). *The Conquest of Don Pedro* (1954).

Vardis Fisher. 📖 *Children of God: An American Epic* (1939). *The Mothers* (1943). *Mountain Man* (1965).

Zane Grey. 📖 *Spirit of the Plain* (1906). *Heritage of the Desert* (1910). *Riders of the Purple Sage* (1912). *The Rainbow Trail* (1915). *The Vanishing American* (1922).

A. B. Guthrie Jr. 📖 *The Big Sky* (1947). *The Way West* (1949). *These Thousand Hills* (1956).

Bret Harte. 📖 "M'liss: An Idyll of Red Mountain" (1863). "The Luck of Roaring Camp" (1868). "The Outcasts of Poker Flats" (1869).

Louis L'Amour. 📖 *Hondo* (1953). *Showdown at Yellow Butte* (1953). *Sitka* (1957). *Last of the Breed* (1986).

Jack London. 📖 *The Call of the Wild* (1903). *Moon-Face and Other Stories* (1906). *White Fang* (1906).

Frederick Manfred. 📖 *The Chokecherry Tree* (1949). *The Primitive* (1949). *The Brother* (1950). *The Giant* (1951). *Lord Grizzly* (1954). *Riders of Judgment* (1957). *Conquering Horse* (1959). *Milk of Wolves* (1976). *Green Earth* (1977).

Cormac McCarthy. 📖 *Blood Meridian* (1985). *All the Pretty Horses* (1992). *The Crossing* (1994). *Cities of the Plain* (1998).

Larry McMurtry. 📖 *Horseman Pass By* (1979). *Lonesome Dove* (1985). *Anything for Billy* (1988). *Buffalo Girls: A Novel* (1990). *Streets of Laredo* (1993). *Comanche Moon: A Novel* (1997). *Boones Lick: A Novel* (2000).

Conrad Richter. 📖 *The Sea of Grass* (1937). *The Light in the Forest* (1953). *The Rawhide Knot and Other Short Stories* (1957). *A Country of Strangers* (1966).

Jack Schaefer. 📖 *Shane* (1949). *The Canyon* (1969).

Frank Waters. 📖 *The Man Who Killed the Deer* (1942). *The Woman at Otowi Crossing* (1966). *The Lizard Woman* (1995).

Owen Wister. 📖 *Lin McLean* (1897). *The Virginian: A Horseman of the Plains* (1902). *When the West Was Won* (1926). *When West Was West* (1928).

Web Site

Western Writers of America. Dedicated to promoting the spirit of the West in works from mainstream fiction to local history; publications include *The Roundup Quarterly*. 💻 www.westernwriters.org

"The Americans have gashed this country up so horribly with their axes, hammers, scrapers and plows that I always like to see a place which they have overlooked; some place before they arrive with their heavy-handed God of Progress."

Frederic Remington

"The west is dead my Friend / But writers hold the seed / And what they say / will live and grow / Again to those who read."

Inscription by Charles M. Russell on a
drawing done for a neighbor's child (1917)

By conveying the masculine bravura and romance of the frontier saga through an intimate knowledge of its landscape and ways, frontier artists and illustrators shaped the cowboy myth of the Old West in the popular imagination. So vivid was this vision that the passing of more than a century and a half has not diminished its impact.

The most prolific and best known of the western devotees is the sculptor and painter Frederic Remington (1861–1909), an avid horseman, hunter, and author (☞ WESTERN FICTION) who first traveled west in 1881 and is known primarily for his animated scenes of mounted cavalry, cowboys, trappers, Indians, and bucking broncos. Finding a good market in such publications as *Outing Magazine* (edited by a fellow Yale graduate) and *Harper's Weekly*, Remington produced thousands of sketches and paintings. These drawings and his twenty-two bronzes tapped into the wave of eastern nostalgia for cowboy life by capturing a sense of drama and adventure.

Among Remington's illustration commissions was the 1888 serialized version in *Century Magazine* of THEODORE ROOSEVELT'S *Ranch Life and the Hunting Trail*. The same year Remington won a silver medal at the Paris Exposition for his painting of Custer's last stand. He illustrated an 1892 edition of Francis Parkman's *Oregon Trail* and numerous stories in *Harper's* by Owen Wister (1860–1938), the popular writer of westerns (☞ WESTERN FICTION). Remington was haunted by what he saw as a dying era, and his ideal was to record the rich panorama of western life for posterity. "I knew wild riders and the vacant land were about to vanish forever," he wrote in 1881. "And the more I considered the subject, the bigger the Forever loomed."

Affectionately known as the "cowboy artist," the self-taught painter and sculptor Charles Marion Russell (1864–1926) left St. Louis for Montana at age fifteen and never

Frederic Remington's bronco-riding cowboy on the cover of Teddy Roosevelt's *Ranch Life and the Hunting Trail* was typical of his spirited illustrations of the Wild West. His bronzes exhibited the same sense of action.

Henry Francis Farny spent his childhood in western Pennsylvania in the 1850s near an Iroquois Indian reservation, an experience that inspired his interest in painting Indians and western scenes. In 1881 he spent three months in the Dakota Territory, sketching and gathering artifacts, which he used back in his Ohio studio. *On the Trail in Winter* dates from 1894.

looked back. His direct experience of life in the Old West was gained by turns as a night wrangler, sheep herder, trapper, and cowhand. Russell was also a serious pupil of the majestic Montana scenery, particularly in the vicinity of his summer cottage in Glacier National Park (☞ GLACIERS), which formed the backdrop for many of his western adventure scenes. Reproduced widely, Russell's first watercolor, *Waiting for a Chinook* (1886), established his reputation as a painter. The artist's first major oil painting, *Breaking Camp*, went on display in 1885, and throughout the decade he sold illustrations to numerous magazines. His masterpiece is considered to be his *Lewis and Clark Meeting the Flathead Indians at Ross Hole* (1912) (☞ CORPS OF DISCOVERY), which displays the artist's gift for recreating historical scenes to preserve the spirit of the vanishing wilds.

French-born Henry Francis Farny (1847–1916) first traveled

west from his home in Cincinnati in 1880 with the idea of painting the Sioux chief Sitting Bull, then imprisoned at Fort Yates on the upper Missouri River. He spent three months in the Dakota Territory making Indian sketches and photographs and collecting weapons, clothing, and other tribal artifacts that later served as studio props. A long association with *Harper's Weekly* widely disseminated Farney's work. In 1884 he and the journalist Eugene Smalley were commissioned to produce an account of a journey down the Missouri River and across the range to the Yellowstone Valley (☞ YELLOWSTONE NATIONAL PARK). The trip produced seven illustrations for *Century Magazine* and countless sketches of landscapes and Indians that Farny used in paintings over the ensuing years. ☞ *also* FRONTIER GENRE PAINTERS, ROCKY MOUNTAIN SCHOOL ARTISTS

Amon Carter Museum ✉ 3501 Camp Bowie Boulevard, Fort Worth, TX 76107. *Contacts*
☏ 817-738-1933. 🖥 www.cartermuseum.org
■ The museum was established to house an extensive private collection of paintings and sculptures by Frederic Remington and Charles Russell.

Charles Russell Museum ✉ 400 Thirteenth Street North, Great Falls, MT 59401. ☏ 406-727-8787. 🖥 www.cmrussell.org
■ Included in the collection are Russell's house, log cabin studio, research library, and galleries.

Eiteljorg Museum of American Indians and Western Art ✉ 500 West Washington Street, Indianapolis, IN 46204. ☏ 317-636-9378. 🖥 www.eiteljorg. org/index2.html
■ The collection is strong in works by George Catlin, Albert Bierstadt, Frederic Remington, and Charles Russell, as well as the Taos Society of Artists.

Gilcrease Museum ✉ 1400 Gilcrease Museum Road, Tulsa, OK 74127. ☏ 918-596-2700. 🖥 www.gilcrease.org
■ Albert Bierstadt, George Catlin, Alfred Jacob Miller, Thomas Moran, Frederic Remington (18 of 22 bronzes), and Charles Russell are well represented.

Montana Historical Society ✉ 225 North Roberts, Helena, MT 59620. ☏ 406-444-2694. 🖥 www.his.state.mt.us/front.html
■ A museum highlight is the Mackay Gallery of Charles M. Russell Art.

R. W. Norton Art Gallery ✉ 4747 Creswell Avenue, Shreveport, LA 71106. ☏ 318-865-4201. 🖥 www.tfaoi.com/perm12a.htm .
■ Well known for its collection of American western art, the museum includes works by Charles Russell and Frederic Remington. Its collection of Russell's bronze sculptures (136 subjects) is one of the largest and most complete. Holdings also include *The Trappers' Last Stand* (1899), one of Russell's largest oil paintings.

Whitney Gallery of Western Art ⊠ Buffalo Bill Historical Center, 720 Sheridan Avenue, Cody, WY 82414. (307-587-4771. ⌨ www.bbhc.org

■ Featured here are George Catlin, Alfred Jacob Miller, Thomas Moran, Albert Bierstadt, Frederic Remington, Charles Russell, and N. C. Wyeth. Remington's reconstructed studio is also on display.

White Mountains

"Nothing in the United States so nearly approaches the wild scenery of Switzerland, as the Alpine region of New Hampshire."

Henry Marsh, *The White Mountain and Winnepisseogee Guide Book* (1848)

"Let us hope that the lumberman's axe will long spare these beautiful sylvan retreats; that the sun will not shine down with fervent heat upon a desolate and wasted region."

Benjamin Champney (1894)

The earliest known attempt to explore this New Hampshire segment of the APPALACHIAN MOUNTAINS was made in 1642, when an Englishman named Darby Field successfully ascended Mount Washington. This was no mean feat. Mount Washington is the highest peak (6,288 feet) in what is the highest range east of the Mississippi River and north of the GREAT SMOKY MOUNTAINS. Even in the summer the weather at the summit can be perfectly hideous. In the winter Mount Washington claims some of the worst conditions anywhere in the United States: the record low is minus 47 degrees Fahrenheit with the wind gusting at 231 miles per hour (these statistics were clocked in 1934).

The White Mountains, which encompass the Presidential Range, run about 80 miles across the north-central part of New Hampshire into a small fragment of western Maine. Their name first appeared in print in John Josselyn's *New England Rarities Discovered* (1642) and tantalized explorers with rumors of gemstones sparkling on their slopes. The legend of a gigantic garnet guarded by evil spirits held that anyone who spied the stone in its cavern hiding place was doomed to a lifetime of madness wandering the range in search of more treasure.

Giants in the Hills

The real treasure of the White Mountains proved to be the scenery, which helped build one of the first wilderness tourist trades in the country, despite the fact that the area was one of the last in New England to be settled. Among its distinctive features are the glacier-carved passes called notches (☞ GLACIERS). The long-sought Crawford Notch, a deep defile between the coast and the Connecticut River valley, was rediscovered in 1771 and made somewhat more accessible by a rough, heart-stopping wagon road in the 1790s. The notch was the stomping ground of the Crawfords, a famous family

Tourists in the White Mountains about 1910 gape at the famous rock formation widely known as the Old Man in the Mountain. The old man can just be seen looking left, jutting out near the top of the outcropping in the distant notch.

of grizzled New Hampshire mountain guides who kept a series of rudimentary inns at the notch well into the nine- teenth century. Ethan Allen Crawford, the "giant of the hills," was something of a tourist attraction himself, well known for a menagerie that included wild wolves, bears, and a moose.

In 1792 the historian Jeremy Belknap (1744–98) extolled the range's "aged mountains, stupendous elevations and rolling clouds," declaring that "almost anything in nature, which can be supposed capable of ideas of the sublime and beautiful, is here realized." Artists and writers began following their muses to this "thick wilderness" in the 1820s and continued to do so through the 1840s. Nathaniel Hawthorne (1804–64), who stayed at Crawford's Notch, wrote several popular romantic works inspired by the Indian legends of the region, including "The Great Carbuncle" (1837). RALPH WALDO EMERSON, HENRY DAVID THOREAU, and Thomas Cole (1801–48) were also paying guests at the Crawford House Inn. Among the other Hudson River painters who helped establish an artists colony of considerable renown around the North Conway studio of Benjamin Champney (1817–1907) were Champney's friend John Frederick Kensett

(1816–72) and Asher B. Durand (1796–1886), who first came to New Hampshire with Cole in 1839 and painted several views of Franconia Notch. Albert Bierstadt (1830–1902) and Frederick Church (1826–1900) also painted in the White Mountains.

Because they were so evocative of America's wild marvels, the White Mountains figured prominently in early European histories of America. Engravings made from several views of the region by Thomas Cole illustrated *The History and Topography of the United States* (1831), by John Howard Hinton. The work of the White Mountain School of artists in Champney's circle was made widely accessible to the public through such commercial printers as Louis Prang (1824–1909) and Currier and Ives. Chromolithographs of White Mountain paintings were a thriving tourist trade from the 1860s to the 1890s. The rise of stereopticon photography also had a huge impact on public interest in the area. In the 1880s the Littleton, New Hampshire, studio of Benjamin and Edward Kilburn was producing 300,000 stereopticon photos a year; views of the road up Mount Washington counted among the most popular.

The porch of the Crawford House frames a view about 1900 of the narrow divide through Crawford Notch in the White Mountains. The arrival of a rail line through the notch in 1875 brought thousands of visitors to the area's hotels; the rustic P&O (Portland and Ogdensburg) Railway depot is visible in the distance.

As early as 1901, a small group of citizens established the Society for the Protection of New England Forests to fight CLEAR-CUTTING and the rapidly growing pulp industry in the region. Intense lobbying by the society was influential in the passage of the Weeks Forest Purchase Act (1911) (☞ NATIONAL FOREST SYSTEM). This watershed legislation authorized federal purchase of much of the White Mountain region and led directly to the creation of the White Mountain National Forest (New Hampshire and Maine), which now covers about 780,000 acres, an area larger than the state of Rhode Island. This national forest encompasses more than 114,000 acres of land in the NATIONAL WILDERNESS PRESERVATION SYSTEM, nine scenic areas managed to protect outstanding views, and more than 1,200 miles of hiking trails. ☞ *also* HUDSON RIVER SCHOOL ARTISTS, PHOTOGRAPHERS, ROCKY MOUNTAIN SCHOOL ARTISTS

Contacts

Mount Washington Observatory ⊠ P.O. Box 2310, North Conway, NH 03860. ℂ 603-356-2137. ▯ www.mountwashington.org
▪ The only continuously staffed weather observatory in the Western Hemisphere is maintained here. Programs tackle summit environmental education, aviation research, weather science, and backcountry search and rescue. The Weather Discovery Center is open year-round in the Mount Washington valley.

New Hampshire Historical Society ⊠ Tuck Library, 30 Park Street, Concord, NH 03301-6384. ℂ 603-225-3381. ⊠ Museum of New Hampshire History, Eagle Square, Concord, NH 03301-6384. ℂ 603-226-3189. ▯ www.nhhistory.org
▪ The White Mountain Collection (1780–present) emphasizes the White Mountain School artists, including Thomas Hill, Benjamin Champney, Thomas Doughty, Frederick Church, Jasper Cropsey, and Albert Bierstadt. Holdings are also strong in souvenirs, photographs, hotel business records, maps, and railroad advertising.

Society for the Protection of New Hampshire Forests ⊠ 54 Portsmouth Street, Concord, NH 03301. ℂ 603-224-9945. ▯ www.spnhf.org
▪ Campaigns focus on protective land reservation purchases (more than 24,000 acres), low-impact forestry management, natural resource education, a permanent statewide funding program for the protection of open space, and political advocacy throughout New England. Publications include *Forest Notes*.

White Mountain National Forest ⊠ Supervisor's Office, 719 Main Street, Laconia, NH 03246. ℂ 603-528-8721. ▯ www.fs.fed.us/R9/white
▪ The forest offers campgrounds, trails, and scenic drives.

Reading

▣ Jeremy Belknap, *The History of New Hampshire* (1792). ▣ Benjamin Willey, *Incidents in White Mountain History* (1856). ▣ Tom Wessels, *Reading the Forested Landscape: A Natural History of New England* (1999).

Walt Whitman

Walt Whitman (1819–92) published the first edition of *Leaves of Grass* at his own expense in 1855. This compendium of twelve then-untitled poems was written in free verse, and its unconventional form further shocked the public in its celebration of the body and assertion of universal love. The poet's plea for faith in the divinity of human individuality is defined as the immediate sensual and physical expression of nature, the substance of all of the joy of human existence and sense of self. Among Whitman's contemporaries, *Leaves of Grass* garnered praise only from RALPH WALDO EMERSON, who saw Whitman's oeuvre as an answer to his own call for an original, native body of work in a country itself born anew. Emerson's positive

"Oh truth of the earth! Oh truth of things!"

Walt Whitman, *Leaves of Grass* (1855)

When *Leaves of Grass* was published in 1855, it was received largely unfavorably by literary reviewers. Walt Whitman was paralyzed by a stroke in 1873, but he continued to write until his death in 1892.

response inspired Whitman to revise the work for a second edition, published in 1856, which included twenty new poems underscoring the themes of a common human experience. "Song of the Open Road" evokes the credo of self-reliance and the idea of life as a journey composed of everyday encounters that define each person's unique place in the universe.

Throughout his life Whitman revised and rearranged *Leaves of Grass* for some nine different editions; at least one of these, the 1881–82 Boston edition, was withdrawn from publication after censorship by local authorities. In the various versions the poet's own optimism about the American experience ebbed and flowed. The sixth edition, which appeared in 1876, when Whitman was suffering from stroke-induced paralysis, expressed faith in the future as part of the continuance of time—the quintessential message of nature—that defines all people. "Song of the Redwood Tree," Whitman's eulogy to a dying redwood, hears the voice of the tree's soul as "that chant of the seasons and time, chant not of the past only but the future." ☞ *also* WRITERS (NINETEENTH CENTURY)

Selected Works

📖 *Franklin Evans; or, The Inebriate* (1842). *Leaves of Grass* (1855, 1856, 1860, 1867, 1870, 1876, 1881, 1891). *Drum Taps* (1865). *Sequel to Drum Taps* (1865). *Passage to India* (1870). *Democratic Vistas* (1871). *Memoranda During the War* (1875). *Specimen Days and Collect* (1881). *November Boughs* (1888). *Good-Bye, My Fancy* (1891). *Complete Prose Works* (1892).

Contact

Walt Whitman Birthplace ✉ 246 Old Walt Whitman Road, Huntington Station, NY 11746. ☎ 516-427-5240. 🖥 www.fieldtrip.com/ny/64275240
■ The house and visitor center offer exhibits of Whitman memorabilia, photographs, and books. Poetry readings and lectures are also held.

Wild Horses and Burros

Although certain horse species roamed across the North American continent in prehistoric times, those and many other mammals, camels among them, were extinct—for reasons that remain a scientific mystery—by the time of the last glacial retreat about 8,000 to 12,000 years ago (☞ GLA-CIERS). Beginning in the late 1400s, however, Spanish explorers reintroduced horses from the Iberian Peninsula. These small-ish, sturdy animals, which included the horses now known as Sorraias, were swift of foot and well adapted to carrying a rider in full armor and could survive by foraging for their own food. Captive Indians were sometimes trained as stable hands at Spanish stock ranches near the Rio Grande River, and gifts of horses were made to Christianized tribe members. Indians also learned to capture and ride the Spanish horses, and their use spread from the Southwest to the Great Plains tribes, pro-foundly affecting their cultures by altering hunting, trading, and raiding patterns and changing the nature of Indian warfare.

The Sorraia gene pool has been preserved in a few isolated bands of wild horses, and their characteristics are particularly evident in the Kiger mustangs of Oregon, the Sulphur Springs mustangs of southwestern Utah, and the Pryor Mountain mus-tangs of Wyoming and Montana. These and the other wild horses and burros that now roam the West are the descendants of animals that escaped into the wild or were purposely released, some by the U.S. Cavalry. Unclaimed, unbranded

Burros forage for food in the seemingly unlikely locale of Death Valley National Monument in California. The Bureau of Land Management runs an adoption program to ensure preservation of wild horses and burros.

horses and burros are now found in herd-management areas administered by the BUREAU OF LAND MANAGEMENT in Arizona, California, Colorado, Idaho, Montana, Nevada, New Mexico, Oregon, Utah, and Wyoming. Often known generically as mustangs, from the Spanish *mesteño* (wild horse or cattle), they represent no special breed and are predominantly sorrels, bays, and browns that typically stand about 14 or 15 hands.

By the mid-1800s an estimated 250 million wild horses lived west of the Mississippi River, but within a century the population was reduced to a few herds, mainly because of grazing competition from domestic stock and the effects of bounty hunting. The first federal statute to protect wild horses was the Wild Horse Annie Bill (1959), which outlawed the use of aircraft to hunt wild horses on PUBLIC LANDS. The Wild Free-Roaming Horse and Burro Act (1971) declared that wild burros and horses "are living symbols of the historic and pioneer spirit of the West" that enrich the lives of Americans. Amended by later acts, this statute placed the animals on lands under the authority and control of the Bureau of Land Management and set management standards for their protection against harassment, branding, and inhumane treatment.

Wild Horse and Burro Adoption

As a provision of the Wild Free-Roaming Horse and Burro Act, the BLM offers healthy "excess" wild horses and burros for adoption by qualified individuals. While a goal is to ensure free-roaming behavior, management of the wild populations is necessary because modern wild horses are a nonnative species whose only natural predator is the rare cougar (mountain lion). The herds thus tend to outgrow their food supplies and face death from thirst and starvation.

In 1999 the bureau placed almost seven thousand mules and horses in adoptive families. Qualified adopters can take home a maximum of four animals a year but must be able to provide adequate facilities for them. In general there are no federal restrictions on how the adopted animals are used other than that they cannot be exploited for commercial purposes that "take advantage of the wildness of the animal." After leaving the range all wild animals are protected by state livestock and humane treatment laws.

Contacts

American Mustang and Burro Association ✉ P.O. Box 788, Lincoln, CA 95648. ☎ 916-633-9271. ▤ www.bardalisa.com

■ This group provides services and information to adopters, focuses on public education, and also maintains a registry of wild horses and burros and their offspring.

Bureau of Land Management ✉ National Wild Horse and Burro Program, P.O. Box 12000, Reno, NV 89520. ☎ 775-861-6711. ▤ www.wildhorseandburro.blm.gov.

■ The BLM program finds qualified adoptive families for wild mules and horses threatened by starvation.

Least Resistance Training Concepts/Wild Horse Mentors ✉ P.O. Box 648, Knightsen, CA 94548-0648. 🖥 www.whmentors.org
■ The national coordinators of the Wild Horse Mentors, this group provides training information and organizes annual wild horse workshops.

Lifesavers ✉ 23809 East Avenue J, Lancaster, CA 93535. 📞 661-727-0049. 🖥 www.wildhorserescue.org
■ Committed to protecting wild horses from abandonment and abuse, Lifesavers oversees an adoption program for rescued mustangs and offers education programs.

Wild Horses and Burros. Outlines adoption events, training, workshops, and clinics. 🖥 www.kbrhorse.net/whb/blmhorse.html

Web Site

World Heritage Sites

Sites of international cultural and historical importance are included on UNESCO's World Heritage List in accordance with the Convention Concerning the Protection of the World Cultural and Natural Heritage (World Heritage Convention), adopted by the UNESCO General Conference in 1972. The convention's provisions are based on the acknowledgment that the deterioration or loss of any item of a country's cultural or natural heritage constitutes a "harmful

Kilauea Volcano in Hawaii Volcanoes National Park is the world's most active volcano, offering scientists insights into the birth of the Hawaiian Islands. More than half of the park, which was created in 1916, is designated as part of the National Wilderness Preservation System.

impoverishment of the heritage of all nations of the world."
The purpose is to prevent such a loss by ensuring national
and international protection of that heritage, defined as monuments (architecture and works of monumental sculpture
and painting); groups of buildings; sites (man-made works as
well as those created by a combination of human and natural
efforts, including archaeological sites); and natural features and
geological formations. All are deemed of outstanding universal value from a historical, aesthetic, ethnological, anthropo-
logical, or scientific point of view.

As of 2000, 158 nations have adopted the convention. Each
of these states parties agrees to adhere to a general policy that
integrates heritage protection and to develop research and
other measures to preserve and rehabilitate the sites. The
required inventories of property constituting the cultural and
natural heritage that are submitted by the signatories to the
World Heritage Committee form the basis of the World Heritage List. Composed of twenty-one specialists from member
nations elected for six-year terms, the committee administers
the convention and recognizes nominated sites for inclusion
on the list. No site can be included without the consent of
the country in which it is located. As of 2000, the list numbered 690 properties.

The World Heritage Committee also administers the World
Heritage Fund, which is made up in part from voluntary con-
tributions and a percentage of UNESCO member dues; the
monies are used to supply assistance to countries requesting
it for their sites. The United States, which has dropped its
UNESCO membership, volunteered $450,000 (from the for-
eign operations appropriation) in fiscal year 2000. In recent
years controversy has arisen over naming U.S. national parks
and monuments to the World Heritage List. Critics contend
that the current UNESCO listing policy undermines Congress's role in governing American PUBLIC LANDS. The World
Heritage Convention, however, does not give the United
Nations authority over U.S. sites.

World Heritage Sites
in the United States

■ **Cahokia Mounds State Historic Site** (Illinois)
■ **Carlsbad Caverns National Park** (New Mexico)
■ **Chaco Culture National Historical Park** (New Mexico)
■ **Everglades National Park** (Florida) (World Heritage Site in Danger, 1993)
■ **Grand Canyon National Park** (Arizona)
■ **Great Smoky Mountains National Park** (North Carolina and Tennessee)
■ **Hawaii Volcanoes National Park** (Hawaii)
■ **Independence Hall** (Pennsylvania)
■ **Kluane and Wrangell–St. Elias National Parks** (Alaska and Canada)
■ **La Fortaleza and San Juan National Historic Site** (Puerto Rico)

- **Mammoth Cave National Park** (Kentucky)
- **Mesa Verde National Park** (Colorado)
- **Monticello and the University of Virginia** (Virginia)
- **Olympic National Park** (Washington)
- **Pueblo de Taos** (New Mexico)
- **Redwood National Park** (California)
- **Statue of Liberty** (New York/New Jersey)
- **Yellowstone National Park** (Wyoming, Montana, and Idaho) (World Heritage Site in Danger, 1995)
- **Yosemite National Park** (California)

UNESCO ✉ 7, place de Fontenoy, 75352 Paris, France 07 SP 33. ☎ 33-1-45-68-10-0. 🖥 www.unesco.org/whc/nwhc/pages/sites/main.htm — *Contact*

Writers (Contemporary)

The all-encompassing genre of contemporary American literature that might be called "nature" writing embraces novel, short story, essay, verse, lecture, criticism, and memoir—with many authors working in more than one form and sometimes weaving them together in a single work. The contributors in fact defy categorization. Their work is so individualistic that as a body it also defies inclusion in a single genre save for the overlapping themes of nature and land as solace, gift, legacy, and source of sanity. Voices might be strident, like that of Edward Abbey (1927–89), a vocal objector to the Glen Canyon Dam (☞ GRAND CANYON), who emerged as a rebellious and irreverent defender of the American West against overpopulation and development. Or quiet, like the reasoned prose of Annie Dillard (b. 1945), who calls herself "a wanderer with background in theology and a penchant for quirky facts," or of Terry Tempest Williams (b. 1955), a Utah descendant of Mormon pioneers who writes of the passages of life and the passages of nature. The unifying thread among all is a role as literary advocates for moral conscience whose writing cultivates—directly and indirectly—a consensus for responsible environmental stewardship. ☞ *also* WRITERS (NINETEENTH CENTURY) *and specific historic writers*

Edward Abbey 📕 *Desert Solitaire* (1968). *Black Sun* (1971). *The Monkey Wrench Gang* (1975). *The Journey Home* (1977). *Hayduke Lives!* (1990). *The Serpents of Paradise* (1995). — *Selected Works*

Rick Bass 📕 *The Ninemile Wolves* (1992). *In the Loyal Mountains* (1995). *The Lost Grizzlies* (1995). *The Book of Yaak* (1996). *Wild to the Heart* (1997). *The New Wolves* (1998). *Colter: The True Story of the Best Dog I Ever Had* (2000).

Charles Bowden 📕 *Killing the Hidden Waters* (1985). *Blue Desert* (1988).

Annie Dillard 📖 *Pilgrim at Tinker Creek* (1974). *An American Childhood* (1987). *The Writing Life* (1989). *The Living* (1992). *Mornings Like This* (1995). *For the Time Being* (1999).

Ivan Doig 📖 *This House of Sky: Landscapes of a Western Mind* (1978). *Winter Brothers: A Season at the Edge of America* (1980). *The Sea Runners* (1982). *Heart Earth* (1993). *Bucking the Sun* (1996). *Mountain Time* (1999).

Gretel Ehrlich 📖 *To Touch the Water* (1981). *The Solace of Open Spaces* (1985). *Drinking Dry Clouds: Stories from Wyoming* (1991). *Islands, the Universe, Home* (1991). *Arctic Heart: A Poem Cycle* (1992). *A Blizzard Year* (1999).

Teresa Jordan 📖 *Cowgirls: Women of the American West* (1982). *Riding the White Horse Home: A Western Family Album* (1993). *Graining the Mare: The Poetry of Ranch Women* (1994).

William Kittredge 📖 *We Are Not in This Together* (1984). *Owning It All* (1987). 📖 *Hole in the Sky: A Memoir* (1992). *Who Owns the West?* (1996). *Waste Land: Meditations on a Ravaged Landscape* (1997). *The Portable Western Reader*, ed. (1997).

Barry Lopez 📖 *Desert Notes: Reflections in the Eye of a Raven* (1976). *Of Wolves and Men* (1978). *Arctic Dreams: Imagination and Desire in the Northern Landscape* (1986). *The Rediscovery of North America* (1990). *Lessons from the Wolverine* (1997). *About This Life: Journeys on the Threshold of Memory* (1998).

John Madson 📖 *Stories from Under the Sky* (1961). *John Madson, Out Home* (1979). *Where the Sky Began: Land of the Tallgrass Prairie* (1982). *Up on the River: An Upper Mississippi Chronicle* (1985).

Bill McKibben 📖 *The End of Nature* (1989). *The Age of Missing Information* (1992, 1994). *Hope, Human and Wild: True Stories of Living Lightly on the Earth* (1995). *Return of the Wolf* (2000). *Long Distance: A Year of Living Strenuously* (2001).

John McPhee 📖 *A Sense of Where You Are* (1965). *Encounters with the Archdruid* (1971). *The Survival of the Bark Canoe* (1975). *Coming into the Country* (1977). *Basin and Range* (1981). *In Suspect Terrain* (1983). *Table of Contents* (1985). *Rising from the Plains* (1986). *The Control of Nature* (1989). *Assembling California* (1993). *Annals of the Former World* (1998).

Gary Paul Nabhan 📖 *The Desert Smells Like Rain* (1982). *Gathering the Desert* (1985). *Desert Wildflowers* (1988). *Enduring Seeds* (1989). *Counting Sheep: Twenty Ways of Seeing Desert Bighorn* (1993). *Desert Legends* (1994). *The Forgotten Pollinators* (1996). *Cultures of Habitat* (1997).

Leslie Marmon Silko 📖 *Ceremony* (1977). *Storyteller* (1981). *After a Summer*

Rain in the Upper Sonoran (1984). Almanac of the Dead (1992). Sacred Water (1993). Laguna Woman (1994). Yellow Woman and a Beauty of the Spirit (1996). Gardens in the Dunes (1999).

Annick Smith 📖 The Last Best Place: A Montana Anthology, ed. with William Kittredge (1990). Homestead (1995). Big Bluestem: Journey into the Tall Grass (1996).

Gary Snyder 📖 The Back Country (1968). Blue Sky (1969). Earth House Hold (1969). Turtle Island (1974). He Who Hunted Birds in His Father's Village (1979). Left Out in the Rain (1986). The Practice of the Wild (1990). No Nature (1992). A Place in Space (1995). Mountains and Rivers without End (1996).

Wallace Stegner 📖 Fire and Ice (1941). Mormon Country (1942). The Big Rock Candy Mountain (1943). Beyond the Hundredth Meridian (1954). The Gathering of Zion: The Story of the Mormon Trail (1964). The Sound of Mountain Water (1969). Angle of Repose (1971). The Spectator Bird (1976). American Places (1981). American West as Living Space (1987). Crossing to Safety (1987). Where the Bluebird Sings to the Lemonade Springs (1992).

Charles Wilkinson 📖 American Indians, Time, and the Law (1987). The American West (1989). Crossing the Next Meridian (1992). Eagle Bird: Mapping the New West (1992). Fire on the Plateau (1999).

Terry Tempest Williams 📖 Between Cattails (1981). Pieces of White Shell (1984). Coyote's Canyon (1990). Refuge (1991). An Unspoken Hunger: Desert Quartet (1995). Leap (2000).

Ann Zwinger 📖 Beyond the Aspen Grove (1970). Land above the Trees (1972). Run, River, Run (1974). Wind in the Rock (1978). A Conscious Stillness: Two Naturalists on Thoreau's Rivers (1982). The Mysterious Lands (1989). Downcanyon (1995). The Near-Sighted Naturalist (1998).

Gary Snyder — Earth House Hold

The first three words of the title of Gary Snyder's *Earth House Hold: Technical Notes and Queries for Fellow Dharma Revolutionaries* (1969) play on the root meaning of *ecology*. William Suttle's photograph is called *Homage to Edward Weston*.

"Is it true that Emerson is going to take a gun? Then somebody will be shot!"

Henry Wadsworth Longfellow, declining an invitation to join the 1858 Follensby Pond camping trip to the Adirondacks, as quoted by William James Stillman in "The Philosophers' Camp," *Autobiography of a Journalist* (1901)

Writers (Nineteenth Century)

America's wilderness has provided writers with a subject for an ongoing moral discourse that both shaped a literary genre and ultimately became a catalyst for environmental reform. The major themes of this literary tradition reflect an evolution from the Puritan concept of wilderness as a symbol of humanity's innate sinfulness to an appreciation of nature as godly and sublime: panacea, wellspring of inspiration, origin of renewal and pleasure, and incontrovertible source of a universal code of human ethics. That America's wildlands could be regarded as a heritage equal if not superior to the ancient artistic treasures of other countries did much to bring American literature out from the shadow of the European model in the nineteenth century.

By the early 1800s it had become rather fashionable in Boston academic circles to spend time traveling or living in the wilds and then emerging to write about the experience. Thus the foundation for an American genre was laid in New England. As writers and poets reconsidered the place of human beings in the universe, the desire for direct contact with both nature and the land fueled interest in published accounts, scholarly and otherwise, of the surveyors and frontiersmen who were exploring the trans-Allegheny West. Such works proved a remarkable literary influence. *Algic Researches* (1839), for example, a well-known study of Indian culture by the GREAT LAKES explorer and ethnologist Henry Rowe Schoolcraft (1793–1864), directly inspired the 1855 poem *The Song of Hiawatha*, by Henry Wadsworth Longfellow (1807–82).

The emerging cult of the "noble savage" was no better exploited than by JAMES FENIMORE COOPER. As a product of nineteenth-century romanticism, Cooper's oeuvre celebrates a return to the primitive ways of nature and finds virtue in the "uncivilized" heroes of pioneer scout and long-suffering Indian. The writer was in fact the first American to use the word *pioneer* (originally denoting a miner or a laborer) as it is now understood. WASHINGTON IRVING joined Cooper and Sir Walter Scott (1771–1832) as one of the most influential writers of the time and was the first American to be recognized as a significant literary figure abroad. If Cooper and Irving were the great romantics, then HENRY DAVID THOREAU and RALPH WALDO EMERSON and by extension WALT WHITMAN were the true philosophers of the age. Their transcendentalist call for personal revelation through the intuitive experience of nature was in turn a major influence on JOHN BURROUGHS, ALDO LEOPOLD, and JOHN MUIR, the triumvirate who forged the vanguard of the American environmental movement. ☞ *also* WRITERS (CONTEMPORARY) *and specific historic writers*

The cult of the "noble savage" in romantic literature praised the honest virtues found in living with the ways of the wilderness. Staged presentations of *The Song of Hiawatha* were popular in the late 1800s and early 1900s. About 1900 an Indian boy named Pulls-the-Bow posed as the poem's Indian hero.

I n 1872 President Ulysses S. Grant signed into law the Yellowstone Act, withdrawing more than 2 million acres of public land on a broad plateau in the ROCKY MOUNTAINS from settlement or sale "to be dedicated and set apart as a public park or pleasuring-ground for the benefit and enjoyment of the people." The designation of Yellowstone National Park established the first national park in the world and set the precedent for a future national policy of reserving land from the public domain for the express purpose of recreation and long-term preservation of the natural resources, wildlife, and scenery therein (☞ NATIONAL PARK SYSTEM).

The park, since designated as a WORLD HERITAGE SITE and an INTERNATIONAL BIOSPHERE RESERVE, measures 3,742 square miles (larger than the states of Rhode Island and Delaware combined) and is located primarily in northwestern Wyoming, although slivers overlap into Idaho (1.4 percent) and Montana (7.6 percent). Within this giant rectangle are some of the earth's more astounding geological curiosities, including ten thousand thermal features, about 250 active geysers (the largest concentration of geysers in the world is found at Upper Geyser Basin), fossil forests, and one of the world's largest calderas, measuring 28 by 47 miles. The hot springs and geysers are evidence of the volcanic activity that created the Yellowstone plateau, most of which was formed from once-molten lava.

Yellowstone National Park

"Paint cannot touch it, and words are wasted."

Frederic Remington, "Policing the Yellowstone," *Harper's Weekly* (1895)

The largest concentration of geysers in the world is found in Yellowstone. This group going off next to the Firehole River was photographed by John K. Hillers in the 1880s, by which time the park had become a popular tourist attraction.

Following the first Lewis and Clark reports of the Yellowstone River (☞ CORPS OF DISCOVERY), fragmentary and unsubstantiated sightings of waterfalls, geysers, sulfur beds, hot springs, volcanoes, and other "freaks and phenomena of Nature" filtered out of the Yellowstone Valley. These caused much interest but even more skepticism in the years before the first formal expeditions of 1869–71. Fear of Indian attacks limited penetration into the region to the scant trapping and prospecting forays of trappers and prospectors. The first reliable written account of Yellowstone's weird "decorations," by Daniel T. Potts of General W. H. Ashley's expedition, dates to 1822; Jedediah Smith (1799–1831), one of the famous mountain men, was there by 1824. An 1850 journey up the north-flowing Yellowstone River to Yellowstone Lake and Falls and across the CONTINENTAL DIVIDE to the Madison River led another party of prospectors, including Jim Bridger (1804–81) and Kit Carson (1809–68), to the Lower Geyser Basin. Bridger provided important information about the region to mappers, but the fact that he was also one of the greatest and most entertaining tellers of "trappers' tales" clouded the issue over what was real and what was fiction with regard to Yellowstone's incredible geothermal features.

Reports were intriguing enough to generate the Yellowstone surveys led by David Folsom and Charles Cook (1869, 1870),

Henry Washburn and Gustavus Doane (1870), and Ferdinand V. Hayden (1871). Various members of these survey parties—notably, Nathaniel Langford, Cornelius Hedges, and Hayden—are credited with leading the movement to set aside the plateau as a public reserve (☞ SURVEYS). Historians minimize the role of wilderness preservation in the park's creation because the surveys were motivated largely by political struggles in the Montana Territory and the Northern Pacific Railway's effort to create a tourist destination to which it would be providing sole rail access. The banking house of Jay Cooke and Company, which had controlling interest in Northern Pacific stock, engaged Langford as a lecturer, the idea being to build popular interest to expedite sale of rail bonds. Articles by Langford also appeared in *Scribner's Monthly* in 1871, and four hundred copies of the magazine were circulated to members of Congress.

   Legislation followed the model of the Yosemite Land Grant Bill (1864), but Yellowstone differed from the earlier YOSEMITE VALLEY reservation in that Yellowstone was put under federal rather than state jurisdiction, partly because neither Wyoming nor Montana was yet a state. One main concern was to prevent private acquisition and depredation of the geothermal curiosities and ensure public access to them. Although recreation took precedence over wilderness preservation, protection of Yellowstone's natural features was implicit in the legislation. Care and maintenance of the park was assigned to the secretary of the interior, who was charged with framing regulations to "provide for the preservation, from injury or spoliation, of all timber, mineral deposits, natural curiosities, or wonders within said park, and their retention in their natural condition." The dual responsibilities of protecting the natural environment while making the park accessible and safe for the public have set a precedent for a NATIONAL PARK SERVICE policy that is often seen as leading to a contradictory mission.

   Although commercial hunting and fishing were supposed to be prohibited, poaching and vandalism went on unchecked for years after the park designation. In 1886 the secretary of war dispatched a U.S. Cavalry detail to enforce the rules before the NATIONAL PARK SERVICE was created in 1916. The Yellowstone Park Protection Act (1894) finally made illegal killing any wildlife in Yellowstone Park and outlined penalties for offenders.

William Henry Jackson's view of the Lower Falls on the Yellowstone River is half of a stereograph image. When seen through a special device, photographs of such wonders as this Wyoming cascade appeared in three dimensions, enthralling viewers in parlors across the country.

Wildlife Preservation

The diverse Yellowstone ecosystem supports about 60 species of mammal, 309 bird types, 18 fish species (5 are non-native), and 10 reptile and amphibian types. Of these, the whooping crane and gray wolf are listed as endangered (☞ ENDANGERED SPECIES), and the bald eagle, grizzly bear (☞ BEARS), and lynx are listed as threatened. Until recently, one of the major human threats to wildlife habitats here has been the use of recreational snowmobiles. However, in late 2000 the National Park Service indicated that it would phase out snowmobiles in Yellowstone National Park by the winter of 2003–4. A primary threat to wildlife in the greater Yellowstone ecosystem comes from subdivision of large tracts of open land for residential use; more than a million acres have recently been subdivided in the region.

Bison

Regeneration efforts have increased the bison herd to about 3,500 wild buffalo, which are permitted to range freely in the park. That they also migrate out of it has become the focus of controversy. The fear is that the bison may carry the bacterium *brucellosis,* which is dangerous to domestic cattle and a threat to Montana's *brucellosis*-free livestock designation, although there is no documented case of a buffalo causing the infection. Attempts to force the animals back into Yellowstone Park are seldom successful, and many of the bison migrating into Montana are killed. During the winter of 1996–97, the Montana Department of Livestock authorized the slaughter of 1,100 bison, or about one-third of the Yellowstone herd. The action was precipitated by harsh weather conditions that forced the animals to search for winter forage on lands immediately north and west of the park. Despite milder winters since then, state officials have continued the practice. The total of buffalo killed under the government plan in the last decade numbers more than 2,400. In 1999 the federal government completed a purchase and exchange of land to secure public ownership of a tract immediately north of Yellowstone Park that is a habitat for buffalo and other wildlife. The Modified Preferred Alternative plan issued under the Clinton administration in 2000, however, leaves open the possibility of continued slaughter over the next fifteen years. ☞ *also* BISON

Elk

The 20,000 elk living in Yellowstone National Park constitute its largest large-mammal population. Well into the 1900s the park's administering agencies provided for the feeding and protection of the herds to the point of overpopulating the habitat. A reduction program began in the 1920s, when elk were relocated outside the park or slaughtered outright. Culling was ended by the National Park Service in 1969 in a

policy move that emphasized natural population controls, including weather and predators. The elk population is closely tied to that of the gray wolf, which favors elk over other prey. According to the U.S. FISH AND WILDLIFE SERVICE, a revitalized wolf population could reduce the elk herds by as much as 30 percent.

Grizzly bear management in the greater Yellowstone region is coordinated by an Interagency Grizzly Bear Committee, comprising representatives from the National Park Service, U.S. Fish and Wildlife Service, U.S. FOREST SERVICE, BUREAU OF LAND MANAGEMENT, and the Fish and Game Departments of Montana, Idaho, and Wyoming. Since 1975 about three hundred of the bears have been radio-collared for monitoring. The total estimated population is between three and six hundred bears, which are protected in Yellowstone Park under the proviso of the Endangered Species Act. In recent years there has been a controversial move to take the grizzly bear off the Endangered Species List. Opponents cite the danger of loosening the safety net of habitat protection. The population is believed to be about the same as it was when the grizzly was listed, but habitat destruction has increased. Forest roads and associated CLEAR-CUTTING are considered a primary danger to grizzlies. If the grizzly bear is taken off the list, management of its population would fall to the states, which do not have the authority to manage the habitat on federally administered public lands. ☞ also BEARS

Revised park regulations allowed the six-story Old Faithful Inn to be built in 1904 close to its namesake geyser.

Grizzly Bears

Trumpeter Swans

The increasingly compromised habitat of this subspecies has made Yellowstone a refuge for trumpeter swans. The birds are the subject of a pending petition for listing under the Endangered Species Act (1973) and are included on the Birds of Management Concern list maintained by the U.S. Fish and Wildlife Service. Nevertheless, in 2000 the service announced a plan to open a permanent hunting season for these rare swans and for the similar-looking tundra swan. Under the plan hunters in Idaho, Wyoming, Montana, Nevada, and Utah may kill the swans, despite the declared concern of the superintendent of Yellowstone National Park that such hunting could eliminate the already declining population that uses the park.

Wolves

Avidly sought by early trappers, gray wolves were gone from New England and Pennsylvania by the early 1900s. The Rocky Mountain wolf, exterminated from the Yellowstone Valley by the 1930s, has been reintroduced to the area.

The greater Yellowstone area is one of three gray wolf recovery areas managed by the U.S. Fish and Wildlife Service in the ROCKY MOUNTAINS. Largely because of predator-control efforts instituted by the U.S. Biological Survey, precursor of the Fish and Wildlife Service, gray wolves were completely extirpated from the park and surrounding area by the late 1930s. The animals gained legal protection under the Endangered Species Act and began recolonizing on their own in northern Montana in the 1980s. The Fish and Wildlife Service reintroduced 66 wolves into Yellowstone National Park in 1995 and 1996, and by 1999 there were at least 118. Many have radio collars for monitoring. The Yellowstone wolf population is classified as "nonessential experimental"; this means that there is more flexibility in their management and treatment than for packs in other recovery areas considered more fragile and allows for the extermination of wolves under certain circumstances, such as when the animals cross into private land. All but one of the confirmed losses (twenty-four) of livestock and dogs to predatory wolves in the region in 1999 in fact occurred on private land. Crop damage from livestock and wild elk displaced by wolves and scattered cattle herds are related problems. In 1997 a U.S. district court ruling declared that wolf reintroduction in the greater Yellowstone area actually violates the Endangered Species Act because of the discrepancy in management between the special experimental recovery areas and other wolf habitats, which are not geographically separated. The wolves were ordered removed from the park, but a final decision in 2000 upheld the reintroduction.

Contacts

Greater Yellowstone Coalition ✉ 13 South Willson, Suite 2, Bozeman, MT 59771. ☎ 406-586-1593. 🖥 www.greateryellowstone.org

■ The coalition participates in a variety of campaigns: protecting wolves and grizzly bears, ending buffalo slaughter, and passing legislation to preserve geothermal

features by preventing development in the hot-water aquifers that extend beyond the Yellowstone Park boundaries. A strong voice for recreation reform, the group has been a major supporter of several wilderness bills.

Montana Historical Society ✉ 225 North Roberts, Helena, MT 59620-1201. (406-444-1645. 🖥 www.his.state.mt.us
■ A major holding is the collection of photographs of Yellowstone National Park, including the archive of F. Jay Haynes, the park's first official photographer.

Western Heritage Center ✉ 2822 Montana Avenue, Billings, MT 59101. (406-256-6809. 🖥 www.montana.edu/wwwmor
■ Interpreting life in the Yellowstone Valley is the center's mission. Its collection includes more than 1,000 photographs documenting the social history, architecture, and development of the region.

Yellowstone National Park ✉ P.O. Box 168, Yellowstone National Park, WY 82190. (307-344-7381. 🖥 www.nps.gov/yell
■ The park covers more than 2.2 million acres and attracts 3 million visitors a year.

Yellowstone National Park Archives ✉ P.O. Box 168, Yellowstone National Park, WY 82190. (307-344-2261. 🖥 www.nps.gov/yell/technical/museum/index.htm
■ The history of the park is documented through more than 200,000 objects, natural science specimens, a herbarium, hotel furnishings, souvenirs, objects relating to park rangers, and works of art by Thomas Moran and others. The archives, which is affiliated with the National Archives, also contains more than 80,000

An Elk Pursued by Wolves appeared in the New Sporting Magazine in 1840. Reintroducing wolves to the Yellowstone Valley could have similar repercussions for the elk population.

historic photographs; records pertaining to the 1988 fires; and historic film footage. Many of these objects are exhibited in park visitor centers and museums; the remainder are found in study collections available to researchers year-round.

Yellowstone Park Foundation ⊠ 37 East Main Street, Suite 4, Bozeman, MT 59715. (406-586-6303. 🖳 www.ypf.org

■ The foundation helps fund projects that are beyond the resources of the National Park Service. Donations have been made for the restoration of wolves, relocation of Pelican Valley Trail out of grizzly bear habitat, and continuation of the Yellowstone Youth Conservation Corps for summer employment.

The 3,593-foot-high granite buttress El Capitan is one of Yosemite's most famous sights and inspired early efforts to set aside the area as a reservation in the 1800s. One of the first supporters of this idea was the landscape architect Frederick Law Olmsted. The national park was created in 1890, and Yosemite Valley became a World Heritage Site in 1984.

Yosemite Valley

Beginning with the Yosemite Land Grant Bill (1864), the legislation surrounding the placement of California's Yosemite Valley and the Mariposa Big Tree Grove of giant sequoias (☞ TREES) in the public trust is considered to have been the primary impetus for the NATIONAL PARK SYSTEM in America. Although the statute, signed into law by Abraham Lincoln, neither established nor provided for a national park, no tract of federal land nearly so large (39,200 acres) had ever been set aside for public enjoyment and preservation. The legislation was especially significant for creating a land reservation for strictly nonutilitarian purposes, thus establishing a precedent for the creation of the country's first national park in the Yellowstone Valley in 1872 (☞ YELLOWSTONE NATIONAL PARK).

Although other non-Indians had almost certainly seen it from afar, the first to actually enter, explore, and name the Yosemite Valley of the Merced River were members of a volunteer militia known as the Mariposa Battalion in 1851. Among this band of ex-Texas Rangers was Lafayette Houghton Boutelle, whose written account of the events surrounding the battalion's campaign to subjugate Indians in the gold-mining region of the southern Mother Lode was published in 1880 as *Discovery of the Yosemite and the Indian War of 1851 Which Led to That Event*. Boutelle's initial encounter with the valley and the granite buttress known as El Capitan found them shrouded in haze, which did nothing to diminish the power of the scene. "This obscurity of vision but increased awe with which I beheld it," wrote Boutelle, "and as I looked, a peculiar exalted sensation seemed to fill my whole being, and I found my eyes in tears with emotion."

The American press was instrumental in creating a prominent role for Yosemite Valley in the national environmental movement almost as soon as the valley was discovered. The first of many journalists to write about it was James M. Hutchings of San Francisco, who published an article about Yosemite, illustrated by the artist Thomas Ayres in his *California Magazine* in 1856. Hutchings claimed squatter's rights, became the proprietor of a hotel in the valley, and challenged the state ruling against private ownership of property there. The completion of the transcontinental railroad in 1869 opened up tourist access, although the last leg of the journey to one of the haphazard assortment of tent camps and lodges that followed the first hotel in the mid-1850s still required a 30-mile trip by horse or mule.

Public support for the creation of Yosemite National Park in 1890 was largely due to the influence of the newspaper and magazine articles of the writer and environmental advocate JOHN MUIR. Protecting an area of subalpine meadows, the original 1,512-square-mile national park encircled but did not include the state-owned Yosemite Valley and Mariposa Grove. California receded these tracts to the federal government in 1905, and they were incorporated into the national park in 1906. Pressure

Of all the wonders of America that *Doan's Directory* could have chosen for the cover of its medicine guide, Yosemite Valley earned the honor.

from private claims and management issues had actually reduced the national park by 38,000 acres the year before, but much of that private land was later purchased by conservationists and donated back to the park. Yosemite National Park now measures 1,169 square miles and was declared one of UNESCO's WORLD HERITAGE SITES in 1984. More than 94 percent of the park is included in the NATIONAL WILDERNESS PRESERVATION SYSTEM.

Hetch Hetchy Reservoir

In the first decades of the 1900s, an effort to dam the Tuolomne River and create the Hetch Hetchy Reservoir put Yosemite National Park at the center of one of the country's bitterest battles in the early history of the American environmental movement. Immediately after the earthquake of 1906, San Francisco reactivated a previous application for water rights to the Tuolomne Valley and nearby Lake Eleanor within the national park, secured preliminary permits from the U.S. DEPARTMENT OF THE INTERIOR, and passed a $45 million bond issue to build the dam and create an artificial reservoir. Led by John Muir, the ensuing fight to preserve the valley produced the first environmental debate to seriously test wilderness preservation in the context of a political showdown over whether a water supply served the greater public good. The decision that ultimately permitted the dam in 1913 was also the first of its kind to catch the attention of the American public, which bombarded Congress with letters of protest.

San Francisco's dismissal of the idea that the Tuolomne Valley's unspoiled wilderness might have an intangible but valid national worth of equal or greater importance than its value in hard currency was underscored when the city refused to consider other viable dam locations because the Hetch Hetchy location would be the cheapest. The city sidestepped the issue of recreational benefits by promoting the reservoir as a scenic addition to the park and promising public access.

At issue were the same philosophical arguments, waged widely in the national press, that form the fundamental tension in environmental policy debate today. Does wilderness have any value if it is simply left alone? Opponents of dam development in effect argued for the greater social good of beauty as inherent in the unspoiled wilderness. As Muir put it, beauty is in fact as God-given and essential as bread; everybody needs it, as well as "places to play in and pray in where Nature may heal and cheer and give strength to body and soul alike." Proponents of dam development, among them the nation's chief forester, Gifford Pinchot (1865–1946) (☞ NATIONAL FOREST SYSTEM), reasoned that greater good was measured by maximum use of resources whenever those resources were needed. The basis of the nation's conservation policy, Pinchot

The Hetch Hetchy Reservoir near Yosemite Valley was created after a dam for the Tuolumne River was approved in 1913. "These temple destroyers," wrote John Muir in 1912 of the dam supporters, ". . . seem to have a perfect contempt for Nature."

testified, is that of use, "to take every part of the land and resources and put it to that use in which it will serve the most people." Although the Raker Act, which authorized the O'Shaughnessy Dam at Hetch Hetchy, was signed into law by President Woodrow Wilson in 1913, the issues raised by the fight for protection helped coalesce the movement for wilderness preservation. ☞ *also* SIERRA NEVADA RANGE

Friends of Yosemite Valley ⊠ P.O. Box 702, Yosemite, CA 95389. ☏ 209-379-9337. 🖥 www.yosemitevalley.org
■ Devoted to the protection and restoration of Yosemite "through advocacy, education and action," this nonprofit grassroots organization focuses on curtailing road building and other development in and around the park.

Contacts

Yosemite Association ⊠ P.O. Box 230, El Portal, CA 95318. ☏ 209-379-2317. 🖥 www.yosemite.org
■ The association, authorized by Congress, operates in cooperation with the National Park Service to provide services and promote park stewardship. It supports interpretive, educational, research, scientific, and environmental programs.

Yosemite National Park ⊠ P.O. Box 577, Yosemite National Park, CA 95389. ☏ 209-372-0200. 🖥 www.nps.gov/yose
■ Highlights include Yosemite Valley, with its high cliffs and waterfalls; the Ahwahnee Hotel; the Mariposa Grove of ancient giant sequoias; and Tuolumne Meadows, a large subalpine expanse surrounded by mountain peaks.

Zion National Park

Opposite: This photograph of the distant rock formation called the "Three Patriarchs" was probably taken in 1872. Forested side canyons are among Zion's many micro-environments.

Mormon pioneers named this canyon, composed of nine layers of porous sandstone, limestone, and shale in southwestern Utah, for the Hebrew word *Zion* (a place of safety or refuge). (However, after the Mormon leader Brigham Young declared the scenery beautiful but not Zion, the canyon was for some time actually known as Not Zion in deference to Young's opinion.) The sedimentary rock formations that distinguish this landscape of cliffs and canyons date mostly from the Triassic through the Jurassic periods (250 million to 150 million years ago) and include the Kolob arch, the world's largest natural arch. It spans 292 to 310 feet (depending on who is measuring) near the top of the cliffs of Navajo sandstone located on the north side of La Verkin Creek.

The 229-square-mile park began its life as a public reservation as the Mukuntuweap National Monument in 1909, became Zion National Monument in 1918, and was established by Congress as Zion National Park in 1919, just months after the Grand Canyon National Monument was redesignated as Grand Canyon National Park in a similar process (☞ GRAND CANYON). Zion's striking formations are largely the product of the Virgin River, which annually sifts about 3 million tons of pulverized rock out of the park and into the Colorado River as the Virgin bores its way through Zion Canyon. The area is also remarkable for its diverse fauna; the change in elevation, from about 3,700 feet to almost 9,000, means that some eight hundred species can thrive here—from cactus in the desert to pines in the higher plateaus and mesas. Differences in temperature and the amounts of sunlight and rainfall also help create microenvironments, including hanging "gardens" and miniforests in protected side canyons, which account for the varied plant species. Among the rare and endangered animal species found here are peregrine falcons, Mexican spotted owls, and the Zion snail, which is found nowhere else in the world. Opened in 1930, the Zion–Mount Carmel Highway, running west from the high plateaus of Mount Carmel Junction down to lower Zion, was considered one of the major engineering feats of the era.

Zion National Park ⊠ State Road 9, Springdale, UT 84767. ℂ 435-772-3256.   *Contact*
▯ www.nps.gov/zion

▪ The park has two visitor centers: one at the Kolob Canyons entrance and the other at Zion Canyon near the south entrance.

Illustration Credits

Every effort has been made to locate the copyright holders of images used in this book. Please contact the publisher with any additions for future editions.

3: Library of Congress, Prints and Photographs Division, LC-USZ62-90560
12: National Archives, Records of the U.S. Department of the Interior, Ansel Adams Photographs
13: Adirondack Museum
14: Library of Congress, Prints and Photographs Division, Detroit Publishing Company Photograph Collection, LC-D4-33235
15: Adirondack Museum
18 top: Library of Congress, Prints and Photographs Division, Detroit Publishing Company Photograph Collection, LC-D418-31589
18 bottom: Adirondack Museum
19: Library of Congress, Prints and Photographs Division, Detroit Publishing Company Photograph Collection, LC-D4-14885
22: Library of Congress, Prints and Photographs Division, Jerry Rotundi and Bob Matheo, Environmental Action, PO6-U.S., 1246
25: Manuscripts, Special Collections, University Archives, University of Washington Libraries, Harriman, 43
26: U.S. Geological Survey, S. R. Capps, 1071
28: Colorado Historical Society, William Henry Jackson Collection, CHS-J1154

31: Carol M. Highsmith
32: Carol M. Highsmith
33: U.S. Geological Survey, Topography A, 492
34: Library of Congress, Prints and Photographs Division, LC-Z62-095231
35: © B. and C. Alexander, Photo Researchers, Inc.
36: National Geological Survey, A. Post, 4
38: Carol M. Highsmith
39: Adirondack Museum
40: Frederic H. Kock, from *Woodcraft*, by Bernard S. Mason (New York: A. S. Barnes, 1939), p. 229, fig. 119
41: Jeanne Van Etten
43: Johnny Johnson, © Tony Stone Images
44: Jeanne Van Etten
47: Beinecke Rare Book and Manuscript Library, Yale University
49: Charleston Museum, Charleston, South Carolina
50: Library of Virginia
51: Washington University Gallery of Art, St. Louis. Gift of Nathaniel Phillips, 1890. Oil on canvas, 36 × 50 in.
53: Library of Congress, Prints and Photographs Division, LC-USZ62-50181
55: Newberry Library, Chicago
56: National Archives, Records of the U.S. Department of the Interior, Ansel Adams Photographs

59: Library of Congress, Prints and Photographs Division, LC-USZ62-103950
62 top: Yale Collection of Western Americana, Beinecke Rare Book and Manuscript Library
62 bottom: Jeanne Van Etten
64: © Corbis
65: Library of Congress, Prints and Photographs Division, Detroit Publishing Company Photograph Collection, LC-D4-72410
66: Frank Lerner, General Research and Humanities Division, New York Public Library
67: Courtesy Old Town Canoe Company, Maine
68: Title page, *Silent Spring*, by Rachel L. Carson. Copyright © 1962 by Rachel L. Carson, renewed 1990 by Roger Cristie. Reprinted by permission of Houghton Mifflin Company. All rights reserved
69: U.S. Geological Survey, C. L. Dreidger, 10
70: Yale Collection of American Literature, Beinecke Rare Book and Manuscript Library
72: Library of Congress, Prints and Photographs Division, Illinois WPA Art Project, LC-USZ62-105105
73: Library of Congress, Prints and Photographs Division, Detroit

Publishing Company
Photograph Collection,
LC-D4-12614

76: Jeanne Van Etten

78: Jeanne Van Etten

81: Library of Congress,
Prints and Photographs
Division, Farm Security
Administration, Office
of War Information
Photograph Collection,
LC-USF34-058354-D

82: Library of Congress,
Prints and Photographs
Division, Cabinet of
American Illustration,
LC-USZ62-8323

83: Jeanne Van Etten

84: Jeanne Van Etten

86: Library of Congress,
Prints and Photographs
Division, LC-USZ62-
112464

88: Yale Collection of
Western Americana,
Beinecke Rare Book and
Manuscript Library

89: Missouri Historical
Society, St. Louis, Clark
Family Papers

91: Library of Congress,
Prints and Photographs
Division, LC-USZ62-
96189

94: Library of Congress,
Prints and Photographs
Divsion, Farm Security
Administration, Office
of War Information
Photograph Collection,
LC-USF34-065549-D

97: National Archives,
Records of the U.S.
Department of the
Interior, Ansel Adams
Photographs

98: Denver Public
Library, Western
History Collection

99: Buffalo Bill
Historical Center,
Cody, Wyoming. Gift
of I. H. "Larry" Larom
Collection

102: Adirondack Museum

105: Yale Collection of
Western Americana,
Beinecke Rare Book and
Manuscript Library

107: Manuscripts, Special
Collections, University
Archives, University of
Washington Libraries,
Barnes, 1589

111: Carol M. Highsmith

114: U.S. Department of
the Interior, Fish and
Wildlife Service

118: Library of Congress,
Prints and Photographs
Division, Farm Security
Administration, Office
of War Information,
LC-USF34-073159-D

119: Carol M. Highsmith

121: U.S. Department
of the Interior,
National Park Service,
Harpers Ferry Center,
hpc-000774

122: Metropolitan
Museum of Art,
Morris K. Jesup Fund,
1933 (33.61). All
rights reserved

123: Paul Mellon
Collection, © 2001
Board of Trustees,
National Gallery of
Art, Washington

125: Wyoming Division
of Cultural Resources

127: Adirondack Museum

129: U.S. Department
of the Interior, Fish and
Wildlife Service

130: Manuscripts, Special
Collections, University
Archives, University of
Washington Libraries,
Harriman, 31, detail

131: Manuscripts, Special
Collections, University
Archives, University of
Washington Libraries,
Harriman, 31, detail

132: © Corbis

135: U.S. Department
of the Interior,
National Park Service,
Harpers Ferry Center,
hpc-000004

137: U.S. Geological
Survey, J. K. Hillers, 66

140: Adirondack Museum

143: Buffalo Bill Historical
Center, Cody, Wyoming.
Gift of Mrs. Karl Frank

144: U.S. Geological
Survey, N. K. Huber, 29

146: U.S. Geological
Survey, A. Keith, 291

150: Adirondack Museum

152: Grand Canyon
National Park, 16412

153: National Archives,
Records of the U.S.
Department of the
Interior, Ansel Adams
Photographs

154: Library of Congress,
Prints and Photographs
Division, Farm Security
Administration, Office
of War Information
Photograph Collection,
LC-USF33-010020-M2

159: © Galen Rowell,
Corbis

160: U.S. Department
of the Interior,
National Park Service,
Harpers Ferry Center,
hpc-000005

161: Library of Congress,
Prints and Photographs
Division, Illinois WPA
Art Project, LC-USZC2-
860

163: Collections of the
New York Public Library,
Aster, Lenox and Tilden
Foundations

166: Michigan State
University Museum

168: Yale Collection of
Western Americana,
Beinecke Rare Book
and Manuscript Library

170: Yale Collection of
American Literature,
Beinecke Rare Book
and Manuscript Library

172: U.S. Geological
Survey, W. H. Jackson,
586

174: American
Philosophical Society,
B. S. Barton Collection

176 top: Library of
Congress, Prints and
Photographs Division,
Frank and Frances
Carpenter Collection,
LOT 11453-4, 16

176 bottom: Jeanne
Van Etten

177: Jeanne Van Etten

180: American
Philosophical Society

182: U.S. Department
of the Interior, Bureau
of Reclamation

183: Yale Collection of
Western Americana,
Beinecke Rare Book and
Manuscript Library

185: Library of Congress,
Prints and Photographs
Division, Farm Security
Administration, Office

of War Information
Photograph Collection,
LC-USF34-073188

186: Yale Collection of
Western Americana,
Beinecke Rare Book and
Manuscript Library

189: Aldo Leopold Foundation Archives

190: Beinecke Rare Book
and Manuscript Library,
Yale University

193: General Research
Division, New York
Public Library, Astor,
Lenox and Tilden
Foundations

195: Newberry Library,
Chicago

196: Jeanne Van Etten

199: Yale Collection of
Western Americana,
Beinecke Rare Book and
Manuscript Library

201: Jeanne Van Etten

203: Adirondack Museum

205: U.S. Geological
Survey, M. H. Staatz,
281

206: U.S. Geological
Survey, M. H. Staatz,
210

208: Library of Congress,
Prints and Photographs
Division, LC-USZ62-
36760

210: Manuscripts, Special
Collections, University
Archives, University of
Washington Libraries,
Barnes, 2003

212: Darius R. Kinsey,
*Building a Logging Railroad Bridge Over a
Canyon, Using Fir Beams
100 Feet Long,* from
untitled album of
logging photographs,

ca. 1908. Gelatin silver
print, 11 × 14 in. © San
Francisco Museum of
Modern Art. Purchased
through a gift of Robin
Moll and Accessions
Committee Fund

213: Yale Collection of
Western Americana,
Beinecke Rare Book and
Manuscript Library

215: U.S. Geological
Survey, J. K. Hillers,
95

217: National Archives,
Records of the U.S.
Department of the
Interior, Ansel Adams
Photographs

219: U.S. Geological
Survey, J. K. Hillers, 44

220: U.S. Department
of the Interior,
National Park Service,
Harpers Ferry Center,
Asahel Curtis, hpc-
000222

222: U.S. Geological
Survey, J. A. Holmes, 42

223: National Archives,
Records of the U.S.
Department of the
Interior, Ansel Adams
Photographs

225: Yale Collection of
Western Americana,
Beinecke Rare Book and
Manuscript Library

226: JKM Collection,
National Museum of
Wildlife Art, Jackson,
Wyoming. Oil on
canvas

229: U.S. Department of
the Interior, Fish and
Wildlife Service

230: Denver Public
Library, Western
History Collection

233: Yale Collection of
Western Americana,
Beinecke Rare Book and
Manuscript Library

234: Yale Collection of
Western Americana,
Beinecke Rare Book and
Manuscript Library

236: Library of Congress,
Prints and Photographs
Division, New York
World Telegram and the
Sun Newspapers Photograph Collection, LC-
USZ62-118433

238: Beinecke Rare Book
and Manuscript Library,
Yale University

241: Manuscripts, Special
Collections, University
Archives, University of
Washington Libraries,
Barnes, 1361

242: U.S. Geological
Survey, J. H. Barks, 1

244: National Park
Service, *Park Structures
and Facilities,* 1935

245: Grand Canyon
National Park, 17010b

246: Carleton Knight III

247: Haynes Foundation
Collection, Montana
Historical Society,
Helena, Montana

249: Library of Congress,
Prints and Photographs
Division, LC-USZ62-
20328.

250 top: U.S. Department of the Interior,
National Park Service,
Harpers Ferry Center,
W. H. Jackson, 76-78

250 bottom: U.S.
Geological Survey,
J. K. Hillers, 545

251: U.S. Geological
Survey, J. K. Hillers,
1020

253: U.S. Department of
the Interior, Fish and
Wildlife Service

254: U.S. Department of
the Interior, National
Park Service, Harpers
Ferry Center, George A.
Grant, hpc-000013

259: Michael Peake

262: © Pat O'Hara,
Corbis

264: Denver Public
Library, Western
History Collection

265: Newberry Library,
Chicago

267: U.S. Department
of the Interior Museum,
Washington, D.C. Oil
on canvas

269: Theodore Roosevelt
Collection, Harvard
College Library

271: Library of Congress,
Prints and Photographs
Division, Detroit
Publishing Company
Photograph Collection,
LC-D4-10574A

273: Library of Congress,
Prints and Photographs
Division, LC-USZ62-
25362

276: U.S. Department of
the Interior, Fish and
Wildlife Service

277: U.S. Department of
the Interior, Fish and
Wildlife Service

278: Library of Congress,
Prints and Photographs
Division, Frank and
Frances Carpenter
Collection, LC-USZ62-
123548

279: Denver Public Library, Western History Collection, Collection of D. F. Barry

280: Jeanne Van Etten

281: U.S Geological Survey, W. H. Jackson, 102

282: U.S. Geological Survey, J. K. Hillers, 109

284: U.S. Geological Survey, W. H. Jackson, 282

286: U.S. Geological Survey, C. B. Hunt, 988

287: Ellsworth Jaeger, from *Wildwood Wisdom*, by Ellsworth Jaeger (New York: Macmillan, 1955), p. 112, plate 63

289: U.S. Geological Survey, W. T. Lee, 1084

292: National Archives, Records of the U.S. Department of the Interior, Ansel Adams Photographs

293: Library of Congress, Prints and Photographs Division, LC-USZ62-90560

294: Library of Congress, Prints and Photographs Division, LC-USZ62-90561

295: Library of Congress, Prints and Photographs Division, Detroit Publishing Company Photograph Collection, LC-D4-13529

296: U.S. Geological Survey, G. K. Gilbert, 1973

299: Diplomatic Reception Rooms, U.S. Department of State

302: Library of Congress, Prints and Photographs Division, Ruthven Deane Collection, LC-Z62-102417

303: Library of Congress, Prints and Photographs Division, Farm Security Administration, Office of War Information Photograph Collection, LC-USF34-073195

304: U.S. Geological Survey, M. H. Staatz, 226

306: © Lynda Richardson, Corbis

308: Yale Collection of Western Americana, Beinecke Rare Book and Manuscript Library

310: Newark Museum/Art Resource, New York

311: Yale Collection of American Literature, Beinecke Rare Book and Manuscript Library

312: University of California, Berkeley, Bancroft Library Photo Collection

315: Western History Collections, University of Oklahoma Library

316: Rockwell Museum of Western Art, Corning, New York. Photograph © James O. Milmos

319: Library of Congress, Prints and Photographs Division, Detroit Publishing Company Photograph Collection, LC-D419-39

320: Library of Congress, Prints and Photographs Division, Detroit

Publishing Company Photograph Collection, LC-D4-72410

322: Yale Collection of American Literature, Beinecke Rare Book and Manuscript Library

323: U.S. Geological Survey, C. B. Hunt, 1048

325: U.S. Geological Survey, D. A. Swanson, 26

329: Cover, *Earth House Hold,* by Gary Snyder. Courtesy New Directions Publishing Corporation

330: Library of Congress, Prints and Photographs Division, LC-USZ62-94944

332: U.S. Geological Survey, J. K. Hillers, 134

333: U.S. Geological Survey, W. H. Jackson, 695

335: Library of Congress, Prints and Photographs Division, Portraits of America Collection, LC-USZ62-119577

336: U.S. Department of the Interior, Fish and Wildlife Service

337: Beinecke Rare Book and Manuscript Library, Yale University

338: U.S. Geological Survey, J. K. Hillers, 40

339: Collection of the author

341: © Galen Rowell, Corbis

343: U.S. Geological Survey, J. K. Hillers, 1024

Index

Page numbers in **bold** refer to entries in this book. Page numbers in *italics* refer to photographs or illustrations.